THE BRIEF & BRILLIANT LIFE
of John Thomas Geary

Copyright © 2021 by Lisa Michele Church and Kaye Page Nichols

All rights reserved.
No part of this publication may be reproduced, distributed, or transmitted in any form or by any means, including photocopying, recording, or other electronic or mechanical methods, without the prior written permission of the publisher, except in the case of brief quotations embodied in reviews and other noncommercial uses permitted by copyright law.

Copy Editing by Laurieann Thorpe
Cover design by Lisa Michele Church

Front Cover Photographs: Witherley Parish Church, Leicestershire, England https://wikipedia.org/Witherley (top left); Geary Family Seal, courtesy of Sonny Bailey (center left); Toquerville, Utah, courtesy of Kaye Page Nichols (bottom left); Big Mountain in the Wasatch Mountains near Salt Lake City, Utah, courtesy of Kaye Page Nichols (center right); digital image of the John Thomas Geary 1850s portrait, courtesy of Brian Kemp Bowler (center).

Back Cover Photographs: (left to right) Jason S. Anderson at 44 Duncan Terrace, Islington, London, England, 2018, courtesy of Katherine Anderson; digital image of the Sophia Fryer Geary 1850s portrait, courtesy of Brian Kemp Bowler; interior of Southwark Cathedral, London, England, 2015, courtesy of Lisa Michele Church.

Published by Relentless History
Salt Lake City, Utah
Contact us at www.relentlesshistory@gmail.com

THE BRIEF & BRILLIANT LIFE
of John Thomas Geary

Lisa Michele Church
Kaye Page Nichols

CONTENTS

INTRODUCTION		7
TIMELINE		9
CHAPTER ONE	**BEGINNINGS**	11
CHAPTER TWO	**A GENTLEMAN AND A SCHOLAR**	41
CHAPTER THREE	**EN ROUTE**	69
CHAPTER FOUR	**OPTIMISM IN THE MOUNTAINS**	98
CHAPTER FIVE	**HEADED DOWN SOUTH**	125
CHAPTER SIX	**CLOUDS OVER THE SUN**	145
CHAPTER SEVEN	**AFTERMATH**	171
CHAPTER EIGHT	**HONORABLE REMEMBRANCE**	184
ACKNOWLEDGEMENTS		211
APPENDIX		213

INTRODUCTION

Sometimes a story just demands to be told. Each of us spent years researching and writing about our common ancestor, John Thomas Geary, without knowing about the other! We both descend from John's oldest daughter, Sophia Ann, we both love family history, and we both believe we will meet John again in another realm, so we needed to know his story. We first met in front of the ghostly mansion still standing at Sophia Ann's Page Ranch home in southern Utah. Lisa Michele was conducting tours at the house to raise money for a collapsing roof and Kaye came for a tour. As soon as we began talking, we knew we needed to combine our efforts to write the story of John Thomas Geary.

Five years and hundreds of emails later we are finally publishing this book. John's story still contains tantalizing mysteries but we've taken it as far as current resources will let us and we'd like to leave some research opportunities for the next generation! Miracles occurred all along the way. Some examples include the public release of Brigham Young's letter files so we could use John's priceless 1857 letter in his own hand, the discovery of a journal entry from a witness to the Gearys' 1852 London wedding, and the offers from countless Geary descendants to provide their insights and mementos. The story practically wrote itself as these miracles cascaded down around us. Many, many Geary descendants are fascinated by John Thomas and Sophia Fryer Geary. It is as John's patriarchal blessing promised, "you shall have posterity upon the earth and they shall call you blessed."

In today's digital age, we were able to find far more out about John Thomas and Sophia than was available to earlier researchers. Nevertheless, we owe a heavy debt to the previous family historians, especially Bessie Snow and Maree Higbee Gardner; we built on the foundation they laid. We can now verify old records half a world away, they are online and searchable. Many of the letters, diaries and journals of our pioneer settlers previously hidden away in family attics are now digitized and posted online. We can cross-check dates with historical digitized newspapers. We hired Patty Swenson, a professional genealogist, to go back in time and walk with the Gearys from the 1700s. Our story is detailed and documented. But we also hope it captures the spirit of our ancestors. While we don't know everything about their lives, we feel closer to them. If you know additional information, we solicit your suggestions for future editions of this book.

It is our hope, as authors, that this volume will expand your understanding of these venerated pioneers and bring their stories alive in the 21st century. Become acquainted with them!

Lisa Michele Church
lmhchurch@gmail.com

Kaye Page Nichols
kayep722@aol.com

JOHN THOMAS GEARY

SOPHIA FRYER GEARY

TIMELINE

February 5, 1823	John Thomas Geary born in Atterton, Leicestershire, England
July 12, 1829	Sophia Fryer born in Yarmouth, Isle of Wight, England
November 24, 1838	John enters into Articles of Clerkship to become an attorney
June 11, 1845	John admitted to the Queen's Bench as an attorney
January 11, 1849	John's father mortgages the family's land in Leicestershire
April 20, 1851	Sophia is baptized into the Church of Jesus Christ
May 20, 1851	John is baptized into the Church of Jesus Christ
August 20, 1852	John and Sophia are married at Southwark Cathedral
September 17, 1852	Geary family lands in England are lost to foreclosure
January 17, 1853	Sophia sails from Liverpool to America
February 5, 1853	John sails from Liverpool to America
March, 1853	The Gearys reunite in St. Louis, travel to Keokuk, Iowa
June 10, 1853	Sophia Ann Geary is born in Keokuk, Iowa
July 17, 1853	The Geary family arrives in Council Bluffs, Iowa
August 25, 1854	Thomas Fryer Geary is born, likely in Council Bluffs
January 15, 1855	Thomas Fryer Geary dies
1856	The Gearys cross the plains to Utah
December 9, 1856	Echo Workman Geary is born in Echo Canyon, Utah
December 15, 1856	The Geary family reaches Salt Lake City
April 6, 1859	Eliza Jane Geary is born; Gearys live in Cedar City, Utah
1860	John works part of the year in Salt Lake City as a store clerk
October 19, 1862	John and Sophia are called to settle southern Utah
December 12, 1862	Leah Fryer Geary is born
1863-1865	The Gearys live between Toquerville and Salt Lake City
February 29, 1864	Sarah Ann (Annie) Geary is born in Toquerville
October 16, 1866	Sophia writes Brigham Young requesting a divorce from John
November 13, 1866	Brigham Young responds, advising Sophia to stay with John
December 31, 1866	John is accidentally shot in a Salt Lake City backyard
January 5, 1867	John dies of his gunshot wound, is buried in Salt Lake City
June 15, 1867	Sophia marries Joshua Thomas Willis in Toquerville
May 27, 1872	Sophia dies in childbirth with her third Willis child

BEGINNINGS

"I intend to take hold of the very first thing which may present itself."
JTG

John Thomas Geary stood at the crossroads, looking toward the mountains. The landscape couldn't be more different from his British birthplace and he paused to find a connection to this bleak view. Utah Territory in the dead of winter did not feel welcoming. But he had made his choice. It took John and his wife, Sophia, the better part of three years to make it across the American plains to Great Salt Lake City and he intended to make it his home.

When John arrived in Utah in December, 1856 he was 33 years old with two small children. John and Sophia came to the remote desert for religious reasons – they were Mormon emigrants following their prophet. They left England and their extended families behind, knowing they would never see them again. It seemed both a privilege and an immeasurable price to pay for their beliefs. Both were optimistic that the rewards would be worth the cost.

THE GEARYS: A LAND-OWNING FAMILY

The Geary family, from which John Thomas Geary descended, was a land-owning family for several generations in Leicestershire, England. Through a series of fathers and sons all named "John Geary" they formed a solid line of agricultural endeavors for at least two hundred years. The Geary men fit the definition of a "yeoman" – a farmer who owned the land he cultivated but still worked for a living. Until the early 1700s, Leicestershire was a rural county with few towns or industries. Farming was the chief industry in the area. The Geary men continued to farm their modest holdings themselves or with a few employees, occasionally adding acreage during their lifetimes, then passing it to their sons or male heirs at death.

An English historian describes the county as follows:

Leicestershire was, until the early eighteenth century, an almost purely farming county with no towns of any size (Leicester itself had about 4,500 to 5,000 people at the end of the seventeenth century) and no industries beyond those of the local crafts and trades; and it was until the later decades of the seventeenth century a great corn country…Fully 95 percent of Leicestershire was being cultivated in some form or other in this period. Leicestershire had been one of the most highly cultivated and densely populated regions of England from the thirteenth century onward.[1]

The earliest John Geary on local land records, birthdate unknown, died in 1712 and wrote a will in which he left his land in Atterton to his son, John Geary.[2] Atterton was a small hamlet in the county of Leicestershire, having a population of fewer than 50 people, as it does even today.[3] Atterton is located in the English Midlands, about 100 miles from London, on the southwest corner of the county border with Warwickshire. Towns nearby to Atterton in the 1860s were similarly small: Ratcliffe Culey (population, 208), Atherstone (population, 3,857), Witherley (population, 528), Dadlington (population, 216), and Fenny Drayton (population, 134). The largest city in the area would have been Market Bosworth with a population by the mid-1800s of 26,000.[4]

This first John Geary on record was married to Mary (Marie) Weaver and they had three children: Mary, born in 1697, John, born on January 19, 1698 and Thomas, born in 1699. When writing his will, this first John Geary first commended "my soule into ye hand of All mighty God my Creator and of Jesus Christ my Blessed Savior and Redeemer" and then provided for that "portion of Worldly Goods and estate which God of his mercy hath made me a steward of for a time." The oldest son, John Geary/1698, became his father's heir to the Leicestershire family land.[5] (From this point forward, we will refer to each "John Geary" by his birth year due to the repetitious names.)

The other son, Thomas inherited from his father a bed and 110 pounds; a daughter, Mary, inherited a bed, shelf, chest of drawers, round table and 100 pounds.[6] This first John Geary was buried at Witherley on April 22, 1712.

In 1724, John Geary/1698 married Sarah Lynes. Soon thereafter, his Geary land was consolidated and re-appropriated into more efficient parcels by an Act of Enclosure, finalized on April 25, 1729. John Geary/1698 would have been about 31 years old at the time of the consolidation.

Parliament passed Acts of Enclosure throughout England beginning in the 1400s to make the farmers' fields more efficient to operate. Prior to this time period, a family might own odds and ends of fields which were not contiguous, making them difficult to cultivate and limiting productivity. "There is little doubt that enclosure greatly improved the agricultural productivity of farms from the late 18th century by bringing more land into effective agricultural use. It also brought considerable change to the local landscape. Where there were once large, communal open fields, land was now hedged and fenced off, and old boundaries disappeared."[7]

Enclosure required that all sections of a particular district were combined into one area, one or more surveyors were chosen to map the land, and then three to five independent commissioners would allocate the specific plots back out to each land holder. If an owner were fortunate, he would receive back a consolidated piece of land roughly equal to the acreage of his previously-owned separate parcels. Sometimes smaller tenants were displaced altogether. Landowners such as the Gearys were able to keep their land and improve its productivity. In a document entitled "Supplemental Abstract of Title DE322/13/2 recorded at The Record Office for Leicestershire, Leicester and Rutland" the parties to the Geary enclosure explain the need for the enclosure: 'Several freeholders Owners & occupiers of Lands in Atterton…had & stood severally seized of several yard lands & [other] p(ar)cels of land meadow & pasture with the appurts (appurtenances) in Atterton aforesd [lying] promiscuously & interming (intermingling) one amongst the other in the Common

& open fields of Atterton aforesd insomuch that no man [could] make the best profits of his own land…"[8]

A published record from 1813 shows the results of the enclosure and notes that a map and survey was taken by Mr. Henry Beighton in 1720, then given to Captain Weaver.[9] The results of the legal documents recorded in the Leicestershire title office are shown in "Appendix to the History of Leicestershire" page 156, with an effective date of April 25, 1729, and this chart, although the math does not tote, itemizing the following acreage ("roods" are one quarter acres and "perches" are 1/160 of an acre):

	ACRES	ROODS	PERCHES
Charles Jennens (Copsall),	189	3	15
Robert & Catherine Charnels (Packington)	53	0	32
John King (Old Hayes)	135	0	17
John & Mary Weaver (Horeston Grange)	63	1	35
Elizabeth Harris – widow of Randle Harris (Shustock)	94	0	10
John & Sarah Geary (Atterton)	61	3	29
Titheable land	597	2	18
Glebe	16	3	24
Total of Lordship	614	2	2

John Geary/1698 now owned 61 contiguous acres of the total 614 acres of land – not as many as his neighbor, Charles Jennens, who owned 189 acres, but more than Robert Charnels, who owned 53. The Act of Enclosure came at a good time for John Geary/1698 and his wife, Sarah Lynes, who was also from a landed family. Sarah was the daughter of John Lynes of Tooley Park. The enclosure enabled the Gearys to consolidate their holdings and add to it with some of Sarah's own inheritance and purchases.

John and Sarah Geary had two children, Mary Geary (1728-1769) and John Geary (1730-1816). Parish records show that John Geary/1698 was the Churchwarden of the Atterton Parish. The Churchwarden was a lay officer who looked after the secular affairs of the church, and who, in England, was the legal representative of the parish. Geary's signature appears on some pages of the parish registers. The only freeholder listed for Atterton in the 1741 Poll book Leicestershire, Sparkenhoe Hundred, was John Gery [sic], and as a result he was the only male in Atterton to have a vote. These things indicate that John Geary held an important position in the small hamlet of Atterton, and in the parish of Witherley as well.[10]

When John Geary/1698 died he left a will written March 11, 1754, in which he gave his land to his son, John Geary/1730. This heir, John Geary/1730, was probably the wealthiest of the Geary men. He not only had the combination of lands from his father but also some from his maternal Lynes relatives, and then he added significantly to his land holdings during his lifetime.[11]

Although John Geary/1730 was only in his mid-twenties when he inherited his land, he was industrious and worked hard to increase his estate. He married Ann Sharman in 1758 and they had two sons: John Sharman Geary (1763-1826) and Thomas Geary (1767-1853). Both the Sharman and Geary families included landowners and gentlemen. Because there was land in both families, John Geary/1730 decided not to leave his Geary family land directly to his two sons.

The oldest son, John Sharman Geary/1763, inherited lands from his paternal Sharman grandfather instead of inheriting any part of the Geary lands from his own father. The younger son, Thomas Geary/1767, was granted an annuity from his father but not given ownership of the land itself. Instead, the Geary ancestral land, which by then included hundreds of acres in Atterton, Witherley, and Ratcliffe Culey, skipped a generation. John Geary/1730 left that land to his grandson, Thomas Geary (1792 -1865), the son of John Sharman Geary. This grandson would become the father of our subject, John Thomas Geary (1823-1867).[12]

THOMAS GEARY, THE LAST TO INHERIT THE GEARY LANDS

Thomas Geary, who inherited the family lands from his grandfather, was born September 27, 1792 at Dadlington, Leicestershire, the youngest son born to John Sharman Geary and Mary Elton. He had a twin brother, John, and sisters, Mary and Ann. His twin brother inherited John Sharman Geary's lands, because Thomas was already in line to inherit his grandfather Geary's lands.[13] Thomas' mother died in 1803 when he was just 11 years old and his father remarried Susannah Tookey Brotherhood on September 18, 1811.[14] Thomas was raised in Atterton and came into his inheritance when he was 25 years old. He likely knew from a young age that he would inherit his Grandfather Geary's ancestral lands. He would have been told that his inheritance would include the responsibility of providing for his uncle, Thomas Geary/1767 by paying him an annuity. The younger Thomas was directed by his Grandfather Geary's will to pay Uncle Thomas 200 pounds per year out of the income of the land. In addition, a special codicil to the will entitled Uncle Thomas to receive a one-time legacy of 1,000 pounds, worth more than $150,000 in today's dollars.[15]

In 1820, when Thomas Geary was 28 years old, he married Sarah Ann Elton, a 17-year-old girl from Maidstone, Kent. Thomas' mother was also an Elton. It appears that Sarah's father, John Elton, was friends with Thomas' father, John Sharman Geary.[16] Thomas Geary obtained a marriage license on November 20, 1820 which reads: "Thomas Geary of Witherley Leic. Bach. & Sarah Ann Elton of Maidstone, a minor (mother Eliz E wid) at Maidstone, Kent." The witnesses to the marriage were Nehemiah Ford and Sarah Clements.[17]

Thomas Geary referred to himself as a gentleman and he did own family land, but he was more correctly a middle-class farmer, often called a yeoman.[18] The yeoman class in Britain fit between the gentry and the labourers because the landholder helped work on his own land. The Geary family could afford to hire farm laborers to work alongside them on the farm. They were certainly much better off than the typical member of the working or labor class, but they were not wealthy. Almost every one of the male Gearys left a will, at a time when only about 10% of the British population made a will. That, in itself, is remarkable and shows some sophistication. And when leaving a will, these Geary men left substantial sums of money to their heirs.

There was a Geary family seal passed down from father to son – portraying an olive branch across a lyre in a striking image of harmony and peace. A family seal puts a distinctive wax imprint

```
                    John (Gery) Geary of Atterton
                            Died 1712
                       md. Mary (Marie) Weaver
```

- Mary (Gearie) b. 1697
- John (Gearie) Geary 1698-1754 md. Sarah Lynes
- Thomas (Gearie) 1699-1715

Children of John (Gearie) Geary and Sarah Lynes:
- John Geary 1730-1816 md. Ann Sharman
- Mary Geary 1728-1769 md. Thomas Neal

Children of John Geary and Ann Sharman:
- John Sharman Geary 1763-1826 md. Mary (Elton)
- Thomas Geary 1767-1853

Children of John Sharman Geary and Mary (Elton):
- John Geary 1790-1791
- John Geary 1792-1868
- Thomas Geary 1792-1865 md. Sarah Ann Elton
- Mary Geary 1794-1796
- Ann Geary 1796-?

Children of Thomas Geary and Sarah Ann Elton:
- John Thomas Geary 1823-1867 md. Sophia Fryer 1829-1872
- Henry Geary 1825-1880
- Thomas Edmund Geary 1825 to ?
- Frederick Geary 1830-1901
- Elton Geary 1835 to ?

Charles Geary Browne 1857 to ?
(Thomas Geary's son by Mary Browne)

Children of John Thomas Geary and Sophia Fryer:
- Sophia Ann Geary Page 1853-1934
- Thomas Fryer Geary 1854-1855
- Echo Workman Geary Hanley 1856-1936
- Eliza Jane Geary Keele 1859-1931
- Leah Fryer Geary 1862-1898
- Sarah Ann (Annie) Geary Davis 1864-1921

on signed documents. This indicates a literate life. Each Geary family was prominent in the local Church of England parish. However, the Gearys were a prominent family in a small society of a few hundred local people, not thousands. None of them appears in the history books written about the Leicestershire area. The fact that they owned land, paid taxes, sometimes collected the taxes, and married well, indicates they were comfortable but not rich.[19]

Despite some family stories to the contrary, there is no evidence that this Geary family was involved in Britain's House of Lords.[20] Historically the Lords who served in that house of Parliament carried titles granted by royalty to earlier generations and lived in manor houses with extensive real estate ownership. Tenant farmers worked that land to provide income for the Lord.[21] Leicestershire, where the Gearys lived, did have a manor house in the 1800s, but it was occupied by Sir Wolstan Dixie. Bosworth Hall was built in the 1500s and the Dixie family lived there for more than two centuries.[22]

BIRTH OF JOHN THOMAS GEARY AND SIBLINGS

Three years into the marriage of Thomas Geary and Sarah Elton, their first child arrived on February 5, 1823. He was named John Thomas Geary, after a long line of male relatives with the same names. John's brothers were born in rapid succession: Thomas Edmund in 1824, Henry in December, 1825, Frederick in July, 1830 and Elton in January, 1835. The three oldest sons were baptized in the Witherley Parish Church in Leicester by an Anglican Rector on December 14, 1825, probably near the time of Henry's birth. The two youngest sons were christened years later, on January 6, 1837, at the Independent Chapel (Non-Conformist) of Atherstone in the Parish of Mancetter, Warwickshire.[23] The Geary family's inconsistency in terms of chosen religions may have set the stage for John Thomas Geary's later openness to the Mormon faith.

There are no records of the Geary brothers attending school near their childhood home but they most likely attended the neighborhood school. Certainly, John's adult writings demonstrate that he had a solid education, given his sophisticated use of language, references to literature, and his elegant penmanship. Children in the area usually went to school at the Witherley Parish School from a very young age, which was a free school operated by the Church of England. After the early grades, these children often transferred to the Market Bosworth School in middle childhood.[24] This was a well-respected school, originally called the Market Bosworth School, later known as the Dixie School, after the local family headed by Sir Wolstan Dixie. It is speculation, but if John attended this school, he would have gained an above-average education for the 19th century, learning several foreign and classical languages, mathematics, science and literature.

The Market Bosworth School is described as follows:

"The earliest records we have of the School's existence date from 1320, but The Dixie gained its present name when it was re-founded in 1601 under the will of an Elizabethan merchant and Lord Mayor of London, Sir Wolstan Dixie. The most distinguished of the School's former pupils is Thomas Hooker, founder of Hartford, Connecticut, and Father of American Democracy. The best known of its teachers is undoubtedly Dr. [Samuel] Johnson, moralist, poet and author of the famous dictionary, who taught at the School in the mid-eighteenth century. The main building of today's School was built in 1828 and faces the historic market square of Market Bosworth, making a distinctive landmark."[25]

John and possibly his brothers, Henry and Thomas Edmund, could have attended Market Bosworth School, only eight miles from their home in Atterton. There, they would have encountered the long-time Headmaster, Arthur Benoni Evans (1781–1854) who led the school from 1829 until his death in 1854. Evans was from a well-educated family; his father was a professor of mathematics and a well-known astronomer. Evans himself attended St. John's College at Oxford, graduating with a Doctorate of Divinity in 1829. He was well-versed in the classical languages – Latin and Greek – and was also fluent in Hebrew, French, Italian, Spanish, German, and Icelandic. (John Thomas Geary was reported to know seven languages – this may be the source of his language education. His clerkship in law may have taught him some Latin.) Headmaster Evans was also fascinated with geology, botany and history. He served as both a cleric and a headmaster and was reported to be one of the most successful in the school's history.[26]

Boys in mid-1800s England who attended a typical grammar school curriculum for free public schools would have had classes which included a study of languages. "From the 1830s, French and German began to be offered in the emerging major Public Schools… French was widely taught in private schools catering to the emerging middle classes, German seems to have been taught only in the so-called Dissenting Academies of non-conformist Protestant groups, where modern languages were taught alongside Latin, Greek, English, Mathematics and a science; the number of these and similar schools increased after 1779, when non-conformists were legally allowed to be teachers …" Therefore, it is possible that John and his brothers, having a non-conformist mother and good access to the Market Bosworth free public school, were taught by Headmaster Evans.[27]

When John was fifteen years old, his father arranged with a local attorney, Stafford Stratton Baxter, of Atherstone, to take John on as a legal apprentice. The papers for John's official clerkship were drawn up and signed on November 24, 1838. Baxter signed the papers along with "Thomas Geary, Farmer and Grazier of Atterton in the county of Leicester and his son John Thomas Geary, also of Atterton, Leicester."[28] The process for becoming a lawyer in England at that time required a young man to be an apprentice to an experienced attorney and pay a fee for a period of five years, minimum. The two would enter into Articles of Clerkship to commit to the arrangement. Once trained, the young man would be admitted to the Law Lists and embark upon his own practice. In 1823 the Law Society was formed in England and given a charter in 1831 to regulate the profession. Thereafter apprentice arrangements were handled formally and an annual certificate of admission was required. Attorneys were known as either Barristers or Solicitors in England at this time. Barristers generally represented people in court proceedings while Solicitors were usually assisting people with transactions and other non-court related matters.

By 1841, John was still living at home with his family in Atterton while working as Baxter's legal apprentice in Atherstone. He was seventeen years old. The family also had two farm laborers and two household servants living there. The 1841 British Census record for Witherley Parish, Leicester County, Atherstone Registration District 20, residence of Atterton shows the following people in the home:[29]

Thomas, age 45
Sarah, age 35

John, age 17
Thomas, age 15
Henry, age 13
Frederick, age 10
Elton, age 6
George Starkey, age 15, agricultural laborer
James Smith, age 15, agricultural laborer
2 female servants

This Geary family grouping indicates that they were prosperous enough to have servants and farm employees, but still living close to the land that they owned and they were involved with farming labor themselves. With limited mechanization for the farm, the Gearys required considerable hired physical labor to manage this size of farm, which was approximately 186 acres. The Geary's centuries-long family history of owning land in the English countryside was about to come to an abrupt halt when Thomas Geary made a difficult decision.

THOMAS GEARY MORTGAGES THE ANCESTRAL LANDS

As John and his brothers got closer to adulthood, their father, Thomas Geary, was in the process of taking out a loan and mortgaging his ancestral Geary family land. It is not clear what would have led him to this momentous decision, but financial need may have played a part. Thomas was still required to make the large annuity payments owing to his Uncle Thomas. This obligation could have created cash flow problems if the Geary land wasn't producing enough income to support both Uncle Thomas and the Gearys' growing family of five boys. The 1840s was also a time when the Industrial Revolution was causing many people who previously worked in agriculture to move to the cities and work in factories. That situation could have created a labor shortage for this farming family. Given that Thomas wanted to provide a meaningful future for his five sons, he may have decided that raising money for their education and training through a mortgage was a better use of the main family asset than continued farming.

It is also possible that Thomas Geary was seeking a mortgage for his family lands because he had made a poor investment in railroad stock. In the mid-1840s England was swept into "Railway Mania," a period of widespread railway expansion that drew many investors into speculative schemes. "Railways transformed English finance as surely as they changed the face of the English landscape...In 1845 Parliament sanctioned 2,816 miles of new railway line... The Mania of the mid-forties drew in the whole nation of investors. The aristocracy and gentry became heavily involved in railway shareholding since they were often given large blocks of shares to secure their goodwill for lines crossing their estates."[30]

There is evidence that Thomas invested in a proposed railway spur between Coventry and Nuneaton in 1846. The company he invested in was called the Oxford, Coventry, Burton on Trent Junction Railway. In November, 1845, that company published a Book of Reference Containing the Names of Owners, Lessees, and Occupiers of the Lands, Houses, and Hereditaments to be taken for the purposes of building a Line of Railway. In other words, it was a prospectus to potential investors. Thomas Geary is listed on three pages concerning land he owned in Witherley, Atterton, and Ratcliffe Culey.[31] It is not clear how much he would have invested or if he was somehow trading for the rights to cross his land, but it appears he had an interest in the railway line being built. One writer describes how heady the environment of railway-building was: "Men who went to church as devoutly as their counting houses - men whose word had ever been as good as their bond - joined the pursuit. They entered the whirlpool, and were carried away by the vortex."[32]

Unfortunately, this particular railway spur between Coventry and Nuneaton was never built. A competitor, North-Western Company, got there first. In 1847, the House of Commons approved a proposal by the North-Western Company to build a branch diverging from their main line between Coventry and Nuneaton. The House struck out the part of the proposal that recited terms of an arrangement with the Oxford, Coventry and Burton on Trent Railway Company relative to providing the necessary funds for construction.[33] With this action, Thomas Geary's investment became worthless in a company unable to build a railway line.

Two years after the railway investment fell through, Thomas asked his oldest son, John Thomas Geary, to help him create an abstract of title to the family lands. In 1849, John Thomas Geary had been studying law for more than a decade and practicing for four years. He passed the exams and was admitted to the Law Lists in 1845. As he went to work on his father's request, John assembled a large collection of property documents related to the farm. He created an abstract of title that detailed the title chain by which the Geary ancestral land had been acquired through inheritance during more than one hundred years. This was a process similar to a modern-day title search.

Thomas Geary then took that title report to his lender, Lord Thomas Thorpe Fowke, and obtained a mortgage on the Geary lands. On January 11, 1849 Thomas Geary and Lord Fowke recorded an Abstract of Mortgage against the property for 5,000 pounds (roughly a quarter of a million US dollars in today's values).[34] It is not clear how Thomas Geary would have known Fowke nor how they came to do business together. Thomas Thorpe Fowke was an esquire and gentleman described as a Lord of the Manor in Midgham, which was several counties away from Leicestershire.[35] The Fowke family had a long and prominent history in British naval admiralty. Fowke was also one of the magistrates for Berks County, having been appointed in December 16, 1842.[36] At the time of the loan and mortgage, John was working as a legal apprentice in London and may have had business experience that helped him connect Lord Fowke with his father. The terms of the mortgage required Thomas Geary to make annual payments to Lord Fowke.

When Thomas received the 5,000-pound loan in cash, he may have used it to benefit himself and each of his sons. At the beginning of the 1850s, the Geary sons were seeking their own paths in life. As mentioned, John was pursuing a career in law, having been a legal apprentice since he was 15 years old and a practicing lawyer since 1845. His next younger brother, Thomas Edmund Geary, 25, was operating the family farm on the mortgaged Geary lands. Henry, 23, had become a physician with a medical practice in Market Bosworth. Frederick, 19, also wanted to pursue a career in law, and Elton, 15, was to become a banker's clerk. It is possible that Thomas used some of the borrowed 5,000 pounds to fund each son's ambitions.

Thomas also likely used some of the mortgage proceeds to change his own lifestyle by moving from the farm into the city. In the 1851 British Census, Thomas and his wife Sarah were living at St. Mary, Tower Street in Leicester. They also had a 16-year-old servant, Ann Law, living with them.[37] Leicester was a town of 60,584 in 1851, just on the verge of an industrial expansion. Railway connections prompted factory building and the town was on track to pass 200,000 in population by the turn of the century. The main manufacturing industries there were clothing, boots, shoes, hosiery, along with engineering and waterworks. Thomas, at 58 years old, probably did not work after the move, but he did remain in Leicester for the rest of his life.[38]

Thomas Edmund remained on the family lands when his father moved to Leicester. Thomas Edmund was the only one of the Geary boys who continued farming at Atterton as an adult; it is not known if he was aware of his father's mortgage or its implications. Two months after the mortgage was placed on the land, Thomas Edmund, 25, married Jane Ann Neal, 23, the daughter of John Neal on 20 March 1849 at St. Martin's, Birmingham, Warwickshire, England. Her residence is listed as Atherstone on the Parish Register.

On the 1851 British Census, Thomas Edmund is shown as the Head of Household and he employs two farm servants, two general servants and a nurse living in his home. Thomas Edmund is listed as 26 years old living in Atterton with his wife, Jane Ann Geary, 24 years old, a one-year-old daughter, Anne Mary Geary, and a newborn son, John Thomas Geary. He is also listed as having numerous other people in his household – John Arnold, 22, servant; William Fording, 21, servant from Ireland, Mary Falkner, 22, servant, Sarah Jane Smith, 20, servant and Emma Adcock, 13, servant.[39]

Despite Thomas Edmund's farming endeavors, no payments were made on the Fowke mortgage from 1849 to 1851 and therefore, Thomas Geary's mortgage fell into default. In 1851, Lord Fowke foreclosed on the mortgage and took clear title to the Geary property. He then transferred the mortgage to Sir John Edward George Bayley and George Brockman for 5,000 pounds plus accrued unpaid interest.[40] Sir John Edward George Bayley was a 2nd Baronet and member of the peerage. He played amateur cricket. His father, Sir John Bayley, was 1st Baronet and a prominent Solicitor and Judge at the King's Bench. He also served as Baron of the Exchequer.[41]

The transfer by Fowke to Bayley eliminated the Geary family's interest in their Atterton lands. Although the mortgage technically gave Thomas Geary a right to come forward and redeem the mortgage by curing the default, he did not do so.[42] The land passed to Bayley and the personal property, crops and animals were sold at auction. The Leicester Chronicle dated October 30, 1852 carried an advertisement which read: "Valuable Farming Stock, Horses, Corn, Hay, Clover, Grass Seeds, and Stubble Keeping, Turnips, Implements, etc." to be sold at Atterton near Witherley, Leicestershire. "W. Berridge is honoured with instructions from Mr. T.E. Geary of Atterton Field, to sell by auction on Thursday, November 11th, 1852, on the premises… sale to commence at eleven o'clock."[43] As the last Geary brother left Atterton, it was a sad but possibly transformative end to at least a six-generation history of Geary property ownership.

ECONOMIC CONDITIONS IN BRITAIN 1840s AND 1850s

During the period when Thomas Geary lost the family's ancestral lands, the economic and social conditions in and around London during the 1840s and 1850s reveal a society in transition. Thomas and his five Geary sons probably realized that the future was not bright for farming. Beginning in the late 1700s, the Industrial Revolution changed economic conditions for the entire world. Innovations such as steam power, mechanized textile production, and iron and coal mining, began in England and spread to the European continent. During the 1840s, factories were built all over the country to manufacture locomotives, steamboats, telegraph machinery, and large-scale production of machine tools. This transformed the formerly agrarian society of England into an industrial powerhouse, expanding opportunities for young men such as the Geary boys.

The enclosure movement, which affected the Geary family lands in the mid-1700s, was completed by the first part of the 19th century and it left many small farmers dispossessed. Some early Mormon missionaries who visited the English countryside in the 1840s wrote a vivid description of the changes: "A few years since, and almost every family had their garden, their cow on the common & their pig in the Stye, which added greatly to the comforts of the household; but now we seldom find either Garden, Cow or Pig…"[44]

During this Victorian era, English society still consisted of strict class distinctions with an Upper Class of royal families, Lords and officers, wealthy men and business owners, a Middle Class of skilled tradesmen, merchants, shopkeepers, and white collar professions such as clerks or lawyers/solicitors, a Working Class of unskilled laborers working in brutal and unsanitary factory conditions, and an Under Class, those dependent on the support of others, such as orphans or single women living on the streets.[45] Unlike America, where movement between classes in even one generation was possible, the English system restricted one's ability to move from the class to which you had been born. If you were born poor, you usually died poor in Victorian England. The middle class did expand dramatically during the 1800s with industrialization, as formerly agrarian families sought better lives in cities.

Three of the Geary brothers moved to London while still young men. They were seeking their fortunes in the world's largest port and city. London had a population of more than 3 million in the 1850s. The Great Irish Famine caused an influx of immigrants during the 1840s. "The vast majority of the migrants who fueled London's remarkable population growth were from Britain, and in particular, from counties and regions of the South East. As a result, Londoners continued to be both younger and more likely to be female than the inhabitants of other British regions…the first half of the nineteenth century also witnessed a steady decline in both child and adult mortality, primarily as a consequence of better sanitation, building standards and food supplies."[46]

There was an "insatiable demand for capital investment in railroads, shipping, industry and agriculture" which drove the growth of financial services in London.[47] The 1862 Bradshaw's Guide to London listed 83 banks, 336 stockbrokers, 37 currency brokers, 248 ship and insurance brokers and 1500 different merchants in London. The Bank of England employed hundreds of people and did millions of pounds of business each day. The great railways were built throughout England in the mid-1800s, such as Euston station in 1837 and King's Cross station in 1852.

The Geary brothers were not reduced to poverty with the loss of their ancestral land holdings or the changes in the British economy. If their father distributed to them some of the 5,000 pounds received for the mortgage on his land, it provided them with options. Rather than going into factory or manual labor jobs, each of the Geary boys pursued a profession and stayed solidly in the middle class. They may not have been in the highest class of London society, but neither were they in the lowest.

As of 1851, the five Geary brothers were on paths away from Leicestershire. John Thomas was in London practicing law. His two younger brothers were living with him; Fred was also studying law and Elton was a bank clerk. Henry was listed as a partner in a medical practice in Market Bosworth, Leicestershire, England.[48] Thomas Edmund was moving his young family to Australia sometime in the 1850s after the loss of the farm. All of the Geary boys landed on their feet after losing their family lands.

THE GEARY FAMILY'S RELIGIOUS BACKGROUND

Consider the religious circumstances that existed in the Geary household at the time the sons were reaching manhood. It appears that the family was originally involved in the Church of England (also referred to as the Anglican Church) when the children were small. The three older boys' baptism in 1825 attests to that. On December 14, 1825, the three older boys of Thomas and Sarah Geary were all baptized (christened) in the Church of England. However, a few years later, in 1837, the parents chose to baptize the two younger boys in a Non-conformist Church.

At this period of time in England, an active reformation was taking place amongst the many religious persuasions of the day. Parliament passed a law in 1832 law – between the baptisms of the two groups of Geary boys – which granted additional rights to Non-conformists. This might have prompted the change in affiliation for at least part of the Geary family. Perhaps their mother's family, who had a history in the Non-conformist church, influenced some of the Geary brothers in religious matters.

In 19th Century England, where church and state were combined, the Anglican Church was the approved church of the English government. There were those who advocated only an internal revival of 'true religion' and they were termed Conformists. There was another group – about a third of Anglican clergy from within the church - who called themselves Evangelicals, advocating for social reform such as temperance, help for the poor, and opening up the education system.[49] Another group felt that a new Christian emphasis outside of Anglicanism was necessary, and classed themselves Non-conformists or Separatists who attended what was known as the Independent Churches.

Beginning in the 1600s, Non-conformists were treated as dissenters in England and represented the groups that became Baptists, Congregationalists, Presbyterians, Methodists, or Unitarians by the 1800s.[50] Until 1832 Non-conformists could not hold office in England nor have baptisms recorded in English churches, but the Great Reform Act of 1832 changed that.

In the mid-1800s, Non-conformists grew in political power. They advocated for increasing the separation between Church and State and allowing their members to attend state-sponsored universities. As people in England became more willing to identify as Non-conformist, the group increased dramatically at this time. "[T]he Church of England is shown to have lost almost one-fifth of its affiliation market share during this period…Non-conformity more than quadrupled."[51]

There is evidence that the extended Geary family had traditionally been active in religious affairs. The family members were usually baptized in their local churches and married by their local church leaders. Their life events are recorded at the parish churches where they lived. The Geary Family Bible was a treasured piece of their family property, one which John's father, Thomas, inherited through his paternal Geary line.

The Geary Family Bible, still in the family to this day, is a rare 1629 first edition of the King James Bible published only a few years after the original edition. It is not known if that particular Bible was in the Geary family since 1629, but it was in the family many generations because it contained a written genealogy on papers inside the front cover of the book dating back at least to the 1700s.[52] Per family tradition, Thomas Geary gifted the Bible to John Thomas Geary, his oldest son, sometime in the years prior to 1853. When Thomas Geary gave the Bible to his son John Thomas, he instructed to him to keep the family Bible with him always and to only sell it if his children were hungry and in need of food. At the same time, Thomas entrusted to John Thomas the Geary Family Seal, which is made of Carnelian agate and displays the family crest.

During this time of great religious upheaval in England, the newly-formed Mormon Church from America was making its first inroads into the local faith community. As early as 1837, five years after the 1832 British legal change regarding Non-conformist rights, Mormon Prophet Joseph Smith was inspired to send Heber C. Kimball and Orson Hyde as missionaries to the British Isles.[53] Kimball baptized the first convert in London on August 31, 1840 at the Public Baths. "It was "Father Conner" who offered himself as a convert to the Elders, and it was Heber C. Kimball who baptized him. The ceremony was performed at the Public Baths, after which the new member was confirmed under the hands of the three Apostles at his own house."[54] Henry Connor, a watchmaker, became the first London Mormon. London served for many years as the headquarters for the church in Britain.

Additional Mormon missionaries arrived in subsequent years and, by 1841, there were a total of 5,864 Mormon converts in and around London. That year even Queen Victoria had her own copy of the Book of Mormon, richly-bound and presented to her by Mormon Elder Lorenzo Snow during a private audience.[55] The number of Mormon converts continued to grow. Sometimes entire congregations of Separatists or Non-conformists were converted to Mormonism. In 1850, there were 30,747 Mormon Church members in England about the time that John Thomas Geary would have first encountered them.

ENDNOTES FOR CHAPTER ONE

1   Hoskins, W. G., <u>Four Centuries of Leicestershire Farming, Studies in Agrarian History</u>, 1939, cited by Patty Swenson in Swenson, Patty, "Research Report - Geary Family, For: Kaye Page Nichols & Lisa Michele Church, May 5, 2019, The Socioeconomic Status of the Geary Family who lived in Atterton, Witherly and Ratcliffe Culey, and Dadlington in Leicestershire England from About 1680 to 1880". This self-published report contains professional genealogy research commissioned by the authors to provide documentation on the Geary family history prior to 1850. Original in possession of authors. Hereinafter "Patty Swenson Research Report 2019". Selected excerpts appear in the Appendix herein.

2   Patty Swenson Research Report 2019.

3   Coke, Charles Anthony, <u>Population Gazetteer of England and Wales, 1864</u>, www.Google Books.com, accessed May 24, 2020. Even at the time of this book's writing, the population of Atterton in Leicester County, England is listed at a mere 40 persons. https://en.wikipedia.org/wiki/Atterton, accessed September 29, 2020.

4   *Ibid.*

5   Patty Swenson Research Report 2019. Note: to avoid confusion, each subsequent John Geary mentioned in this chater is referred to by his birth year.

6   *Ibid.* See Appendix for a copy of the will of John Geary who died in 1712.

7   "Enclosing the Land" article, at the UK Parliament website, https://www.parliament.uk/about/living-heritage/tranformingsociety/towncountry/landscape/overview/enclosingland, accessed September 29, 2020.

8   Estate Document 2, was located in British land records and transcribed from the original document by Kaye Page Nichols - Supplemental Abstract of Title DE322/13/2 post 1800, Of Thomas Geary, Esq. to a portion of an estate at Atterton. The Estate Documents were obtained in 2009 by Kaye Page Nichols from The Record Office for Leicestershire, Leicester and Rutland, Long Street, Wigston Magna, Leicester LE18 2AH, Tel: 0116 257 1080 Fax: 0116 257 1120, recordoffice@leics.gov.uk. It appears to be the set of documents which John Thomas Geary prepared an "Abstract of Title" for his father in 1849 in preparation for mortgaging the family lands.

9   Nichols, John, <u>The History and Antiquities of the County of Leicester including The Hamlet of Atterton in The Same County</u> (1813), page 1026. <u>The History and Antiquities of the County of Leicester, Vol. 4</u> (1811). Cited in Patty Swenson Report, Chapter 1, pages 1-3. The "glebe" land is the land owned by the Church of England to support the local parish priest.

10   Patty Swenson Research Report 2019.

11   *Ibid.*

12   *Ibid.*

13   *Ibid.*

14   *Ibid*, citing Record Office for Leicestershire, Leicester & Rutland: Leicestershire Burials; DE2599/5; Dadlington. MaryGeary Image found at www.findmypast.com.

15   *Ibid.* Uncle Thomas Geary lived in Leicester most of his adult life, married twice, and did not work. Because Uncle Thomas lived to be 87 years old, dying in October, 1853, the value of this annuity obligation would grow to be more than 8,000 pounds during his lifetime, quite a burden on the younger Thomas Geary's inheritance.

16   Sarah Elton's father, John Elton, died in 1811 when she was a child, but his will names John Geary of Dadlington, a grazier, as one of his executors. It is likely that the two families were connected through the Elton family, as John Sharman Geary's wife was also an Elton.

17   Patty Swenson Research Report 2019, citing Kent, Surrey, London: Canterbury Marriage Licenses, 1810-1837, Vol. 35, folio 135, 1820.

18   https://www.britannica.com/topic/yeoman, accessed September 29, 2020.

19   Patty Swenson Research Report 2019.

20   https://www.parliament.uk/business/lords/lords-history/history-of-the-lords Accessed September 29, 2020.

21   https://archives.parliament.uk/collections/search?s=geary Accessed September 29, 2020. Kaye Page Nichols wrote letters to the House of Lords Information Office in 2008 and their replies confirmed that there are 'no records of a past member of the House of Lords with the surname/title 'Geary' nor a record that Geary was 'a speaker of either House of Parliament.' House of Lords Information Office, Mathew Purvis at www.parliament.uk. Dated, August 14, 2008, and History of Parliament, Paul Seward, Director, 18 Bloomsbury Square, Lond WC1A 2NS, pseaward@histpart.ac.uk, dated August 22, 2008.

22   Tomlin, Arthur, *The Hinckley Times*, "Past Times: A history of Market Bosworth", 11 Sep 2016. https://www.hinckleytimes.net/news/local-news/past-times-history-market-bosworth-11853085

23   England and Wales Non-Conformist Record Indexes (RG4-8), 1588-1977, accessed at www.FamilySearch.org., Frederick Geary, (1830-1901), K2FC-92Z and Elton Geary, K2FC-W1M.

24   https://en.wikipedia.org/wiki/Witherley

25   http://www.dixie.org.uk/Our-History The Market Bosworth School is now called the Dixie School and it still stands in its original 1820s building. "The village school, Witherley Church of England Primary School, is located next to the church. Usually, children attending the school will transfer to Market Bosworth School at the appropriate age." Witherley entry, www.wikipedia.com. Accessed December 11, 2019.

26   Reports from commissioners, 1869, House of Commons, page 40 West Leicestershire, cited in https://en.wikipedia.org/wiki/Arthur_Benoni_Evans. See also Gent. Mag. January 1855, pp. 100–2; Men of the Time (1887), p. 360, cited in the Dictionary of National Biography volume 18.djvu/60. (2018, August 16). In *Wikisource*. Retrieved 02:28, October 5, 2020, from https://en.wikisource.org/w/index.php?title=Page:Dictionary_of_National_Biography_volume_18.djvu/60&oldid=7902466.

27   McClelland, Nicola, French and German in British Schools (1850-1945), pages 109-124, retrieved on October 5, 2020 from https://journals.openedition.org/dhfles/4089.

28   See Appendix for a transcription of Geary's Articles of Clerkship, copy in possession of Kaye Page Nichols. They are located online at www.ancestry.com/family-tree/person/tree/10612501/person/6404827772/facts.

29   "England and Wales Census, 1841," database with images, FamilySearch (https://familysearch.org/ark:/61903/1:1:MQYL-RMP : 24 May 2019), accessed September 29, 2020.

30   Robb, George, White Collar Crime in Modern England, Financial Fraud and Business Morality, 1845-1929, Cambridge University Press, 1992, Chapter 2 - Railway Mania, pages 30-32, accessed at Googlebooks.com on October 10, 2020.

31   Patty Swenson Research Report 2019.

32   Robb at page 145.

33	The Monthly Railway Record, edited by John Robertson and J.W. Brooke, March 1847, accessed on Googlebooks.com, October 10, 2020.

34	See Appendix for a Transcript of Thomas Geary's 1849 Mortgage, located and transcribed from the original document by Kaye Page Nichols - Supplemental Abstract of Title DE322/13/2 post 1800, Of Thomas Geary, Esq. to a portion of an estate at Atterton. The Estate Documents were obtained in 2009 by Kaye Page Nichols from The Record Office for Leicestershire, Leicester and Rutland, Long Street, Wigston Magna, Leicester LE18 2AH, Tel: 0116 257 1080 Fax: 0116 257 1120, recordoffice@leics.gov.uk. Hereinafter "Thomas Geary's 1849 Mortgage."

35	Clarke, Benjamin, British Gazeteer: Political, Commercial, Ecclesiastical, and Historical, 1852, London: H.G. Collins, Vol. 111 L-Z, accessed at Googlebooks.com, December 13, 2019.

36	Accounts and Papers of the House of Commons, Vol 33, 1846, accessed at Googlebooks.com, December 13, 2019.

37	"England and Wales Census, 1851," database with images, *FamilySearch* (https://familysearch.org/ark:/61903/1:1:S-GF3-Z73 : 9 November 2019), Thomas Geary, St Marys, Leicestershire, England; citing St Marys, Leicestershire, England, p. 19, from "1851 England, Scotland and Wales census," database and images, *findmypast* (http://www.findmypast.com : n.d.); citing PRO HO 107, The National Archives of the UK, Kew, Surrey. See www.familysearch.org, Thomas Geary, (1792-1865), MG5D-6TF.

38	www.familysearch.org, Thomas Geary (1792-1865), MG5D-6TF.

39	"England and Wales Census, 1851," database with images, *FamilySearch* (https://familysearch.org/ark:/61903/1:1:S-GZK-LPQ : 8 November 2019), Thomas Edward Geary, Hamlet Of Atterton Witherley, Warwickshire, England; citing Hamlet Of Atterton Witherley, Warwickshire, England, p. 4, from "1851 England, Scotland and Wales census," database and images, *findmypast* (http://www.findmypast.com : n.d.); citing PRO HO 107, The National Archives of the UK, Kew, Surrey. See www.familysearch.org, Thomas Edmund Geary, (1825-deceased), L7X2-R84.

40	See Appendix for a Transcript of Thomas Geary's 1849 Mortgage.

41	Sir John Edward George Bayley, 2nd Baronet (23 December 1793 – 23 December 1871) was an English baronet and amateur cricketer. Born December 23, 1793 in London, he was the son of Sir John Bayley, 1st Baronet and his wife Elizabeth, the youngest daughter of John Markett. Bayley was called to the bar by the Inner Temple in 1835 and went then to the Northern Circuit. He succeeded his father as baronet in 1841. He died December 23, 1871. He was listed as a member of the peerage in England. Rt Hon Sir John Bayley was a lawyer of 2 Essex Court Temple, a judge on the kings Bench and Baron of the Exchequer. https://www.ucl.ac.uk/lbs/person/view/45435, https://en.wikipedia.org/wiki/Sir_John_Bayley,_2nd_Baronet http://www.thepeerage.com/p49428.htm

42	See Appendix for a Transcript of Thomas Geary's 1849 Mortgage.

43	*Leicester Chronicle, or Commercial and Leicestershire Mercury*, Leicester, Leicestershire, London, England, 30 October 1852, Saturday, page 2. www.Newspapers.com/Ancestry.com, accessed August 8, 2019. Copyright 2019, All Rights Reserved.

44	Walker, Ronald W., "The Willard Richards and Brigham Young 5 September 1840 Letter from England to Nauvoo," *Brigham Young University Studies*, Vol. 18, No. 3, Spring 1978, pages 466-475, published by Brigham Young University, .https://www.jstor.org/stable/43040774

45	https://www.oldbaileyonline.org/static/London-life19th.jsp "If the eighteenth century had started the process of creating ever more solid social and geographical boundaries between classes, the nineteenth century completed the job."

46	https://sites.udel.edu/britlitwiki/social-life-in-victorian-england/

47	https://en.wikipedia.org/wiki/19th-century_London, accessed October 10, 2020.

48   "England and Wales Census, 1851," database with images, *FamilySearch* (https://familysearch.org/ark:/61903/1:1:S-GFG-QXV: 9 November 2019), Henry Geary, , Leicestershire, England; citing , Leicestershire, England, p. 2, from "1851 England, Scotland and Wales census," database and images, *findmypast* (http://www.findmypast.com : n.d.); citing PRO HO 107, The National Archives of the UK, Kew, Surrey. See www.familysearch.org, Henry Geary, (1825-1880), K2FC-H3X.

49   https://www.museeprotestant.org/en/notice/Protestantism-in-england-in-the-sixth-century

50   https:\\www.Britannica.com/topic/nonconformists. Accessed November 4, 2019.

51   Field, Clive D., "Counting Religion in England and Wales the Long Eighteenth Century," *The Journal of Ecclesiastical History*, Cambridge.org, Accessed, 17 Sept 2012. Cambridge University Press www.liberalhistory.org.uk/history/conformists/.

52   See Appendix for images of the Geary Family Bible and also the image at the end of this chapter. The original Geary Family Bible is currently in possession of Geary descendant Kirk Bailey of Brigham City, Utah.

53   Allen, James B., Esplin, Ronald K., Whittaker, David J., Men With a Mission 1837-1841, The Quorum of the Twelve Apostles in the British Isles, Deseret Book Company, Salt Lake City, Utah, 1992, page 20.

54   Whitney, Orson F. The Life of Heber C. Kimball, An Apostle: The Father and Founder of the British Mission, Published by the Kimball Family and printed at the *Juvenile Instructor* office, Salt Lake City, Utah, 1888, page 303.

55   www.wikipedia.org/wiki/The_Church_of_Jesus_Christ_of_Latter-day_Saints_in_England. Note: the authors herein refer to The Church of Jesus Christ of Latter-day Saints as "Mormons" in this book due to the time in which our story is set. During the middle part of the 19th Century, the church was known as and referred to most often by the colloquial term "Mormons" although the proper name was and is "The Church of Jesus Christ of Latter-day Saints."

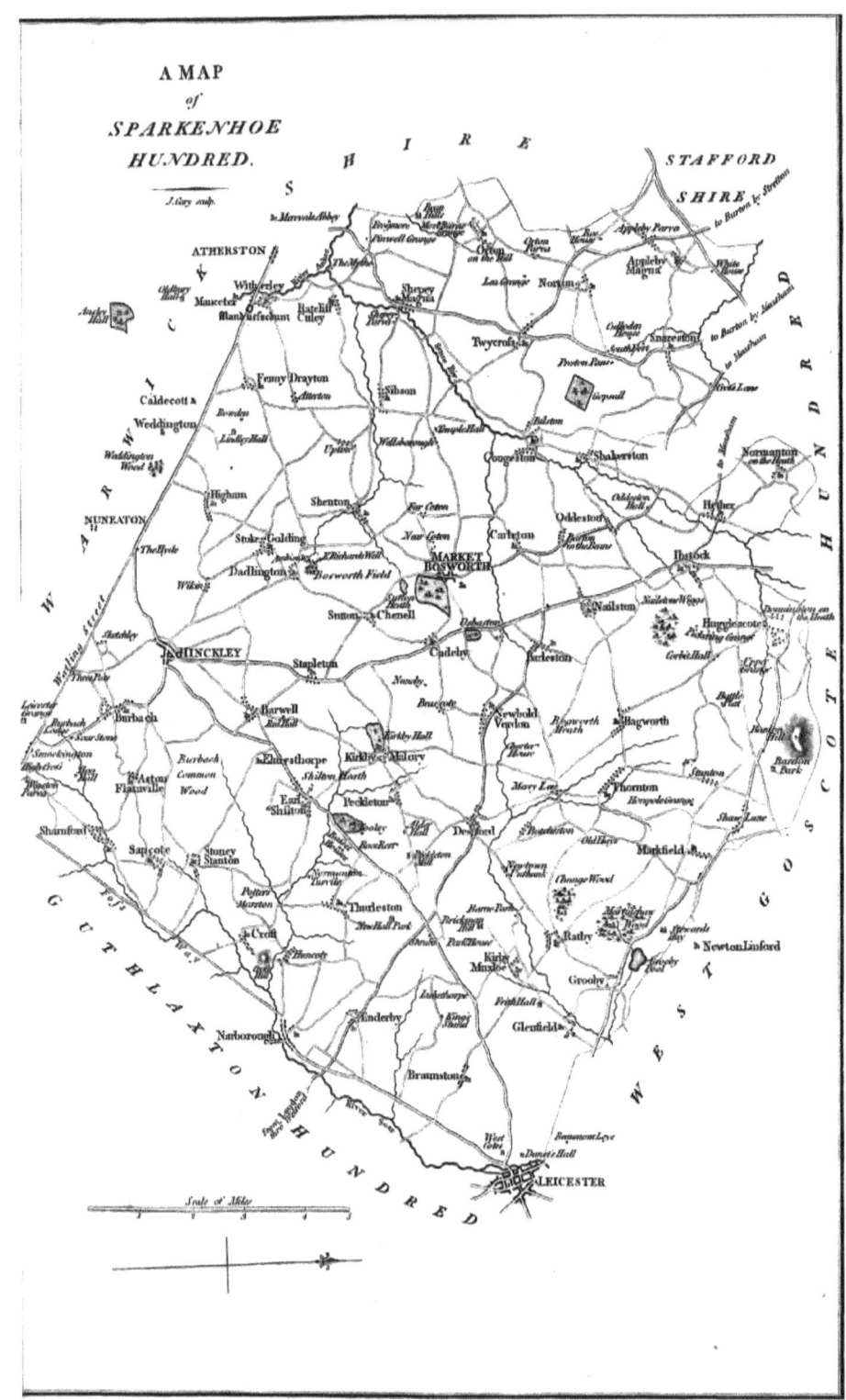

This map shows the area of the English Midlands where the Geary family was located for generations. It is taken from a history of Hinckley, a town at the left center of the map. The map is titled "The Sparkenhoe Hundred" because English areas were organized in groups of 100 "hides," meaning 100 parcels of land big enough to support a family, usually 120 acres each. "The origin of the Sparkenhoe hundred is thought to have dated from the first half of the fourteenth century…" The area shown on the map in 1811 was supporting about 100 families, including the Gearys, who lived near Atterton in the upper left quadrant of the map.

This enlarged section of The Sparkenhoe Hundred map shows the Leicestershire settlements in which the Gearys were involved during the 1600s-1800s in England. Atterton is the small hamlet where the Gearys lived and where most of their farmland was located. John Thomas Geary was raised there. Dadlington is the parish church where John's father, Thomas Geary, and his Geary grandparents are buried. Witherley is the location of the parish church attended by the Geary family and where John and two of his brothers were baptized in the Anglican Church on December 14, 1825. Atherston (or Atherstone) across the county line in Warwickshire is where John served his apprenticeship to become a lawyer with Stafford Stratton Baxter from 1838 forward. It is also the location of the Independent Chapel of Atherstone where John's two younger brothers were christened in a Non-conformist Church.

References are made in the Geary documents to land in the areas of Ratcliffe Culey, Shepey Parva, and Fenny Drayton. For scale, Atterton is about two miles from Witherley and about four miles from Dadlington. According to an article written by Hugh Beavin in the Hinckley Historian Magazine, "Sparseness and barren waste was the characteristic of the Sparkenhoe hundred in medieval times and the late creation of its separate identity…It was certainly in medieval times the poorest part of Leicestershire. This was due to the fact that it was mainly heavy clay and the only settlements were on the islands of gravel in this clay morass."

A typical view in the rural Atterton countryside where John Thomas Geary grew up. This photo was taken in 2014.

The Witherley Parish Church where John was baptized on December 14, 1825 by an Anglican rector. His two brothers, Thomas Edmund and Henry, were also baptized that day. Witherley Parish includes Atterton, Fenny Drayton, and Ratcliffe Culey just as it did when John lived there in the mid-1800s. The church, also called St. Peter's, dates back to the 1600s.

The Atherstone Independent Chapel where John Thomas Geary's two younger brothers, Frederick and Elton, were christened on January 6, 1837. This chapel was built in 1827 as the Independent Chapel (Non-conformist) of Atherstone in the Parish of Mancetter, Warwickshire, England. Atherstone had a history of dissenting, Non-conformist ministers throughout the 1600-1800 time period. One of them was Obadiah Grew (1607-1689) who was imprisoned for preaching doctrines other than those of the Church of England. The local people continued to seek out Non-conformist beliefs throughout the 18th century.

In 1792, the community of Atherstone built its first Independent Chapel and Mr. R.M. Miller served as the minister for 32 years. Membership increased significantly and younger men took up the ministry. The group purchased this land on North Street in 1822 and built the new chapel 5 years later. The Thomas Geary family chose to have their two young sons christened here in the new chapel, although their three older boys had been christened at the Church of England's Witherley Parish Church. The Independent Chapel at Atherstone still stands today and it is used for residential housing.

> **BROMPTON HOSPITAL FOR CONSUMPTION.**—Yest[er]day a well attended meeting of the board was held at [the] above institution, and the routine business having been [dis]posed of, it was stated that the list of stewards for [the] forthcoming anniversary festival is rapidly filling up. Be[nja]min Disraeli, M.P., will preside on the occasion. The n[um]ber of patients at present within the walls of the hospit[al] (both sexes included) eighty one.
>
> **APOTHECARIES HALL.**—The following gentlem[en] passed their examination in the science and practice of [me]dicine, and received certificates to practise, on Thursd[ay] March 22, 1849:—George James Thurston, Southampt[on] street, Bloomsbury; Henry Geary, Atterton, Leicestersh[ire]; William Carroll Satchell, Newport, Isle of Wight.

This March 24, 1849 <u>Morning Chronicle</u> newspaper clipping indicates that Henry Geary, the younger brother of John Thomas Geary, passed his exams to become a medical doctor on March 22, 1849, the same year their father, Thomas Geary, mortgaged the family lands.

> **SPARKENHOE FARMERS' CLUB.**
>
> The annual ploughing match and dinner of this club took place on Wednesday at Market Bosworth, and being favoured with extremely pleasant weather, attracted a considerable number of visitors. The ploughing took place in two fields on opposite sides of the road leading from Bosworth to Sutton Cheney, belonging to Mr. Abel and Mr. Wood, and there were twenty-three competitors, all whose work exhibited an improvement upon that of previous seasons, and, allowing for the unfavourable state of the land, was in most respects highly commendable. The match presented the novel feature in some instances of ploughs with three horses and a driver competing with ploughs with two horses abreast, without a driver.
>
> At the dinner, which took place at the Dixie Arms, and which reflected the greatest credit upon the establishment, about seventy gentlemen sat down, among whom were Messrs. Harrison, Ward, (Appleby,) J. Mayne, Geo. Kilby, Richard Allen, (Waltham,) W. Baker (Moorbarns), S. S. Pilgrim, W. Thompson, H. Chamberlain, T. Smith, E. Wood, J. Arnold, S. Abell, sen., E. Clementson, J. Thorpe, T. Ragg, J. W. Hubbard, S. Kirkman, J. Grundy, C. Noel, Jas. Croaher (Bagworth), J. Nixon, J. Moxon, T. Moxon, jun., R. Chapman, M. Taverner (Upton), Jas. Taverner, W. Cooper, J. Bladon, H. Geary, J. Bucknall, J. Thorpe, J. N. Gimson, J. J. Burbury, T. E. Geary, J. Lowe, J. Atkin, E. Taverner, T. C. Browne, W. Pettifor, T. Johnson, C. D. Britton, &c. &c. Mr. Mayne occupied the chair, and Mr. Chamberlain the vice-chair.
>
> After the cloth had been drawn, the musical grace of Non nobis Domine was sung by a party of musical friends who were present, and the Chairman then gave the usual loyal toasts, "The Queen," "Prince Albert" coupled with an allusion to the Great Exhibition, "The Prince of Wales and all the Royal Family," which were drunk with much enthusiasm. These were followed by "The Bishop and Clergy of the Diocese," and the good order of the people, which, according to Lord Palmerston, had attracted the attention of foreigners, was attributed not so much to the source to which he had traced it as to the teachings of the administrators of the Gospel.
>
> The Rev. R. Vernon Whitby, being called upon to respond to the toast, expressed his pleasure at meeting the company, his belief that they were all interested in the welfare of the country, and his coincidence in the sentiments uttered by the chairman.

This 1851 <u>Leicester Chronicle</u> newspaper clipping indicates that Thomas Edmund Geary ("T.E. Geary") and Henry Geary ("H. Geary"), two of John's brothers, attended the annual ploughing match and a dinner at the Sparkenhoe Farmers' Club. The "seventy gentlemen" toasted to the success of the recent Great Exhibition occurring in London, sponsored by Queen Victoria and Prince Albert. The Great Exhibition was open from March to October, 1851 so it would have just concluded at the time of this dinner. The brothers were members of The Sparkenhoe Hundred which was a unit of English government that included the 100 land-owning families within a certain district, in this case the northern corner of Leicestershire. The hundred would be the unit of local government that resolved disputes and made collective decisions about taxes and other public matters.

Thomas Edmund would have been 26 years old at the time and was still working the Geary family farmlands, although they were heavily mortgaged and about to be lost to foreclosure. He would soon emigrate to Australia. Henry was 25 years old, practicing as a London doctor in 1852 and soon after moving to Australia as well.

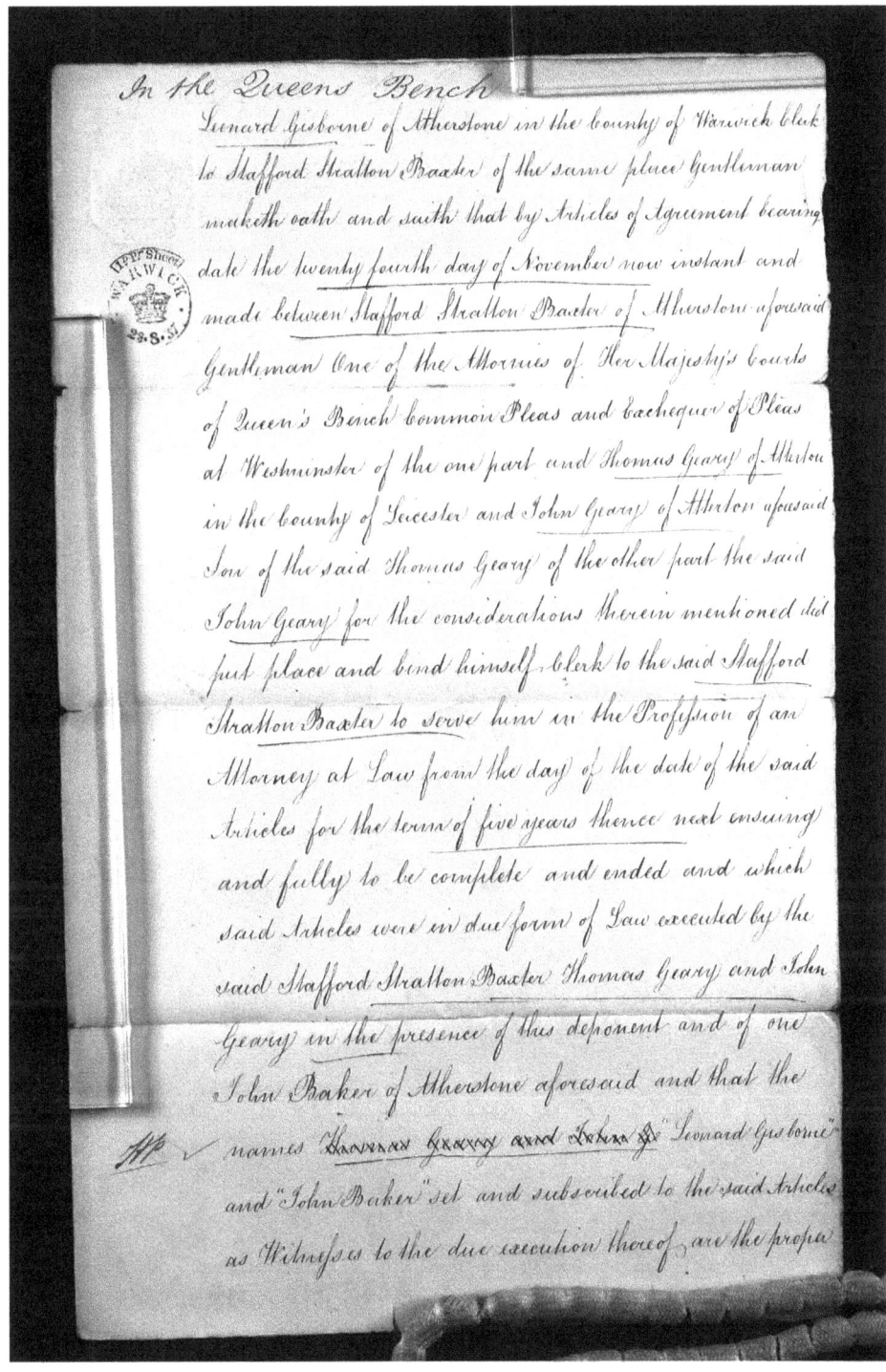

This is a copy of the first page of John's apprenticeship documents with attorney Stafford Stratton Baxter in 1838. John was only 15 years old when he agreed to "bind himself" to Baxter for a term of five years in order to become an attorney himself. This document is part of his "Articles of Clerkship" agreement between John's father, Thomas Geary, and Mr. Baxter, who was an attorney in a town near Atterton called Atherstone. The date of the agreement is November 24, 1838.

A full transcript of this document is included in the Appendix.

The next three pages show a copy of the original handwritten January 11, 1849 Mortgage which Thomas Geary granted to Thomas Thorpe Fowke on his Leicestershire lands in exchange for 5,000 pounds.

The title indicates it was "a mortgage on the whole of Mr. Geary's property."

A typed transcription of the mortgage appears in the Appendix for reading convenience.

Note the tables which show each parcel of Geary land being mortgaged, including the "state of cultivation" such as "arable," "pasture," or "meadow."

Declar[ati]on as to the mode of applic[ati]on of the proceeds of such Sale & that purchaser shou[l]d not be bound to see to the applic[ati]on of purchase mon[e]y &c & that his receipts sho[ul]d be a good disch[arge]

Power of distress & entry in case[s] in[to] in arrear for 1 cal[endar] month

Cov[enan]ts by s[ai]d T Geary (pty to now abstract[e]d Indre) with s[ai]d T.T. Fowke his exrs ads & as[sign]s for p[a]y[men]t of princ[ipa]l & int[eres]t as afores[ai]d

That he had good right to convey

For quiet enjoym[en]t by s[ai]d T.T. Fowke after default

Free from incumb[rance]s (the s[ai]d Ann[uit]y excepted)

And recit[in]g that s[ai]d T Geary (pty to now abs[tracte]d Indre) many years ago caused s[ai]d messes or tenem[en]ts erections or build[ing]s upon s[ai]d premis[e]s to be insured ag[ains]t loss or damage by Fire in the Phœnix Fire Office in the City of London by a cert[ai]n Policy of Insce No 299509 & dated the 5 day of March 1801 for £500 & that same policy was then in full force & virtue

The s[ai]d Thos Geary (pty thereto) did by those prests bargain sell assign transfer & set over unto s[ai]d T.T. Fowke his exrs ads & ass[ign]s

All that the same policy & all benefit to arise to be derived therefrom

And all & ev[e]ry sums & sum of mon[e]y due or to become due or payable in respect thereof

To hold same unto s[ai]d T.T. Fowke his exrs admors & ass[ign]s to & for his & their own use & benefit but subj[ec]t nevertheless to the same or the like proviso for redemption as was in now abstr[acte]d Indre before could convey s[ai]d premises

Cov[enan]t by s[ai]d T Geary (party thereto) for himself his his exrs & admors with s[ai]d T.T. Fowke his exrs ads & ass[ign]s to keep s[ai]d premises insured during contin[uan]ce of now abstract[e]d Secy in Su[m] at the least & to pay premiums produce receipts &c with the usual power for Mr Fowke to insure in case of Mr Geary's neglect & any mon[e]y put by him for p[remiu]ms &c to be a chge on the prop[er]ty

Declar[ati]on that Ins[urance] mon[e]y sho[ul]d be applied in rebuild[in]g &c or in f[ur]ther paym[en]t of s[ai]d princ[ipa]l & int[eres]t in M[ortgage]es' discre[ti]on

Cov[enan]t by s[ai]d T Geary for further Assurance

Power for m[ortga]gee to appoint receiver (which has not been done) af[ter] default in paym[en]t of Int for 3 cal[endar] mos

Declar[ati]on that such Receiver's rects should be suffic[ien]t discharges with a provis[i]on as to applic[ati]on of mon[e]ys rec[eive]d by him & such ov[e]r Clauses & especially an Agreem[en]t on the p[ar]t of the

M[ortga]gee reducing the int. from 5£ to £4.10.- per cent on punctual payment & for quiet enjoym[en]t by the M[ortga]gor until default

Cov[enan]t by T.T. Fowke that the said principal sum of £5000 should remain on sec[urit]y of these presents for 5 y[ea]rs from the date that except in the events therein ment[ione]d & that he would not proceed for a sale or enter into pos[sessi]on or receipt of the rents or institute any pro[ceedin]gs at Law or in equity until after the expir[ati]on of 5 years next & perfect enjoym[en]t of s[ai]d p[re]pty or until default of paym[en]t of princ[ipa]l & int[erest] or unless sd Thomas Geary &c...

contd or untill said Thos Geary should become Bankrupt or take the benefit of the Insolvent Act.

Cov[enan]t from said T Geary not to recover [on] premiss or pay off all or any part of said £5000 during [the] term of 5 y[ea]rs without consent of T.T. Fowke his exrs &c &c in writ[in]g under their respective hands

The Schedule to which the above abstracted Mortgage refers

Name or description	State of cultivation	Quantity		
In Atherton		acres	roods	perches
Site of Buildings Yards & Garden		2	1	24
Kingsmoor Hill	Pasture	24	2	33
Darbys Meadow	Meadow	4	1	14
Hill Meadow	Meadow	2	2	11
Dinner Meadow	Meadow	1	0	28
Far Snipes	Arable	6	2	17
Near Do	Arable	8	3	13
Top Meadow	Meadow	2	1	1
Far Acres	Arable	8	1	25
Near Do	Pasture	10	3	3
Townsends Leys	Meadow	3	1	29
Home Close & Site of Cottages	Pasture	8	0	1
Garden at Village		.	"	36
Slade Meadow	Meadow	5	2	20
Middle Close	Pasture	11	1	1

Name or description	State of cultivation	Quantity		
...?	Arable	6	2	17
Near Do	Arable	8	3	13
Top Meadow	Meadow	2	1	1
Far Acres	Arable	8	1	35
Near Do	Pasture	10	3	3
Townsends Leys	Meadow	3	1	29
Home Close Site of Cottages	Pasture	8	0	1
Garden at Village	—	.	"	36
Slade Meadow	Meadow	5	2	20
Middle Close	Pasture	11	1	1
Bush Close	Arable	7	3	5
Roberts Hill	Arable	8	1	34
Ozier Beds		.	2	11
Two Doles in Town Meadow	Meadow	1	3	14
Lane		1	2	34
In Witherley		120	3	39
Little Atherton Close	Pasture	6	1	32
Great Do Do	Arable	9	2	21
Atherton Meadow	Meadow	4	1	20
Lane		1	0	18
In Ratcliffe Culey		21	2	16
Far Close	Arable	2	3	"

Name or description	State of cultivation	Quantity		
Middle Close	Arable	5	0	1
Far Hill	Arable	5	1	3
Near Hill	Arable & pasture	2	1	36
House Close with site of Buildings	Pasture	4	1	10
Ratcliffe Close	Pasture	4	2	30
Sexall Close	Arable	3	0	38
Long Meadow	Meadow	4	1	35
Hunters Meadow	Meadow	7	0	0
Hinckley Leys	Pasture	2	3	27
		42	0	20

Executed by Thomas Leary & Thomas
Thorpe Duke duly attested & except for common
endorsed..

Abstract of an Indenture of the 17th day of Septr 1852
being a Transfer of a Mortgage on Estates of Mr. Thomas Geary
at Atherton Witherley and Ratcliffe Culey in the County of Leicester
for securing L5000 & Interest

17th September 1852

    By Indenture of this date made between Thomas Thorpe Fowke of Midgham in the Coy of Berks Esqre of the one part

    and Sir Jno Edward George Bayley of the Middle Temple in the City of London Barrister at Law & George Brockman of the Junior United Service Club Chas St. St. James in the Coy of Middex Esqre of the other part.

Reciting that by Indre bearing date on or about the 11th day of Jany 1849 & made between Thos Geary therin described of the one part & said Tho. Thorpe Fowke of the ot part All & signr the messes or tent pieces or parcels of land farms & heredits descd or mentd & compd in certain Indres in the now reciting Indrementd & recited situate in the parishes of Atterton Witherley & Ratcliffe Culey in the Coy of Leicester with their appurts & wch were then in the posson of the said Thos. Geary the site of wch said messes or tent & said lands & heredits are expressed to have been then recently surveyed & measured & were found by such survey & admeasd to be divided into the several fields closed & parcels of land & were called or known by the several names & contd the several quantities mentd in the Schedule to the now reciting Indre

And also all other (if any) the lands tent & heredits described or compd in the said Schedule were conveyed unto said Tho. Thorpe Fowke his heirs & asss for securing the repayment by the said Tho. Geary of the sum of L5000 & intt thereon at or after the rate of L5 for every L100 for a year payable half yearly on the 15th Jany & the 15th July in each & every year (subject to a provision for reducing the same to L4 10/. per cent if paid within the time therein specified)

And in the now reciting Indre were contd the usual powers of sale & of powers provisos condons & agreements.

And reciting that said principal sum of L5000 still remains due on the sec..y of the thrnbefore recited Indre with an arrear of intt from the 15th day of July 1851 amounting to L 281..0..2 after deducting the Income tax thereon & that...

This partial transcription shows the first page of the Geary mortgage foreclosure document prepared in September, 1852 for non-payment. This transcription added red highlights to the text showing that the 1849 mortgage was not being paid by Thomas Geary and the first few payments were in arrears, plus interest: "the sum of L5000 still remains due on the [second year] of the [thereinbefore] [Indenture] with an arrear..." The mortgage-holder, Thomas Thorpe Fowke, subsequently transferred the foreclosed mortgage to Sir John Edward George Bayley and George Brockman and the Geary family no longer owned an interest in the lands.

<u>Ab</u>ove, a 2008 photo of Atterton Road, illustrating that the area of the Geary ancestral land holdings continues to be rural, even today.

<u>Below</u>, a July 5, 2001 photo of the footbridge over the River Anker, looking towards Witherly. It also illustrates the rolling countryside of the area where John Thomas Geary grew up. The River Anker is just north of Atterton and the Geary farmlands.

Atterton, near Witherley, Leicestershire.

Valuable Farming Stock, Horses, Corn, Hay, Clover, Grass, Seeds, and Stubble Keeping, Turnips, Implements, &c.

W. BERRIDGE

Is honoured with instructions from Mr. T. E. GEARY, of Atterton Field,

TO SELL BY AUCTION,

On Thursday, November 11th, 1852, on the premises, THE whole of his truly valuable FARMING STOCK, CORN, HAY, TURNIPS, KEEPING, &c.

The Stock consists of a herd of forty-one very superior long and short-horned beast, viz., eighteen superior in-calf dairy cows, six drawing heifers, ten barren cows, four barren heifers and three yearlings; forty in-lamb black-faced ewes, bred with great care from the best flocks in the county; four superior draught horses, very useful half bred mare, cart colt foal, ditto filly, nag filly foal; one breeding sow, three in-pig gilts, seventeen strong store pigs, and a young boar of the Tamworth breed. The implements comprise in part three narrow wheel waggons, three six-inch carts, one narrow wheel ditto, single plough, land-roll, three cow cribs, three iron pig troughs, two ladders, forks, rakes, &c., &c.

Also, the Stacks of Corn, Hay, and Clover, superior grass, seeds, and stubble keeping, and swede turnips, to go off the ground.

Sale to commence at eleven o'clock.

Descriptive catalogues will be ready for delivery fourteen days previous, and may be had at the principal Inns in Atherstone; at Mrs. Davis's, stationer, Atherstone; at the Auctioneer's Offices, Market-place, Leicester; and at the place of sale.

By Messrs. BURTON & CLARKE.

This October 30, 1852 newspaper clipping from the Leicester Chronicle advertises the remaining farm stock of the Geary family for sale at auction. John's brother, Thomas Edmund, who was left to run the farm when his brothers moved into professions, is selling out. The land itself was subject to a mortgage which was being foreclosed, but the farm stock, equipment, and crops would have been sold separately as personal property.

This advertisement shows a considerable operation including 41 "superior long and short-horned" cattle, plus 18 "superior in-calf dairy cows, six drawing heifers, ten barren cows, four barren heifers and three yearlings." The Gearys also had sheep, horses, pigs, and a young boar.

The title page of the Geary Family Bible, a 1629 edition of the King James Bible which has been in the family for generations. John's father, Thomas Geary, gave it to him as the oldest Geary son in about 1850 when he was a young adult. Thomas told John to never let it out of his possession unless his children were starving. John brought it with him across the Atlantic Ocean in 1853 and as he trekked 1,000 miles across the American plains in 1856. John passed it down to his daughter, Sophia Ann Geary Page, and it is now in possession of one of her descendants who lives in Utah. Additional images of the Bible can be found in the Appendix herein.

A GENTLEMAN AND A SCHOLAR

*"I was admitted to the practice of Law,
in which Profession I was successfully engaged..."*
JTG

John Thomas Geary's career as a London attorney was well underway in 1852 when the Geary family lands were sold. Having begun as a teenager, he trained with two experienced attorneys then took the required exams and was admitted to the bar. John was successful enough to live in a nice neighborhood and sponsor his younger brothers in their careers. The years he spent in London would be eventful in John's life; that is where he would meet the woman he would marry and make a bold decision to join a new church.

STUDY OF LAW

John began his law career as a young man of 15. His father obtained Articles of Clerkship for him to study the law in 1838 in the Trinity Term under the apprenticeship of Stafford Stratton Baxter, a local Atherstone attorney. Because John Thomas was a minor, the contract was signed by Baxter, John and John's father, Thomas.[1] Thomas paid Baxter a fee for the apprenticeship. Baxter was a well-known attorney who worked in Atherstone a few miles from John's birthplace. He could give John diverse learning experiences. Stafford Baxter had just passed his own exam to become a Barrister in 1838 when he sponsored John Thomas Geary in his legal work.[2]

There were essentially two pathways to becoming a lawyer in 19th century Britain. A man could attend a university and then enter into training with one of the lawyer guilds – known as Inns of Court. There were Inns such as Gray's Inn or Lincoln's Inn in London where students lived and studied and attended court while they trained. That background usually led to the person becoming a Barrister, which is the type of attorney who appears often in Court. The other pathway was to become a legal apprentice. "Outside London, attorneys were found only in the main towns in each county, particularly those where the assizes or quarter sessions were held. Without traditional guilds, apprenticeship became the only means of entry into the profession."[3] Once a man entered an apprenticeship, he was required to work for a minimum of five years before being eligible to enter the profession. This pathway led more people to becoming Solicitors rather than Barristers. A Solicitor would spend time working on documents and transactions instead of going to Court.

As new laws were passed in the mid-1800s, the legal profession became more regulated and developed a better reputation. There were 13,000 attorneys and solicitors in Britain by the 1870s. After completing the original Articles of Clerkship, the apprentice lawyer would need to file for admission to the bar and take an oath. "The status of the attorney rose with the reforms of the 19th century when the more successful made further money from property and transport speculations; they [attorneys] became valuable members of town corporations and other governing bodies, and many married into land-owning families."[4] Prior to 1871, no "man of the law" was allowed to stand for election to Parliament.

This timeline illustrates the progress of John Thomas Geary's legal studies:

1838 November 24	The original Articles of Clerkship[5] were drawn up and entered into by Attorney Stafford Stratton Baxter of Atherstone, Warwick, and Thomas Geary, Farmer and Grazier of Atterton in the county of Leicester, and his son, John Thomas Geary, also of Atterton, Leicester. John Thomas Geary was 15 years and 9 months old when the first papers for his Clerkship were drawn up.
1839 February 15	Leonard Gisborne was an Attorney's Clerk for Stafford S. Baxter and he drew up the paper work and signed the Affidavit, legally witnessing the beginning of the Articles of Clerkship for John Thomas Geary.
1839 February 18	The Articles of Clerkship for John Thomas Geary were formally registered with the County, which certified that John Thomas Geary had begun his Clerkship.
1843 March 31	Approximately four years into his apprenticeship, the parties made an Indenture of Assignment for John Thomas Geary's Articles of Clerkship. It was made and agreed to by the original Attorney, Stafford Stratton Baxter, Thomas Geary and John Thomas Geary, wherein John Thomas Geary was assigned over to attorney Robert Michael Baxter to complete his unexpired term of Clerkship. Robert Michael Baxter, of Lincoln's Inn Field of the County of Middlesex in which London is situated, was a practicing attorney and also the son of Stafford S. Baxter. Thus, John Thomas Geary left Warwick and moved to the largest city in England to complete his training as an attorney.
1843 April 1	Stephen Pilgrim signed the Affidavit as a Deponent witnessing the Indenture of Assignment of John Thomas Geary to Attorney Robert Michael Baxter.
1843 April 5	Charles Cooke, the younger, signed the Affidavit as a Deponent witnessing the Indenture of Assignment of John Thomas Geary to Attorney Robert Michael Baxter.
1845 June 1	John Thomas Geary completed his Articles of Clerkship and signed an Affidavit before the Commissioner, William Whytman, attesting to his completion of his apprenticeship.
1845 June 11	John Thomas Geary of Number 14 Denmark Street, Islington, Middlesex, London, is sworn, admitted, and enrolled an Attorney of Her Majesty's Court of Queen's Bench at Westminster. When John Thomas Geary officially became an Attorney, he was 22 years, 4 months and 6 days old. Thus, it took six years and seven months for the full completion of his apprenticeship.

1845 March to October	The Law Times, Volume V, March 1845-October 1845, published at the Office of the Law Times, 20 Essex Street, Strand, London, lists John Thomas Geary as one of the Attorneys to Be Admitted in the Trinity Term, on page 160.
1845 May to October	The Legal Observer or Journal of Jurisprudence, Published Weekly by Edmund Spettigue, London, lists John Thomas Geary as one of the "Candidates who passed the Examination" for the Trinity Term 1845, on page 222.
1851	The Law List, Being a List of the Judges and Officers of the Different Courts of Justice… and the "only authentic and complete list of certificated Attorneys, Notaries, Etc. in England and Wales"…was published in London by V & R Stevens and G.S. Norton. It is known as the Law List and it shows "Geary, John Thomas, 44 Duncan Terrace, Islington" on the List.[6]

Once John Thomas Geary was successfully established as a London lawyer, he agreed to take on his younger brother, Frederick, as an apprentice. On February 4, 1850, while John was living at Number 5, Three Crown Square, High Street, Southwark, Surrey, he entered into Articles of Clerkship for Fred to be his apprentice. John Hudswell is one of the deponents who witnesses the Clerkship. Hudswell was listed as a Sealing Wax and Wafer Manufacturer living at the same address as John.[7] The area where John was living, immediately south of the Thames River near the London Bridge, was known for having many inns along High Street (now called Borough High Street). John and his witness may have both been residents at an inn. Three Crowns Square is near the Borough Market, an open-air market still operating after hundreds of years. Next to that market stands the majestic Southwark Cathedral, where John and Sophia would be married in 1852.[8]

LIFE AT DUNCAN TERRACE

In about 1851, John, Fred, and their other brother, Elton, moved into a roomy four-story home at 44 Duncan Terrace in the Islington area of London. Elton was working as a Clerk in a Merchant House (or bank). Islington was and is a district in Greater London extending from High Street to Highbury Fields, and from Upper Street Essex Road to Southgate Road. By the mid-1800s, it was a rapidly growing area with population in the hundreds of thousands. This growth was partly due to the introduction of horse-drawn omnibuses in 1830. Once transportation to the "suburbs" was convenient, many large brick rowhouses and fashionable squares were built. These neighborhoods drew clerks, artisans and professionals to the district.[9]

Duncan Terrace, the street where John lived, was named after Admiral Adam Duncan (1731-1804) who commanded the British fleet against the Dutch at the Battle of Camperdown in 1797.[10] Duncan Terrace itself was a developing area near the river that contained small groups of contiguous homes next to winding parks and waterways. John lived at 44 Duncan Terrace, a four-story rowhouse that still stands today, in 2021, in a well-maintained neighborhood.

Duncan Terrace is a long line of brick row houses in the four-story model. They were built in a series starting in 1794 with units 46-49, then units 1-10 by 1817, and units 11-32 by 1839. In 1843 a large brick church was built at the end of the rows named St. John the Evangelist Roman Catholic Church.[11] It was built during the time of religious upheaval when Roman Catholics were given additional rights under British law. Prior to this time, the Church of England did not allow

Roman Catholics certain privileges to meet, worship or serve in public office. In 1828, Parliament repealed the Sacramental Test Act, which required public officials to take communion in the Church of England in order to qualify for many privileges. Once that restriction was moved, a new mood of inclusion swept the country and Catholics were able to worship more openly.[12]

The house where John lived was among the last units built on Duncan Terrace next to the Catholic Church. Units 33-39 and 40-45 were begun by 1841 and finished by 1851.[13] The Geary brothers may have been some of the first occupants of the house at 44 Duncan Terrace. Other occupants of the neighborhood were mostly people who worked at the Catholic Church.[14]

Today, Duncan Terrace is a group of 75 houses and flats with "an average current value of 2,729,039 pounds" each. There have been 13 property sales on Duncan Terrace over the last 5 years with an average house price paid of 2.2 million pounds. The actual unit where the Gearys lived was last sold in May 2000. It is described as a "4 bed freehold terraced house, rent for 575 pounds per week."[15]

JOHN THOMAS GEARY JOINS THE MORMON CHURCH

On May 20, 1851, John Thomas Geary was baptized a member of the Church of Jesus Christ of Latter-day Saints in the Theobald's Road Branch of London, England by "Elder Hyde".[16] He is listed as member #928 in the Theobald's Road Branch of the London Conference, British Mission.[17] Around that same time, he probably met the woman he would marry – Sophia Fryer -- also a recent Mormon convert. Stories abound about how John came in contact with the Church and its missionaries, but no specific records have been found to confirm what occurred.

It is interesting to consider what would have drawn John to the Mormon religion. In 1851, he was embarking on a promising and already somewhat successful professional career in London. He was helping his younger brothers to be launched in professions as well. He was living in a fairly new and growing neighborhood. He does not seem in need of economic or social opportunity. However, he was raised in a religious household and possibly he was either attending an Anglican or Non-conformist church service in his neighborhood or investigating religion for himself.

One or both of John's brothers might have been upset about his baptism. Six days after the baptism, on May 26, 1851, Fred's clerkship was re-assigned from John to Attorney Ebenezer Benham of Number 18, Essex Street, Strand, in London. John Thomas Geary, Thomas Geary, and Frederick Geary all agreed to it.[18] Was this due to Fred's reaction to John's baptism? John later describes this period as a contentious one in his household: "At the period of my baptism, some of my relations were living with me. They immediately became my most bitter enemies, and did all in their power (which however was not much) to injure me in my business."[19]

From surviving letters written by John, especially his 1857 letter to Mormon President Brigham Young, John's devotion to the gospel sounds strong and deeply felt from the beginning. As he tells President Young, "I obeyed the Gospel about 7 years ago…"[20] In letters to his relatives, he expresses sophisticated and beautifully-worded declarations of the spiritual strength he receives from his religious beliefs. John was an intellectual who was well-read and well-spoken. Changing his entire lifestyle, beliefs, affiliations, family relationships and, most of all, eventually leaving

England forever, could not have come easily. He must have been powerfully drawn to make this religious decision despite the sacrifice it would entail. From the limited record we have, there is no evidence that John struggled with his decision to join the Church - he sounds intensely committed to Mormonism and the gospel of Jesus Christ – but the results of that decision were to challenge and haunt him for the rest of his life.

There are several possibilities for his conversion scenario. John, who came from a mixed family that included both Anglicans and Non-conformists, may have been attending a Non-conformist congregation where the Mormon missionaries preached. Occasionally, entire congregations in England were converted by the Mormon missionaries invited to address existing congregations.[21] Another possibility is that Elder John Hyde, Senior, who baptized both John and Sophia's sister, Jane, that spring, brought the families into social contact with each other and with the church. Finally, it is possible that John Hyde, Senior, knew John professionally. Hyde worked as a Solicitor's Clerk and John was a Solicitor; perhaps they met each other in law circles and discussed religion.[22]

London was not a particularly fruitful mission for Mormon missionaries in the early days although it became more successful during the 1850s. Missionaries had much greater success in outlying areas such as Herefordshire, Staffordshire, or Lancashire. The early apostles, Wilford Woodruff, George A. Smith, and Heber C. Kimball, found their time in London "to be the most frustrating of their entire mission."[23] The missionaries did not spend time proselyting door-to-door as became the custom in the 20th century; most early London converts were found through mutual friends or by attending religious or street meetings.[24]

THE JOHN HYDE FAMILY

The man who baptized John Thomas Geary led a colorful religious life. In 1851, John Hyde, Sr. was 40 years old and lived with his wife, Martha, and 9 children in Windsor Place, Saint Luke's, London. This area is less than a mile from John Thomas Geary on Duncan Terrace, Islington, about a twenty-minute walk. At this time, John Hyde, Sr. had been a Mormon for about three years and was serving as the Branch President of the largest branch in London, the Theobald's Road Branch, with 413 members.[25] John Hyde, Sr. was originally from Dublin, Ireland and grew up with a varied religious history. In 1833, in his early twenties, he was baptized in the Non-conformist Church at Bishopsgate, London.[26] There was a well-known Non-conformist chapel in Islington. John Hyde christened one of his children, John, Jr., as an "Irvingite" that same year. The Hyde family may have been active in the Irvingite movement before joining the Mormon Church in 1848.

Irvingites were a fascinating sect originating in Scotland during the early 1800s. One of their key concepts was that Christ's Second Coming was imminent. They were known by the name of their charismatic leader, Edward Irving. Irving and the group built an Irvingite Church in 1832-1834 on Duncan Street not far from where John would live on Duncan Terrace.[27] Edward Irving and the founders of the group believed strongly in restoring the Council of the Twelve Apostles and other aspects of the early Christian Church. They later changed their name to the Catholic Apostolic Church.[28] Mormon Prophet and leader Joseph Smith was visited by two Irvingite men in America in 1839: "Two Scottish men visited Mormon Prophet Joseph Smith in 1839 and discussed with him the ideas of Edward Irving. Joseph opined that they 'counterfeited the truth' but that they were 'perhaps the nearest of the sectarians.'"[29]

It appears that John Hyde, Sr., was a seeker of religious truths and may have found the Mormon Church's message while he attended another sect. As historian Lynne Watkins Jorgensen explains in her article about the Hydes and other London converts, "The Non-conformist movement reflected anti-establishment religious dissent against the state church and professional clergy. Non-conformist ministers were usually lay members without formal religious education. Between 1840 and 1845, shortly before the Hawkins, Piercy, and Hyde families were baptized, over four hundred identifiable Londoners joined the Mormon Church. Ninety percent can be identified as Non-conformists, although most were also listed in records of the state church, the Church of England. Most were young with some education, many had successful occupations, and half (210) emigrated to America. Thus, a tradition of dissent was an important precondition for interest in Mormonism, and their conscious cosmopolitanism as Londoners seems to have given them a special confidence and sophistication."[30]

John Hyde, Sr., his wife, Martha Marmoy Hyde, five of their seven sons and five daughters all joined the Mormon Church in 1848 and became members of the Theobald's Road Branch. The London Conference British Mission Record of Members, 1841-1850, lists John Hyde, Sr. as member #487. His son is member #455 and his daughter, Martha, is #518.[31] Most of the Hyde family members were baptized by John Banks, an American missionary then serving as president of the London Mission and president of the Theobald's Road Branch.[32] Banks lived next door to another family converted at nearly the same time as the Hydes – Frederick and Angelina Piercy. The Piercy and Hyde families would interact with John Thomas Geary in interesting ways in the future.

John Hyde, Jr., who had been christened an Irvingite as a child, remembers his Mormon baptism on September 4, 1848, in this way: "I had an ideal of what religion and the worship of God might be; I imagined that this system, as I then heard it expounded, realized that ideal; and, in the love of that ideal, I embraced it and was accordingly baptized on the 4th of September, 1848, being then a boy of fifteen years... In December of the same year I was ordained a Priest, and commenced to preach Mormonism."[33] Unfortunately, John Hyde, Jr. would become a rebellious Mormon later in life and seek to damage the cause he earlier embraced.

JOHN THOMAS GEARY BECOMES A MORMON LEADER

At baptism, John Thomas Geary became a member of Theobald's Road Branch, London Conference, of The Church of Jesus Christ of Latter-day Saints. Theobald's Road was about 1-1/2 miles from John's home on Duncan Terrace. Three months later, on August 11, 1851, John Thomas received the Melchizedek Priesthood and was ordained an Elder in the Theobald's Road Branch.

By 1850, there were 30,747 members in Britain, approximately the same size as the total membership in the United States at that time. This was only twenty years into the Church's history on either continent. According to historian Jorgensen, "In the late 1840s the London Conference was divided into: Theobald's Road Branch, meeting in a hall off Gray's Inn Road in Holborn; the Skinner Street Branch, founded by Albion (Non-conformist) which may have been meeting in Castle Street near Finsbury Square Clerkenwell; and the dedicated and faithful Woolwich group...By 1850 there were thirty-three branches of the Church in the London Conference."[34]

John did not stay in the Theobald's Road Branch for more than a few months. Later in 1851, John was appointed President of the Paddington Branch. In the Church Archives, the Paddington Branch is listed as being located at 54 Bell Street, Edgeware Road, with Sunday meetings at 11 a.m., 2:30 p.m. and 6:30 p.m. and Wednesdays at 8 o'clock. Paddington is in the area of Bell Street and Edgeware Road about 3 miles away from Duncan Terrace, toward Hyde Park. On the reverse of John's membership card is written, "Appointed President".

John was also given another large church responsibility during the December 6-7, 1851 London Conference of the Mormon Church. The recently-baptized John Thomas Geary was appointed Assistant-Secretary for the Conference, nominated by Elder Eli B. Kelsey, President of the London Conference. John was 28 years old at the time and had been a Mormon about six months.

The printed cover of the "Half Yearly Report of the London Conference" shows J.T. Geary as a Secretary along with T.C. (Thomas) Armstrong.[35] The fact that John was promoted to positions of responsibility just a few months after his baptism speaks highly of his character and of the respect that his fellow church leaders had for him. The printed Conference Report also lists John Thomas Geary as the President of the Paddington Branch of the Church, which had been organized on March 21, 1850 and had 102 members. The Paddington Branch met at the Literary Institution on Great Carlisle Street in Middlesex County.

President Eli B. Kelsey was highly regarded by Orson Pratt, who wrote of him in the church publication, *The Millennial Star*: "It has been the blessed portion of but few men to acquire that unstudied fame and undivided confidence which were bestowed upon Elder Kelsey by all the British Saints who had the pleasure of his acquaintance, strictly exemplary in all his ways and councils."[36] The conference was a twice-yearly event held by Church authorities to organize church business and hear from visiting Church authorities. It was held in the Eastern Lecture Hall on Church Lane in Whitechapel. In this instance, the visiting authorities were Lorenzo Snow and Franklin D. Richards of the LDS Quorum of the Twelve Apostles. Elders George B. Wallace and Levi Richards served as counselors to President Kelsey and also spoke at the conference.

As part of his conference clerk duties, John wrote down in the Conference Report some inspiring speeches given by Church leaders. The meeting began on Saturday at 3 p.m. in the afternoon and didn't adjourn until after 11 p.m. Lorenzo Snow encouraged the British converts to stay strong: "I perceive it is with you as it is with us all – work! Work! Work! It is a privilege which we all enjoy, that we have a constant increase of care." Indeed, much of the business discussed at the Conference was how to provide for the Church members and how to take up collection to support those in need. Elder Snow also admonished them about their burdens: "It is pleasant to swim in deep water, if we know how to swim – it is peculiarly the case with the Latter-day Saints. You are called to bear heavy burdens…The work of the Lord has greatly increased in this place; and still it is your privilege to do much good. You are now great. There are many of you who have charge over far more people than I had when I was the President of the London Conference ten years ago…We have gone forth in the name of Israel's God, and we have sown the seed of eternal truth, and it will germinate and grow in defiance of the combined hostility of the powers of earth and hell."[37] The leaders asked John Thomas Geary to "call upon the Presidents of Branches to give in their reports."[38]

The following day, which was Sunday, the speeches continued with rousing sessions in the morning, afternoon, and evening. President Kelsey said good-bye to those in attendance, noting, "I shall this day close my labours as President of the London Conference" and he recognized the good efforts of Elders Speakman, Hyde, Squires, Lewis, and Savage. President Kelsey asked that Elder Geary write them letters of commendation on the group's behalf. (It is presumably Elder John Hyde, Jr., to which the speaker refers, as he was then serving as a missionary to France.)

Geary is on a list with 68 other Branch Presidents who received specific instruction about their considerable duties from the newly-sustained President of the London Conference, James Marsden:

> "You are a highly privileged body of men. You hold authority from the Ruler of the Universe – a power for good unto your fellow men, and all your legal administrations are sanctioned by the high court of Heaven… You are appointed to counsel the saints in all things – to teach them to obey those whom God has placed over them…Now is the time for you to distinguish yourselves as confidential men in the kingdom of God, men who will do their duty. You have now the privilege of shewing who and what you are – your pedigree, character, and destiny…With your special calling to the presidency of branches, is given spirit and power to enable you to discharge the duties, which do, or may in time to come, devolve upon you…The presidency of a branch is the main-spring of action to the particular organization with which he stands connected, and when he acts diligently and in righteousness he gives life and energy to the body."[39]

The attendees at the London Conference were asked to give an offering to the Church to be used to build "a Glorious Temple in Great Salt Lake City" and they were forthcoming with their offerings.

Six months later, another large conference was held in London on June 5, 1852. In the records of that conference, John Thomas Geary continues to be shown at the President of the Paddington Branch, with the only change being that the branch is now meeting at 65 Great Carlisle Street at the Portman Market and they are up to 131 members.[40] The group heard reports concerning the increase in membership of the church in London, now totaling more than 2,300 members in 33 branches. There were 3 Seventies, 114 Elders, 56 Priests, 36 Teachers, and 23 Deacons in attendance. Eloquent speeches were given by Elder John Hyde, Jr., President James Marsden, Elder Jacob Gates, and Apostle Lorenzo Snow, who made a surprise appearance.

Elder Snow said, "I rejoice in the opportunity of seeing the saints once more. It is as unexpected to me to see you as it is to you to see me." The report goes on to say that he made "many other instructive remarks" to the group.[41]

Elder Gates noted, "The London saints have done well. The financial affairs of this Conference are in good condition…We have done well and we shall do better, for we are a progressive people. We have received some intelligence and we want more…It is no small thing to be a saint. Show yourselves worthy. Do your duty, and win a crown of celestial glory. We want to gather and we will do it. Wake up and see if you are prepared to gather up to Zion. Leave your native land, show your perseverance and endurance. Realize your position. Accomplish your duty, that you may obtain a great reward – a celestial crown. Make up your minds to run the whole race of the Christian."[42]

Another record about John Thomas Geary during 1852 is found in the journal of Curtis E. Bolton. Bolton grew up in Pennsylvania among a prosperous educated family who had sent him to study in Europe as a teenager, where he learned several languages.[43] He converted to the Mormon

Church in 1842 as a young man living in New Jersey. After spending some time in Nauvoo, Bolton emigrated to the Salt Lake valley in 1848 and was called to accompany John Taylor on a mission to France in 1850. During the summer of 1852, Bolton was serving as the Mission President in France. He became acquainted with John Thomas Geary, a new convert in London. Bolton apparently traveled from Paris to London for church meetings regularly and stayed at John's home on Duncan Terrace:

CURTIS BOLTON JOURNAL EXCERPTS:

August 1852, Monday 23 – arrived in London – went to Jervin Street – met Elder Stenhouse – went with him to see Bro. Capt. Stayner, a splendid man, spent ½ and hour then retired to Bro. Geary's with Elder Stenhouse to sleep. Bro. Geary is a lawyer…the night was far advanced before we fell asleep.

August 1852, Tuesday 24 - …I am satisfied with everything I have done and verily believe God is pleased with me also. Left Elder Hart at 5 P.M. and returned to 35 Jervin St. and met Elder Stenhouse and again slept with him at Bro. Geary's after spending an hour in the evening at Capt. Stayner's.

August 1852, Thursday 26 – Dined with Sister Sutherland. Her husband is on a mission to Dublin. Called on Sister Jordan, met Elder Hyde there. Spent the evening with Capn Stayner.

August 1852, Friday 27 – Spent the day with Fred Piercy – went to a warm swimming bath.

Tuesday November 22, 1852 – Arrived at 7 at Southhampton (in the morning) – determined to go at once to London…when I arrived at 12 and went at once to see Sister Hart – whom I found still very will…Laid hands on her and blessed her and having letter to deliver I went to the Portland Place and took tea, then went to Jervin Street and saw two Brethren going to Gibralter and Bro. Gates, Bro. Hyde, Sen…Spent the evening at Bro. Geary's…

Wednesday [November] 23 [1852] – Spent the morning until ½ past 11 with Sister Hart – left her in good spirits and proceeded to Jervin street. Saw Bro. Levi Richards and several other brethren…Dined with Bro. Geary – left London at ½ past 8 for Southhampton…[44]

These Bolton journal entries paint a good picture of church affairs being conducted in London around the six months John was active in London church leadership. Bolton was involved in some disagreement involving the leaders and frequently mentions Samuel W. Richards, Levi Richards, both John Hyde, Sr. and John Hyde, Jr., as well as Louis Bertrand, a French Mormon who seems to have caused some trouble. Bolton is a colorful and entertaining writer who developed a friendship with John Thomas Geary that would endure into the coming years when both would live in the Utah Territory.

DEATH OF SARAH ANN ELTON GEARY

In 1852, John's mother, Sarah Ann, moved to London to join her three sons. Her husband, Thomas Geary, continued to reside in Leicester. This was some months after John became a Mormon. The census shows that Sarah Ann's cousin, Charlotte Wright Hall, was also living at 44 Duncan Terrace, possibly as a caregiver or housekeeper. Charlotte would later play a pivotal role in the Geary family.

Tragically, on June 10, 1852, Sarah Ann Elton Geary died at 48 years old. Her death certificate indicates that she was still living with her sons at Duncan Terrace at the time of her death.

"Apoplexy, sudden, a previous attack 6 months ago followed by paralysis" are listed as the causes of her death. Thus, Sarah may have moved to London due to her health issues. Sarah Ann Geary is buried at Highgate Cemetery in London.[45]

SOPHIA FRYER AND HER FAMILY

Presumably John Thomas Geary met Sophia Fryer in either 1851 or 1852 when they were both newly-converted Mormons in London. No records indicate how long John and Sophia courted or whether they met at the Mormon Church, but it seems likely they would have done so. In 1852, John was 28 and Sophia, 23.

Sophia was living at 33 Old Bond Street that year, working as a servant in the home of John Mitchell, a 43-year-old bookseller.[46] John Mitchell and his wife, Emily, had three children, ages 12, 10, and 9, plus a governess and two other servants living there. The neighbors included a china dealer and a carpet manufacturer. It was a neighborhood where most families had at least one servant. This residence was in the parish of St. James in the Hanover Square area of Westminster in downtown London. There is a distance of three miles between John's Duncan Terrace address and Sophia's Old Bond Street address. The building where Sophia lived is still there today and appears to be a very upscale building, which is called the Swan House, at 32-33 Old Bond Street.

Sophia met the typical profile of a young woman Mormon convert for this time. According to historian Lynne Watkins Jorgensen, "domestic service was the largest single occupation listed for young female converts [in London] who identified some employment…moderately wealthy families would employ eleven women including a housekeeper, lady's maid, nurse, two house maids, laundry maid, kitchen maid, and scullion, and thirteen men, including a butler, house steward, coachman, three grooms, two footmen, gardeners, and possibly a laborer."[47]

As previously described, John was baptized by Mormon elder John Hyde, Sr., in May, 1851. Elder John Hyde, Sr. also baptized Sophia Fryer's older sister, Jane, a few months before John. Jane was baptized on February 25, 1861 in the Theobald's Road Branch of the London Conference.[48] Jane was the first member of the Fryer family to join the Mormon Church.[49] At the time of her baptism, Jane, 28, had been married to Francis Jorden for 10 years and they had a son, Frank Jr., who was 8 years old, and a daughter, Annie who was 6. Three other children of Jane and Frank Jorden died in infancy. The Jordens were living at Doughty Street near Mecklenberg Square in London and Frank, Sr. was a successful carpenter and woodworker.

Later in his life, Jane's son, Frank, Jr. (a disaffected Mormon by then) described his family's conversion this way:

FRANK JORDEN, JR.:

"When I was about seven years of age the Mormon Elders visited London, England where they found my parents and my Mother was soon enlisted in the new developments of Bible teachings, and was persuaded to join them. Following close upon this demand – I ought to say command – that all who accepted the revelation of Joseph Smith should emigrate to America, thence to Salt Lake City. Some of my Mother's friends united with them. At least my Father, though very reluctantly and doubtful of the issue, was induced by my Mother's determination to emigrate whether he consented to go or not, to join them."[50]

Sophia Fryer was baptized in the Mormon Church on April 20, 1851, a few months after her sister, Jane, and a month before John.[51] She was baptized by "Priest McCoughie," according to the Church records. This is likely a reference to Thomas McCaughie who served as the Branch President of the Southwark Branch in 1852. The Southwark Branch met in the Octagon Rooms, on Mount Street in Westminister, about three blocks from where Sophia lived on Old Bond Street.[52] Jane's husband, Frank, Sr. was baptized by McCaughie on the same day as Sophia.[53]

Sophia and Jane were both children of the Moses and Eliza Fryer family of Yarmouth, Isle of Wight, England. Sophia was born on July 12, 1829 in Yarmouth, the 4th oldest in a family of 11 children with several step-siblings. She was christened in the Church of England at the Hampshire Parish on November 1, 1829.[54] Her father was a house painter and/or plumber. As soon as the sisters were old enough, they left home to work for other families as servants.

When Sophia was about 12 years old she began to help her older sister, Jane, who was a domestic servant in Yarmouth. On the 1841 British Census, Sophia is living with Jane in the home of John Stephens at Market Square in Yarmouth. Jane is 15 years old and listed as a "F.S." or family servant.[55] The Stephens family had three small children, who were 5, 4 and 8 months old. On October 24, 1841, Jane Fryer married Frank Jorden at Millbrook, Hampshire on the Isle of Wight. It is not known if Sophia continued working for the Stephens family at that time.

After marriage, Jane and Frank Jorden lived in the Hampshire area at Shirley Common in Millbrook for the next few years from 1841-1845. During that time, they had a boy who died in infancy and a son, Frank, Jr., who was born in 1844. About 1845, the Jordens moved to the St. Pancras area of London.[56] Sophia, who would have been 16 years old, may have gone to London with them or soon after.

Jane and Sophia left most of their siblings back in Yarmouth when they moved to London. Of their nine siblings, only one, Richard, joined them in converting to Mormonism and emigrating to America. Another, William, moved to Australia and died in 1880. Three siblings, Edward, Ann, and Victoria, died young. One sibling, Eliza, moved to America temporarily in the 1870s then returned to England. Three others, George, Leah, and Albert, continued to live on the Isle of Wight for the rest of their lives. They lived into the 20th century and corresponded with their Mormon siblings in America, never understanding or agreeing with their religious convictions.[57]

MARRIAGE OF JOHN AND SOPHIA AT THE CATHEDRAL

Just two months after the sad death of John's mother, John and Sophia were married in London's Southwark Cathedral on August 20, 1852.[58] It is interesting that they chose to hold the wedding ceremony in an Anglican Church; early British Mormons didn't own church buildings in London.

Southwark Cathedral, also known as St. Saviour's Collegiate Church, is a magnificent and ancient church building with a very illustrious legacy. A Southwark religious community is mentioned in the Domesday Book of 1086. A priory (monastery) was built on the site in 1106 and it later became known as St. Mary Overie under the Diocese of Winchester. Much of the building currently known as the cathedral was built between 1220 A.D. and 1420 A.D. as the first Gothic-style church in London. In the 1390s it was devastated by fire and was rebuilt about 1420 by the Bishop of Winchester, Henry Beaufort. King James I of Scotland married his bride, Joan, at Southwark in 1423.

In 1555, Queen Mary I held heresy trials in the Galilee Chapel at Southwark and six clergymen were condemned to death there. The church was also associated with the theater community during the time of William Shakespeare because the Globe Theater was nearby. In 1607, William Shakespeare buried his deceased brother, Edmund, in the cathedral. The building today contains a 19th century large stained-glass window dedicated to Shakespeare. The window depicts scenes from all of the Shakespeare plays at the base of which is a statue of a reclining William Shakespeare holding a quill. The original nave of the cathedral was in decay during the 1700s but was rebuilt in the 1800s and a new nave was installed in 1841 designed by Henry Rose.[59] This would have been a few years before John and Sophia's wedding. Southwark has been a place of worship for more than 1,000 years and became a cathedral in 1905. It sits in a marshy area south of the River Thames near where London Bridge was now located.

The Geary marriage certificate reads, "Married in the Parish Church according to the Rites and Ceremonies of the Established Church, by license."[60] The entry of "by license" differentiates the event from a "bann" where the parties publish their intent to marry in a public forum. The witnesses to the marriage listed on the certificate are Jane Jorden, John Hyde, Sr., and Curtis Bolton. Jane is Sophia's sister. John Hyde, Sr. is the man who baptized John. Curtis Bolton is John's friend and occasional lodger. The license lists John as a "bachelor" and Sophia as a "spinster". On the marriage certificate, John's father is listed as a "gentleman." Sophia's father is listed as a "plumber."

It is possible that other people also attended John and Sophia's wedding, as not all attendees at the wedding would have been listed as witnesses. John's father was still alive and living in Leicestershire at the time. John's brothers, Fred and Elton, were living with him at Duncan Terrace. There may have been other Fryer relatives in attendance as well; the Isle of Wight is about 90 miles from London.

Sophia Fryer received a beautiful book as a gift from Mormon Church leader Samuel W. Richards at the time of her wedding. The book is approximately 6 inches by 8 inches, leather-bound in pinkish leather and embossed in gold, with the title "A Bridal Gift." The title page of the book reads "By the editor of 'A Parting Gift to a Christian Friend'" and includes the following quote:

> "Oh if there is aught that can stable be,
> 'midst the endless round of earth's vanity,
> 'Tis the love, true love, which can two hearts bless,
> With a glimpse of the phantom happiness."[61]

Richards was serving as the President of the British Mission in 1852, succeeding his brother Franklin D. Richards who served in that same position. Richards must have known Sophia and John personally to give them such a gift. The book is a collection of poems and essays on the power of love. It is not from a Mormon source; it is written by a Christian group with the explanation inside that, "The work is intended as an elegant little present to those who have recently entered into the state of holy Matrimony…many would gladly avail themselves of a MANUAL, as the vehicle through which they may express their kindly feelings to the newly wedding pair." Richards' handwritten letter accompanying the book reads:

SAMUEL W. RICHARDS LETTER TO SOPHIA:

Liverpool 1852
Mrs. J.T. Geary,

Dear Sister,

Please accept the accompanying "Bridal Gift", as a small token of the good wishes, and esteem, of your friend and brother; whose earnest prayer is, that you may fully realize the brightest hopes portrayed by the richest sentiments that it contained.

Yours faithfully,
S.W. Richards
London

Curtis Bolton, also a wedding attendee, wrote in his journal contemporaneously about the Geary wedding:[62]

August 28 1852 "Went today to the Wedding of Bro. Geary – to the sister of Sister Jordan accompanied by Elder Hyde, Sen. and Sister Jordan. After the ceremony at the Church near London Bridge we went per Rail Road to Gravesend and spent the afternoon and evening. Spent the evening at the Gardens. I gave away the bride. Saw fireworks – dancing, Gipseys [sic]. A Gipsey [sic] told me I am to have 14 children. When Elder Hyde and Sister Jordan and I returned to town we met Sister Jordan's Husband, who acted like a devil…"

This is a delightful firsthand description of John and Sophia's wedding day. One can picture Sophia walking down the aisle of the great cathedral on the arm of Curtis Bolton. It is wonderful to hear that they had a festive celebration for their marriage.[63] The group of at least five (John, Sophia, Jane, Bolton and Hyde) apparently rode the train from London down the Thames River to Gravesend, a journey of about 30 miles. Gravesend is an ancient city located on the Thames and was famous in the 1800s for its pleasure gardens:[64]

As was usually the case in most seaports, inns and places of refreshment abounded. In the first half of the 19th Century, with the coming of the steamboats and the construction of the piers at Northfleet and Gravesend thousands of day-trippers poured in from London. This was Gravesend and Northfleet's "Golden Age". Business boomed and bathing establishments and pleasure grounds opened up, the most famous of these being Rosherville Gardens, which rivalled the Vauxhall Gardens in London and attracted thousands of visitors.

When Curtis Bolton writes that the wedding party "spent the evening at the Gardens" he is likely referring to Rosherville Gardens.

[Rosherville Gardens] were a place of surpassing beauty and a favourite resort of Londoners. Adorned with small Greek temples and statuary set in the cliffs, there were terraces, and archery lawn, Bijou theatre, and Baronial Hall for refreshments, and at one time a lake. At night the gardens were illuminated with thousands of coloured lights and there were fireworks displays and dancing. Famous bands such as the American Sousa were engaged during the season. Blondin, the trapeze artist, performed … In 1857 as many as 20,000 visitors passed through the turnstiles in one week.[65]

"Rosherville Gardens was one of the largest and most popular Victorian pleasure gardens."[66] It opened in 1837 and closed during the First World War about 1915. "George Jones, a businessman from Islington, formed the 'Kent Zoological and Botanical Gardens Company' and persuaded people to become shareholders in 1837. The gardens were laid out with a terrace, a bear pit, an archery ground, a lake, a maze, flower beds, statues, a lookout tower on a spur of rock and winding paths…Visitors flooded in from London the steamboats, landing at the nearby Rosherville Pier." "The Gothic Hall was used as a restaurant, ballroom and theatre…Other entertainments at the Rosherville Gardens included fireworks, tightrope walkers, balloon ascents, and a gypsy fortuneteller."'

It is interesting that Bolton specifically mentions that the group talking to the "Gipseys" that night at Rosherville. The fortuneteller's prediction that Bolton would have 14 children is eerily close. Before he died, Bolton's 3 polygamous wives in America had given birth to a total of 13 children by him.[67] At the time of this 1852 prediction, only 8 of those children had already been born.

While Curtis Bolton notes that he and the guests returned to London, it is possible that John and Sophia spent a honeymoon at the Rosherville Hotel, also known as Rosherville Shades. It was built in 1835 at a location just off Pier Road. The hotel was open for many years and closed in 1914; it was demolished in 1968.[68]

THE GEARYS DECIDE TO EMIGRATE TO AMERICA

John and Sophia made the decision to emigrate to America within four months of their marriage. Mormon Church leaders were vigorously asking British Mormons to emigrate to Utah. An article in the church publication, *The Millennial Star*, appeared in England the same year as their marriage, which read, in part: "For the Saints to get themselves to the Valley is a good thing. Few of them can be worse off there than they are here…There, all would have necessaries, and most would obtain many of the comforts. As a whole, the Saints of Utah are far better fed and clothed than their brethren and sisters in this country. Then how unwise it is for anyone to delay gathering till he gain sufficient means here to make himself what he thinks comfortable on the journey…"[69]

This portrayal of Utah life may have been slightly rose-colored. Mormon leader Jedediah Grant noted in a Utah discourse in 1854: "The imagination of some Saints has been so exalted by the Elders who preached to them, that they suppose that all our pigs come ready cooked, with knives and forks in them."[70]

Nevertheless, the literal gathering of Israel was and is a primary tenet of the Mormon faith and the church leaders put their money where their mouth was. Mormon leaders combined church assets and private donations to form the Perpetual Emigration Fund (PEF) in 1849 to fund emigration expenses of converts, mostly from Europe. "Between 1852 and 1855 the PEF helped approximately 10,000 Latter-day Saints come to Zion. By 1870 the fund had assisted more than 38,000 from the British Isles…"[71]

John Thomas Geary himself described his emigration decision in his 1857 letter to Brigham Young by writing: "I was counseled to emigrate, which I did without bidding farewell to my father, except by letter. We, however, still regularly correspond together." In 1852, John's father, Thomas, was living in Leicester with a housekeeper who became his common-law wife after Sarah's death. None of the father-son correspondence has been located.

Sophia had two family members joining her in America. Her younger brother, Richard, 15, was ready to seek his fortune in America, and her sister, Jane, was emigrating with her husband and two living children. On December 16, 1852, John Thomas Geary's records were removed from Holborn (Theobald's Road) Branch and he is officially shown as "emigrated to America" as of January 6, 1853.

ENDNOTES FOR CHAPTER TWO

1   See John Thomas Geary Articles of Clerkship with Stafford Stratton Baxter https://www.ancestry.com/family-tree/person/tree/10612501/person/6404827772/facts John Thomas Geary Articles of Clerkship with Robert Michael Baxter https://www.ancestry.com/family-tree/person/tree/10612501/person/6404827772/facts, a transcript appears in the Appendix, hereinafter "Articles of Clerkship."

2   *The Legal Observer or Journal of Jurisprudence,* Published Weekly, May to October 1845, inclusive, 1845, volume 30, London, Published for the proprietors by Edmund Spettigue, Law Bookseller and Publisher, 67 Chancery Lane. See entry at page 222 for John Thomas Geary. Stafford Stratton Baxter, Athersone. Robert Michael Baxter, Lincoln's Inn Fields. accessed at www.Google books.com.

3   https://www.familysearch.org/wiki/en/Lawyers_in_England_and_Wales

4   *Ibid.*

5   See Articles of Clerkship.

6   *The Law Times and Journal of Property*, March 1845 to October 1845, Volume 5, London, published at the office of The Law Times, 30 Essex Street, Strand. See entry at page 160 for John Thomas Geary.

7   See Articles of Clerkship.

8   "Borough High Street is one of the oldest roads in the London area and from the earliest times of which we have any knowledge it has been well supplied with inns for the convenience of travellers. A number of these were used in the 18th and 19th centuries as depots for carrier wagons and for passenger coaches to and from Kent, Surrey, Sussex and Hampshire. 'Borough High Street', in Survey of London: Volume 22, Bankside (The Parishes of St. Saviour and Christchurch Southwark), ed. Howard Roberts and Walter H Godfrey (London, 1950), pp. 9-30. *British History Online* http://www.british-history.ac.uk/survey-london/vol22/pp9-30 [accessed 6 March 2021].

9   See Wikipedia entry for Islington, https://en.wikipedia.org/wiki/Islington

10   See Wikipedia entry for Adam Duncan, https://en.wikipedia.org/wiki/Adam_Duncan,_1st_Viscount_Duncan

11   "After the final emancipation of Catholicism in the Relief Act of 1829, in 1837 a school was built in Duncan Street. It was used for worship until it was replaced by the NeoRomanesque St. John the Evangelist RC church. This was built 1841-3 to designs of J J Scoles with twin towers, the northern one only completed in 1877 by F W Tasker. Construction of the houses either side – nos. 33-39 and 40-45 had begun by 1841 and had been finished by 1851. The Roman Catholic institutions occupied a long piece of ground north of Duncan Street between the backs of Islington High Street and Duncan Terrace, up to Charlton Crescent which has changed little today apart from the rebuilding of the school in the late C20." https://planning.islington.gov.uk/NorthgatePublicDocs/00161186.pdf page 6 of Planning Document.

12   See Wikipedia entry, https://en.wikipedia.org/wiki/Sacramental_Test_Act_1828.

13   Design, Access & Heritage Statement, July 2012, 45 Duncan Terrace, Islington, London, https://planning.islington.gov.uk/NorthgatePublicDocs/00161186.pdf, accessed December 10, 2019.

14   1851 British Census, https://search.ancestry.com/collections/8860/records/2518083 Class: HO107; Piece: 1501; Folio: 54; Page: 23; GSU roll: 87835.

15   https://www.zoopla.co.uk/house-prices/london/duncan-terrace/?q=44%20Duncan%20Terrace%2C%20islington%2C%20London%20&yr=15055622. Accessed February 28, 2021.

16   Family History Library, British Film 87013, Record of Members, 1841-1946, accessed by Kaye Page Nichols.

17   *Ibid.*

18   Swenson, Patty, *Frederick Geary, 8 July 1830 to 4 July 1901*, Report by Patty Swenson, April 2020, for Kaye Page Nichols and Lisa Michele Church, copy in possession of authors. https://www.ancestry.com/imageviewer/collections/2380/images/40180 612057 0149-00902?treeid=10612501&personid=6421279203&rc=&usePUB=true& phsrc=puN1& phstart=successSource&pId=855.

19   Letter from John Thomas Geary to Brigham Young, March 11, 1857, Church History Library, Brigham Young Office Letter Files. Brigham Young office files, 1832-1878 (bulk 1844-1877); General Correspondence, Incoming, 1840-1877; General Letters, 1840- 1877; F-G, 1857; John T. Geary letter; Church History Library, https://catalog.churchofjesuschrist.org/assets?id=1df-2b02e-b337-4b1f-a644-4891b8f481a0&crate=0&index=0 (accessed: February 14, 2021) (hereinafter "John Thomas Geary Letter to Brigham Young, March 11, 1857")

20   *Ibid.*

21   Jorgensen, Lynne Watkins, *The First London Mormons: 1840-1845: "What Am I and My Brethren Here For?* (1988). All Theses and Dissertations. 4841. https://scholarsarchive.byu.edu/etd/4841. See Chapter IV, Non-Conformist London and the Mormons.

22   www.familysearch.org, John Hyde, Sr., (1811-1892), KLXK-5TK.

23   Allen, James B., Esplin, Ronald K., Whittaker, David J., Men with a Mission, 1837-1841, The Quorum of the Twelve Apostles in the British Isles, Deseret Book Company, Salt Lake City, Utah, 1992, page 190.

24   Family legend as recorded by Geary descendants Bessie Snow and Eva Geary Page Higbee in the 1970s states that "John Hyde was one of the elders who knocked on the Geary's door in London. At first turned away by the butler, then beckoned back by John, they spent a pleasant two hours together in his study. They said this was something they had been looking for all their lives." The source of this story is likely through John's daughter, Sophia Ann, who told it to her daughters, Eva, decades after the event in question. It includes at least one inaccuracy because it suggests John was already married to Sophia Fryer when he first heard about the Church. They were married more than a year after each being baptized. It is also unlikely that John Hyde, Sr. would have been knocking on doors randomly as a middle-aged professional man on the streets of London. Missionaries during that period were using other methods of proselytizing.

25   *Half-Yearly Report of the London Conference of the Church of Jesus Christ of Latter-day Saints,* Held in the City of London, Saturday and Sunday, May 31st and June 1st, 1851., Printed by W. Aubrey, 25, Brandon Street, Walworth, London, page Historian's Office Library, M204.6 L847 1851, May. Church History Library. (hereinafter "*Half-Yearly Report June 1851*".)

26   www.familysearch.org, John Hyde, Sr., (1811-1892), KLXK-5TK.

27   Thornbury, Walter, Old and New London: Volume 2 (London, 1878), see Islington, pp. 251-268. *British History Online* http://www.british-history.ac.uk/old-new-london/vol2/pp251-268 [accessed 6 March 2021].

28   "Catholic Apostolic (Irvingites): Revd. Edw. Irving, after expulsion from National Scotch Church in 1832, preached in the open in Britannia Fields and other parts of Islington. Irvingite Church in Duncan Street built 1834 by Duncan Mackenzie of Barnsbury Pk., former elder at Irving's Regent Sq. Scotch Church and one of 12 Apostles of Catholic Apostolic Church from 1835 to 1840. Designed and built by Messrs. Stevenson & Ramage of Theobalds Rd. in Holborn, seating 350 in 1835, 300 in 1851. Church was closed between 1964-1975." https://www.british-history.ac.uk/vch/middx/vol8/pp101-115#fnn54c
See also, A History of the County of Middlesex: Volume 8, Islington: Protestant nonconformist, pages 101-115, published by Victoria County History, London, 1985, A P Baggs, Diane K Bolton and Patricia E C Croot, 'Islington: Protestant nonconformity', in A History of the County of Middlesex: Volume 8, Islington and Stoke Newington Parishes, ed. T F T Baker and C R Elrington (London, 1985), pp. 101-115. *British History Online* http://www.british-history.ac.uk/vch/middx/vol8/pp101-115 [accessed 3 March 2021].

29   Buchanan, Frederick S. (1987) "The Ebb and Flow of Mormonism in Scotland, 1840-1900," *BYU Studies Quarterly:* Vol. 27 : Iss. 2 , Article 4, page 29. Available at: https://scholarsarchive.byu.edu/byusq/vol27/iss2/4. In a footnote to that article, Buchanan mentions that there is also a record of a delegation of Irvingites from England visiting Joseph Smith around 1835 "with the intent of offering the Mormons financial assistance" if their religious views could be reconciled. The Irvingite movement was strong in Canada as well as England. They did call a Council of Twelve Apostles who led the church until the last one died. See also Lancaster, John, "John Bate Cardale, Pillar of Apostles, A Quest for Catholicity," published as a Thesis at the University of St. Andrews, 1977, http://hdl.handle.net/10023/12046.

30   Jorgensen, Lynne Watkins, "John Hyde, Jr., Mormon Renegade," *Journal of Mormon History, 17*, 120-144, 1991. Retrieved March 1, 2021, from http://www.jstor.org/stable/23286428.

31   *Ibid*. See also London Conference British Mission Record of Members, 1841-1850 (FHL film 87,014). John Hyde, Jr., is member #455, John Hyde Sr., is member #487, and Martha Hyde, baptized by David Shorten, was #518.

32   See Jorgensen's, "John Hyde, Jr., Mormon Renegade" at page 125. She includes the following footnote in her article: London Conference British Mission Record of Members, 1841-1850 (FHL film 87,014). "All of the converts I list are included in these records semi-alphabetically. Banks lived next door to Frederick and Angelina Piercy on Tonbridge Avenue and is identified as the baptizing missionary for most of the Hawkins, Piercy, and Hyde family members. He returned to Utah in 1856, became a leader of the schismatic Morrisite movement, and was killed 5 June 1862 in Weber Canyon, Utah, during the so-called Morrisite War." Andrew Jenson, comp. Encyclopedic History of the Church (Salt Lake City: Deseret News Publishing Company, 1941), 540.

33   *Ibid.*

34   See Jorgensen's, "The First London Mormons," at pages 34 and 78.

35   *Half-Yearly Report of the London Conference of the Church of Jesus Christ of Latter-day Saints*, held in the City of London, Saturday and Sunday, December 6th & 7th, 1851. Printed by Brother J.B. Franklin, 5, Northhampton Street, King's Cross, London, Historian's Office Library, P M204.6, L847m, 1851, Dec. No. 2, Church History Library. (hereinafter "*Half-Yearly Report December 1851*".)

36   www.familysearch.org, Eli B. Kelsey,

37   *Half Yearly Report December 1851* at page 8.

38   *Ibid.* at page 1.

39   *Ibid.* at page 15.

40   *Half-Yearly Report June 1852. of the London Conference of the Church of Jesus Christ of Latter-day Saints,* held in the City of London, Saturday and Sunday, June 5th & 6th, 1852. Historian's Office Library, P M204.6 L847m, 1852, Church History Library. (hereinafter "*Half-Yearly Report June 1852*").

41   *Ibid.* at page 7.

42   *Ibid.* at page 5.

43   Jenson, Andrew, Latter-day Saint Biographical Encyclopedia, A Compliation of Biographical Sketches of Prominent Men and Women in the Church of Jesus Christ of Latter-day Saints, Volume IV, Salt Lake City, 1901, entry for Curtis Bolton, p. 334-335. Accessed at www.archive.org/details/latterdaysaintbi04jens. Brigham Young University Harold B. Lee Library digital collection.

44   *Curtis Bolton Reminiscences and Journal, 1849-1852*, Journal MS_1424-Journal_1852_February-1853_ORIGINAL Curtis Bolton, Church History Library. See also www.familysearch.org, Curtis Bolton (1812-1890), KWJ1-R32.https://catalog.churchofjesuschrist.org/assets?id=e251d241-3587-422b-8da8-e971a28a71f8&crate=1&index=23

45   www.familysearch.org, Sarah Ann Elton Geary, (1806-1852), LZV6-5Z7.

46   www.familysearch.org, Sophia Fryer (1829-1872), LLHM-Z2G. "England and Wales Census, 1851," database with images, *FamilySearch* (https://familysearch.org/ark:/61903/1:1:SGFR-TNY : 9 November 2019), Sophia Foyer in household of John Mitchell, Saint George Hanover Square, Middlesex, England; citing Saint George Hanover Square, Middlesex, England, p. 16, from "1851 England, Scotland and Wales census," database and images, *findmypast* (http://www.findmypast.com : n.d.); citing PRO HO 107, The National Archives of the UK, Kew, Surrey.

47   See Jorgensen's "The First London Mormons," at pages 27-28.

48   The name of the branch was Theobald's Road and it met in the Holborn area so the names were sometimes used interchangeably to refer to this branch.

49   www.familysearch.org, Jane Fryer Jorden Harrison, (1823-1880), KWNY-6XQ.

50   Snow Bessie, The Fate of the Fryers, self-published, 1973, at page 76, copy in possession of authors. Hereinafter "Snow, Fate of the Fryers". Snow had access to a document written by Frank Jorden, Jr. entitled "for the Religious Herald - A True Story by Reverend Frank F. Jorden." Snow notes in her book that she was given this document by Mrs. Merton E. Doolittle and Lucy Doolittle Keeler, the granddaughters of Frank Jorden, Jr. It appears to be an undated news article written in six installments by Jorden. It is consistently critical of the Mormon Church. The document is reproduced in Snow's book but the original has not been located.

51   www.familysearch.org, Sophia Fryer Geary Willis (1829-1872), LLHM-Z2G.

52   *Half-Yearly Report December, 1851*, See Table of Branches in the London Conference.

53   During their marriage, Jane Fryer and Frank Jorden had lived at 1 Red Lion Square, 18 Doughty Street and 6 Wakefield Street in London. The house on Doughty Street was on Mecklenburg Square and was a four-story brick house a few doors down from where Charles Dickens lived. It was while at Doughty Street that they were introduced to missionaries and joined The Church of Jesus Christ of Latter-day Saints, according to an entry on Family Search by Suzanne Swindle Johnston.

54   "England, Hampshire Parish Registers, 1538-1980," database, *FamilySearch* (https://www.familysearch.org/ark:/61903/1:1:QGQG-6ZHL : 13 February 2021), Sophia Fryer, 01 Nov 1829; citing Christening, Lancashire Record Office and Hampshire Record Office, England; FHL microfilm 1,470,893.

55   "England and Wales Census, 1841," database with images, *FamilySearch* (https://www.familysearch.org/ark:/61903/1:1:M79D-P9F : 6 March 2021), Sophia Fryer in household of John Stephens, Yarmouth, Hampshire, England, United Kingdom; from "1841 England, Scotland and Wales census," database and images, *findmypast* (http://www.findmypast.com : n.d.); citing PRO HO 107, The National Archives, Kew, Surrey.

56   www.familysearch.org Jane Fryer Jorden Harrison entry, including the useful history of Frank and Jane Jorden written by Suzanne Swindle Johnston.

57   Snow, Fate of the Fryers at pages 25-27, for examples of letters from Albert Fryer and Eliza Fryer to Richard Fryer in "about 1862" according to Bessie Snow.

58   Marriage entry given at the General Register Office, Application No 926307/1 in the Registration District of St. Saviour, Surrey, 10th day of February 2009. Copy in possession of Kaye P. Nichols, February 20, 2009.

59   See the official Southwark Cathedral website at https://cathedral.southwark.anglican.org/about-us/our-history/ and the Wikipedia entry on Southwark Cathedral at https://en.wikipedia.org/wiki/Southwark_Cathedral.

60   *Ibid.*

61   See digital images at the end of this chapter for A Bridal Gift, Seventh Edition, Liverpool, Published by D. Marples: and

by Hamilton, Adams, & Co., & Simpokin, Marshall, & Co., London. The book is currently in possession of a Geary descendant, having been handed down by Sophia to her daughter, Sophia Ann Geary Page.

62	Curtis Bolton Reminiscences and Journal, 1849-1852, Journal MS_1424-Journal_1852_February-1853_ORIGINAL Curtis Bolton, Church History Library. https://catalog.churchofjesuschrist.org/assets?id=e251d241-3587-422b-8da8-e971a28a71f8&crate=1&index=23

63	Family stories, including those of 20th century descendants Bessie Snow and Golda Page, tell a different, more embellished tale of the Gearys' wedding day. They describe a wedding parade in the streets of London occurring, but a check of London newspapers for the week before and after the Fryer-Geary wedding did not yield any record of such events.

64	http://www.discovergravesham.co.uk/architecture/a-brief-history-of-the-area.html. Accessed March 9, 2021.

65	www.wikipedia.org, Gravesend entry, citing Hiscock, Robert, A History of Gravesend (Phillimore, 1976).

66	www.DiscoverGravesham.co.uk/northfleet/rosherville-gardens. Accessed Jan 20 2020.

67	www.familysearch.org, Curtis Bolton (1812-1890), KWJ1-R32.

68	www.Dover-kent.com/2014-project-a/Rosherville-Hotel-Northfleet. Accessed Jan 20 2020.

69	Arrington, Leonard J. and Bitton, Davis, The Mormon Experience – A History of the Latter-day Saints, New York, Vintage Books, 1980, pages 128-129.

70	Grant, J.M., Journal of Discourses, Volume III , September 24, 1854, 65-67, www.journalofdiscourses.com/Jedediah_M_Grant.

71	Arrington and Bitton at page 131.

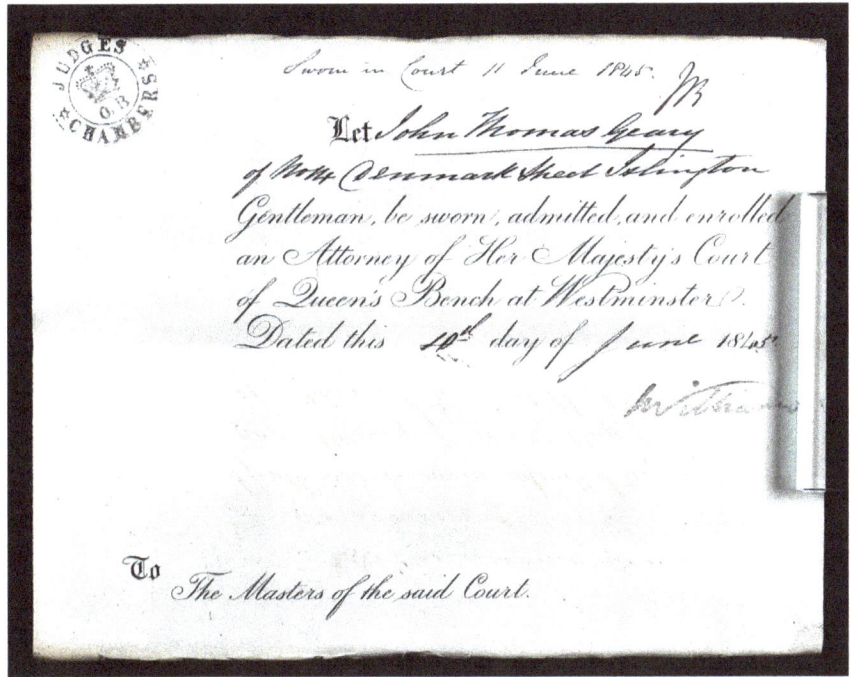

Document from the English Court records showing that John Thomas Geary was sworn in as an attorney on June 11, 1845.

"Let John Thomas Geary of No. 14 Denmark Street, Islington, Gentleman, be sworn, admitted, and enrolled an Attorney of Her Majesty's Court of Queen's Bench at Westminister.

Dated this 10th day of June, 1845.
Williams

To: The Masters of Said Court."

Left: Record showing John Thomas Geary passed his legal examinations in the Trinity Term 1845 and was an apprentice of both Stratton Stafford Baxter of Atherstone and Robert Michael Baxter of Lincoln's Inn Fields in London.

Above: The Geary family seal given to John by his father. It contains the image of the lyre and the olive branch with the words "Paiz Et Harmonie." The seal is still in the Geary family today. Look carefully at the graphic design of this book and echoes of the Family Seal will be found throughout.

44 Duncan Terrace in Islington, where John lived with his brothers in the early 1850s, is still there in London today. It is an upscale neighborhood with elegant townhomes that sell for several million pounds each. The units are four stories high.

In this photo, John's great-great-great-great grandson Jason S. Anderson visits Duncan Terrace in 2018.

<u>Below</u>, an exterior view of the Duncan Terrace block of homes, with the tower of St. John's Catholic Church at one end. Many of the early residents were affiliated with the church. The unit John lived in, No. 44, was completed in the late 1840s. Currently there are 75 houses and flats at Duncan Terrace.

Duncan Terrace is about 1-1/2 miles from Theobald's Road, where the Mormons held their branch meetings when John was baptized in 1851.

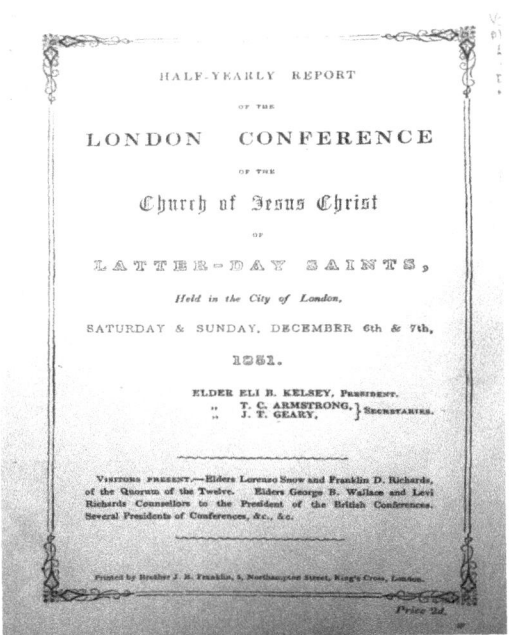

Cover of the Half Yearly Report of the London Conference of the Church of Jesus Christ of Latter-day Saints, Held in the City of London, Saturday & Sunday, Dec. 6-7, 1851. Note J.T. Geary is shown as Secretary.

Franklin Dewey Richards (1821-1899), Mormon apostle and President of the British Mission in 1849; later he served as President of the European Mission. He attended the 1851 London Half-Yearly Conference.

Lorenzo Snow (1814-1901), Mormon apostle and later President of the Church In 1849, he was called to the Italy/Switzerland mission. He attended the 1851 London Half-Yearly Conference.

Samuel Whitney Richards (1824-1909). He served as President of the British Mission 1851-1854 and gave John and Sophia a book of poetry as a wedding gift with an accompanying letter.

> On the 4th inst. at No. 44, Duncan Terrace, Islington, London, at the residence of her son, Mr. J. T. Geary, in her 49th year, Mrs. Sarah Ann Geary, the beloved wife of Mr. Thomas Geary, of Belgrave, in this county, and the second daughter of the late Mr. John Elton, formerly of this town.

Above: The death notice for John's mother, Sarah Elton Geary, who died in John's home at Duncan Terrace. Leicestershire Journal and Midland Counties Advertiser, June 12, 1852.

Below: Pages from the December, 1851 London Half-Yearly Conference Report showing John's involvement and his status as the Paddington Branch President in 1851.

BRANCHES IN THE LONDON CONFERENCE, DECEMBER 7, 1851.

Those marked thus * do now belong to the Reading Conference; those marked thus † to the Kent Conference; those marked thus ‡ to the Essex Conference; and those marked thus § to the Lands End Conference.

No.	BRANCHES.	ORGANIZED.	PLACE OF MEETING.	COUNTY.	NAME OF PRESIDENT.	ADDRESS OF PRESIDENT.
1	Theobalds Road	Nov. 10, 1841	Queen's Square Assembly Rooms	Middlesex	David Shorten	5, Hand Court, Holborn
2	Whitechapel	Oct. 21, 1848	Eastern Lecture Hall, Church Lane	,,	Thomas C. Armstrong	35, Jewin Street, City
* 3	Newbury	June 27, 1843	Latter-day Saints' Chapel, St. Mary Street	Berkshire	Thomas Squires	8, Waterloo Place, Newbury
4	Woolwich	Oct. 10, 1841	Thomas Street	Kent	Thomas Fisher	8, Albert Place, Charlton, Woolwich
5	Somers Town	July 2, 1848	16, Aldenham Street	Middlesex	William Bowring	16, Aldenham Street, Somers Town
6	Old Kent Road	Jan. 14, 1849	Crown Wharf, Canal Bridge	Surrey	Henry Manistre	19, St. James Street, New Hatcham
7	Kennington	June 15, 1848	Rackham's Academy, Bowling Green St.	,,	John Hawkins	1, Robert Street, North Brixton
§ 8	Devonport	May 19, 1850	104, Fore Street	Devonshire	James Caffall	2, Cornwall Street, Devonport
9	Paddington	March 21, 1850	Literary Institution, Great Carlisle Street	Middlesex	J. T. Geary	44, Duncan Terrace, Islington
10	Finsbury	,, 6, 1850	Providence Chapel, Cumberland St., Shored.	,,	J. Maiben	52, Gloucester St., Queen's Sq., Bloomsbury
11	Southwark	,, 5, 1850	Octagon Rooms, Mount St., Wesminster	Surrey	Thomas Macaughic	7, Berry Street, Sutton Street, Clerkenwell
12	Deptford	July 21, 1849	1, Collier Street [Road	Kent	John Griffiths	1, John Street, Woolwich New Town
† 13	Dover	1846	10, Chapel Place		Thomas Barton	1, Chapel Place, Dover
† 14	Brighton	Nov. 1849	Richmond Buildings, Richmond Street	Sussex	Henry Hollist	7, Wellington Place, Great Russell Street
15	Islington	Jan. 20, 1850	23, Ratcliffe Terrace, Goswell Street Road	Middlesex	William Cook	2, Redcross Square, Jewin Street, City
* 16	Cold Ash	July 30, 1848	William Ballard's, Cold Ash	Berkshire	Joseph Kimber	Cold Ash
17	Chelsea	Nov. 1849	Beulah Chapel, Pond Place	Middlesex	Cornelius Bagnall	5, Cumberland Street, Chelsea
18	Poplar	April 18, 1847	Literary Institution, High Street	,,	Samuel Purdy	11, Willis Street, Poplar New Town
19	Camden Town	July 7, 1850	School Room, 15, Grange Road	,,	Charles Norton	6, Upper Hartland Road, Camden Town
20	Globe Fields	June 30, 1850	41, Globe Road, Mile End	,,	Thomas Hilliker	41, Globe Road, Mile End
† 21	Sheerness	March 1840	Meeting Room, 1, Mile Town	Kent	Edward Bools	Hope Street, Mile Town
† 22	Faversham	July 24, 1850	Bridge Place, Brents, Faversham	,,	Edward Spillett	Bridge Place, Faversham
23	Notting Hill	Disorganized				
24	Notting Dale	Aug. 8, 1851	10, Crafter Terrace, Latimer Road, Shep-[herds Bush	Middlesex	James P. Grinham	8, Crafter Terrace, Latimer Road
‡ 25	Watford	Feb. 1, 1848	Jones' Yard, High Street	Herts	Richard John Caffall	New Street, Station Road
26	Welling	July 21, 1849	Mr. Jones', Welling	Kent	William Morrison	3, Albert Place, Charlton, Woolwich
‡ 27	St. Albans	April 1, 1849	Holywell Hill, St. Albans	Herts	Daniel Brown	Old London Road
* 28	Windsor	Aug. 20, 1850	Dorney, near Windsor	Berkshire	David Blair	1, Keppell Terrace, Windsor
29	Battersea	July 1848	King Street Chapel	Surrey	George Sims	6, Caroline Place, Queen's Elms, Brompton
30	Vauxhall	April 6, 1851	Bapt. Chapel, Coburg Row, Rochester Row	Middlesex	Samuel Priday	9, Pond Terrace, Chelsea
‡ 31	Boxford	Oct. 8, 1849	Ebenezer Chapel, Stone Street	Essex	Ebenezer Gillies	Bure, near Colchester, Essex
32	Bromley	June 2, 1850	Meeting Room, Bromley Common	Kent	Samuel James	Bromley Common
33	Isle of Dogs	Feb. 21, 1850	7, Tooke Street, Mill Wall, Poplar	Middlesex	Eli Hull	6, Bowen Street, Poplar New Town

The impressive and ancient Southwark Cathedral in London where John and Sophia were married on August 20, 1852. The cathedral has stood since medieval times and is famous for a number of reasons, including the fact that William Shakespeare buried his brother, Edmund, there. It contains beautiful stained glass windows and is in operation today along the banks of the Thames River near the London Bridge.

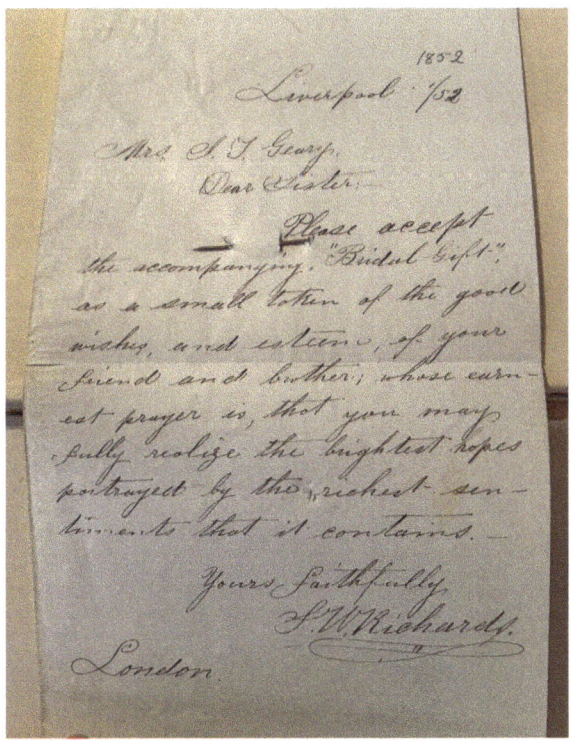

A letter from Mormon Church leader Samuel W. Richards to Mrs. J.T. Geary. He sent the letter to Sophia with his wedding gift to the Gearys in August, 1852. Richards was then serving as President of the British Mission and appears to have been acquainted with John and Sophia.

Right: The grand interior of Southwark Cathedral, originally built between 1220 AD and 1420 AD and rebuilt after a fire in 1420. In 1555, heresy trials occurred in this building under the reign of Queen Mary I. When John and Sophia were married here in 1852 their guests included Sophia's sister, Jane Fryer Jorden, and John Hyde, Sr., the man who baptized John into the Mormon Church.

Below: Photos of the book given to Sophia at the time of her wedding by then-President of the British Mission, Samuel W. Richards. It is a book of poetry and advice to young couples. The book is still treasured in the family of Geary descendants.

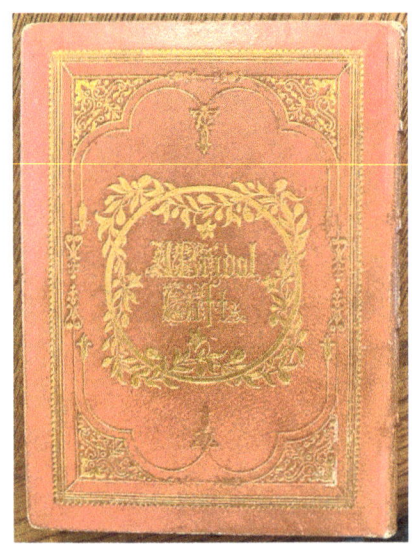  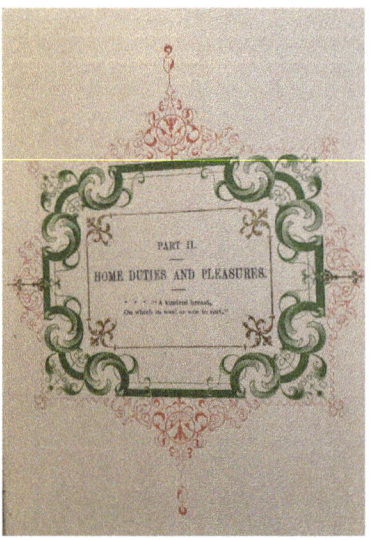

Handwritten journal entry by Curtis E. Bolton on Saturday Aug 28, 1852 when he attended the wedding of John Thomas Geary and Sophia Fryer. Bolton, then serving as the President of the French Mission, was visiting London on church business and became friends with John. He notes that he "gave away the bride." The wedding party then traveled to Gravesend where they "spent the evening in the Gardens," likely Rosherville Gardens.

Rosherville Gardens was a well-known Victorian Pleasure Garden along the Thames River a few miles from London. It was at the height of its popularity in the mid-1800s when the Geary wedding party would have visited.

The newspaper clipping is from The Observer, Sunday, August 15, 1852, advertising to Londoners about the appeal of the gardens.

ROSHERVILLE GARDENS.—Admission, 6d. each.— To the fascinating beauty of these unrivalled grounds, the first artistic skill is added, for the gratification of parties whose visits are limited to the afternoon.—Signor Silran, the great trampoline sprite, will go through his astonishing performances twice every day, commencing at 3 o'clock. A pleasing display of hydraulics will take place at 4. Military and quadrille dancing on the lawn and in the Gothic Ball Room at 5 o'clock; Baron Nathan Master of the Ceremonies. On Mondays, Wednesdays, and Saturdays, brilliant fireworks; concluding with the Grand Pyrotechnic Spectacle, Tam O'Shanter, designed by Gellini—the bard's vision embodied.—Refreshments by Winch and Calder.

Above: The record of the marriage of John Thomas Geary and Sophia Fryer at the Parish Church of St. Saviour, Southwark, in Surrey County. It shows that Curtis E. Bolton and Jane Jorden and Jos. Hyde were witnesses. The ceremony was performed by R. Bickerdike, Curate.

Below: A postcard drawing of the Rosherville Gardens in the 1800s where John and Sophia took their wedding party to Gravesend to celebrate the wedding in August, 1852.

EN ROUTE

"I resolved to go as far as that place, at all events
believing that the Lord would open the way further."
JTG

After deciding to emigrate to America, John and Sophia took the train to Liverpool on January 3, 1853 with Sophia's younger brother, Richard Fryer, who was 15 years old. They found lodgings at Grant Crosshall Street. They were planning to travel together on the ship *Ellen Maria* which was due to leave January 10 for New Orleans. On January 8, the three of them went to look at the ship and see what lay in store for them. On January 9, they attended a church meeting and heard Elder Orson Spencer preach "on the Plurality of Wives," according to Richard Fryer's journal. (It is fortunate that Richard kept such a good journal as he records many important events in John and Sophia's life from this time forward.)[1]

On January 10, the Gearys and Richard boarded the ship *Ellen Maria* with their luggage. Richard noted that "Brother Young" had forgotten to secure a berth for him.[2] The ship was delayed in leaving Liverpool due to wind conditions not being satisfactory, so the Gearys decided to remain in port a few extra days while the other emigrants waited on board the ship. Richard writes in his journal that, on January 12, 1853, "A Sheriff's Officer and Policeman came on board and examined the ship. Mr. Geary and me went on shore in the evening to get some necessaries for the voyage. He also got his head shaved." It appears John was trying to make it more difficult to recognize him; he feared that the policeman was looking for him. It is not clear why John was so afraid of being recognized.

Two days later, on January 14, the ship was still in port and a man came on board the ship with a letter for Richard Fryer. Richard and John refused to identify themselves. Richard writes in his journal that, "I knew better than to take it, and I informed Mr. Geary of it. There was a policeman on board the rest of the day." Finally, on January 15, 1853, John became too nervous that "his brother and a policeman would come on board" and he insisted that he should leave Sophia on the ship and try to catch up with it at another port. This suggests that John was fearful of his younger brothers, either Frederick or Elton Geary, who had both lived with him in London. Richard decided to disembark with John; the *Ellen Maria* sailed without them.

As a result of this last-minute decision, John and Richard were never able to catch up with the *Ellen Maria* in any other port and had to wait for another boat on which to emigrate to America. This left Sophia Fryer Geary, in the early stages of her first pregnancy, to sail to America alone. She sailed from Liverpool on January 17, 1853 and arrived in New Orleans on March 6, 1853. She then sailed up the Mississippi River to St. Louis to wait for Richard and John.[3]

Another of Sophia's siblings -- her sister, Jane Fryer Jorden -- was also emigrating from Liverpool at the same time with her little family. Jane and her husband, Francis, 31, left London sometime in early 1853 and may have been in Liverpool at the same time as John, Sophia, and Richard. The Jorden family, including Jane and Francis with their children Frank, 8, and Anne, 6, are listed on the ship *International*, which sailed on from Liverpool on February 28, 1853 and arrived at New Orleans on April 25, 1853.[4]

JOHN AND RICHARD TRY TO FIND A SHIP

Richard Fryer wrote about the confusing days in January, 1853 while he and John traveled from port to port seeking a plan for emigration:[5]

RICHARD FRYER JOURNAL

January 15: "Mr. Geary, thinking that his brother and policeman would come on board, resolved upon going to Holyhead and meet the ship there. He left the ship about 1 o'clock went over the River to new Brighton Ferry. After it was dark we went to Berkenhead Railway Station. On our way we met a man who remarked that Brother Geary was very much like a gentleman he had took over to Liverpool during the day. Brother Geary, thinking it was his brother, asked the man several questions about this gentleman and he gave a correct description of Mr. Fred Geary." [John and Richard found lodgings that night in Chester. They boarded a train to Holyhead the next day.]

January 16: We arrived at Holyhead about 1 o'clock in the morning, but Mr. Geary thinking he was [illegible] telegraphed to Holyhead, resolved to go on to Ireland…" [John and Richard then went to Dublin.)

January 17: "Mr. Geary thinking he was not safe, went to a Law Station to read the English Common Law Act, but he found he was quite safe."

January 20: "Mr. Geary and a Brother went to some reading rooms to look for advertisements of shipping but they could not find one for New Orleans. We left Dublin for Glasgow at 2 o'clock in a steamer."

John and Richard searched Glasgow and then Greenock for a ship that would take them back to Liverpool, as they decided they would have a better chance of emigrating from there. After a few days they made a deal with a ship's captain to take them to Liverpool as crew members instead of passengers.

January 29: "We rose early next morning and were soon on our way to the railway station, but as we passed the Post Office I remarked to Brother Geary that there might be a letter for us. He put down his bundle and went into the Post Office to see and there was a letter from Brother Samuel Richards informing Brother Geary of Brother John Hall's arrival and also counseling him to go to Liverpool. So we left Glasgow for Liverpool about 4 o'clock in the afternoon. We had a very rough night. The wind was blowing right ahead. We were up all night."

What exactly was John afraid of? Why would his brother, Fred, be looking for him and trying to stop his emigration? Why was he told to meet with Brother John Hall?

In family stories as well as in Bessie Snow's self-published book, *Fate of the Fryers*, there are suggestions of danger and controversy surrounding John's departure from London. Bessie Snow opines that she believes it was due to persecution of the Mormon converts occurring in England at this time.[6] Some persecution of Mormon converts did occur, but there is no evidence that John Thomas Geary was singled out for this treatment among an entire ship of Mormon converts.

Another theory is that there may have been trouble on the Fryer side of the family. There is evidence that Sophia's family was not happy with her younger brother, Richard, possibly joining the Mormon Church. Richard Fryer was only 15 years old at the time and, being a minor, his parents could have prevented him from leaving England without their consent. Three of the 11 Fryer children became Mormons (Jane, Sophia, Richard), but the family that remained in England were strongly opposed to Mormonism and pleaded with them to change. Still, it is John, not Richard, who expresses concern at the time of departure.

John himself gave the best explanation for his nervousness and delay in Liverpool when he wrote a letter to Brigham Young in 1857: "At the period of my baptism, some of my relations were living with me. They immediately became my most bitter enemies, and did all in their power (which however was not much) to injure me in my business." [7]

The "relatives" living with John at the time of his baptism were his two brothers, Fred and Elton, and his older cousin, Charlotte Hall (mother of the above-mentioned John Hall). There are intriguing indications that the Hall family, Fred Geary, and John Thomas Geary were in the middle of an issue over deeds that somehow involved Mormon Church leaders in England.

THE HALL FAMILY

Charlotte Hall and her family were to play a key role in the life of John Thomas Geary. Charlotte was born in 1798 and christened on March 17, 1798 in Selling, Kent, England.[8] On March 24, 1819, Charlotte married Thomas Johnston Hall, a coal merchant. They were married in Holborn, London. Thomas and Charlotte had two daughters born to them, but both died in infancy. They had two sons who lived to adulthood: John Charles Hall and Thomas Charles Hall. Charlotte's husband abandoned his family in 1827, reportedly moving to Canada. Charlotte placed her boys in boarding schools and moved to London.

When John C. Hall became a young man, his mother sent him to America to look for his father. John C. Hall did not find his father in America, but he did meet the Mormon missionaries and joined the Mormon Church in 1847, making his way to Utah. Therefore, in 1852 when his mother was living with John Thomas Geary in London, the two distant male cousins were both members of the Mormon Church on different sides of the world.[9]

DEED DISPUTE IN LONDON INVOLVING HALLS AND LDS CHURCH

Clues to this mystery around John Thomas Geary's departure for America are found in the missionary journal of John Charles Hall, Charlotte Hall's eldest son.[10] By the early 1850s John Hall was living in Salt Lake City with the large group of the Saints. Fortuitously, he was called on a mission back to London at the very time that John Thomas Geary was preparing to emigrate to America as a Mormon convert. The cousins, John Hall and John Thomas Geary, crossed paths for at least two critical days in Liverpool on January 30 and January 31, 1853.

John Hall's journal notes the following about a letter he received from John Geary just as Hall was getting on the boat in New York to sail for England: [11]

JOHN HALL JOURNAL

Jan 3 [1853]. At daylight this morning went to Logan office. Saw the provisions for the voyages packed all right, then recollected there might be a letter for me in the post office. Upon going there ascertained there was one. I saw it. The postmark was Islington, a black envelope also 25 cents to pay. Having but 15, ran up to Sister Hicks in some anxiety of mind to know whose death it announced, to borrow the money, also with no little fear that the ship might move off from the pier. Upon procuring the letter there was no account of any death but was merely one from J T Geary stating that he would leave for America in Feb. As soon as I got on board the ship moved off and anchored out in the river, the wind blowing from the east rather fresh.

This Hall journal notation confirms that John Hall knew he could possibly meet with John Thomas Geary in Liverpool while both were in transit. It is also intriguing that Samuel Richards, the church official in London, had already sent John Thomas Geary the letter at Glasgow – mentioned above in Richard Fryer's journal - counseling him to meet with John Hall in Liverpool. Why was this necessary? Why did a Mormon church leader need to arrange the meeting between Hall and Geary? There is some indication that John Hall thought Church disciplinary action might be needed to resolve the "deed dispute" involving John Thomas Geary. After the two cousins met in Liverpool, they were able to resolve whatever issues existed between them. They remained friends and would associate with one another later in Utah.

Richard Fryer writes in his journal that the two men met in Liverpool on January 30, 1853 as they arrived from Glasgow:[12]

RICHARD FRYER JOURNAL

January 30, 1853 [Liverpool, England] It was tremendous rough today and we were both very sick until we arrived at [illegible] Brother John Hall came and met us and took us to a lodging house. We were very tired and went to bed.

January 31st, 1853 [Liverpool, England] Brother Hall went to the Office and brought back some stars [likely referring to the Mormon Church newspaper *The Millennial Star*].

February 1, 1853 [Liverpool, England] Brother John Hall went to London and Brother Geary went to the office.

It is not clear what business transpired between John Thomas Geary and John Charles Hall during these two days of encounter described in Fryer's journal. The next day, Geary apparently boarded the ship, *Jersey*, to sail to America with Richard, and John Hall went on to London.

Once in London, John Hall's journal describes a specific assignment he has to fix some dispute related to John Thomas Geary in London. The dispute involves a "land deed" or "papers" that must be corrected. "Brother Marsden" is the same President James Marsden who was the presiding church officer of the London Conference when John served as the Paddington Branch President under him. Hall suggests that the deed was the central point in "the affair with John":

January 25 [1853 London] We had a warm greeting and a short conversation with Brother Richards. He said he could tell me something about J T G. I said I would call in the morning.

Feb 4 Went to Brother Marsden in the morning. He seemed very kind. Promised to do everything that 'was right in regard to the papers'. From there passing through the Thames Tunnel, went to Maria's and from there to Martha, meeting with Mother and aunts where we spent the evening.

Feb 5 At home till the afternoon, Wrote to Tom [*John C. Hall's younger brother, Thomas Charles Hall, who also joined the Church and later emigrated to Utah*] and went to Brother Marsden. Saw the papers but was requested to leave them for a day or two longer. I consented. He also requested me to mention his willingness to do something that was right to Mother and Aunt.

Feb 10 [1853 London] Over to Brother Marsden's. Succeeded in getting the land deed, but on my arrival home found I did not have the deed of settlement. Went to Jervin St in the afternoon, saw Brother Marsden. He told me I might search for the papers myself tomorrow. On my way home called and delivered the letter to Sister Allen, which I received from Brother Gaulten.

Feb 11 [1853 London]. Once more to Brother Marsden's. Looked for the papers I found Aunt's. From thence through the Thames Tunnel to Maria's. Bid Maria good-by, promised to write to all. Returned home, calling on Jervin St. where I received 10/ by order of Brother Marsden, promising to return it at earliest convenience. Arose about 5:00 this morning and went to the railway station. Fred and Elton accompanied me. Before I left Mother's, interested that Mr Fuller has suspicions that I knew where John was. In answer to this I said that if I did know where he was I should not reveal it until an action of the church had been taken. I am sincerely sorry about the affair with John. It has brought much reproach upon the church and has shut my mouth while here. The fact of getting the deeds has done something towards softening feelings against the church…

John C. Hall was visiting extended family in London. His mother, Charlotte Wright Hall, has one sister still living in 1853 – Rebecca Sarah Wright Fuller.[13] She is presumably the "Aunt" to whom he refers. "Maria" and "Martha" could be references to female cousins. Charlotte also has at least two nieces living in 1853, the daughters of her deceased sister, Ann Wright Gorham: Martha Ann Gorham (1820-1883) and Maria Gorham (1824-1875).[14] Finally, Hall mentions the Geary brothers, Fred and Elton Geary, who apparently have some interest in the matter. Charlotte Wright Hall is living with them.

The deed dispute seems to center on the Hall-Elton-Geary family connection. Charlotte Wright Hall and Sarah Ann Elton Geary were cousins. Perhaps there was a dispute within the Elton family that involved both women and some land or property they owned in common? John Thomas Geary apparently had deeds in his possession at some point that belonged to Charlotte Hall and/or her sisters. Could John Thomas Geary, in his role as an attorney, have advised the women on the matter?[15] Why would the presiding officer of the Mormon Church be needed to resolve a non-Mormon family's property dispute? Were the activities of John Charles Hall with Brother Marsden in London designed to get the deeded property back to the Elton/Wright relatives and out of the Church's hands? Or could it have been simply a legal paperwork matter John promised to complete but left town without finishing?

Hall's journal entries seem to say that Hall eventually received the deeds from Brother Marsden on February 10 and received his Hall relatives' related paperwork on February 11. The matter appears to be resolved with those actions. After Hall's entry on February 11, 1853, Hall no longer mentions the deeds, so he was able to close this chapter to the satisfaction of the Elton-Wright-Hall relatives and to the satisfaction of the Mormon Church leaders.

FREDERICK PIERCY

Frederick Piercy was born January 27, 1830 in Portsea, England, the eighth of nine children. Piercy joined the Church of Jesus Christ of Latter-day Saints on March 23, 1848. In 1849 he was married to Angelina Hawkins, a fellow Londoner. The Hyde, Piercy, and Hawkins families were all early English converts to the Mormon Church and appear to have known each other. Frederick is shown as a member of the Holborn Branch in London where John and Sophia Geary resided in the early 1850s. Frederick served as the secretary of the London Conference in 1849 and 1850. The Hyde family included John Hyde, Sr., who baptized John into the church, and John Hyde, Jr., who became first a supporter and then a detractor of the church.

On February 5, 1853, Piercy, along with John Hyde, Jr., Joseph Hyde, and about 300 other immigrants, set sail from Liverpool on the ship Jersey, bound for the port of New Orleans. They were headed to join church members in Salt Lake City. Piercy was 23 years old, John Hyde, Jr. was 20 years old and his brother, Joseph, was about 9. John Thomas Geary and Richard Fryer were on the boat with Piercy and the Hydes in the same sleeping berth. Piercy's purpose in the trip was not to stay in America, but to travel with this company as an artist to sketch images of the West and publicize the Mormon migration. He faithfully kept a journal and a sketchbook of his trip. This resulted in the publication of his illustrated travel book, "Route from Liverpool to Great Salt Lake Valley." It was first published in fifteen monthly parts from July, 1854 to September, 1855 in England to encourage British Mormons to emigrate to Utah. Piercy skillfully sketched immigration in the American West; his works and writings are often used to represent the time period.

Fred Piercy's Journal Excerpt from his ocean voyage:

"After looking round the good ship, and taking a peep at the passengers who were to be my companions during the voyage to New Orleans, I selected a berth quite to my taste in the second cabin, a small house on deck fitted up with single berths for eight persons. I found, much to my satisfaction, that there were five or six pleasant fellows, of whom I already knew something…the Steerage passengers of whom there were three hundred, were composed one half of English and the other half of Welsh, causing a confusion of tongues quite amusing until you were personally interested in what was said. They, however, managed very well, and most heartily and lustily helped each other in all kinds of work where more than one pair of hands were necessary for its accomplishment."

Piercy went on to mention that the ship was "quickly towed down the Mersey, past the Rock Lighthouse and the Fort at the mouth, and the wind being fair, the sails were soon unfurled and filled, and we stood out to sea. Thoughts crowded my brain; of course, I thought of old England. It is impossible to leave the land of one's birth without regret, or to leave one's kindred and friends, even for a few months, without a sigh. I wondered if I should ever see them again…"

Piercy came across the plains earlier than the Gearys and returned to England in 1854. Piercy spent most of his life as an artist and teacher in London. He reportedly left the Mormon faith. The 1861 England Census lists Piercy as an artist and professor of drawing. Piercy suffered from paralysis the last ten years of his life, dying on June 10, 1891 in London.

SAILING ON THE SHIP *JERSEY* FOR AMERICA

John Thomas Geary and Richard Fryer finally boarded a ship for America from Liverpool at the end of January, 1853. John was 30 years old and Richard was half his age. John and Richard were not listed on the manifests of any of the known LDS Emigrant Ships that traveled from Liverpool to America during 1852 or 1853. It is most likely they are not listed on ship manifests because they signed on as sailors for the ship instead of passengers. As they did in Glasgow, they may have volunteered that they would sign on as sailors in exchange for free or reduced passage. Or they may have traveled under assumed identities due to their fears. Richard Fryer states in his journal that he and John Thomas Geary came on the ship *Jersey*; in a later part of his journal Richard Fryer writes that he suspended journal writing during their time on the seas.

There is additional evidence that the ship John and Richard sailed on was known as the *Jersey*, which departed Liverpool on February 5, 1853 for New Orleans. Contemporaneous diaries from another shipmate mention the men and Richard Fryer's journal corroborates several details.[16] It is particularly interesting that – after trips around British ports for two weeks – John and Richard ended up on the same Mormon emigrant ship as Elder John Hyde, Junior, whose father, John Hyde, Senior, baptized John almost two years prior in London and was a witness at the Gearys' Southwark Cathedral wedding. John Hyde, Jr., and his 9-year-old brother, Joseph Hyde, were emigrating to Utah themselves, along with a friend and fellow British convert, Frederick Piercy. The Hydes and Piercy were baptized in 1848 and might have known John Geary as Church acquaintances in London at the Theobald's Road Branch or other locations.

RICHARD FRYER JOURNAL

February 2nd [1853 Liverpool] Brother Geary went and got the tickets.

February 3rd [1853 Liverpool] Brother Geary went to the ship and secured his berth.

February 4th [1853 Liverpool] Brother Piercy and Brother Geary took the bundles to the ship and in the afternoon Brother Geary came in a cab and we went to the ship. After we had passed the Doctor, Brother Geary, Piercy and Hyde went on shore to buy provisions for the journey. They came on board late in the evening with bedding etc. and they intended on going on shore in the morning to buy the rest, so we all went to bed. However, we had not been in bed long when Brother Piercy said he would have a joke with Brother Hyde making him believe it was morning. Well, he got out of bed and dressed himself then Brother Piercy and Brother Geary jumped into bed again and we had a good laugh at him.

February 5th [1853 Liverpool] All hands were called on the quarter deck to count them and the tug towed us out of the dock.

There are interesting records of the voyage of the ship *Jersey* from both Frederick Piercy (see sidebar) and the Mormon leader aboard ship, George Edward Halliday, who supervised the 300 emigrants. The voyage lasted from February 5, 1853 until March 22, 1853.

HALLIDAY'S GENERAL VOYAGE NOTES

…with a company of 314 Saints, sailed on board the Jersey, on the 5th instant, for New Orleans, on their way to their mountain home of the Israel of God. Thus are the elders and Saints, flocking to the Lord's hiding place, as doves to their windows, that they may dwell in safety when judgments shall make the nations desolate…[17]

Piercy describes a scene in his berth that matches with the Richard Fryer journal note about the group of men traveling together. This occurred soon after departure from Liverpool, when the passengers were first feeling the effects of seasickness. "John H." is most likely John Hyde. Mention is made of his brother, "Joe H.", or Joseph Hyde. Piercy also mentions a man named "Leary" with a shaven head, which could be John Thomas Geary, who had shaved his head in Liverpool to avoid being recognized and probably didn't give his real name.[18]

FREDERICK PIERCY JOURNAL

I went to the cabin where I found my fellow passengers already assembled, sitting on their boxes with all the gravity of men momentarily expecting the visitation of a grievous calamity. Young Joe H. was already in his berth, hugging a tin basin, and I thought, from the noise he was making, that he would soon be relieved. His brother John was sitting on his box, with is large eyes wide open, looking at Leary [Geary] and seeming to say, 'Am I! Am I going to be sick?' While Leary [Geary] with his shaven head (he had a fever), his hands on his knees, without a vestige of color in his cheeks, did not answer audibly, but in the same language seemed to say, 'Ditto! Ditto!' I turned into my berth and presently saw Leary [Geary] start from his seat and rush out of the cabin; very soon John [Hyde] followed his example."

"Considering all things, however, the little world behaved itself remarkably well. After a few days all became used to the motion of the ship. Sickness disappeared, and was only remembered to be laughed at. Merry groups assembled on deck, and, sitting in the sunshine, told stories, sang songs, and cracked jokes by the hour together, and generally with a propriety most unexceptionable.[19]

ARRIVAL IN AMERICA

The ship *Jersey* landed at New Orleans on March 2, 1853. The Hydes and Piercy separated from John at this point, following their own path to make their own way across the plains to Utah. John Hyde, Jr. became disaffected with the church within a few years and was excommunicated. Joseph Hyde, his younger brother, went on to Utah and lived the rest of his life there as an active member of the Mormon Church. The Hyde family back in England, including John Hyde, Sr. who baptized John, eventually fell away from the church over a dispute about whether they should emigrate to Utah. Fred Piercy returned to England and published his illustrated book about the Mormon emigrant experience to wide acclaim. He also left the Mormon Church later in life.

After landing in America, John and Richard were seeking to unite with their other family members. Richard Fryer paints a vivid picture of arriving in America and the journey he and John took once they landed at New Orleans on March 21, 1853.

RICHARD FRYER JOURNAL

Today the Saints were busily employed getting their luggage on board the "John Simonds" Steamboat, and left New Orleans at dusk on our way up the Mississippi. The next day presented to our view such a scene as I never before witnessed, to see the steamers going up and down the River, the ---- at work in the plantations, the thick long Woods as we passed with new and then a large piece of farming land with a bustling little town. It was truly beautiful. We were 6 days coming up the River, during which time John was our President, and we had a good time. We arrived at St. Louis on the morning of the (illegible). Met my Sister, Sophia who I was glad to see, she having come in the same ship that we intended coming in. I stayed in the city of St. Louis about 6 weeks, during which time I worked at painting, received 1 dollar per day wages. The time for us to leave being close at hand, Geary started up the River to get cattle and a Wagon.

It is notable that - as they traveled up the Mississippi River - John served as president of their Company of Saints while they were traveling, consistent with the duties he had performed as Mormon Branch President back in London, England. When they reached St. Louis, John parted company with Richard Fryer to reunite with his wife, Sophia, as soon as possible. This must have been a joyful reunion, as Sophia had been waiting for John since her arrival in America March 6.

Sophia was nearing the end of her first pregnancy, having left England three months before. Though they had been married less than a year, John and Sophia had spent only four months together in England and now had been apart about three months. Sophia apparently survived her solo journey on the *Ellen Maria* well. Richard writes that he stayed in St. Louis for 6 weeks, "during which time I worked at painting, received 1 dollar per day wages. The time for us to leave being close at hand, Geary started up the river to get cattle and a wagon."[20] Presumably John and Sophia were with Richard in St. Louis. Sophia was likely waiting for her sister, Jane, who arrived in New Orleans with her family a few weeks later on April 25, 1853.

After the Jordens and Gearys were reunited, Sophia and John traveled to Keokuk, Iowa, across the river from the earlier Mormon Church headquarters in Nauvoo. This particular year, 1853, was the only year that the Mormon Church used Keokuk as an outfitting point for the pioneers. Keokuk was a small rural area that could easily handle an influx of hundreds of European immigrants. A recent steamboat tragedy on the Mississippi River caused Church officials to prefer Keokuk over having Saints take a steamboat from St. Louis across Iowa.[21]

When the Gearys arrived at Keokuk, the newly-settled community of Saints was getting ready for a journey across the American plains to Great Salt Lake City in the Utah Territory.

RICHARD FRYER JOURNAL

In a few days I received a letter from him [Geary], wishing me to come to Keokuk. Consequently, I started by the Next boat, arrived at Keokuk late in the evening of the next day, found Geary who delivered into my hands a yoke of cattle, which I found to be a very troublesome job. There was about 1200 of the Saints camped here in their wagons and tents and on the arrival of Geary and my Sisters we joined with them. We stayed here a fortnight during which time they organized 3 companies, but Geary not being ready we were organized in the last company, John Brown, Captain.

On June 10, 1853, Sophia delivered her first baby while she and John were living in the Keokuk camp. She had been in America about two months. With her at the birth were her husband, John, and her siblings and family: Richard Fryer, Frank and Jane Fryer Jorden, and the Jordens' two children, Annie and Frank, Jr. The story recorded by Bessie Snow describes a situation where Sophia's delivery became problematic and Church President Brigham Young got involved:

FATE OF THE FRYERS:

"While they were here, Aunt Sophia took sick. President Brigham Young came to Grandmother [Jane Fryer Jorden] and told her she must deliver her sister's child. He brought Dr. Willard Richards. In those days it was considered improper for a man to deliver a baby and care of a woman in confinement. That was the work of a midwife. Grandmother told them she couldn't handle the case because she had never done such a thing in her life and didn't know what to do. President Young told her they would bless her and she would get along all right. So she sat down on a wagon tongue and he and Dr. Richards placed their hands on her head and blessed her and set her apart as a nurse and midwife to work among the Saints. She took care of Aunt Sophia and she got along all right." [Jane received this "calling" as a midwife and performed these duties for the rest of her life.][22]

John and Sophia named their baby girl Sophia Ann Geary. Within a few days, the Gearys' new little family was starting out on a wagon journey across the country. Richard Fryer traveled with them in the same John Brown Company for hundreds of miles to Council Bluffs, Iowa.

RICHARD FRYER JOURNAL

Undated: "After considerable trouble yoking up our cattle, owing principally to our want of experience in that line, we succeeded, however, in making a start. We traveled over a considerable extent of country chiefly prairie land, distance about 500 miles which took us a fortnight to travel and during which time I had some little experience in driving team, watching cattle, and camping out in tents. We arrived at Council Bluffs on the Missouri River on 17th of July, camped just below the city and drove the cattle 2 miles off to feed."

When they reached Council Bluffs, Iowa on July 17, 1853, after 500 miles of difficult travel, John and Sophia decided to remain there for a while. Sophia needed to recover her health and stabilize the new baby. No doubt she was struggling with the effects of giving birth in such unsettled and remote circumstances. The rough travel would have been difficult on a new mother and baby. John sold his cattle and wagon and they moved into the city of Council Bluffs, Iowa where Sophia would end up staying for three years.

FATE OF THE FRYERS:

"It was at Council Bluffs that Uncle John Geary decided to remain for some time because Aunt Sophia was ill. Frank Jorden Jr. tried to get Grandmother [Jane] to stay also but she wouldn't. So Uncle Richard helped to get Grandmother and her family transferred to another wagon. Both the Geary and Jorden families had been well off when they joined the church. Uncle John and Aunt Sophia lost most of theirs before they left England. Uncle John brought with him a family Bible that was over 300 years old. It had been given to him by his father who told him to never sell it unless 'his children were crying for bread.' He also brought a "Seal" in a gold frame that both he and his father had used in their business for letters and documents."[23]

RICHARD FRYER JOURNAL

July 18th: Herding cattle till noon, afternoon helping my sister Jane to remove to another wagon. Geary was making preparations to stay because his wife was sick. Jorden was trying to induce Jane to stay but could not.

July 19th: Mr. Stewart came to camp inquiring for men. I engaged myself to him to drive team across the plains for my board, preferring this to staying another year, which Geary intended doing. Today he sold his cattle and wagon, and moved into the city.

July 20th: Hunted up the Cattle, drove through the City where Geary run after me and bid me farewell.

Jane Fryer Jorden, Frank Jorden, their children, and Richard Fryer continued across the plains to Salt Lake City with the Stewart Company. They arrived in late summer, 1853.[24] Back in Couneil Bluffs, Sophia was already pregnant with her second child. John had returned to St. Louis to work, 430 miles away.

JOHN WORKS IN ST. LOUIS

A few years later in writing about this period, John described the ensuing situation this way in his 1857 letter to Brigham Young:

"In consequence, however, of Sister G's sickness I sold my wagon and team to my President, and retraced my steps back to St. Louis, a course which I now know, by experience, was a very unwise one. In that City,

SAINTS IN SAINT LOUIS

St. Louis, Missouri played an important part in the history of the early Mormon Church, especially in terms of housing the flood of European immigrants that headed for America during the 1840s to 1860s. Originally, emigrants would land in New Orleans and come upriver to St. Louis on their way to Nauvoo, the church's headquarters in the 1840s. It was a more cosmopolitan part of Missouri. After the Mormons began the trek to the Utah Territory in the 1850s, St. Louis was a key place for emigrants to work and organize supplies before they embarked on travel across the American plains.

"Church leaders chose St. Louis as the most logical 'safety valve' city for the emigrants from Europe. Emigrants who ran out of funds (and there were thousands) could easily obtain work in growing St. Louis until they could earn the money necessary to buy the wagons and other outfitting supplies needed for the journey west to Utah. For many years after the initial Mormon trek, the exodus of the Saints evolved into a highly organized mass migration with St. Louis as one of its most crucial hubs. The Mormon Trail passed through St. Louis and by steamboat up the Missouri River to various overland trail heads, which shifted from year to year."

"Mormons felt safe in St. Louis during the mid-nineteenth century. First, they were not planning on permanent residency; second, they were not a threat to the city's political powers; third, they were skilledworkers; and finally, the general population was large, and the Mormons were dispersed throughout the metropolis. Approximately 22,000 Mormons passed through St. Louis between 1847 and 1855 on their way to Utah. For some, the stay in the city was only as long as necessary to transfer to another steamboat heading up river to the Mormon overland trail head on the banks of the Missouri. However, others were forced to remain in St. Louis for months or even years, and a church organization was created to assist with both temporal and spiritual needs. The church procured housing in various sections of the city. Employment was found to enable the emigrants to earn the money they needed to pay for the overland journey to Utah. Local lay leaders were assigned to care for each church member staying in the city.

"By April 1854, Brigham Young and other church leaders in Salt Lake City had designated St. Louis as a location where the 'Saints might gather with approbation who were unable to go directly through to Utah.' Young chose Apostle Erastus Snow to journey to St. Louis, organize a stake, preside over the region, and oversee general emigration matters in Iowa and Missouri…"

"…St. Louis remained a vital part of the Mormon journey to Utah until the threat of yellow fever and cholera along the Mississippi forced another change. Due to direction from Brigham Young, by 1856 the Saints began to use the eastern ports of Boston, Philadelphia, or New York, from which they rode the rails to Iowa City, the newly designated trail head for Mormon handcart and wagon companies. Handcarts were used up until 1860. With the coming of the first transcontinental railroad in 1869 and its proximity to Salt Lake City, transportation by handcart and wagon was discontinued."

Farmer, Thomas L. and Woods, Fred E., "Sanctuary on the Mississippi – St. Louis as a Way Station for Mormon Emigration", The Confluence, Spring/Summer 2018, pages 42-53. The Confluence is a journal published by Lindenwood University in Saint Charles, Missouri.

> I lost, in one way or another, the greater part of my luggage, and was, from necessity, alternately, a furniture-cleaner and polisher, stove-polisher, and gas-pipe-layer, at a salary of 5 dollars per week. I also drove Messrs Harlow's and Co's furniture van, during my residence in St. Louis. At length, I became school-teacher, at a monthly salary of 25 dollars, which, before leaving, was increased to 40. But, although my income thus kept increasing, my prospect of getting an outfit for the Plains, kept as gradually decreasing i.e. my means, somehow, or other, actually became more and more limited every year."[25]

For an educated man like John Thomas Geary, the rough 1800s culture of the American plains presented a tough dilemma. While he was willing to work hard and learn any number of new trades, he couldn't establish a business anywhere because he was intent on joining the rest of the religious pilgrims in the Utah Territory. He couldn't practice his legal profession in these transitory circumstances. It must have been challenging for him to provide for his family in such uncertain times. He may not have wanted to leave his wife and baby for months at a time, but he was forced to go to a larger city to find work.

During the three-year period that John lived in St. Louis – 1853-1856 – the city was experiencing an influx of Mormon emigrants. Of the 100,000-plus residents in that city, several thousand Mormons were staying there temporarily. The Church organized a stake with Stake President Erastus Snow presiding there. The members held church meetings in a building they rented from the Methodist Chapel at 4th and Washington Street. Services were conducted in English, French, German, and Danish for the Mormon pioneers.[26] John worked, among other jobs, at the Harlow's Furniture Store in St. Louis driving a van; the store was known for its piano sales.

JANE FRYER JORDEN FAMILY IN UTAH

By 1854, Sophia's sister, Jane, was already living in Utah, and having her own difficulties due to her husband's desertion. After their 1853 arrival, Jane's family initially settled in Salt Lake after and Frank worked as a woodworker on some prominent projects. Family historian Bessie Snow recorded that Frank was a cabinetmaker in England and used his skills in Utah to carve the beautiful woodwork in the Gardo House.[27] (The Gardo House wasn't built until 1873 but it is possible Frank worked on similar houses in Salt Lake.)

Frank Jorden, Jr. later explained "My father found employment with the Mormon leaders, *viz*, Lorenzo Snow, one of the Twelve Apostle, D.H. Wells, Superintendent of Public Works, and also Brigham Young, from whom he found it very difficult to collect his pay."[28] After just a few months of work, in the spring of 1854, Frank Jorden, Sr., left Jane and the children to pursue a career in the gold fields of California. For all they knew, he would never return.

Jane had few options to support herself and her two small children. She was introduced to Richard Harrison, a married man, during a social event in early 1855. Harrison was a prominent businessman and Territorial Delegate who was reportedly asked by Brigham Young to marry Jane as a polygamous wife because she was abandoned by her first husband.[29] However, Harrison wrote a personal letter to Mormon Church President Brigham Young seeking permission to marry Jane, which may indicate that marriage was his idea.[30] In the letter, Harrison notes "As I will be leaving for the North on Monday if matters permit, I would be obliged if you would attend or appoint one of the Brethren to marry Sister Jordan to me tomorrow."

Jane and Richard Harrison were married on February 25, 1855 by Brigham Young in his Salt Lake City home, called The Lion House. She became Harrison's second wife; his first wife Mary Ann had given birth to a child three weeks before, on February 3, 1855. Richard and Mary Ann Harrison made their home in Cedar City at the time, so he took Jane and her children back to live with them in polygamy in Cedar City. Bessie Snow wonders in her family history if Jane really knew what she was doing: "None of us will ever know just how Grandmother felt about President Young telling her and Grandfather, who were perfect strangers, to marry each other and he performing the ceremony when they had known each other barely six weeks."[31]

THE GEARYS HAVE A BABY BOY

John and Sophia's second baby, Thomas Fryer Geary, was born in Council Bluffs on August 25, 1854. It is not clear if John was with Sophia at the time of the birth or still working in St. Louis. Unfortunately, the baby boy only lived five months, dying on January 15, 1855.[32] Sophia's granddaughter wrote an account many years later in which she states, "he died of cholera after only a short time. He had been ill for so many days that Grandmother bathed and dressed him before she realized he was dead."[33]

The Gearys likely buried their baby boy in the Council Bluffs (Kanesville) pioneer cemetery now known as Fairview, although there is no official record of burial site or the cause of his death. This death of the Gearys' only son is particularly sad on several levels. For parents to lose a baby in those primitive frontier circumstances, far from anything familiar, was heart-breaking. For John, who wanted a son and had grown up with four brothers, it was the end of his own family name in America. And for both John and Sophia, they had endured so much already, and this additional loss could have depleted their will to continue across the plains further.

JOHN AND SOPHIA START ACROSS THE PLAINS

In the summer of 1856, after three years of waiting and preparing for their journey across the plains, John, Sophia, and their toddler, Sophia Ann, decided to start out for Utah at exactly the worst possible moment. Not only did they begin their journey in August of 1856 when Sophia was already pregnant with her third child, but they started too late in the season.

The little Geary family started the journey as part of the Andrew Siler Independent Wagon Company which rode in wagons alongside the ill-fated Martin and Willie handcart companies. The wagon company was assigned to help supply the handcart companies during the 1,000-mile journey. Interestingly, given the Gearys' background as part of the Mormon community in London, a considerable portion of London Mormons were part of the Martin handcart company. They may have known John and Sophia from their days at the Theobald's Road Branch in London.

Six London branch presidents and their families, along with 50 other London Mormons, were in the company: William L.S. Binder, David Blair, James Godson Bleak, Robert Clifton, Sr., John Griffiths, and Henry Augustus Squires.[34] Because John served as president of the Paddington Branch during 1851-52 he may have known some or all of these men. Sadly, three of the six presidents (Blair, Griffiths, and Clifton) died on the trail.

HANDCART AND WAGON COMPANIES CROSSING THE PLAINS

The idea of asking Mormon converts to cross the American plains pulling handcarts instead of riding in wagon trains was proposed by Church leaders not only as a money-saving tactic, but with the hope that it would allow them to make the trip in less time. In an announcement by President Brigham Young to the entire church in the January 26, 1856 Millenial Star, he wrote, "Let the Saints...who intend to immigrate [in] the ensuing year understand that they are expected to walk and draw their luggage across the plains, and that they will be assisted by the [Perpetual Emigration] fund in no other way."

The 1856 emigration season - when the Gearys crosssed the plains - was a year with a particularly high number of immigrants - 4,326. Handcart pioneers were given certain weight and other restrictions: five people were assigned to each cart and only 17 pounds of personal belongings were allowed in the cart. The weight of the 3 foot by 5 foot cart itself was between 60-75 pounds and, once food and supplies were added, the total weight was about 160 pounds. Mormon leader Franklin D. Richards, who had known the Gearys in England, was in charge of the handcart plan. He was overly optimistic about it, writing, "When we allow our imaginations to wander into the future and paint the scenes that will transpire on the prairies next summer, they partake largely of the romantic."

The first two handcart companies left in June and traveled successfully across 1,300 miles, keeping a pace of 25 miles per day and arriving in early fall. But the remaining handcart companies delayed their departure from Iowa until July. They arrived in Florence, Nebraska on August 11, 1856 with 1,031 miles to go. These later handcart companies were organized into four companies: 1) The Willie Handcart Company; 2) the Martin Handcart Company; 3) the Hunt Wagon Company; and 4) the Hodgett Wagon Company. There was an additional company of five wagons called the Siler Independent Wagon Company which included the Geary family. The Siler Independent Wagon Company was originally attached to the Willie Handcart Company for support. Support wagons assisted if any people became injured or sick; the wagons also helped carry provisions too large for the handcarts, such as tents and poles.

By the time the Willie Handcart Company reached Ft. Laramie at the first of October, the Siler Independent Wagons decided to delay and rest their animals. The handcart companies were determined to proceed without the wagon support. The Geary family then joined the Hodgett Wagon Company with whom they travelled most of the remaining journey. When the snowy weather conditions became so severe in the late fall that the various companies were stalled in their forward progress, the Willie Handcart Company had proceeded the furthest toward Salt Lake, with the Hodgett and Martin companies about 100 miles behind and the Hunt company even farther behind them. All companies were unable to move any further due to weather and deprivation.

During October, 1856 General Conference, Brigham Young called for volunteer rescuers to travel from Salt Lake City back east over the mountains to rescue the trapped handcart companies and bring them safely home. Months later, after the rescue was completed, hundreds of lives had been lost en route and many others suffered crippling injuries. Due to the disastrous experience of the handcart companies that year, the practice was discontinued by the church in 1860. When the Transcontinental Railway connected America in 1869, pioneers could make the trip by rail.

The Siler Wagon Company began its journey from Florence, Nebraska, a few miles from Council Bluffs, Iowa along the Missouri River. It was specifically assigned to support the Willie Handcart Company. In addition to the Geary family, the others in the Siler Company of four or five wagons included the James Sherlock Cantwell and John Alexander Jost families, Christina Anderson, Ravinia Mount Leason and her baby, Lucinda Melissa Davenport, and William Wilford Allen.[35] The entire Company was delayed just a few days after leaving Council Bluffs along the Platte River: "Staid in camp all day. Bros. Jost and Geary returned to Florence with Bro. Cantwell's oxen."[36] John Thomas Geary was driving one team of oxen for a wagon in the Siler Wagon Company and, when Brother Cantwell's oxen became difficult to work with, John helped take them back to Florence, Nebraska to exchange for more manageable animals.

On August 22, 1856, the Company Journal records, "During the afternoon, Sister Sophia Geary had her left foot run over by Brother Wilford's wagon. She was administered to in the evening by Bros. Siler, Cantwell and Geary, Capt. Siler officiating.[37] He sealed the blessing of health and strength upon her and promised that inasmuch as she would exercise faith she would walk tomorrow." The next day's entry reads, "Sis. Geary walked a considerable distance pursuant to Bro. Siler's promise."[38] In the absence of another reference to Sophia, we can assume that she healed and was able to continue her journey, but walking many miles a day would be challenging for anyone, even without a pregnancy and a foot injury.

Capt. Andrew Lafayette Siler (1824-1898) was a good traveling partner for John Thomas Geary to work with in the Siler Independent Wagon Company. They were both attorneys and well-read. Siler was a tall man, standing six feet, six inches tall and weighing 185 pounds. He had served in both the Mexican War and the Mormon Battalion. He was a convert from Georgia. Siler was known for his honesty, hospitality, generosity and justice. He was also a botanist and a schoolteacher. One can imagine Siler and Geary getting along well as they worked side by side in the Siler Independent Wagon Company coming across the plains for more than 500 miles between Iowa and Wyoming.[39]

One especially trying circumstance that occurred on the way to Fort Laramie was a cattle stampede on the evening of September 3, 1856 when the group was about halfway across Nebraska. A violent storm arose in the night and more than 30 cattle went missing, many of them being the oxen that pulled the supply wagons. The Siler and Willie companies lost valuable days searching in vain for the missing animals. One woman in the group, Ann Rowley, described the terrible effect this had: "This was the beginning of our great hardships and probably was the cause of most of them, for we had spent valuable time looking for the oxen. This loss in turn reduced our meat supply, and because there weren't enough cattle to pull the supply wagons, a hundred pounds of flour was placed in each handcart. Our handcarts were not designed for such heavy loads and were constantly breaking down."[40]

The handcart group arrived at Fort Laramie in the Wyoming Territory on September 29, 1856. The Siler Independent Wagons, with whom the Gearys were traveling, decided to stay at Fort Laramie for a few days. According to James Cantwell, the Siler company decided to stay due to the poor condition of their cattle and the fact that Cantwell's daughter was healing from a rattlesnake bite.[41]

The Gearys then joined the Hodgett Company to continue their trek and moved on as well. The Hodgett Wagon Company, with 150 emigrants and 45 wagons, was led by William Benjamin Hodgett (1831-1860) a 23-year-old man from a wealthy English family who converted to the Mormon Church in the 1840s.[42]

Early snowstorms plagued the Gearys and other travelers as they made their way across Wyoming. They had started too late in the season to coordinate properly with the supply wagons and so all were running low on food. During October the snow began to fall heavily. "Fighting through it, the Hodgett wagon company traveled 10 miles to Red Buttes on October 20, 1856, the day after the last crossing of the Platte. Slowed by weather, weakness, and burials, the Martin company took four days to travel those 10 miles, finally arriving on October 23." [43] The Martin and Hodgett companies could go no further. The next leg of the journey required them to undertake a 40-mile overland drive to the Sweetwater River and they were too weak to make it. Freezing temperatures and low supplies further depleted them. As the travelers, including the Geary family, hunkered down at Red Buttes the daily rations at the camp fell to four ounces of flour per day. During the 11 days that the Gearys and others waited at Red Buttes, at least 56 people died. [44] It was an unimaginably sad and harrowing situation.

One of the pioneers with the Gearys in the Hodgett company, John Bond, described the scene at Red Buttes where some died "lying side by side with hands entwined, showing the last agonies and suffering of life with a gasp of love and affection, facing each other in death's embrace…Some died sitting by the fire: some were singing hymns or eating crusts of bread."[45] Most, if not all, of the suffering Saints had given up hope, including possibly the Gearys. One cannot imagine how Sophia felt, eight months pregnant and caring for a three-year-old toddler, Sophia Ann.

Bond describes what happened when the suffering people saw the first rescuers riding up on October 28, 1856: "All came to the conclusion that they must die, far away from the civilized world, all for the reason and sake of truth. Along in the afternoon, I was playing in front of Sister Scott's… wagon with her son Joseph…His mother was looking to the westward. All at once, Sister Scott sprang to her feet in the wagon and screamed out at the top of her voice, 'I see them coming! I see them coming! Surely they are as angels from heaven!'" [46] John, his pregnant wife, Sophia, and their tiny daughter, Sophia Ann, had renewed hope that they would yet make it to Utah.

RESCUE OF THE HANDCART AND WAGON COMPANIES

At first, President Brigham Young had little knowledge of the Martin/Willie handcart groups stranded on the plains. Elder Franklin Richards and several missionaries traveling west passed the companies in early September and noted their struggles.

When Elder Richards arrived in Salt Lake City on October 4, 1856 to discover that the companies he passed on the plains still had not arrived, he alerted Brigham Young. The next morning at Sunday morning services in the Bowery, President Young announced: "Many of our brethren and sisters are on the plains with hand-carts…and they must be brought here…Go and bring in those people now on the plains, and attend strictly to those things which we call temporal…otherwise your faith will be in vain."[47]

The attendees at Conference obeyed Brigham Young and quickly organized rescue parties. They donated blankets, stockings, shoes and clothing, along with food and supplies from their own meager stores. By October 7, the first rescue party of 16 wagons was on its way, and more volunteers were joining every day. By the end of October, 250 rescue teams were on the road, not realizing it would be two months before all the handcart companies could finally be safely brought into the valley.

The rescuers first encountered the suffering members of the Willie Handcart Company whom rescuers reached on October 21, 1856 by the Sweetwater River near Rocky Ridge. They rescuers stayed there only briefly to help them and tell them another team would be arriving soon. The rescuers then pressed on 45 more miles east to Devil's Gate and another 50 miles to Red Buttes on the Platte River. Once the rescuers arrived at Red Buttes - where the Gearys were suffering - they shored up the depleted situation of the Hodgett and Martin companies as best they could. But the rescuers needed to keep going eastward to rescue the wagons in the Hunt company which were still stranded a few miles east at the last crossing of the Platte. The rescuers gradually rounded up all the companies together. By October 29, 1856, all the companies were finally heading west back to Salt Lake City with rescuers.

In early November, the rescuers and their various companies straggled in to Devil's Gate, where the snow was about fourteen inches deep. "Five miles west of Independence Rock, Devil's Gate is a well-known landmark of the trail. Here the Sweetwater River flows between rock walls nearly 400 feet high."[48] Thousands of people went by this spot during the summer traveling season because all the major westward trails, such as the Oregon Trail, came through the Devil's Gate. But this winter, the scene was grim.

People in the handcart companies were continuing to die even as they made their way slowly across the plains with the rescuers, so the rescuers considered keeping all four companies at Devil's Gate for the winter and taking them to Utah the next spring. After a few days and more snowstorms, all concluded that they must press on. Captain George D. Grant held a council on November 3, 1856 at Devil's Gate to make a plan. Joseph Young, a son of Brigham Young, was at the council. "At one point Captain Grant asked Joseph Young, 'What would your father do now if he were here?' Joseph answered, 'If my father was here, he would take all the books and heavy material and cache them in order to save the lives of the people.' That is what Captain Grant decided to do; empty some of the wagons of the Hodgett and Hunt companies, store freight in the cabins at Devil's Gate, and use those wagons to carry the sick and incapacitated members of the Martin company to Salt Lake City."[49]

The Gearys, along with about 40 other wagons and owners, took their possessions out of their wagon and stored them in dilapidated log buildings that remained from an old abandoned fort known as Fort Seminoe near Devil's Gate. The temperatures at that time were well below zero. Not all could be accommodated to ride in the wagons, so some walked alongside.[50] Perhaps some of the Geary family walked the remaining 325 miles to Salt Lake City. Sophia, being nearly nine months' pregnant, would have been a good candidate for a wagon ride.

Sophia's brother, Richard Fryer, who was already in Salt Lake City, wrote in his journal on November 6, 1856 that he received a note from John Geary saying they were short on provisions on the plains. In the next entry, November 9, 1856, Richard Fryer writes, "I met a church company who arrived in Salt Lake. They said Geary was in the next company."[51]

As the weary groups trailed westward in constant snowstorms, they were finally met by additional rescuer wagons on November 16, 1856 as they crossed Rocky Ridge and then South Pass. With more supplies and resources, the groups again reorganized into companies of tens by wagons, and everyone could ride in a wagon, although it was crowded. In this way, they were able to make better time and they had more food to sustain them.

BIRTH OF ECHO WORKMAN GEARY

Captain Cornelius Ceazar Workman was the rescuer who helped the Geary family on this last part of the journey. Workman was one of hundreds of rescuers that voluntarily left Salt Lake City within days of President Brigham Young's announcement at October General Conference to "Go and bring in these people!" Workman led a company that departed Salt Lake City on the 7th of October, 1856. Workman and his team rescued and brought back 363 individuals to the Salt Lake Valley on December 15, 1856, including the Geary family.[52]

Cornelius Workman was born on March 21, 1826 in Carlisle, Kentucky to John and Lydia Workman. He moved to Tennessee with his parents as an infant when they converted to the Mormon Church. They all emigrated to Salt Lake City, then on to California, and back to Salt Lake in 1854. Cornelius was an experienced overland traveler, having gone back and forth across the western plains many times in his young life. He traveled back to Illinois to marry his wife and lived in many different states, including Montana, California, and Idaho, finally settling for good in Springville, Utah.

When Captain Workman rescued the Geary family along with several others, he recognized immediately the severity of Sophia's health condition. She was very close to delivering her baby. In fact, just a few miles from the Salt Lake Valley, at the mouth of Echo Canyon, the group decided to stop. Sophia delivered her second daughter there and named her "Echo" after the canyon of her birthplace. The baby's middle name, "Workman," was in recognition of Cornelius Workman, the hero who had rescued her family from a terrible winter on the American plains. Echo Workman Geary was born December 9, 1856, six days before her family entered the Salt Lake Valley. [53] The exhausted family of four finally arrived in the Salt Lake Valley on December 15, 1856.

ENDNOTES FOR CHAPTER THREE

1   See Excerpts from the Diary of Richard Fryer in the Appendix herein. A copy of this diary was given to Kaye Page Nichols by Dale Clawson, a descendant of Richard Fryer. Portions of Fryer's journal also appear throughout Bessie Snow's 1973 self-published *Fate of the Fryers*, in possession of authors. It appears that Bessie Snow had possession of the original Richard Fryer diary and retyped or summarized certain entries when she wrote her book; those original records have not been located. In this reference, Fryer is mentioning Orson Cornelius Spencer (March 14, 1802 – October 15, 1855) who was a prolific writer and prominent member of The Church of Jesus Christ of Latter-day Saints. Spencer served a mission to Britain and was sent on another mission to Prussia in the 1850s. He was a former Baptist minister who was baptized into the Church in 1841, according to Roberts, B.H., The Comprehensive History of the Church, Brigham Young University Press, Provo Utah, 1930, Volume IV, page 118, footnote 20.

2   "Brother Young" was likely Brother Joseph Watson Young (1829-1873), a nephew of Brigham Young and a Mormon Church leader returning from a British mission at the time. Brother Young was in charge of Mormon emigrants' travel arrangements from Liverpool. He was just finishing his mission and he sailed from Liverpool on the ship, *Elvira Owen* on February 7, 1853, Church History Library, Joseph W. Young Papers 1849-1872, MS 1529 p. 65-70, entries, Missionary database.

3   Although Sophia Fryer Geary is not listed on the *Ellen Maria* manifest, nor any other Mormon emigrant ship during this period, it can be surmised that she sailed on the *Ellen Maria*. The ship's Voyage Notes state: "The ship *Ellen Maria* sailed from Liverpool, January 17, 1853, after being detained in port several days by contrary winds… On the sixth of March, 1853, the *Ellen Maria* arrived with her precious cargo in New Orleans, making the passage from Liverpool in forty-seven days. From New Orleans the emigrants continued the journey to St. Louis, Missouri, where they arrived March 18, 1853, and later proceeded up the river to Keokuk, in Iowa, from which place the journey across the plains was commenced. (Millennial Star, Vol. XV, pp.90, 253, 282.)» https://saintsbysea.lib.byu.edu/mii/account/337?netherlands=on&europe=on&sweden=on&mii=on&scandinavia=on&keywords=ellen+maria.

Because we know from Richard Fryer's diary and Bessie Snow's records that the Gearys first boarded the ship on January 10, 1853 and then waited in port for several days due to weather, the departure date matches. Because we know from those same sources that Sophia Geary made her way to St. Louis, on March 18, 1853, where she met up with John Geary on about the last week in March, the date of her arrival on the *Ellen Maria* on March 6, 1854 also aligns.

It is surmised from Richard Fryer's diary that Richard Fryer and the Gearys were travelling under duress in January, 1853. Due to John's belief that civil authorities were looking for them, Sophia may have been traveling under an assumed identity. Richard Fryer's Journal states that he and John came to America on the ship *Jersey*. All evidence points to John Geary and Richard Fryer traveling on the ship *Jersey*, which arrived in New Orleans on March 21, 1853. However, they are not shown on the *Jersey* manifest either and may also have used another identity. Fred Piercy, a fellow passenger on the *Jersey*, refers to John Geary in his diary as "Leary."

4   https://saintsbysea.lib.byu.edu/mii/account/621?netherlands=on&europe=on&sweden=on&mii=on&scandinavia=on&keywords=international
          https://www.churchofjesuschrist.org/study/ensign/1997/01/backman-faith-in-every-footstep?lang=eng†
There is an interesting story concerning the voyage of the ship *International*, which left Liverpool, England, on 25 February 1853 with the Fryer-Jorden family aboard. It carried a Latter-day Saint immigrant company of 425, including a number of unbaptized friends and relatives and a crew of 26. The ship ran into violent storms, delaying the crossing and making it necessary to ration food. In four weeks only one-third of the distance to New Orleans, Louisiana, had been covered. Thanks to the faith and prayers of the valiant Saints, a miracle occurred: favorable winds made it possible to make up time lost. The *International* docked in New Orleans after a 54-day voyage across the Atlantic Ocean. Christopher Arthur presided over the company of Latter-day Saints aboard the *International*. In his official report to the British Mission president, President Arthur wrote: "I am glad to inform you, that we have baptized all on board except three persons. … We can number the captain, first and second mates, with eighteen of the crew, most of whom intend going right through to the valley. … The number baptized in all is 48, since we left our native shores" (quoted in William G. Hartley, "Voyage on the Ship *International*," *New Era*, Sep. 1973, 9).

5   Snow, Fate of the Fryers at pages 6-7.

6   Snow, Fate of the Fryers at page 4, "At one period so many skilled workmen began leaving England that the government passed a law against them leaving the country, and many of the seaports were guarded and ships searched to stop these men from taking their families out of the country."

7   John Thomas Geary Letter to Brigham Young, March 11, 1857.

8   www.familysearch.org, Charlotte Wright Hall, (1798-1881), 2NMX-S65.

9   www.familysearch.org, John Charles Hall, (1821-1890), KWNK-J2K. Thomas Charles Hall, (1825-1907), KWVQ-FZS.

10   Charlotte Hall and John's mother, Sarah Ann Elton Geary, were identified as cousins on the 1851 British census. One possible but unconfirmed familial relationship: Charlotte's father was Thomas Wright (1760-1815), he was married to Martha Elton (1765-1818). Sarah Ann's father was John Elton (1776-1817) and married to Elizabeth Tiptaft (1777-1839). If Martha Elton and John Elton were related, that could be the source of the cousin relationship.

11   Richard Fryer Journal, Entry for January 3, 1853

12   Richard Fryer Journal. Also Snow, Fate of the Fryers at page 6.

13   www.familysearch.org, Rebecca Sarah Wright, (1802-1875), L3SZ-WBF.

14   www.familysearch.org, Ann Wright, (1786-1839), L3SQ-SPV.

15   Some of these theories arise from the research of Hall descendant Patty Swenson, also a professional British genealogist, who has researched the Hall family extensively. In a March 4, 2021 email to the authors, Swenson states in part, "Thomas Wright and Martha Elton had only daughters. Typically, women did not inherit, but because there was no male heir the Wright sisters did inherit jointly. (A male would have to act for them in matters concerning the property.) Thomas Wright's will specifically states in a codicil, 'And after the decease of my said wife my will is that the property remaining shall be divided equally between my five daughters namely – Ann, Maria, Mary, Charlotte, and Sarah share and share alike'". Only Charlotte and [Rebecca] Sarah were living by 1853. Copies of Swenson's unpublished Hall research is in the possession of the authors.

16   Richard Fryer Journal, entry February 4, 1853 refers to Piercy by name, and see also Piercy, Frederick, Route from Liverpool to the Great Salt Lake Valley, Illustrated, Published by Franklin D. Richards, 36, Islington, London, Latter-day Saints Book Depot, 35 Jewin [sic] Street, City, 1855, pages 22-27.

17   https://saintsbysea.lib.byu.edu/mii/account/673?netherlands=on&europe=on&sweden=on&mii=on&scandinavia=on&keywords=jersey

18   Richard Fryer Journal, entry January 12, 1853, where Fryer notes that Geary shaved his head.

19   Piercy at page 24.

20   Richard Fryer Journal. Also Snow, Fate of the Fryers at page 5.

21   Farmer, Thomas L. and Woods, Fred E., "Sanctuary on the Mississippi – St. Louis as a Way Station for Mormon Emigration", *The Confluence,* Spring/Summer 2018, pages 42-53. *The Confluence* is a journal published by Lindenwood University in Saint Charles, Missouri.

22   Snow, Fate of the Fryers at page 8.

23   Snow, Fate of the Fryers at page 9.

24   Snow, Fate of the Fryers at pages 10-11.

25   John Thomas Geary Letter to Brigham Young, March 11, 1857.

26 Farmer and Woods at pages 42-53.

27 Snow, <u>Fate of the Fryers</u> at pages 8 and 76. Bessie Snow had access to a document written by Frank Jorden, Jr. entitled "For the Religious Herald, A True Story by Reverend Frank F. Jorden". Bessie Snow notes in her book that she was given this document by Mrs. Merton E. Doolittle and Lucy Doolittle Keeler, the granddaughters of Frank Jorden, Jr. It appears to be an undated news article written in six installments and is consistently critical of the Mormon Church. The document is reproduced in Snow's book but the original has not been located.

28 Snow, <u>Fate of the Fryers</u> at page 11.

29 Snow, <u>Fate of the Fryers</u> at pages 14-15.

30 Brigham Young office files, 1832-1878 (bulk 1844-1877); Ecclesiastical Files, 1841-1877; Files Relating to Marriage and Other Ordinances, 1845- 1877; Letters, 1845 -1877; 1855; Richard Harrison letter; Church History Library, https://catalog.churchofjesuschrist.org/assets?id=22df4ba1-eaa9-4523-b8c5-9473df4c88e6&crate=0&index=0 (accessed: February 14, 2021)

31 Snow, <u>Fate of the Fryers</u> at page 56.

32 Snow, <u>Fate of the Fryers</u> at page 17.

33 Gardner, Maree Higbee and Zeenati, Eva Gardner, <u>My Father Called Me Yebbie</u>, Custom Family Publishers, St. George, Utah, 1996, page 467.

34 Jorgensen, Lynne Watkins, "The Martin Handcart Disaster: The London Participants," *Journal of Mormon History,* No. 2, Fall, 1995, pages 175-176.

35 Allphin, Jolene S., <u>Tell My Story Too</u>, 8th edition, 2nd printing, 2018, digital edition, www.tellmystorytoo.com, Frances Cantwell, pages 13-17.

36 *Ibid*, referring to Cantwell Journal.

37 *Ibid.,* Allphin, Jolene S., <u>Tell My Story Too</u>, James Sherlock Cantwell (1813-1887) <u>Tell My Story Too</u>, Sophia Fryer Geary, page 32. https://history.churchofjesuschrist.org/overlandtravel/sources/7439/james-g-willie-emigrating-company-journal-1856-may-november

38 *Ibid.*

39 *Ibid*. Allphin, Jolene S., <u>Tell My Story Too</u>, Andrew Lafayette Siler, page 123.

40 Olsen, Andrew D., <u>The Price We Paid, The Extraordinary Story of the Willie & Martin Handcart Pioneers</u>, Deseret Book, Salt Lake City, 2006. Pages 90-91, quoting Rowley, Ann, "Autobiography of Ann Jewell Rowley," <u>Some Early Pioneers of Huntington, Utah and Surrounding Area</u>, comp. James Albert Jones (n.p., 1980), page 244..

41 https://history.churchofjesuschrist.org/overlandtravel/sources/14363753061971025091-eng/cantwell-james-autobiography-in-joel-edward-ricks-cache-valley-historical-materials

42 *Ibid.* Allphin, Jolene S., <u>Tell My Story Too</u>, William Benjamin Hodgett, p. 344-345. Benjamin came to Utah alone in 1850 but then returned to England to serve a mission. While there, his mother decided the entire family should emigrate to Utah in 1856. As they boarded the boat in Liverpool and began to sail across the English Channel, the father of the family demanded that the ship drop anchor while he searched it. He found his wife and convinced her to return back with some of the children. Two daughters, Emily and Maria, went on to America where they met up with Benjamin, who had sailed on a boat after they did. Benjamin was made a captain of a wagon company in Iowa and looked after his two young sisters. They made it to Utah where Benjamin married

and had three children, all who died when young. Their family in England helped Ben and his sisters financially in Utah for the rest of their lives. Ben served as a Bishop and died in 1860, not quite 30 years old.

43   Olsen at page 327, quoting Jesse Haven's journal, 23 October 1856, Church Archives, Salt Lake City, Utah.

44   *Ibid.* at page 328, Red Buttes is on a bend of the Platte River known today as Bessemer's Bend. It is about 10 miles east of Casper, Wyoming on Highway 220.

45   *Ibid.* at page 335, quoting John Bond, Handcarts West in '56, un-published, page 20.

46   *Ibid,* at page 340, quoting John Bond, at page 25.

47   *Ibid,* at page 116.

48   *Ibid.* at page 337.

49   *Ibid.* at page 369, quoting Journal History, 13 Nov 1856, Church Archives, Salt Lake City, Utah.

50   *Ibid.* at page 370.

51   Snow, Fate of the Fryers at page 19.

52   The Gearys' progress across the plains was part of a report on "Immigration To Utah" in the *Deseret News* on October 15, 1856 as "Wagon Company Organized at Florence with the Fourth Handcart Company [the Willie Company], FROM ENGLAND, J.S. Cantwell and family, J.T. Geary and family, FROM THE UNITED STATES, A.L. Siler, N.L. Christianson, Ruvinia Leason and son, J.A. Jost and family, C. Anderson." http://digitalnewspaper.org. In a December 17, 1856 *Deseret News* article the paper reported that "The Hodgetts and Hunts companies with those who went to their relief have been arriving within the past few days and are now, Dec 16, all in except a few who will tarry at Fort Supply during the winter and the small company previously mentioned as being stationed at Devil's Gate." (Immigration article). http://digitalnewspapers.org. See also the Family Search entry on Cornelius Ceazer Workman, www.familysearch.org.

53   "The Second Birth in Echo Canyon," A Research Report by Kaye Page Nichols, 2010. The Church of Jesus Christ of Latter Day Saints, The Church History Library, Digital Collection Call Number MS 23018.

Portrait of John Thomas Geary. This appears to be a professional photograph with hand colorization. It was likely done in London shortly before John emigrated to America in 1853, as Sophia had a simliar portrait taken. It is the only known photograph of John which has been found. The original is treasured by a Geary descendant today.

Portrait of Sophia Fryer Geary, likely done in London before she emigrated to America in 1853.

Jane Fryer Jorden Harrison, Sophia's older sister, who also emigrated to America in 1853. Jane was the first Fryer family member to join the Mormon Church. Jane's daughter, Effie May Harrison, is also shown here in the photo with her.

Richard Fryer, Sophia's younger brother, who also emigrated to America with John in 1853. Richard lived in Toquerville near John and Sophia during the 1860s.

John Charles Hall, John's cousin, who coincidentally joined the Mormon Church in America while John was investigating it in England. Hall lived in southern Utah near the Gearys.

Above: Vintage Charles Magnus hand-colored lithograph shows a view of St. Louis in the mid-1800s when John and Sophia would have arrived in America. John spent the better part of three years (1853-1856) living and working in St. Louis. There, he lost many of his possessions and worked as a "furniture-polisher, stove-polisher, gas-pipe-layer" and also drove the Harlow and Co. furniture van.

Below: An advertisement for Wm. M. Harlow and Co's Furniture Warehouse, one of John's employers in St. Louis, which appeared in the St. Louis Globe Democrat, January 27, 1855.

Sites Along the Mormon Trail

This map shows the general course of the Mormon migration during the time John and Sophia made the trek. They left from Council Bluffs in July, 1856. They made it to Fort Laramie by October 1. They were snowed in and destitute at Red Buttes, Wyoming when the rescuers found the handcart companies in late October. The rescuers assisted them in completing the rest of the trip. The Gearys were with Captain Cornelius Workman when they stopped at Echo Canyon in Utah to give birth to their daughter, Echo Workman Geary, in early December. They arrived in Salt Lake on December 15, 1856. It was a trip of more than 1,000 miles.

Historic photograph by William Henry Jackson of the 1852 Mormon migration near Council Bluffs, looking toward the Missouri River.

Fairview Cemetery in Council Bluffs, Iowa where John and Sophia Geary's baby boy is likely buried.
He was born August 25, 1854 and died January 15, 1855.
The cemetery address is 308 Lafayette Avenue, Council Bluffs, Iowa.
Many Mormon immigrants lived in Council Bluffs while waiting to cross the plains
and they buried their dead in this cemetery, which dates back to 1820s.

Above: Red Buttes, Wyoming where the Geary family and the Hodgett's Wagon Company were trapped along with the Martin Handcart Company in October, 1856 during early snowstorms. The daily rations at camp fell to four ounces of flour per day. During the 11 days the Gearys were stuck here, 56 people died.

Below: Devil's Gate, Wyoming where the Geary family left most of their belongings during the winter rescue of the handcart companies. Sophia wrote to her sister upon arriving in Salt Lake in December, 1856: "Nearly all our clothing is back at Devil's Gate." Church leaders asked the pioneers to abandon their personal belongings there so more people could ride in the wagons. (Photo by Kaye Page Nichols)

Above: Summit of Big Mountain just east of the Salt Lake Valley, looking west. This would have been a snow-covered route when John and Sophia made their way across the slopes in early December, 1856. Sophia was nine months pregnant and hours away from delivering her baby, Echo, in Echo Canyon. Their three-year-old daughter, Sophia Ann, was also with them. They had been on the trail four months. (Photo by Kaye Page Nichols)

Deseret News - October 15, 1856 article reporting on the handcart emigrants making their way across the plains toward Utah, including "J.T. Geary and family." (Immigration to Utah, page 6.)

Deseret News - November 19, 1856 article featuring Elder Joseph A. Young reporting on the progress of the Gearys and other pioneers crossing the plains.

OPTIMISM IN THE MOUNTAINS

"I am on hand and intend that my actions shall not belie my words -
to do anything and everything (no matter what) which may be in the path of my duty."
JTG

John and Sophia arrived in the Salt Lake Valley in the middle of the cold winter of December, 1856. They were destitute, having left most of their belongings and clothes back in their snowbound camp at Devil's Gate, Wyoming during their overland journey.

As they entered the valley, the Gearys found a well-established city with large ten-acre blocks and extra wide streets laid out by Brigham Young, all surrounding the site for the Mormon Temple. The temple site had been dedicated February 14, 1853 and, while construction began immediately, it was proceeding very slowly due to lack of materials. By 1857, the Mormons had been in the valley for ten years, establishing 90 outlying settlements around the territory. There were almost 40,000 people in Salt Lake and surrounding communities. Businesses were thriving due to the cross-country travelers on the way to California, but Brigham Young, as territorial governor, warned Mormons not to be led astray. He governed the territory using religious principles, organizing their activities with an eye toward building up Zion.

One non-Mormon observer described Great Salt Lake City in this period as follows:

"The city is beyond my power of description. It is beautiful – even magnificent. Every street is bordered by large trees beneath which & on either side run murmuring brooks with pebbly bottoms. Not a sign of dirt of any kind to be seen. The houses are surrounded by large gardens now green with summer foliage. All the houses are built of adobe nicely washed with some brown earth, the public buildings large and handsomely ornamented surrounded by walls of stone…"[1]

President Brigham Young encouraged residents to build stone or adobe brick houses, not wooden shelters, and so most homes looked substantial and well-maintained. Each community had a least one meeting place to host church services, community theater or music performances. The Church leaders sorted the new arrivals when they came into the Salt Lake Valley and gave them homes among existing families. Church historians Leonard Arrington and Davis Bitton describe it this way:

> "The dispersal began with a 'placement meeting' attended by all local bishops. Each was asked how many families could be absorbed into his ward for the winter and what special skills were desirable. The British traveler and editor William Hepworth Dixon told of a placement meeting in which one bishop said he could 'take five bricklayers, another two carpenters, a third a tinman, a fourth seven or eight farm servants, and so on through the whole bench.' In a few minutes, Dixon observed, 'two hundred of these poor emigrants had been placed in the way of earning their daily bread.'"[2]

John and Sophia, with their two little girls, Sophia Ann and Echo, were sent to stay in a home near Emigration Canyon which was owned by Joseph Horne.[3] John immediately began working as a wood chopper until he until he found a better job.

JOHN BECOMES A SCHOOLTEACHER

Within three weeks of arrival, due to John's experience and education as an attorney back in England, he was able to find work as a teacher at the 14th Ward school. John wrote about his first day as a school teacher in the following letter to his sister-in-law, Jane Harrison, who was then living in Cedar City, Utah:[4]

JOHN TO JANE:

January 3, 1857 Great Salt Lake City

My Dear Sister,

Sophy wishes me to embrace the chance of just sending you a line by the present mail, and I am just now moving to a fresh residence. I have this morning obtained a situation as school teacher in the 14th ward under Bishop Oghlan [Hoagland] and Brother Joseph Horn [Horne] and Samuel Richards. It must be but a line as it were. We both would much like to see you at once. But circumstances prevent this for the present. The counsel being to remain in the city if practical for the winter. We came into the place on the 15th and the only employment I have had since arriving is wood sawing which I began to think would be my sole occupation 'till spring. But it is otherwise and I am better off than I expected. We are well and fully alive so trust in the justice of the Kingdom of God which may He grant to be the lot of all the honest in heart. I would say many things but must refrain until another opportunity as Mr. Harrison is waiting while I scribble this as to enclose it in his letter. I hope you will be able to read this scrawl. Sophy joins with me in kindest love to all.

Affectionately yours in the Gospel,
John Thomas Geary

P.S. I must say we have two little responsibilities living. Sophy and another little girl born back at the mouth of Echo Canyon therefore we named her Echo then added the name Workman after our Captain. I think you are aware our little boy, Thomas Fryer, died last January.

John mentions working for the leaders of the 14th Ward as he teaches school. The 14th Ward boundaries covered nine city blocks extending from Main Street to 2nd West Street and from South Temple Street to 3rd South Street.[5] The 14th Ward during the 1850-1860 time period was a promising place to live. Being close to the temple site and the business district, the 14th Ward was one of the largest of the original 19 wards in the Valley. In the 1850 census, the 14th Ward had 88 households; by

1860 it had grown to include 148 households. The 14th Ward was home to many Church leaders and businessmen. Residents included Haden Wells Church, Amasa Lyman, Mathias Cowley, John Taylor, W.W. Phelps, Orson Pratt, Joseph Horne, Wilford Woodruff, Samuel S. Richards, and Franklin D. Richards. John had known the Richards family back in London. There were also several lawyers in the 14th Ward.[6]

Early schools in Utah were organized by each Ward Bishopric and those men also served as the "School Board". When John was teaching in 1857, the 14th Ward school was led by Bishop Abraham Hoagland (misspelled "Oghlan" by John). His counselors were Joseph Horne and John Van Cott. Van Cott had been one of the rescuers as well of the handcart companies. Horne was not only John and Sophia's landlord, but the Superintendent of Public Works and was well-informed about the available jobs and homes in the valley.

John taught school for about three months but then something occurred which required him to discontinue that position. As John described it, "A combination of circumstances will not, however, justify me in retaining this position."[7] It is not clear what occurred. It could have been that other teachers were available and better suited for the position, that the school was being reorganized, or that John had a conflict with the people involved in the school.

Sophia was eager to be reunited with her sister, Jane, whom she had not seen since separating in Council Bluffs, Iowa nearly four years earlier. Jane was living in southern Utah with her new husband, Richard Harrison. In January, 1857, Sophia apparently met Richard Harrison for the first time; he was in Salt Lake to attend the winter session of the Territorial Legislature as a delegate from Iron County. While Harrison was waiting to return south he told her he would take Jane a letter, so Sophia wrote to her sister who was then living in the southern Utah community of Cedar City, 250 miles away:

SOPHIA TO JANE:

January 19, 1857 GSLC

After a long pull and a strong pull and a pull all together, we have managed to fight our way through rivers, roads, creeks, over hills, and dales and snow, and everything else which is good and bad. Anyhow I am thankful we are here and enjoy good health. Since our separation in the states we have passed through some funny things. John has gone and worked at anything he could get to do. He is a first rate good BOY, I mean at sticking to things. At present he is teaching school in the 14th ward for the winter and in the spring I hope we shall wend our way into the country. John is very desirous to be a farmer. He will milk the cows as that is something I am not able to perform yet. I can sew and knit my stockings, work bread, make candles and soap. But I have to learn much more before I can be a good farmer's wife. But take your time, wife Sophia, and by and by I will show you what I can do.

I am glad to hear that you are so comfortably provided for. I wish you every comfort of this life and every honor that you can attain in that which is to come and all those with whom you are becoming united. It is now a time of Reformation in the Valley and I feel like asking your forgiveness of all wrong. I wish that I could see you so that we might have a good chat together for I am afraid I shall not be able to even fill this piece of paper. Echo is at my knee and feels like crying all the time and Sophia is walking around the room saying she can't wait. I must quit writing and give her cornbread. Dick can wait for his supper.

Dick is still at Staples. I want to get him away from there as soon as I can. I do not think he is doing himself much good there. He tells us he has not paid any tithing since he has been in the valley. The amount he now owes to the office is $10 and he now intends to work it off by working at the Public Works. John and he have been to the canyon for wood. The weather is severely cold.

Mary Latrail and Ida Beading are here. I think if Brother Harrison had seen her he would have fallen in love with her right away. I mean Mary. She appears to be more and more interesting than ever. She is very often at T.D. Brown's I think she will get employment at Sister Smith's as she is so very busy. But as to Ideas I can't say anything about her. Edward Southerland is keeping a Bachelor's Hall for the last year. He is working at his business in the 14th Ward.

Today is Monday and your dearly Beloved tells me he is going home. I have to hurry with this scrawl and will promise to give you all the news you may wish to know when we meet which I hope will not be long for you must try to get up here. I want to see you and the children very much. I wanted very much to send you some small present but cannot do so now.

Nearly all our clothing is back at Devil's Gate. I must now wish you goodby with the hope of meeting soon. John says you are a real Brick, a downright good trump. With our united kind love and wishing you good health and plenty of Babies,

I remain your affectionate sister,
Sophia

P.S. John says he is quite ashamed of this writing.

Sophia's letter gives us many insights into the Geary family life during the months after their arrival in the valley. The mention of her young daughters at her feet as she writes tells you something profound about Sophia's character. She sounds worried about her girls. She is touchingly supportive of John's tireless efforts to provide for the family, even though they haven't settled down permanently yet. It is notable that John is planning on becoming a farmer instead of practicing law or working in a trade. Utah's legal community was in its infancy in 1857 but there were frontier lawyers working there and courts operating.

Instead, John and Sophia sounded intent on moving south to join Jane Harrison in Iron County. Sophia is jokingly telling her sister she can learn to be a farmer's wife. While John grew up on farmland back in Leicestershire County in England, he was not necessarily trained in agricultural pursuits. Farming in England, where the land had been cleared and worked for centuries, would be very different than farming in the wilderness. The land the pioneers found in arid Utah was virtually pristine. Irrigation was a challenge and pests of all sorts threatened the crops. John and Sophia were brave to embark on such a challenging venture.

REFORMATION SWEEPS THE UTAH TERRITORY

There was indeed a spirit of Reformation in the Salt Lake Valley during 1856-1857, as Sophia noted in her letter. Church historian B.H. Roberts described it in his 1930 <u>Comprehensive History of the Church</u> as a period of "much needed moral and spiritual awakening" that resulted from the tumultuous 10-year period of unrest and frontier life endured by the Saints.[8] Roberts explained that a certain casualness developed when people were too busy "fighting crickets and grasshoppers and meeting the exigencies of the irrigation system" to observe the Sabbath and he noted other lifestyle lapses. Church leaders such as Jedediah Grant, one of Brigham Young's counselors, first instigated the reformation in a Kaysville, Utah meeting on September 13, 1856 where 500 people were re-baptized to show their renewed commitment. Similar meetings followed throughout the next year across Utah, with President Brigham Young participating in the "enthusiasm of the occasion" during a meeting at the Tabernacle. Roberts admits that the Reformation period accomplished both good and bad; the zeal with which it was approached sometimes lead to "unwarranted interpretations of the scriptures" and "ill-advised things said" which were "more in spirit the severe justice and retribution of the old Mosaic law than spirit of the gospel of Jesus Christ".[9]

Sophia's reference to "Dick" means she is in touch with their brother, Richard Fryer, who is still working in Salt Lake City and - as she mentions - is behind on his tithing. Richard was living at that time in the home of James Staples, a fellow English convert whom the Gearys may have known during their church attendance in London. Sophia's mention of "Mary Latrail" refers to a woman who came with the Gearys in their handcart and wagon trek across the plains; Mary was in the Hunt Wagon Company. Mary Matilda Latrielle was a 21-year-old convert from London, England. As Sophia suspected, Mary was indeed searching for a husband. Later in 1857 she became the 3rd plural wife of Dan Jones, the captain of one of the wagon trains in which she traveled. Mary had two children with Jones prior to his death in 1862. She then married Thomas Vincent, settled in Provo, and had three more children. She died in Provo on March 11, 1916 at 80 years old.[10]

In sum, Sophia's letter establishes that she and John are folding themselves into Salt Lake society while still associating with people they knew back in England or coming across the plains. She sounds optimistic that they will find their path and she is confident in John's abilities.

JOHN WRITES TO PRESIDENT BRIGHAM YOUNG

A few months after Sophia's letter, John must have been feeling pressure to find a more permanent work situation. On March 11, 1857, he wrote to Church President Brigham Young directly to see how he could be of service in his new community:

JOHN TO BRIGHAM YOUNG:

March 11, 1857
To   President Brigham Young

Dear Sir and Brother.

Having but recently come into this City, and having no definite plan of operation for the future yet marked out in my own mind, except that I intend to take hold of the any first thing which may present itself for my acceptance, I feel to lay before you a brief outline of my past history and present position; so as to be open to such counsel or direction (if any) as you may deem it wisdom to give me.

In 1845, I was admitted to the practice of Law, in which Profession I was successfully engaged up to the time of my departure, in Jany, 1853. I obeyed the Gospel about 7 years ago, and, in August, 1852, married my present wife, by whom I have 3 children. At the period of my baptism, some of my relations were living with me. They immediately became my most bitter enemies, and did all in their power (which however was not much) to injure me in my business. After our marriage the fire grew hotter, and all of them, except my father, (who was before, and still is my friend) forsook me. Some of them wrongfully caused legal proceedings to be instituted against me, a game which they soon found to be a losing one for themselves. Thus my presence in the midst of my former friends, being the fruitful cause of their doing evil. I was counseled to emigrate, which I did without bidding farewell to my father, except by letter. We, however, still regularly correspond together.

I arrived at Saint Louis with some valuable freight, and travelled from Keokuk to Council Bluffs under the presidency of Bro. John Brown, in the summer of 1855. In consequence, however, of Sister G's sickness I sold my wagon and team to my President, and retraced my steps back to St. Louis, a course which I now know, by experience, was a very unwise one. In that City, I lost, in one way or another, the greater part of my luggage, and was, from necessity, alternately, a furniture-cleaner and polisher, stove-polisher, and gas-pipe-layer, at a salary of 5 dollars per week. I also drove Messrs Harlow's and Co's furniture van, during my residence in St. Louis. At length, I became school-teacher, at a monthly salary of 25 dollars, which, before leaving, was increased to 40. But, although my income thus kept increasing, my prospect of getting an outfit for the Plains, kept as gradually decreasing i.e. my means, somehow, or other, actually became more and more limited every year. So, having enough to take myself as far as and family as far as Florence, I resolved to go as far as that place, at all events, believing that the Lord would open the way further. I accordingly started, and arrived at Florence with a few dollars in my pocket. During a stay there of about 6 weeks. I continued, by the sale of a few articles, by cellar-digging and so forth, to raise just enough to pay my way though in a brother's wagon. We travelled as far as Fort Laramie in connection with Capt. G. J. Willie's Handcart Company, (he is now my bishop) and from thence, with Captain Hodgetts's Waggon Company, arriving in this City on Monday the 15th of Last December, in good health and spirits, without a full change of clothing for myself.

I had not been here, however, quite 3 weeks, (during part of which time I was engaged in kanyon work and in sawing wood in the City) when I obtained the tutorship of the fourteenth Ward School, in which occupation I am still engaged. A combination of circumstances will not, however, justify me in retaining this position. I am on hand and intend that my actions shall not belie my words – to do anything and everything (no matter what) which may lie in the path of my duty; and if, therefore, you should feel, that my services can anywhere be made available, as Clerk, or in any other position for the upbuilding of the Kingdom of God, I shall cheerfully respond to your call.

    Bros. L. Snow, F. D. Richards, S. W. Richards, and
    G. B. Wallace were acquainted with me in England.
      With respect, I beg to subscribe myself.
       Your faithful servant and brother
        For the Gospel's sake.
         <u>John Thos Geary</u>
          J.T.G.

Live at present, in a house of Bro. Horne's in Emigration Street, next door to Bro Isaac Nash the blacksmith.

There are some notable insights in this letter John wrote. He states that he "obeyed the gospel about 7 years ago" which means he may have been investigating the Mormon Church as early as 1850. He notes that he is still corresponding with his father, Thomas Geary, in March of 1857 when Thomas is living in Leicester with his housekeeper Mary Browne, by whom he has a young son, Charles Geary Browne.

John's 1857 letter to Brigham Young is a heartfelt and forthright plea for direction. Since joining the Church six years prior, John had literally turned his life upside down and left all he ever knew to serve his religion. He established himself as a willing leader in several positions in London and, as he indicates, he knew Church leaders such as Lorenzo Snow and Franklin Richards well from his time in the London Conference. Samuel Richards had given the Gearys that poetry book as a wedding present. "G.B. Wallace" is a reference to George Benjamin Wallace (1817-1900), a Mormon who was converted to the church as a young man in Boston, Massachusetts and served as a London missionary at the time John was baptized in 1851.[11] All of these men were well-connected to Brigham Young and it is important that John invokes their names as references for himself.

EARLY FRIENDS OF THE GEARYS IN GREAT SALT LAKE CITY

Joseph Horne (1812–1897) was born in London and emigrated to Canada with his family when he was 6 years old. Joseph married Mary Hales in 1838. The Horne family was converted to the LDS Church in Canada by Orson Hyde and joined the Saints in Far West, Missouri in 1838. Joseph knew the prophet Joseph Smith and many other leaders while living in Nauvoo during the 1840s. The Hornes came across the plains to Utah with the first immigrant parties in 1847 in the same company as the Hoaglands. In the spring of 1849, Horne and his family moved into the 14th Ward. There, he helped John Geary get a job teaching at the 14th Ward School. From 1854 to 1858, Horne served as Superintendent of Public Works overseeing the labor and team work on the Temple block at Salt Lake City. In 1852, he became a counselor to Bishop Abraham Hoagland of the 14th Ward. He served for many years as a patriarch and died in 1897.

Abraham Hoagland, (1797-1872) was born March 24, 1797 in Hillsborough, Somerset County, New Jersey. He was converted to the LDS Church as a young married man living in Michigan and then moved to Nauvoo in the 1840s. He came across the plains in the first company in 1847 and settled in Salt Lake's 14th Ward where he was appointed Bishop in 1851. He served as Bishop until his death in 1872. He notes in his life story that, in 1856, "the Authorities of the Church began to cry aloud and spare not, and told us we were asleep and that the sword of the Lord was unshielded, ready to fall upon us unless we would return from our backsliding and past wanderings" so Bishop Hoagland led an effort to re-baptize his entire ward during the Reformation. "In the month of March the 23rd, 1857, commenced to baptize the ward, which took two days. A good spirit. On April 2, Thursday, a Fast Day, a few being absent when baptized, the ward baptized 32 more on Fast Day morning." This re-baptism occurred during the time the Geary family was living in the 14th Ward shortly after their arrival in the valley and it is possible that they took part in it.

Isaac Bartlett Nash (1824-1907) "I, Isaac Bartlett Nash Davies, was born in Kidwelly, Carmarthenshire, South Wales, June 14, 1824. My father's name was David Davies and my mother's name was Mary Nash Davies, daughter of Isaac Bartlett Nash and Mary White Nash." Nash heard the message of the Mormons at the White Horse Tavern as a young man and as he described it "The Gospel Net caught me and I was baptized." He and his wife emigrated to Utah and Isaac worked as a blacksmith in Salt Lake. "In the year 1856 I went to work in the Church Blacksmith Shop. During this time, I lived in the Seventh Ward. I had a lot there and a blacksmith shop on it, before I went to California. When I came back, I turned the shop into a dwelling house and lived in it until I built a house next to the shop." Geary lived next to Nash when he first arrived in the valley. Nash helped combat Johnston's Army in 1857-1858 and may have associated with John Thomas Geary during that encampment in Emigration Canyon.

James Staples (1810-1875) was converted to the Mormon faith in 1841 in Cheltenham, England by missionaries he encountered. He attended the same London branch as the Gearys attended - Theobald's Road Branch -- before emigrating to Utah on January 5, 1851. The Gearys may have known Staples in London. Richard Fryer and later, Sophia Geary, lived with Staples at various times when they were in transition. After arriving in Utah, James Staples worked with Joseph Horne on the Salt Lake Temple as a stone mason. "James Staples was chosen as one of ten head masons at 28 cents per hour. He was assisted at first by two masons at 18 cents per hour and two tenders (laborers) at 14 cents per hour...They worked 12 ½ hours per day, six days per week. The normal workweek was 75 hours...President Brigham Young referred to him during a sermon in the Tabernacle when he said 'James Staples is an honest man who works as diligently in one's absence as when one is present.' ...He worked on the Temple until his death in 1875."

The above information was taken from the entries for each person on www.familysearch.org

John expresses hope to Brigham Young that he could be qualified for some position of responsibility in the Great Salt Lake City community. He asks directly about a clerk position similar to when he served as an Assistant Clerk in the London Conference.

In his letter, John gives us a detailed picture of his expertise and experience. He is honest about his mistakes in St. Louis – it is mysterious to know that he lost many of his possessions there - but he remains positive in his outlook. He reveals his character when he indicates that he is willing to do everything from digging cellars to sawing wood: "to do anything and everything (no matter what) which may lie in the path of my duty." He speaks hopefully and confidently. There is no known record of Brigham Young's response to the letter, although Church records are not wholly available to the public on these topics. One wonders if John's life would have been different with more clear direction from Brigham Young as to a job or profession. Nevertheless, John and Sophia remained in Salt Lake City for at least another year. On August 14, 1857, John and Sophia received their initiatory and endowment ordinances in the Salt Lake Endowment House. They were sealed in marriage for time and eternity.

The Gearys may have delayed their move to southern Utah in 1857-1858 due to a tumultuous situation developing in the valley during their first year. From July, 1857 through July, 1858 the Utah Territory was engulfed in a conflict known as the "Utah War" or "Buchanan's Blunder." [See sidebar]. The Utah War was speeding to a climax even as the Gearys came on the scene. It must have been alarming to John and Sophia that the Mormon leaders began to plan for the possible destruction of the entire Utah settlement if the federal troops arrived. On June 29, 1857, U.S. President James Buchanan declared Utah in rebellion due to polygamy and its theocratic style of government. President Buchanan mobilized an Army regiment to travel to the Utah Territory and take control of the area by military force. He ordered 2,500 troops to trek across the country toward Utah in the summer of 1857, while also naming Alfred Cumming as the new Territorial Governor.

Brigham Young and other church leaders resisted this attack on their community, having endured numerous decades of persecution back in Missouri and Illinois. Ironically, Utahns believed they were model American citizens and even presented an application for statehood in 1855. The petition was never considered by the U.S. Congress. The Mormons could not believe their country was attacking them again. Brigham Young addressed his followers in published letters dated October 14, 1857 and October 16, 1857 by saying:

> "I and the people of the Territory universally believe firmly to be the objective of the Administration in the present expedition against Utah, viz: the destruction, if not the entire annihilation, of the Mormon community, solely upon religious grounds and without any pretext whatever." "If you came here for peaceful purposes you have no use for weapons of war. We wish and ever have wished for peace..."[12]

On September 15, 1857, Brigham Young declared martial law in the Utah Territory: "We are invaded by a hostile force who are evidently assailing us to accomplish our overthrow and destruction."[13] Young was willing to negotiate with the government about installing an independent territorial governor but President Buchanan was listening to irate federal officials who returned from Utah frustrated with the church domination over the machinery of government. Eastern newspapers also sensationalized polygamy so many believed the worst about Mormons.

THE UTAH WAR

When President James Buchanan was elected President of the United States in 1856 some of his advisors told him to challenge the authority of Brigham Young and the Mormons in the Utah Territory. Eastern newspapers were featuring sensationalized articles about the scandals of polygamy which provoked federal politicians. Buchanan decided it to assert control over the Utah Territory and to separate church from state. As a result, he appointed Alfred Cumming as the new Territorial Governor, although no one gave Brigham Young notice of that fact because former President Pierce had canceled Utah's mail contract. Buchanan sent an army of 2,500 men under the command of Colonel Albert Sydney Johnston to oversee Cumming's installation as Governor.

Through a series of miscommunications, Brigham Young and the Mormon leaders thought that "Johnston's Army" was coming to take back the Territory by force. Young planned an active military resistance under the command of General Daniel Wells. Some of their tactics included sending out small bands of men to interrupt the Johnston Army wagons in transit. Brigham Young insisted that no lives be lost, but that the Army resources be depleted.

This period of fear and defensiveness is termed "the Utah War" although no formal war was fought. Young ordered teams of Mormon men to build fortifications in the canyons to block entry into the valley. John Thomas Geary and Richard Fryer were part of the contingent that was building those fortifications up the canyon in the winter of 1857.

The families in the valley were instructed to prepare to abandon their homes on a moment's notice if the troops arrived and to burn everything to the ground. Church leaders intended that the Army would find only a wasteland in Salt Lake. Elder John Taylor preached a sermon encouraging "all persons who would apply the torch to their own buildings, cut down their trees, and lay waste to their fields to hold up their hand." According to a <u>Deseret News</u> February 10, 1858 article, "Every hand in the audience numbering over 4,000 persons was raised at the same moment."

The Move South, as it came to be known, meant 30,000 people packed up everything they owned and began moving out of the Salt Lake Valley in the spring of 1858. Bishops organized their wards and the move was conducted in strict military order, wagonload by wagonload. They first planned on going as far south as Parowan, but most groups stopped at Provo.

Fortunately, Brigham Young also pursued a political solution to the crisis by enlisting non-Mormon leaders such as Thomas Kane to negotiate a peaceful end to the Army's plans. The entire episode was sometimes known as "Buchanan's Blunder." Governor Cumming was allowed to take his post as Governor so long as the Army did not accompany him. Brigham Young ensured a peaceful transition to federal control. The Army camped at Camp Floyd for two years and then departed with no further trouble when the Civil War began. Governor Cumming left after a few years himself and the relationship between the Mormons and the federal government became calmer. However, Utah did not receive statehood until 1896 after the Mormons renounced polygamy as a church practice.

Tensions from President Buchanan's actions spread throughout the Utah Territory. Sophia's sister, Jane, and her family down south in Iron County lived very near one of the most tragic and heart-breaking events of early Utah history – the Mountain Meadows Massacre on September 11, 1857. In the tense atmosphere of the Utah War, with fears of mobs and persecution still in their minds, some Mormon leaders in Iron County engaged in a standoff with a wagon train of emigrants from Arkansas and Illinois who were passing through on their way to California. The emigrants were trapped in the meadows southwest of Cedar City and eventually the majority of them were brutally killed, mostly by the Mormons. The tragedy reverberated for generations in southern Utah. It is possible that John and Sophia heard of the massacre during the fall of 1857 and delayed their trip down due to the heightened tensions.

In September, 1857, the U.S. Army sent Captain Stewart Van Vliet in to Salt Lake City as an emissary to meet with Brigham Young and spend six days as his guest discussing the "Utah War." Van Vliet's report was subsequently published in the *Deseret News* on February 10, 1858. Van Vliet's observation was that the Mormons would resist "to the death the entrance of troops into the Valley." He was also alarmed at the Mormons' willingness to destroy all that they had built rather than have it taken by the U.S. government.[14]

Louis Bertrand, a French convert then in Utah, described what he observed in 1857: "It became morally difficult to make war against a people who announce to the whole world their intention of burning from thirty to forty million dollars' worth of property; the fruits of twelve years of work, with such laconic and stoic indifference. To want to subdue such resolute men, capable of conceiving and executing such a plan, is like attempting to put out Vesuvius with a glass of water."[15]

On March 18, 1858, the Church authorities held what historian B.H. Roberts calls "a council of war" in the Church Historian's office. Eight of the twelve apostles and the First Presidency were there and they changed their strategy from one of fight to flight. Roberts notes, "President Young's plan was to go into the desert and not war with the people, but let them destroy themselves."[16] Between March and May, 1858, nearly the entire valley was abandoned, with each bishop organizing his ward into wagon trains and loading up everything they owned. The intention was to burn Salt Lake City to the ground before Buchanan's Army arrived. The entire population was to seek refuge in Parowan during this Move South.[17]

This "council of war" event builds important context around the next two letters written by John and Sophia to their relatives in southern Utah the same month.

JOHN TO RICHARD HARRISON

Great Salt Lake City
March 31, 1858
6th Ward

Dear Brother Harrison:

We are all in commotion here. I start tonight by moonlight for Echo Canyon. A considerable number is called out. A call of 11 men was made on this Ward in the middle of last night and an additional 9 early this morning. The precise object of the expedition is not fully known but I feel satisfied it is all right. The women and children are being moved South as quickly as possible the old men go with them. We have no team but I expect Sophy and the children will be cleared out in some way during my absence – though they may not be able to get far away – they will however get as near Iron County as they can and when I join them we shall go through unless counselled to the contrary. Many I hear contemplate settling in your neighborhood. If you could manage to secure for me 2 to 5 acres of land you would much oblige me as I expect to be with you in time to put in seed. My time for starting is just at hand so please excuse more at present. Our united kind love to Jane and the little responsibilities yourself and all yours and believe me in haste.

Faithfully yours,
John Thomas Geary

John sounds anxious in this letter, but he reiterates his faith in his leaders. Although he does not know much about his mission, he is following instructions despite the personal cost to him and his family. It is inspiring to see his spirit of faith, given the difficulties he had already endured in his travel across the plains. After many separations of their young family, John and Sophia will be separated yet again.

Sophia put her own postscript on the letter:

SOPHIA TO JANE

My Dear Jane,

It would seem that the time is not far distant when we shall have the pleasure of seeing each other. I hope it may be so with all my heart. Dick is going with John and when he returns he will make his way for Iron County. With kind love to all,

Believe me Yours as ever
Sophy.

JOHN AND SOPHIA SEPARATED AGAIN

Although Sophia did leave Salt Lake City for some period of time with her children, the Utah War crisis was soon averted. Alfred Cumming was able to peacefully enter the Salt Lake Valley on April 15, 1858 and meet with Brigham Young; Cumming then became the Territorial Governor. Cumming wrote a report to U.S. President Buchanan which was published in the *Deseret News* stating that he was "universally greeted as the Governor with such respectful attentions as are due" and he was able to verify that all federal and state government offices were intact and well-run.[18] Cumming went on to serve as Territorial Governor and Brigham Young served as President of the Mormon Church. The Army troops were eventually called back east to participate in the Civil War. By the end of April, 1858, Sophia was staying with her children at the home of James Staples in Salt Lake. She wrote a letter to her sister to update her on their status.[19]

SOPHIA TO JANE

April 22, 1858

I received your note yesterday for which I am thankful for I assure you I began to think that something was the matter in that country. But howsoever I am glad to hear that you are doing well and that you have a good

Husband. I expected you up here at conference to get your endowments, but suppose you are pretty busy putting in your grain so that by another harvest you will keep your stomach from growing to your back. I assure you that it has been hard times up here.

I have been living with Brother Staples since they began to station us at the Public and ever since November they would not let us have any provisions at all so from that time to this we have had to catch a little where we could get it which was very little indeed. I have been digging roots which is our provision store. Many times this winter I have rose from my bed not knowing when I could have any breakfast or not. The Bishop cannot give us any because he is in the same fix. Well thank God we have got along and are still alive yet and hope to live, yet it is astonishing when I think how it is that our wants have been supplied but nevertheless and I feel first rate about it if it strengthens my faith in Mormonism. Let hard times come I think I can stand it as well as the rest. But we'll turn over a new leaf.

You say that you did not receive any letters. Yesterday I read a letter from Jorden wrote to Levi Coombs and he stated that he had sent two letters to you and received no answers and by the tenor of his writing I have reason to suppose that he did not receive my letters. But I shall send him again. (There certainly were two letters for you in the Post Office last fall but someone took them out.) I intended to write to Geary and Mother as I have not heard from home. But Brother Geary's cousin came in last fall. His name is Thomas Hall he said they were doing well and were coming on this season if possible. You rather hint that you do not get along as well as could be expected. Well I don't know anyone that has two women that agree all the time and are at peace. We are not any of us perfect but I would like to you to tell me just as matters and things are if there is anything wrong. It is hard for me to get tea or sugar at the best of times, however, I'll send you some as soon as I can get it. I'll send poor Frank five pencils and hope that he won't be afraid to use them, as he will need all he can learn by and by. I'll send Annie some shoes as soon as possible.

Your affectionate sister, Sophia.

Sophia's letter is one of tremendous faith, stating as she does, "Let hard times come, I think I can stand it as well as the rest." This is no casual statement. In light of all her recent trials – death of a child, loss of possessions, loss of extended family, separation from her husband, starvation, deprivation, homelessness, uncertainty – Sophia is making a powerful assertion. She sounds like a person who has gone to hell and back and knows her capacity to survive. Even as she writes this letter she is separated from her husband, caring for two daughters and living under the roof of a family friend.

Her reference to being stationed at "the Public" might mean that she could work at the Public Works in the center of town, where any person not otherwise employed could go to work and obtain assistance with food and clothing.[20] During the Move South her residence must have been temporarily disrupted, but then when the danger passed she was placed at the Staples home while John was away. It is not clear where John is located, but he is not with her as she states she intends to write to him. Sophia's comments encouraging her sister are tender as she advises her to make the best of polygamy, and her kind concern for her niece and nephew – even wanting to send them gifts when she is so poor herself – is extremely poignant.

Earlier in January, 1858, both John and Sophia had received their patriarchal blessings while together in Salt Lake City. John Young, Jr. was the Church Patriarch who gave them the blessings. Young was born in 1791 and converted to the Church along with his brother, Brigham Young. He was ordained a patriarch in 1853 at the age of 62. John Young was the oldest of the Young brothers, with Joseph Young (1797-1881) and Brigham Young (1801-1877) being younger brothers.[21] John Young was trained as a Methodist minister in New England before converting to the Church. It is curious to think about how this blessing was arranged for the Gearys.

Patriarch John Young, Jr. was in a prominent position of leadership, having spoken in Conference or Church meetings at least four times as recorded in the Journal of Discourses.[22] He was serving in the unique role of Patriarch to the Whole Church, as opposed to the Stake Patriarch role we are familiar with today. In the 1850s, Church members were following the guidance of an 1845 editorial by John Taylor that outlined how the duties of a patriarch are carried out. There was a conflict following the martyrdom of Hyrum Smith in 1844, as to who was filling the role of Patriarch to the Whole Church. Taylor wrote the article to clarify that those men who serve as Patriarch of the Whole Church do not necessarily give patriarchal blessings to everyone, but only to the fatherless who have no one to give a father's blessing to them. It appears a special request might have been made to have Patriarch Young give blessings to John and Sophia, as they were indeed 'fatherless' at the time.[23]

THE GEARYS MOVE TO CEDAR CITY

Sophia and John did eventually move to Cedar City in either late 1858 or early 1859. According to Bessie Snow in *Fate of the Fryers*, the Gearys' third daughter, Eliza Jane, was born in Cedar City on April 6, 1859.[24] The two sisters, Sophia and Jane, were finally reunited in southern Utah. Jane had lived in Cedar City since becoming Richard Harrison's plural wife in early 1855. Sophia may have been staying with Jane when baby Eliza was born. It appears that John had obtained a piece of property in Salt Lake by 1859, but it was being sold for unpaid taxes. A Tax Notice in the *Deseret News* on March 23, 1859 states that John Geary of the 10th Ward is among the people who will have city property sold for taxes if not paid before the 11th day of April.[25] He owed 55 cents in taxes.

While the Gearys lived in Cedar City during 1859, it was a town in chaos. The community was originally settled as part of the Iron Mission to produce good quality iron from the extensive chunks of iron ore that could be seen in the hills. The Iron Mission began with a call from the First Presidency in the November 16, 1850. More than 100 men were sent to Iron County and most settled in the area now known as Parowan (formerly Center Creek). Cedar City (formerly Coal Creek) was settled about 15 miles to the south in November, 1851 by a company consisting of mostly English, Irish, Scotch, and Welsh miners and iron workers. "The years 1855, 1856, and 1857 were disastrous, as most crops were lost to grasshoppers and other pests. They lived in isolation and dire poverty, often going without shoes and warm clothing."[26] The tensions of the Utah War during 1857-1858 and the terrible brutality of the Mountain Meadows Massacre in 1857 presented sizable challenges to these Iron County communities.

THE IRON MISSION

Jane Fryer's husband, Richard Harrison, was one of the group of settlers who arrived in 1851 after he received a call to serve from President Brigham Young. Harrison was superintendent of a large iron foundry in Liverpool, England at the time of his conversion to Mormonism in 1840. Richard and his first wife, Mary Anne, emigrated to Nauvoo in 1842 and settled in the Salt Lake Valley in 1849.[27] He was able to work at the Iron Mission during the first wave of sizable investment by the Church (in 1852 more than 4,000 British pounds were invested in the venture from wealthy British saints). "Between September 1852 and September 1853, through experimenting and great effort, the furnace produced about twenty tons of pig iron from approximately fifty tons of ore, even though iron masters were still not satisfied with the quality of the iron. Richard Harrison in March 1853 successfully cast in sand moldings a variety of skillets, flat or hand irons, a kettle, two wheels, and other goods."[28]

Despite its promising beginnings, the Utah iron industry was never successful. In 1858, Brigham Young closed the Deseret Iron Company, explaining, "It would be well to abandon the idea of making Iron for the present and let all the brethren pursue those avocations which they please. Put everything in as good condition for preservation as possible, and let it rest." [29] The mission ended just as John and Sophia Geary arrived on the scene in Cedar City. Most residents were leaving for communities in Washington County or returning to the Salt Lake Valley. With the coming of the transcontinental railroad, iron could be obtained for less cost than it took to produce it in Cedar City. By the 1860 census, the Cedar City population declined from about 1,000 to only 301 and there were 35 unoccupied houses in town. [30]

Richard Harrison and his polygamous wives, Mary Anne and Jane Fryer, were among the families that stayed in Cedar City after the Iron Works closed. According to Bessie Snow, they were still living there in 1859-1860 because Richard and Jane's daughter, Linna Fryer Harrison, was born in Cedar City on December 19, 1860.[31] Richard Harrison had built a house in Cedar that included an orchard, a farm and a garden. Jane's son, Frank Jorden, Jr., wrote that he worked for Richard Harrison there but could never please him: "I found it difficult to please Mr. Harrison, work as faithful as I would, caring for the farm during his long absences I was sure to be found fault with."[32]

John and Sophia and their two little girls (Sophia Ann and Echo) likely lived at the Harrison home in Cedar City when they first moved south in 1858-1859. When they added baby Eliza to the mix in December, 1859 it is possible that they obtained their own home. They may have been able to use one of the many unoccupied homes in Cedar City. The family is shown on the August 1, 1860 U.S. Census as living together in Cedar City at number 1477. The census lists John as a farmer with real estate worth $200 and personal property worth $275. Richard Harrison and Jane are listed on the same census at number 1499 in Cedar City. Within a few months the Gearys were able to get a cow, calf, some sheep, a pig, and some chickens. Sophia must have been busy with three children under 7 years old. Things became even more difficult when, at some point in 1860, John left Sophia and returned to Salt Lake City. On July 15, 1860, John wrote to Sophia in Cedar City:[33]

JOHN TO SOPHIA

G.S.L. City
15 July 1860

My Dear Sophy,

As I have a chance of sending you 2 bunches of cotton yarn &c by Bro. Thompson of Beaver I have thought it best to combine the opportunity lest another such a one should not occur soon. If however, before he starts, I should have a chance to send by someone who is coming nearer to Cedar I shall do so and in that case shall advise you of the fact. In the present I am fixing up Jennings the butcher's books which are very much in arrear. This job will last a few days only just enabling me to make a decent appearance & to pay for my board &c since my arrival.

I am as yet at John C. Hall's – he lives in my old house in the 10th Ward to purchase which he says he has partially made an agreement. I did not go to hard work with Staples because I have a prospect of getting more lucrative & therefore more suitable employment in a store. It is just possible that I may make an engagement for 3 to 4 months with Jennings at all events it will be a good introduction for me – the wedge is now inserted & by God's & my good brethren's help here I will drive it home.

Bros Wells, Hunter, Stenhouse, Long, Bowering, Smith, Armstrong, and others are extending themselves on my behalf. I think that with the exercise of a little patience I shall obtain all that I can reasonably desire – I may however be disappointed in my expectations which in days past has oft been my lot and which may therefore be mine again. So don't get over sanguine on the matter. Ask our Father to bless & prosper us both during our absence from each other and to give to us His Spirit so that we may be able to acknowledge his hand in all things.

God bless you dear Sophy. I wish sometimes you were here to cheer & comfort me in my struggle to obtain the things for which I temporarily have left home and its kindly associations & feelings. I find to be --- verily true the words of the immortal poet who said once of himself, "Absence makes the heart grow fonder. Over this I often ponder. And find that it is true." I am satisfied well satisfied, however, that our present (& future for a while) separation will result in permanent good to both of us in many ways. Pray for me all the time. You & our little ones have been daily remembered by me since my departure from home. It is pleasant and consoling to feel, though absent from the scene some 300 miles, the enlivening influence of those spirits who wish one well and whose heart's desire & prayer to God are that one may be prospered in every lawful undertaking. Such an influence I often experience now and say, "God bless them who entertain such sentiments towards me." I feel well & never did feel much better or more thoroughly satisfied.

No more on this subject for the present. But to business – Please tell me exactly what you received by Bro. Harrison. I sent 2 notes & a quantity of store goods by him but as I felt it rather doubtful whether he would be able to obtain the cotton yard at Spanish Fork I think it will be safer to send you the 2 bunches mentioned at the commencement of this letter. They are No. 8 the highest I can get in the City just now. One is for yourself & the other is for Bro. Gower in case you have not already given him one. If he has had one of course you will keep the 2 now sent for yourself & on no consideration let the fact of your having them transpire except by letting Bro. Stewart have one on account. I would send him one now but cannot get sufficient means. I have borrowed to purchase the 2.

By the bye you will oblige me by keeping my movements quiet with our friends in Cedar rather leading them to suppose that my prospects of success are by no means sure which is the fact and then if I should fail --- you know the rest.

Please look amongst my papers which you will find wrapped a piece of parchment & I believe you will find several of my English Certificates to practice law. Send one of them to me in every letter you write till you have sent all. Be sure you forthwith attend to this & send my last certificate first.

I owe Bro Haight and Bro Morris 15 cents each for postage. If they will take a yard of domestic each instead of the cash which I have not got, please oblige me by paying them. It is getting so dark I can scarcely see to write so excuse me now. I shall write you often & wish you to write me once a week at least & oftener if you feel like it. I will try to send you some postage stamps in my next letter.

Farewell for the present – God bless you & the little ones – Kiss them for me. Sis. DeGray, John, Selina, Keziah, Maria, Tom & his two ladies sent their love, accept of mine.

Believe me Your affectionate husband & true friend
John Thos Geary

This letter illustrates the strain John was beginning to feel during his repeated separations from his family. His confidence in finding a good job situation appears to be waning – "I may however be disappointed in my expectations which in days past has oft been my lot and which may therefore be mine again." He allows himself only one paragraph to describe his feelings, but John is tender in his expressions of love for Sophia and his children. Still, in the same paragraph he states, "I feel well & never did feel much better or more thoroughly satisfied." It is a bit of a paradox that he can be so lonely and satisfied at the same time. Perhaps he is giving himself encouragement.

John's reference to John C. Hall brings back into focus the relationship with his cousin on his mother's side from England. Hall is the man who cleaned up the deed dispute with President Marsden seven years earlier as the Gearys were emigrating to America. Hall's mother, Charlotte Wright Hall, is still living with Geary's brother, Frederick, back in London as of the 1860 census.[34] John C. Hall is in Salt Lake City with his family and apparently made a deal with the tax authorities to buy John's former home in the 10th Ward. This would have been in the area of present-day Liberty Park in Salt Lake City.

In 1860, John C. Hall was married to plural wives – the DeGrey sisters, Selena and Keziah. Hall had converted part of the DeGrey family back in England in 1853 while on his church mission. He married Selena (1837-1905) in England and they had two children – Charlotte and Keziah – before emigrating to Utah in 1857. Selena's mother, Mariah, also emigrated to Utah in 1857 with three other daughters, Maria (1840-1879), Sarah (1945-1926) and Keziah (1837-1905). John married 20-year-old Keziah as his second wife.

When John T. Geary was living with the Halls in 1860 they may have also had John C. Hall's brother, Tom, staying with them. Tom Hall also had plural wives - Marion, whom he married in January, 1860, and his soon-to-be second wife, Selena Dunn. This would account for the people John listed in his letter. The Hall family did not end up staying in the Geary home in the 10th Ward; in 1861 they were called to the Cotton Mission and moved to Rockville, Utah.

In John's letter, the list of Salt Lake City men who will vouch for his character is impressive. Without first names it is difficult to be sure whom he is identifying, but some names are well-known. He lists a Mr. Wells, who is likely Daniel H. Wells (1814-1891), a Mormon apostle and father of 39 children; Mr. Stenhouse could be Thomas Brown (T.B.) Stenhouse (1825-1882), the editor of the *Salt Lake Telegram* and a former missionary in London when John lived there; Mr. Bowering could be Henry Ebenezer Bowring (1822-1906), a British convert who arrived in Utah in 1856 and worked as a saddle and harness maker as well as founding member of the Salt Lake Theater. All were acquaintances of Brigham Young. Some were men John had known in England or on the plains. Wherever John went, he appears to have made friends with prominent and powerful men who could introduce him to opportunities.

Other notable elements in John's 1860 letter are his continued insistence on secrecy about his situation and his request for his law certificates. He did not want Sophia to tell anyone what he was doing in Salt Lake. This is consistent with some of John's secrecy on other occasions, such as his complicated departure from Liverpool or his trouble with the deeds in London. John's request for Sophia to send his law certificates – one by one – is interesting because it indicates that he may want to practice law again instead of farming. Indeed, John was about to file a lawsuit in the coming months.

It is a puzzle why John had not securely established himself in either Salt Lake City or southern Utah after three years in Utah. He appears in these letters as educated, well-spoken, hard-working, an articulate writer, well-connected, and a religious family man. Why didn't he open a law practice? Did he serve in callings in the church? The records are silent on these matters. He mentions "Jennings" in this letter and we will see he does obtain a position with that man, but again it is short-lived. There are also questions about why Sophia and John are living apart for such long periods. John's story is not dissimilar to other pioneers of the time who struggled to make a living, but his unique background should have provided him with an advantage in finding employment.

ENDNOTES FOR CHAPTER FOUR

1	Arrington, Leonard, <u>Great Basin Kingdom – Economic History of the Latter-Day Saints, 1830-1900</u>, University of Nebraska Press, Lincoln, 1958, page 193, quoting Hammond, George P. ed., <u>Campaigns in the West, 1856-1861: The Journal and Letters of Colonel John Van Deusen Du Bois</u>, Tucson, Arizona, 1949, page 69, entry for June 21, 1858.

2	Arrington, Leonard and Bitton, Davis, <u>The Mormon Experience, A History of the Latter-day Saints</u>, New York, Knopf, 1979, pages 135-136.

3	John Thomas Geary Letter to Brigham Young, March 11, 1857.

4	Snow, Bessie, <u>Fate of the Fryers</u>, self-published, 1973, page 17, 22.

5	Wards and Branches of the Church in Salt Lake City, www.familysearch.org

6	1860 United States Census, Great Salt Lake City, www.familysearch.org.

7	Letter from John Thomas Geary to Brigham Young, March 11, 1857.

8	Roberts, B.H., <u>A Comprehensive History of the Church of Jesus Christ of Latter-day Saints, Century I, In Six Volumes, Volume IV</u>, Brigham Young University Press, Provo Utah, 1930, 1965, page 119.

9	*Ibid.*, page 126.

10	www.familysearch.org.

11	https://medium.com/@fieldingwallace/the-life-of-george-benjamin-wallace-37c5004575f1 Wallace, Fielding, <u>The Life of George Benjamin Wallace</u>, Dec. 12, 2019. Wallace served as a counselor to Franklin D. Richards in the Liverpool branch and writes eloquently in his missionary journal about what it was like to serve a mission in England from 1849-1851. He returned from England to Utah on June 1, 1852 and John must have been reacquainted with him in Utah.

12	*Deseret News*, January 13, 1858, www.digitalnewspapers.com.

13	Roberts at page 274.

14	*Deseret News*, February 10, 1858, www.digitalnewspapers.com

15	Bertrand, Louis A., <u>Memoires D'un Mormon</u>, E. Jung-Treuttel, Paris, 1862, Translated by Gaston Chappuis in the Donald R. Moorman Collection, Special Collections, Stewart Library, Weber State University, Ogden, Utah., Cited by Bagley, Will, <u>Kingdom in the West – The Mormons and the American Frontier</u>, Volume 8, On the Way to Somewhere Else, European Sojourners in the Mormon West, 1834-1930, edited by Michael W. Homer, Spokane: The Arthur H. Clark Company, 2006, p. 108. Bertrand (1808-1875) was one of the most fascinating European converts in the early Church. He was a friend of Curtis E. Bolton, the Church leader who attended John and Sophia's 1852 London wedding. Bertrand had been converted by Bolton and John Taylor when they met with him on a Paris street in 1850. At the time, Bertrand was a leading Communist revolutionary and political newspaper editor. He and Bolton worked together to translate the Book of Mormon into French during 1851; Bertrand emigrated to Utah in 1855.

16	Roberts at page 360.

17   Arrington and Bitton at pages 189-193.

18   *Deseret News*, July 28, 1858, www.digitalnewspapers.com

19   Snow, Fate of the Fryers at page 17. This letter is incorrectly dated "April 22, 1856" in Snow's book, but the Gearys had not arrived in the Great Salt Lake Valley in 1856 and the letter describes events consist with 1858.

20   Arrington and Bitton at page 111.

21   https://www.josephsmithpapers.org/person/john-young-jr website Home, People, John Young, Jr.

22   https://www.journalofdiscourses.com/John_Young.

23   See article, "A History of Patriarchs and Patriarchal Blessings", by Church History Library Staff, 26 March 2019, found at https://history.churchofjesuschrist.org/blog/a-history-of-patriarchs-and-patriarchal-blessings?lang=eng. "Patriarchal blessings include a declaration of a person's lineage in the house of Israel and contain personal counsel from the Lord. As a person studies his or her patriarchal blessing and follows the counsel it contains, it will provide guidance, comfort, and protection". https://history.churchofjesuschrist.org/article/chl-pb?lang=eng#what-is-a-patriarchal-blessing. During the October 1979 General Conference, the office [Patriarch to the Whole Church] was discontinued due to the increased number of local stake patriarchs.

24   Snow, Fate of the Fryers at page 24. The official records of Eliza Jane Geary's birth contain conflicting dates and locations of birth.

25   *Deseret News*, March 23, 1859. http://digitalnewspapers.org.

26   Seegmiller, Janet Burton, History of Iron County, Chapter 5, Establishing Cedar City and the Iron Works, Utah State Historical Society, Salt Lake City, 1998, pages 25 and 64.

27   Snow, Fate of the Fryers at page 13.

28   Seegmiller at p 323. The items were displayed by Brigham Young at April 1853 General Conference.

29   *Ibid.* at 325, quoting Brigham Young's letter to Isaac Haight, 8 October 1858, Brigham Young's Letterbook for 1858, LDS Church Archives, Salt Lake City, and Morris Shirts, "The Demise of the Deseret Iron Company," paper delivered at the Mormon History Association Annual meeting, 3 May 1986, Salt Lake City, 23.

30   *Ibid.* at page 74.

31   Snow, Fate of the Fryers at page 28.

32   *Ibid.*

33   See Appendix for a full copy of this letter from John to Sophia dated July 15, 1860. This original letter is in the possession of a Geary descendant, Brian K. Bowler, who posted it on www.familysearch.org, John Thomas Geary (LLHM-Z2I) entry on January 1, 2016. .

34   "England and Wales Census, 1861," database with images, *FamilySearch* (https://www.familysearch.org/ark:/61903/1:1:Q2M2-DZRX : 29 December 2020), Frederick Geary, Islington, Middlesex, England, United Kingdom; from "1861 England, Scotland and Wales census," database and images, *findmypast* (http://www.findmypast.com : n.d.); citing PRO RG 9, The National Archives, Kew, Surrey.

Above: Salt Lake City in 1855, the year before John and Sophia arrived. This is taken from Capitol Hill looking southwest. Temple Square is in the foreground. The 14th Ward meeting house (5) is where John first taught school in 1857. This is the area of town the Gearys lived most often.

Below,: Salt Lake City in 1865, a year before John's death. This view is looking southwest from a building on Main Street toward the Oquirrh Mountains. Walker Brothers store was on the northwest corner of Main Street; the cross street is Second South.

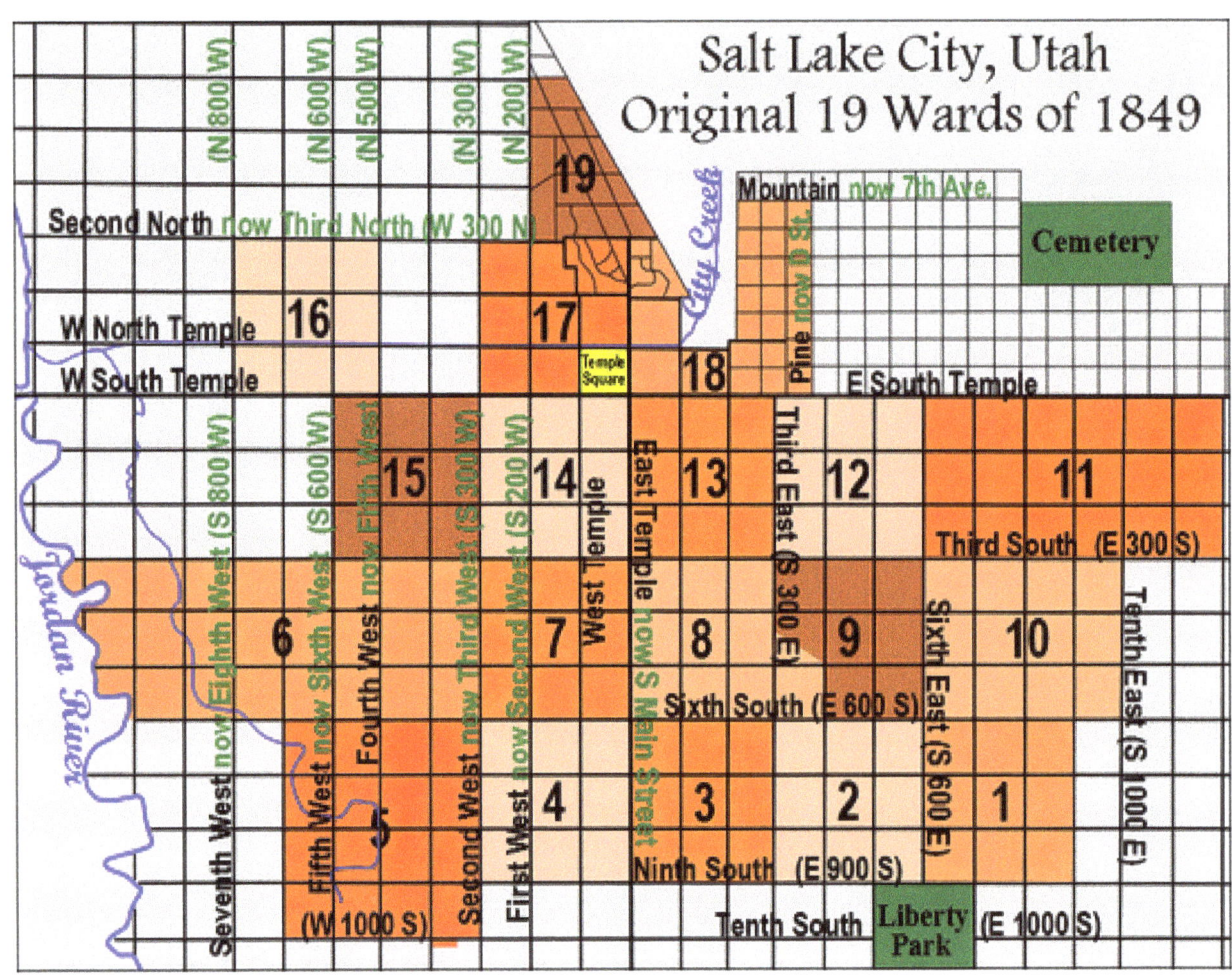

This map shows the locations of the first Mormon wards established in the Salt Lake Valley in 1849. John and Sophia lived most often in the 14th Ward when they were in Salt Lake City. The 10th Ward was another place they lived; John apparently owned property there in March, 1859 because it was noticed up for a tax sale. John was reportedly delinquent on 55 cents worth of taxes. John later stayed in the 10th Ward in the home of his cousin, John Hall.

Echo Workman Geary and Sophia Ann Geary about 1857.
Echo looks about one year old and Sophia Ann about four years old.
The photo shows the girls during the period of John and Sophia's first few years in Utah.

Richard Harrison and his first wife, Mary Ann. Richard married Sophia's sister, Jane, as his plural wife. He helped the Gearys establish a home in Cedar City.

Joseph Horne (1812-1897) was born in London but moved to Canada with his family, and was later converted to the Church in the Nauvoo period. Horne lived in the Salt Lake 14th Ward when the Gearys came to Utah and was helpful in getting them settled.

The Endowment House in Salt Lake City where John and Sophia's marriage was sealed in 1856. It stood on Main Street and North Temple about where the General Relief Society building is today.

Left: The March 23, 1859 Deseret News notice of properties being sold for unpaid taxes. John Geary is shown 5th from the bottom of the left column, living in the 10th Ward and owing 55 cents.

James Staples (1810-1875) a friend of John and Sophia's in Salt Lake City. Staples was a convert from England who attended the London Theobald's Road branch when the Gearys did. James' family emigrated to Utah in 1852 on the Ellen Maria, the same ship on which Sophia sailed from Liverpool.

Abraham Hoagland (1797-1872) was the Bishop of the 14th Ward when John arrived in Salt Lake City in late 1856. Hoagland hired John as a 14th Ward schoolteacher. He remained friends with the Geary family and may have given Leah Fryer Geary her baby blessing in the 14th Ward in 1863.

John Thomas Geary's March 11, 1857 handwritten letter to Church President Brigham Young.

and polisher, stove-polisher, and gas-pipe-layer, at a salary of 5 dollars per week. I also drove Messrs. Barstow and Co's furniture van, during my residence in St. Louis. At length, I became school-teacher, at a monthly salary of 25 dollars, which, before leaving, was increased to 40. But, although my income thus kept increasing, my prospect of getting an outfit for the Plains, kept as gradually decreasing — i. e. my means, somehow or other, actually became more and more limited every year. So, having enough to take myself and family, as far as Florence, I resolved to go as far as that place, at all events, believing that the Lord would open the way further. I accordingly started, and arrived at Florence with a few dollars in my pocket. During a stay there of about 6 weeks, I contrived, by the sale of a few articles, by cellar-digging, and so forth, to raise just enough to pay my way through in a brother's waggon. We travelled as far as Fort Laramie in connection with Capt. G. J. Willie's Handcart Company, (he is now my bishop,) and from thence, with Captain Hodgetts's Wagon Company, arriving in this City on Monday, the 15th of last December, in good health and spirits, without a full change of clothing for myself.

I had not been here, however, quite 3 weeks, (during part of which time I was engaged in kanyon work and in sawing wood in the city,) when I obtained the tutorship of the Fourteenth Ward School, in which occupation I am still engaged. A combination of circumstances will not, however, justify me in retaining this position.

I am on hand — and intend that my actions shall not belie my words — to do anything and everything (no matter what) which may lie in the path of my duty; and if, therefore, you should feel, that my services can anywhere be made available, as Clerk, or in any other position for the upbuilding of the Kingdom of God, I shall cheerfully respond to your call.

Bros. L. Snow, F. D. Richards, S. W. Richards, and G. B. Wallace were acquainted with me in England.

With respect, I beg to subscribe myself
Your faithful servant and brother
for the Gospel's sake,
John Thos. Gears.

live, at present, in a house of Bro. Horne's in Emigration Street, next door to Isaac Nash the blacksmith.

J. T. G.

J. T. Geary.   City 11 March 57
    Lawyer.
                    Jo. B. Young

wants employment as Clerk.
or Counsel what to do,

HEADED DOWN SOUTH

*"It is pleasant enough to have the sun shine upon us,
but if there were no clouds, we could not enjoy the sun."*
JTG

With John living in Salt Lake and Sophia living on the Cedar City farm with their three young children, their marriage was under some financial strain. In early summer 1860, John was able to work as a bookkeeper for William Jennings (1823-1886), a prosperous and well-known Salt Lake City butcher and businessman.

Jennings was British like John was; he emigrated to the U.S. in 1847 for reasons unrelated to the Mormon Church. While working his way west as a butcher, tanner and porkpacker, Jennings met and married a Mormon emigrant named Jane Walker. They arrived in Salt Lake City in 1852 and Jennings joined the Church. He set up a butchering business on the corner of 100 South and Main Street where John worked for him. During 1860, Jennings was beginning to branch out into the mercantile business with large contracts to supply grain. Unfortunately, John left the Jennings shop within a few weeks for unknown reasons. It is possible that John could have been wealthier if he had stayed in Jennings' employ. Jennings built the large Eagle Emporium on the site of his business in 1864 and eventually became mayor of Salt Lake City as well as the city's first millionaire.[1] His building still stands today, as of 2021, in the city's downtown business district.

GEARY V. STAMBAUGH

After leaving the Jennings job, John worked briefly for the Surveyor General of the Utah Territory, Samuel C. Stambaugh. That position lasted from June to August, 1860 while John performed some reviews of property records. An unpleasant dispute arose with the Surveyor's office about whether or not John was paid fairly for his work. John filed a lawsuit against Stambaugh in the Probate Court of Salt Lake County to collect his money. The claim, filed October 1, 1860, requests that S.C. Stambaugh pay the sum of $49.75 to John Thomas Geary "for work and labor" he performed.[2]

125

In the complaint, John stated that he performed work at Stambaugh's request and that Stambaugh "hath hitherto wholly refused and still doth refuse to pay the same…" The personal signature of John Thomas Geary was affixed to the document; he chose to act as his own attorney in the matter.

John claimed in his complaint that he performed the work for Stambaugh as follows: "To 37 days' time (from 20 June till 2 August both inclusive) devoted by me to your service @ $1.75/100 per day $64.75. Credit August by Cash 5.00 and By Cash 10.00 = 15.00. Balance owed, $49.75." In other words, John must have performed 37 days of work for Stambaugh from June 20, 1860 to August 2, 1860 and was supposed to be paid $1.75 per day or $64.75 total. It appears that John was paid $5 on one occasion and $10 on one occasion so he deducted that from the amount owed and claimed a net due of $49.75.

U.S. President James Buchanan had assigned Samuel C. Stambaugh to Utah in September, 1859 to investigate possible government fraud. Stambaugh and Buchanan were friends. The previous Surveyor General in the Utah Territory, David H. Burr, was known for irregularities and was under siege. Stambaugh was an experienced Indian agent in the east who negotiated several treaties with Indian tribes on behalf of the U.S. Government.[3] When he arrived in Utah, the year before John's lawsuit, he brought a crew of men named Wentz, Mason, Jones, Green, and Miller.[4] Stambaugh lived next door to John's old friend, Bishop Abraham Hoagland, in the 14th Ward. There is no evidence Stambaugh was a Mormon but Hoagland might have been aware of the lawsuit between Geary and Stambaugh.[5]

After a few months in Utah, Stambaugh concluded his investigation and found that Burr had, in fact, "perpetrated massive frauds on the federal government and on Utahns".[6] Burr had paid outrageous fees to surveyors for shoddy work. In some cases, the surveys did not have stakes, mounds or any other markers to show they were completed. John, being a lawyer with experience in land matters and title work back in London, may have assisted Stambaugh by examining legal documents and land descriptions in the surveys under investigation. Or John may have performed personal work for Stambaugh unrelated to his fraud investigation, which could explain why John sued him individually and not as a U.S. employee.

On October 20, 1860, John arranged for a Summons to be served on Stambaugh requiring him to defend his actions in court. The Assistant U.S. Attorney for the Utah Territory, Mr. W.W. Broadhead, defended Stambaugh by claiming that the suit was not properly brought. He argued that John's claim was actually against the U.S. Government and not against Stambaugh individually. In layman's terms, he wanted the case dropped because of a legal technicality. He claimed that Geary should have named the U.S. Government as a party to the case. Stambaugh did not deny that the money was owed; he just claimed that John sued the wrong party.

It is understandable that John, having received his legal training and experience in England, may not have been fully versed in the precise concepts of U.S. jurisdictional law. One would hope that Territorial Judge in Utah's Probate Court could see through the technicalities and allow John to amend or re-file his claim if he was truly owed the money, but it was not to be.

The *Mountaineer* newspaper in Utah reported on the case when the first hearing was held October 24, 1860:

> The case of J.T. Geary vs. Samuel C. Stambaugh was called up. Plaintiff, Defendant, and his counsel present. Mr. Broadhead asked leave to withdraw his plea in abatement that he might file another more properly authenticated ---. The plaintiff [Geary] objected to this. The court granted the defendant's request.
>
> The plaintiff [Geary] then asked time to file a replication, which was granted, and the court took a recess till 2 p.m. The court resumed its session at the hour appointed, and the case of Geary v. Stambaugh was again called up, and the plaintiff [Geary] asked for a continuance on the grounds that the plea now filed was a different plea from the first one, and that there was new matter, it was his privilege, he believed, to ask for the continuance in the case.
>
> Counsel for the defendant argued that the motion was not properly brought, that the service rendered had been rendered to the federal government and not to Gen. Stambaugh individually. The judge ordered that the case be continued till Thursday, the 1st day of November next, at 10 a.m.[7]

Thus, at John's first hearing, he lost a few battles. The judge allowed the defendant to file a different plea document, even though John objected. Then the judge asked John to file a reply [replication] to the different plea and John asked for more time. The case was continued for a week so John could prepare his reply to the different plea. But, at the next hearing a week later, the Court actions were not any better for John:

> Court met pursuant to adjournment, the case of Geary v. Stambaugh was called. Mr. Geary filed a replication to defendant's plea in abatement. About three hours' speechifying had to be endured before his honor could get a chance to inform the learned attorney that the strict technicalities of the "common law" could not be introduced into this court.
>
> After a great deal of talk as to which would be heard first, the question of the agency of Gen. Stambaugh, or the pleas in abatement, the court ruled that it was proper to consider the plea in abatement first. Enoch L. Mason, John Miller, George Knowlden, and Richard Treseder were sworn and examined on the part of the defense and Smith Thurston for the plaintiff.
>
> Mr. Geary expressed a wish to have the defendant present. The court declined to gratify the attorney in this particular. Mr. Broadhead then addressed the court in support of the plea in abatement, filed by the defendant. Mr. Geary replied in a lengthy speech. The court ruled that the case was improperly brought, the United States, and Gen. Stambaugh, being the party for whom the labor was performed, and therefore the plea to abate was sustained. The court adjourned sine die.[8]

In the second hearing, John filed his reply as required, but the Court did not let him introduce all his arguments. It is notable that the newspaper describes John's presentation as "three hours speechifying" which had to be "endured" before the judge ruled against John on that point.

Following that presentation, the Court actually heard the meat of the case and ruled against John again. John asked to have Stambaugh present in court, but the judge ruled against him. John then gave another "lengthy speech" but was unsuccessful. He failed to establish his right to payment and there is no evidence he was ever paid for his work. The Utah legal proceedings were likely a discouraging episode for a man such as John, who was sincerely searching for a way to earn money for his family using his professional legal training.

WORK AT STAINES, NEEDHAM & COMPANY

After the legal disappointment during the fall of 1860, John found a different job as a clerk for a mercantile business known as Staines, Needham & Company. This downtown Salt Lake City store opened in 1859 on Main Street near the Jennings butcher shop on Main Street. It was a relatively new business when John was hired; he told Sophia in a letter that he was there only temporarily because their current bookkeeper was a chronic drinker and was trying to reform.

One of the store's owners, William Staines (1818-1881), described the business in his journal:

> "I purchased a stock of goods…in company with [two other men] . . . but they sold out their interest to John & James Needham . . . we purchased goods to the amount of 55,000 dollars and sold more goods in two months than any other house…this induced us to purchase some 20,000 thousand [sic] Dollars worth more."[9]

Staines was so successful that he built the fabulously luxurious home later known as the Deveraux Mansion in Salt Lake City (still standing in 2021 as a historic site). Staines was a Renaissance man interested in agriculture, horticulture, travel, spiritual pursuits, politics, and libraries. He was in charge of the Territorial Library from 1851-1860 and again in 1865-1868.[10] His varied interests and English background would have been a good match for John Thomas Geary's sensibilities. His business partner, James Needham (1826-1890) was also unusually accomplished. Needham was an English convert as well and spent some time in St. Louis, Missouri during 1851-1854. Needham and John may have been acquainted in St. Louis as both men were there during 1853-1854. Needham was a merchant who traveled the plains several times to purchase goods to sell out west.[11] Both Staines and Needham would have had significant influence and connections to help John in his search for a permanent job.

While working at the Staines, Needham store, John wrote Sophia a fascinating "cross-hatched" letter of four pages with two letters written on each page – the first of four pages is written in one direction and then the paper is turned sideways and more is written in a different direction and a different color of ink, with the same approach on all four pages.[12]

JOHN TO SOPHIA

G.S.L. City,
13 September, 1860

My dear Sophy,

I feel quite uneasy on account of not hearing from you. It is now nearly a month since I received your last letter and that was a mighty short one.

Since writing you last I have obtained a situation at Staines, Needham & Co Store through the joint influence directly and indirectly of Bros. J.W. Cummings, J.A. Long and Curtis E. Bolton. I believe too that Bro. Charles Smith spoke formally on my behalf.

I am keeping the books of the firm but, in as much as my retaining the situation for a permanency is somewhat uncertain on account of the great respect and attachment which they feel for their late Bookkeeper who has been discharged for drunkenness but who may nevertheless get reinstated for the reason which I have first stated, I do not feel that it would be prudent to say anything on the matter to the people at Cedar at present. Please therefore not to mention the matter to anyone yet and even your Sister. Do as I wish dearest and all will be well.

I know you wish to keep posted as to my affairs which is the reason why I tell you about this matter now. It is just possible that in the next letter which I write I may have to inform you that I am out of employment altogether for our mutual good. I should much like you to come up at Conference & if I were perfectly certain of keeping my present situation I would say come up on one condition – that you make satisfactory arrangements about everything at home so that if we should have to return nothing would be destroyed in our absence.

I think before posting this I will feel Messrs. S.N. & Co's pulse to find out of what chance there is of permanent employment. I may perhaps ask the plain question whether I shall be justified in sending up for my family. If I can manage to stay where I now am I shall of course leave Cedar altogether – but keep this secret at present – In case you do not come up at Conference in Oct. You will most likely have to wait till next Conference and for my own part I do not wish to act hastily but to do what will really turn out for the best. Ask the Father to direct us both in the matter. I feel in your heart at the time submissive to His will – My prayers since I have been here have been fully answered because I have not asked for anything except what I felt I really needed. Act on the same principle and you shall be blessed with your heart's desire.

In case it should be decided that you remain for the present I want you by return of post to send me a full list of all you require and I will try to supply your wants – Send the list anyhow so that if necessary I may send the things by Bro. Lunt [Henry W. Lunt] or somebody else who may be here at next Conference as I have lost the list I brought with me.

I wish you would send me some sealing wax & a seal the next chance you have as it is useless to buy when I have plenty at home & I wish to spend nothing foolishly. I wish also you would send 'Crittenden on Bookkeeping'[13] which you will find amongst my books. Wrap it up very carefully as it is a borrowed book – I wish to get it as soon as possible. You had better send it by post if Bro. Lunt should not start in a day or so after you receive this. The possession of this book is a matter of importance to me in my present situation. If you send it by Bro. Lunt wrap it up carefully so that its nature cannot be discovered. Know this, be sure.

15 September – my chance of keeping my situation seems to me more certain every day though I do not hold that or anything else otherwise than with a loose hand as I know how in times past my expectation have not always been realized. I like Messr's Staines & Co much so far and do not feel to desire any more comfortable or lucrative Employment in this Territory. I have not yet made any particular arrangements about Salary only that in case I should not remain. I am to receive $3 per day for the time Employed and I have no idea they would think of offering me less than this by the year if I should continue with them. All things seem to be working together for our good and if they continue prosperous as at present I think and hope we shall both know how partially at all events to appreciate the blessing by contrast with just occasional hardships.

I will tell you what has just occurred to me – It is this – If you can make arrangements with Bro. Lunt or Bro. Harrison or anybody else who is coming for Conference to come with him – do so on the condition that you are allowed to return with him if I cannot make arrangements to make you comfortable here during the Winter. You need not say that you are coming up for any other purpose than to pay me a visit and may perhaps stay through the Winter or not according to the circumstances.

You will in case you come, know to make arrangements with somebody to take care of the cow during your absence and I would like somebody to have it that has not one of his own, but I want you to be well satisfied that whoever has it will have plenty of feed for it during the Winter if you should stay so long. I believe Bro Harris has no cow and he is a worthy man. Also Bros. Middleton & Webster too are I believe without cows but leave it with the party who you know has plenty of feed on hand even though you should have to leave it with somebody who has cows. I shall of course expect the party to pay the herd bill for the time he has the cow but he is quite welcome to the use of her free in every other respect if he will take good care of her. I suppose John Adams has herd the cow since I left. I would like to know how much I owe him and will try to send him something at Conference but make no particular promise for fear I should not be able to perform it.

You will have to make arrangements for the calf to be herded to that it can be fed during the Winter. I am willing to pay for it if it can be well attended to. If you cannot get this done in Cedar which to incur? I should think you can do perhaps some of the people at Session would oblige me by taking the oversight of it in connection with their own. As I said before I will pay them for their trouble. I want it put into the hands of a careful man who takes good care of his own stock for it is of great importance to me that I should not lose it. I presume my cattle will be safe on the range.

Both of the sheep will remain with Bro. Seth Johnson as per agreement with him and now about the house and the things therein. You will have to nail up or get nailed up the windows and doors. You had better empty the cellar and put everything into the house. Be sure the house is made secure. Bring with you my double-barreled rifle and moulds also bring with you the silk velvet belonging to your bassinet and all the other good clothing you have. Of course I will be last.

By the bye I have said nothing about the pig and chickens, I think you had better let them out on shares – on halves. I don't think of anything else just now but set to work and do your best to come along and may God help and prosper us both.

I am well and feel well though I have not yet got my money from Stambaugh. I shall sue him as soon as I can find a little spare time. As ever
Your most affectionate John
The moment anything sad comes up I will write you again in case you should not be able to come. Good bye.

There are several notable things about this letter, including the degree of anxiety John expresses about each topic. First, he is nervous about Sophia traveling to see him. Then he asks her again to keep secrets about his situation. He gives extremely detailed instructions as to how Sophia must handle the care of their livestock; one wonders how she would have reacted to being given such a long list of tasks to accomplish all on her own. John also seems to have difficulty managing his own expectations of whether or not his life will stabilize, which is understandable given the twists and turns of the past ten years. He expresses pessimism that he will be able to keep his job: "It is just possible that in the next letter which I write I may have to inform you that I am out of employment…" There is a touch of melancholy in his Postscript "The moment anything sad comes up I will write you again…"

Nevertheless, John is still hopeful that this job will work out and he seems to be enjoying it. He likes the men he works for and he is pleased with the pay. He is considering having Sophia and the family rejoin him in Salt Lake, possibly abandoning their Cedar City farm for good. This indicates that he misses them. He is strong in his religious faith. He mentions to Sophia they should be praying about the direction their lives should take and he is philosophical about the hardships being offset by the blessings.

It is also interesting that John is still in contact with his old friend from British days, Curtis E. Bolton. Bolton was one of the witnesses at John and Sophia's 1852 London wedding and it is good to think he would still vouch for his old friend eight years later. As before, John was relying again on the good word and support of his friends to obtain the Staines Needham job. Besides Bolton, he identifies J.W. Cummings, J.A. Long, and Charles Smith as benefactors. J.W. Cummings was James Willard Cummings (1819-1883) who worked as the owner of a tannery on Main Street in the 15th Ward, was active in politics, and was friends with Brigham Young. Cummings was serving on the city council in 1860 and managing Brigham Young's woolen mills. His granddaughter described him as "a man of large figure, tall and portly, at one time weighing 240 lbs. He possessed a commanding presence, a superior intellect, great force of character…he was an eloquent speaker. One of his outstanding characteristics was charity. Though apparently of a rather stern nature, he was extremely kind-hearted and was especially good to the poor and needy. On many occasions he has taken the needy right into his own home and cared for them."[14]

Finally, it is helpful to read the details of the household issues John worries about, as it sounds like he and Sophia had made a good start at furnishing a new home and farm in Cedar City before he left.

Even though Staines Needham & Co. became financially successful, John's time there was short-lived because the store closed within the year. In the early 1860s, Staines was called by Brigham Young to be the emigration agent for the Church and later, Needham was also called on a mission. There was some speculation that the two men were called away from their business by Church officials because they were viewed as too successful selling merchandise for a profit and competing with church businesses. Brigham Young reportedly said he knew that people "heard that they [Staines and Needham] are sent on this mission because they are speculators" but Brigham denied that was the reason for the mission calls.[15] The closure of their store was a particularly unsatisfying development for John and the Geary family, as this store bookkeeper position was one he described as "comfortable and lucrative" and he seemed happy there.

JOHN AND SOPHIA CALLED TO COTTON MISSION

In any event, John was out of work again by 1861. It is likely that Sophia stayed in Cedar City at least a few more months after the September 13, 1860 letter John wrote her, but she then moved back to Salt Lake City with the children. Her sister, Jane, moved away from Cedar City and it is doubtful that Sophia would have remained to run the farm without either Jane or John for support. Jane's husband, Richard Harrison, was employed at the Great Western Iron and Steel Company at Old Iron Town about 15 miles west of Cedar City. Sometime between the birth of Linna in 1860 and the birth of Jane's next child, Moses, in October, 1862, the Harrison family moved a few miles west to the newly-settled town of Pinto near the iron mine. There, Harrison built them a four-room log house with a dirt roof. Jane had one room and Harrison's first wife, Mary Ann, had the other two rooms.[16]

In the early 1860s, Sophia's brother, Richard Fryer, was living in Johnson's Settlement (modern-day Clover, Utah near Tooele). He had married Theresa Revel on April 7, 1861.[17] Richard and Theresa Fryer had a baby, Eliza Ann, on January 23, 1862 in Johnson's Settlement.

At the October 7-8, 1861 LDS General Conference in Salt Lake City, President Brigham Young read the names of more than 300 people with families who were called to the Cotton Mission in southern Utah. John Geary's cousin, John C. Hall, was among the people called. Hall left Salt Lake City with his two wives and children to help settle the town of Rockville, Utah.[18]

Utah's Cotton Mission in the 1860s is the stuff of pioneer legend. As historians Douglas Alder and Karl Brooks put it, "…the St. George story is pioneering in epic proportions. It is about building a Mormon regional capital in the south. If for no other reason, this was an unusual community in that it was the object of so much planning."[19] In 1858, Brigham Young sent the first group of settlers down to the area which would become St. George, Utah. Conditions there were harsh, with summer temperatures of 100-degrees-plus and winters with snow. Water was either in short supply or flooding out their fields. The desert landscape of southwestern Utah was completely different than the rest of the state, because it is where the Rocky Mountains and the Great Basin meet with the Colorado Plateau. The red sandstone cliffs and extensive volcanic lava make the land less desirable for agriculture, and the steep Virgin River gorge is a temperamental source of water. The early Mormon settlers learned what the Indians long knew; the land was challenging for year-round settlement. But Brigham Young was convinced that the 1861 advent of the U.S. Civil War would result in shortages of cotton which might be solved by cotton farming in southern Utah.

Brigham Young called the first group of 300 families in 1861 to go almost immediately to St. George and set about organizing a city there and planting cotton. Apostle George Albert Smith observed in a speech that, "I have seen faces look longer than a sectarian parson's face…I have seen diseases appear in men that had heretofore been considered healthy…as soon as they heard they were wanted to perform any unpleasant mission."[20] Most of those called were well established in other parts of the Utah Territory, just starting to put down roots and harvest good crops. They were hesitant to pull up stakes again. But they went, and most of them stayed. [21]

When Brigham Young visited St. George again the following year, he realized even more help was needed, so at the LDS General Conference on October 19, 1862 he called another 200 families to move to southern Utah as part of the Cotton Mission. He asked leaders George Albert Smith and Franklin D. Richards to prepare a list of names to read over the pulpit.[22] This time, John T. Geary was on the list. It is possible his prior association with Franklin D. Richards ten years earlier in the London Conference figured into Geary's selection for the mission. John's cousin, Thomas C. Hall, also received a call. Hall was listed as a painter and tinker residing in the 10th Ward; Geary was listed as a clerk residing in the 14th Ward in Salt Lake.[23] John must have found another clerk position similar to the Staines, Needham store job during 1861-1862. The men in the group were called based on their skill set and what it could add to the mix of people building up Washington County. Not all of the people called to the Cotton Mission were required to settle in St. George. Other smaller communities also began to grow in the area such as Santa Clara, Gunlock, Pinto, Virgin, Rockville, Springdale, Leeds, Hurricane, and Toquerville.

TOQUERVILLE

John and Sophia likely did not leave for southern Utah until after the birth of their fourth daughter, Leah Fryer Geary, on December 12, 1862. When they did go south, they ended up living in the small town of Toquerville, which was settled by a group of Iron County pioneers in 1858. The town was located along Ash Creek about midway between Cedar City and St. George. It was at a lower elevation than Cedar City, with a longer growing season, but it did not have quite the blistering summer heat of St. George. Pioneers were able to raise squash, melons, grapes, figs, fruit, sweet potatoes and alfalfa. The original 1858 Toquerville settlers included Isaac C. Haight of Cedar City, his friend, Joshua T. Willis of Fort Harmony, Wesley Willis, Josiah Reeves, John M. Higbee, Samuel Pollock, Charles Stapley, and John Nebeker.[24] John and Sophia had lived near Isaac Haight in Cedar City, according to the 1860 Census and may have known other settlers of Toquerville who came from Cedar City.[25]

By the time of the Gearys' call to southern Utah, St. George had about 500 families, a post office, schools, four Mormon wards, dams, canals, a bowery, a city council, and the construction of the St. George Tabernacle was about to begin.[26] In contrast, Toquerville was still just a small community. In May, 1861, there were ten families living there and Joshua T. Willis was the acting bishop. By December 4, 1861, after the second Cotton Mission call at General Conference, George Albert Smith and Erastus Snow decided to send 10 or 12 more families to Toquerville.[27] The town grew slowly, only reaching a population of 180 in October, 1866.[28]

The date when John and Sophia Fryer Geary actually moved south is unknown. Their daughter, Sophia Ann, recorded in her personal life story that, "I came with my parents to Salt Lake in 1857, moving to Cedar City in 1859, then back to Salt Lake in 1860, and finally to Toquerville in 1861."[29] Sophia Ann also remembered being baptized in a Toquerville ditch about 1862 by her father's cousin, John Hall.[30]

According to family stories, John and Sophia's baby daughter, Leah Fryer Geary, received a blessing from LDS Bishop Abraham Hoagland of the 14th Ward in Salt Lake City in 1863. This indicates that John, at least, was spending considerable time in Salt Lake during 1863 even after having established his family in Toquerville with his Cotton Mission call. He may have been working in Salt Lake and Sophia brought one or more of the children to visit him during the time Leah received her blessing. Apparently, the Gearys still had enough of a relationship with Bishop Hoagland, whom they'd known since their 1856 arrival in the valley, to arrange this blessing. John seems to have stayed with friends in the 14th Ward whenever he was living and working in Salt Lake City. The question arises as to why John didn't baptize or bless his own children? He appears to be a faithful and believing Latter-day Saint, but at least Sophia Ann remembered being baptized by John Hall and that Leah was blessed by Bishop Hoagland.

The records show they were definitely living in Toquerville early in 1864, because their last child, Sarah Ann (Annie) Geary, was born on February 29, 1864 in Toquerville.[31] Sophia Ann told her daughter, Eva, that her father, John, taught school in Toquerville. It would have been a small school with only 20 families in town.

Discovered amongst a few papers of John Thomas Geary are ten pages of his own handwriting, including shorthand, or as it was referred to at the time, phonography. John was keeping books for the Toquerville Ward Tithing Office some of the time. John kept a record of bartering with people for such things as "Dr. Richardson, 1857. Oct. draws 2 teeth for Sis Geary, .75, Nov. 16, paid by 1 bush. Potatoes." (In other words, John paid a doctor with potatoes to pull Sophia's teeth.) An example of his record-keeping for a certain day in 1863 reads as follows:

```
Toquerville, Wednesday, Sept. 16, 1863
Void Minnersly A.       12 ½ beef (July 21) c. 10   000
102     "               11       "          12    132
        "               beef shank   "             25
102     "               2 ½ suet "          25     63
103  Clack  H. Y.       15 beef c  12" Aug 6      180
105  Nebeker John       1 canteen     Aug 12      150
00
91  Sundries    Dr. To Stock
```

133

These writings require some deciphering, but certain themes emerge. John was a meticulous bookkeeper. He was also doing this over a long period of time; his writings include partial entries from the time period starting in 1857 and ending in January-February, 1866. It is plain that the family was living a careful, almost meager, lifestyle in southern Utah. Transactions record everything from a charge for "killing a pig" to "new soles on Sophia's boots." As a school teacher, John was usually paid in food for the time he spent teaching Toquerville children: examples include "9 pints of pears" or "1 peck of onions." The writings tell an interesting story of John's recordkeeping style as well as his daily activities.

John and Sophia now had five daughters to support: Sophia Ann, Echo, Eliza, Leah, and baby, Annie. John may have returned to work in Salt Lake during 1863 or 1864 but was still in communication with Sophia. Sophia wrote an undated letter from Toquerville to her sister, Jane, in Pinto, that appears to be from this time as follows:[32]

SOPHIA TO JANE

(Undated)

Toquerville

Dear Jane

After waiting at Cedar City a week I at last got a chance to get home by the mail. I found them all well and very glad to see their Mother once more. I have got a good cotton warp and will color it and send it to Cedar as soon as I can. I shall not be able to get the other warps for the other folks. Please tell them the needle work will get done as soon as I can and send to you. I found 2 letters waiting for me from John. He is well and doing well but did not say that he was in Bapet [sic] Store. He did not send any calico but a Linsey wrap for each of the children but none for me but this is all right. Please send Dick's pants as soon as you can as Dick's Latter End begins to look Bare. All the settlers in Dixie are to remain as they were. Only a very strong guard is to be kept. But it is supposed that there will be settlers from other parts of the world. I forgot the neck tie you gave me for Dick.

Our kind love to all Every Body
Your affectionate
Sister Sophia

The likely context of the letter is that Sophia was returning home to Toquerville after journeying to Salt Lake to visit John in 1863 or 1864. He may have been working in another store – this letter transcribed by Bessie Snow in *Fate of the Fryers* lists the "Bapet" store, although no Salt Lake City store of that name can be found on the records. The original letter has not been located. Sophia writes about having to wait in Cedar for a ride down the road to Toquerville. She is talking about having obtained fabric in Salt Lake which she is going to use for projects, as well as doing needlework, so she may be sewing items to earn money. She notes that John has written her letters so it is clear they are not together in Toquerville. She jokes about her brother, Richard, and his threadbare pants; she calls him "Dick." Sophia always displays a wry and clever sense of humor in her letters. It is not clear why she speaks of "a very strong guard" to be kept in southern Utah. There may have been an incident with Indians or some other type of passing threat.

By 1864, Richard Fryer was also living in Toquerville when he and Theresa welcomed a new daughter, Annie Fryer, born on February 6, 1864. Richard was teaching school and doing other more creative pursuits at this time, while also working as a plasterer. Richard's family during this time includes wife, Theresa, 26, daughter Eliza, 2, and baby daughter, Annie. They were building a home at 10 North Ash Creek in Toquerville. It was an attractive rock home which is still standing today, as of 2021, and is used as a private home.

John Geary was elected as a Notary Public for Washington County on January 21, 1864. This is further evidence that he was considered a resident of Toquerville in Washington County at that time, although he may not have lived there full-time. The Utah Legislature met in a Joint Session on that date and elected several officers throughout the state, including three men to serve as Notary Public in Washington County: Joseph L. Heywood, John T. Geary, and Eli Whipple.[33] The same election occurred again in 1865 by a joint vote of the Legislative Assembly and numerous state officers were appointed, including James G. Bleak, Joseph E. Johnson, John T. Geary, Joseph L. Heywood, as Notaries Public.[34]

While serving as a Notary Public in the Utah Territory of the 1860s a person would be responsible for administering oaths and affirmations, signing and verifying affidavits, taking the proof and acknowledgements of deeds, mortgages, and verifying any other papers for use or record in the State. John, with his legal training, would have acted as a type of court official, a record-keeper, and a person who could help with official paperwork when a person needed it. The Notaries Public in Utah were nominated by local officials or territorial delegates and then voted on by the Territorial Legislature. This was a position of responsibility and it speaks highly of John that he was elected to serve in this office. He apparently continued to have an excellent reputation among powerful decision-makers in Utah. His fellow notaries, such as Joseph L. Heywood, were well-known and powerful men in their communities. For example, Heywood was a man whose involvement in community leadership dated back to the Nauvoo period. He served as Bishop in Salt Lake before being called to southern Utah. He was serving as an LDS Patriarch in 1860 while living in Panguitch, Utah.[35]

The Geary family life in the early 1860s was centered in Toquerville. John's daughter, Sophia Ann, remembered attending Sunday School and Sacrament Meeting there regularly and enjoying singing. She often sung "solos in Sunday School meetings, at dances and at holiday entertainments. Sophia Ann was a regular member of the choir when she was even so small she had to stand up on the bench by her mother to see. She often recited as well as sang in theatricals…she was very cheerful and, as she grew older, was a regular cutup...Sophia Ann helped her mother with the children and worked for neighbors at a wage of $2.50 a week." [36]

In 1865, John appeared in the newspaper for a light-hearted reason. In the July 26, 1865 issue of the *Deseret News*, he was among the men who served as a community reporter for the newspaper. An item in that issue states:

> THE FOURTH – In addition to the many places previously mentioned, the 4th was in like manner appropriately observed in Parowan and Panguitch, Iron County, and Virgin City, Kane County, as reported by Messrs. William Davenport, A.J. Ingram, John Thomas Geary, and A.J. Workman, for which they will please accept our thanks, and readily discern that dispatches and a crowd of other current items have prevented publishing in full.
>
> TOQUERVILLE – Elder John T. Geary, after an interesting report of the 4th in Toquerville, omitted for reasons given elsewhere, states that "for the first time this summer, rain descended in copious showers during the whole day." "The crops look promising and general peace and good will prevail."[37]

It is charming that John takes time to correspond with the Salt Lake newspapers from his position in southern Utah, even if it is just to report on the weather. John's language and descriptions in all his writings are rich with imagery. These entries also establish that John was living in Toquerville with Sophia at least part of that year.

DEATH OF THOMAS GEARY IN ENGLAND

Thomas Geary, John's father, died at the age of 73 on July 28, 1865 while living at 86 Stanley Street, Leicester, England. His cause of death was listed as "asthma, debility, exhaustion."[38] We do not know if John was still corresponding with his father during this period; no letters have been found. Thomas was living with Mary Browne, possibly his common-law wife at the time, and their young son, Charles. Thomas left a will originally written on July 20, 1860 with a codicil to the will dated June 23, 1863. The codicil provided a one-time legacy of 200 pounds for his 10-year-old son, Charles Geary Browne. The will ensured that Charles and his mother would have no further legal claim on Thomas Geary's estate beyond the 200 pounds. The residue of his estate was to be divided between his sons, Frederick Geary and Elton Geary, with Fred acting as executor. According to probate records, Thomas Geary's estate residue was worth less than 200 pounds. There was no mention of the older Geary sons: John Thomas, Henry, or Thomas Edmund Geary. Thomas Geary was buried in the St. James Church courtyard in Dadlington, near the graves of his parents, John Sharman Geary and Mary Geary, and other grandparents.

As 1865 drew to a close, John and Sophia had lived in the Utah Territory for eight years and John still hadn't found a consistent place of employment. John was then 42 years old and Sophia was 36. John appears to be a respected, competent member of the community with plenty of influential friends. He was certainly working hard at a variety of jobs, some in Salt Lake City. Sophia may have been traveling back and forth from Toquerville to Salt Lake City to visit him occasionally, but her children were being raised in Toquerville. The long periods of separation did not bode well for the family's future.

ENDNOTES FOR CHAPTER FIVE

1   Salt Lake Architecture essay on Eagle Emporium with photographs, accessed February 15, 2021. http://saltlakearchitecture.blogspot.com/2010/08/eagle-emporium.html. Historical Marker Database, Eagle Emporium Building, entry. https://www.hmdb.org/m.asp?m=35804 www.findagrave.com/memorial/37038975/william-jennings; Jenson, Andrew, Latter-day Saint Biographical Encyclopedia, Volume 1, page 244, Jennings, William. The Eagle Emporium building is still standing on southwest corner of 100 South Main, Salt Lake City, Utah as of 2021; it is now owned by Zions Bank. It is the oldest existing commercial building in downtown Salt Lake City. In front of the building stands an ornate clock installed in 1873 and originally powered by a water wheel.

2   Utah State Archives, Series: 373, Reel Number 9, Box Number 07, Folder Number: 089. Also found at the Family History Library, US/CAN Film No. 2258957, Box 7, folder 66 no. 387. Files accessed by Kaye Page Nichols in 2011 while preparing his manuscript, "From Out of England – The Geary and Fryer Families," compiled by Kaye Page Nichols, 2011, in possession of authors.

3   Historical Essay, Samuel C. Stambaugh, Wisconsin History website, citing Wisconsin Historical Collections, Vols 11-12, Stambaugh papers – Pennsylvania Historical Society/National Archives - Letters Received by the Office of Indian Affairs. https://www.wisconsinhistory.org/Records/Article/CS13288, accessed February 15, 2021.

4   *Deseret News*, September 28, 1858. https://digitalnewspapers.org/ Accessed March 4, 2020.

5   1860 U.S. Census, Great Salt Lake City.

6   Alexander, Thomas G., "Conflict and Fraud: Utah Public Land Surveys in the 1850s, the Subsequent Investigation and Problems with the Land Disposal System," *Utah Historical Quarterly*, Volume 80, No. 2, Spring 2012, pages 120-123. Stambaugh was frustrated that he was not authorized to remedy the fraud that he discovered. After the 1860 election of Abraham Lincoln as U.S. President, Stambaugh was recalled back to his home state of Pennsylvania and died shortly thereafter.

7   *Mountaineer*, October 27, 1860, in the Local News section. https://digitalnewspapers.org/ Accessed March 4, 2020.

8   *Mountaineer*, November 3, 1860, in the Probate Court section. https://digitalnewspapers.org/ Accessed March 4, 2020.

9   Evans, Max J. "William C. Staines: English Gentleman of Refinement and Culture," *Utah Historical Quarterly*, Volume 43, No. 4, Fall 1975, pages 410-420. See also information on www.familysearch.org for William Carter Staines, (1818-1881) K2W6-2HQ.

10   *Ibid.*

11   Jenson, Andrew, LDS Biographical Encyclopedia, Vol. 2, pa. 419, Needham, James. See also information on www.familysearch.org for James Needham, Jr.,(1826-1890) KWNT-R1J.

12   See images at the end of this chapter for an example of John's cross-hatched letter and see Appendix for the full image of John's "cross-hatched" September 13, 1860 letter to Sophia. The original is in the possession of Geary descendant Vernetta Page Marshall, copy in possession of the authors.

13   John was probably referring to the book, An Inductive and Practical System of Double Entry Book-keeping, by A. F. Crittenden, Philadelphia, 1847 edition. Crittenden and his brother, Samuel Crittenden, published updates in subsequent years such as 1850 as well. There was an edition for counting houses and one for high schools and academics. The books are referenced in historical textbook collections, including the Walker Collection, Textbook Catalog, at Indiana State University, https://lib.indstate.edu/about/units/rbsc/walker.

14   Taken from a life sketch of James Cummings (1819-1883) written by a granddaughter, Mrs. Clare Cummings Brown, and available at https://www.geni.com/people/James-Cummings/352634616000006486

15   Evans at page 416.

16   Snow, Fate of the Fryers at page 28.

17   Snow, Fate of the Fryers at page 24. Also see information on www.familysearch.org for Richard Fryer, (1837-1875), KWJX-YYF.

18   Barrett, Ivan J., "History of the Cotton Mission and Cotton Culture in Utah" (1947). All Theses and Dissertations. 4506. https://scholarsarchive.byu.edu/etd/4506. Barrett lists John C. Hall's as one of the names called over the pulpit to the Mission on October, 1861 Conference, see page 307 of the document. Hall is listed as living in the 10th Ward and working as a painter. See also information on www.familysearch.org for John Charles Hall, (1821-1890), KWNK-J2X. Consider that – in 1861 - the mother of John Charles Hall, Charlotte Wright Hall, is still shown as living in the London home of John Geary's brother, Frederick, during the same year that Geary and Hall are settling towns in Utah. The families are continually intertwined on both sides of the globe. UK 1861 Census - Islington Finsbury. R.G. folio 9 pg. 128. Digital image at ancestry.com

19   Alder, Douglas D. and Brooks, Karl F., A History of Washington County – From Isolation to Destination, Utah State Historical Society, Washington County Commission, 1996, page 38.

20   Journal of Discourses, Volume 9, Page 200, "Covetousness – Labors of the Elders- Mission to Form a Southern Settlement – Grumbling," Discourse by Elder George A. Smith, delivered in the Bowery, Great Salt Lake City, October 20, 1861. Reported by J.V. Long. https://jod.mrm.org/9/197

21   Alder and Brooks at page 39, "Of the 300 families called to St. George [in 1861], 245 were listed in the census taken in the city in 1862."

22   Barrett at page 316.

23   Barrett at pages 320 and 322.

24   Alder and Brooks at 29.

25   1860 U.S. Census, Cedar City, Iron, Utah Territory; Roll M653_1314, page 755, Family History Library Film: 805314. https://search.ancestry.com/collections/7667/records/34785549

26   Alder and Brooks at page 53.

27   Larsen, Wesley T., *A History of Toquerville*, self-published manuscript, undated, page 8-9, copy in possession of authors. Larsen includes quotes from the Annals of the Southern Utah Mission by James Bleak and the Journal History of the Church.

28   Larsen at page 12.

29   Taken from a handwritten life sketch of Sophia Geary Page distributed at a Page Family Reunion on September 25, 2004. The original or source has not been located; copy in possession of authors.

30   Gardner, Marie Higbee, and Zeenati, Eva Louise Gardner, My Father Called Me Yebbie – Life Story of Eva Geary Page Higbee, Custom Family Publishers, St. George Utah 1996, page 297.

31   Snow, Fate of the Fryers at page 33. Sarah Ann is listed as a 7-year-old in the 1870 census although she is shown mistakenly with the last name of her stepfather, Willis. "United States Census, 1870", database with images, *FamilySearch* (https://www.familysearch.org/ark:/61903/1:1:MNCT-8Z2 : 2 January 2021).

32   Snow, Fate of the Fryers at page 32.

33   *Union Vedette*, January 27, 1864, http://digitalnewspapers.org.

34   *Deseret News*, February 1, 1865, http://digitalnewspapers.org

35   Ipson, Kathryn H., Ever Faithful – The Life of Joseph Leland Heywood, self-published, 1999, pages 204-208, copy in possession of authors.

36   Gardner and Zeenati at page 298.

37   *Deseret News*, July 26, 1865, http://digitalnewspapers.org.

38   Principle Probate Registry Will Index, FHL film #0251177, Research Report by Patty Swenson, 2016, Chapter 2, page 6, copy in possession of authors.

James Willard Cummings (1819-1883) was a friend of John Thomas Geary and assisted him in getting employment. Cummings owned a tannery and was a personal friend of Brigham Young's. He was active in politics, serving on the City Council in 1860.

William Carter Staines (1818-1881) employed John Thomas Geary at his Staines, Needham & Co store as a bookkeeper in 1860. Staines was a man of many talents and built the luxurious home now known as the Deveraux Mansion in downtown Salt Lake.

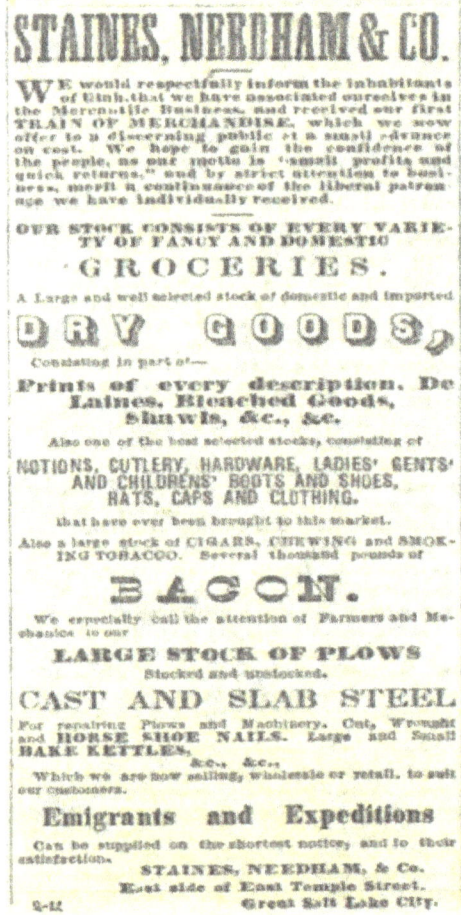

September 28, 1859 advertisement in the Deseret News for the Staines, Needham & Co. store where John worked briefly as a bookkeeper and clerk.

The first page of a "cross-hatched" letter John wrote to Sophia on September 13, 1860. The letter is a total of four sheets of paper, with each page written one direction in one color of ink, then turned 90 degrees and written in another direction with another color of ink. The original letter is in the possession of a Geary descendant, Vernetta Page Marshall. See Appendix for a full copy and transcription.

Toquerville, Utah, where John Thomas Geary and Sophia Fryer Geary settled in about 1862. Toquerville was then a town of about ten families with Joshua Thomas Willis serving as the bishop. At the 1861 October General Conference of the Church, Brigham Young called more families to the Southern Utah Cotton Mission. Church leaders George Albert Smith and Erastus Snow sent 10 or 12 of those families to Toquerville. John and Sophia lived at a home on Ash Creek shown as Lot 4, Block 15. They also had about two and one half acres of fields west of Ash Creek. The Gearys' last child, Sarah Ann (Annie) Geary, was born in Toquerville on February 29, 1864. John taught school in Toquerville during some of the time he lived there from 1862 until 1865. In 1865 he moved to Salt Lake City and never returned. This photo shows Toquerville as it currently appears in 2021 with a population of 1,800.

Photo taken by Kaye Page Nichols.

A newspaper clipping indicating that John Thomas Geary was one of the Notary Public appointments made by the Utah Legislature in early 1864.
Union Vedette, January 27, 1864.

Both of the dispatches above appeared in the July 27, 1865 edition of the Deseret News, referring to information submitted to the paper by John Thomas Geary. He was apparently living in Toquerville at that time.

Above: St. James Church in Dadlington, Leicestershire, England, where John's father, Thomas Geary, was buried in 1865. Thomas died on July 28, 1865 at the age of 73 from "asthma, debiity, exhaustion." He is buried next to his father, John Sharman Geary, his mother, Mary Geary, and his infant brother.

Below: A drawing of the gravestone inscriptions by a local British historian who documented the Dadlington cemetery where the Gearys are buried. Thomas' inscription reads, "Sacred to the memory of Thomas Geary, late of Leicester, Formerly of Atterton, who departed this life July 28, 1865 in the 73rd year of his age."

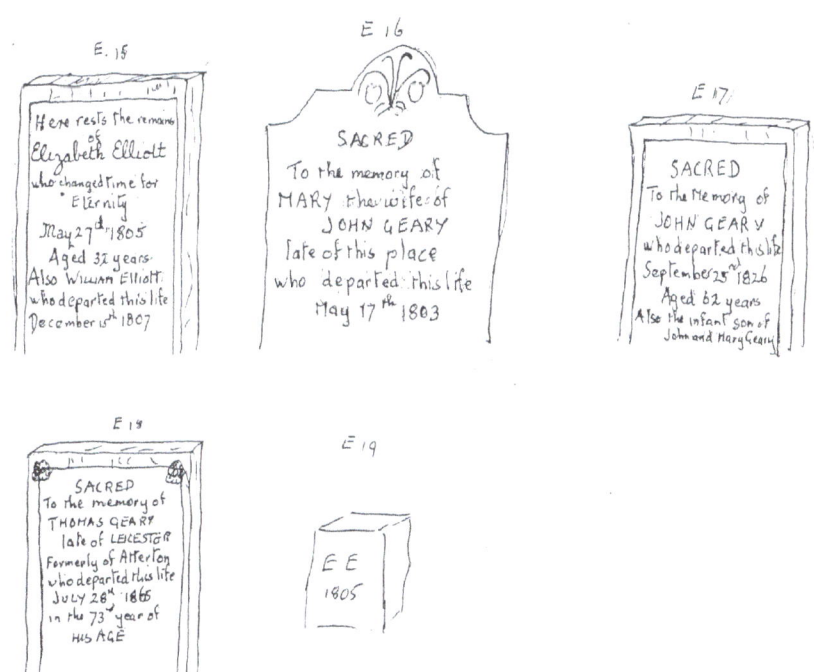

	1			26 50	26 50

1866
Jan 1 To Balance as per
Water Master's a/c   13 35
To am't as agreed
for bal. not © by
him for extra labor
in making out a/c   4 00
error By J. M. Higbee   10 88
By S. Duffin for B.
Bowen   6 47
                                    17 35   17 35

1866
Feb. 13 To above © an error   10 88
By J. M. Higbee   8 10
By John Webeker   2 78
                                    10 88   10 88

1866
Feb. —   By a payment for
dg Hobby Hall   60 «   60 00
By bal. to Ledger fo 15 60 «   60 —
                                   60 «   60 «

An example of John T. Geary's writings when he was a bookkeeper in Toquerville. These entries are from January and February, 1866, the last year of John's life. A complete set of images from John's bookkeeping appears in the Appendix with transcriptions.

CLOUDS OVER THE SUN

"I ask that all of you will try to profit from the few broken hints which I have scattered here and there, as if it were at random..."
JTG

There are many family stories about the events that overcame John and Sophia Geary during 1865-66, but few records exist to either confirm or refute them. One thing is clear; the Geary marriage was in trouble. Bessie Snow, Jane Fryer Harrison's granddaughter, believes their marriage disintegrated due to interference by the Toquerville bishop, Joshua Thomas Willis, and she implies some ill intent by him in her story.[1] Eva Geary Page Higbee, Sophia's granddaughter, wrote a different story, explaining that "John Thomas left home [in 1861-1863] because of the trouble that continually fermented between him and Sophia...John Thomas finally went to Salt Lake City, as it was so hard for him to be near his family and not permitted to see them. He loved his children and wife very much, but could not get along with Sophia."[2]

JOHN'S SIBLINGS

As John was living out his pioneer experience in Utah, his family back in England was also going through some upheaval. It is not clear whether John kept in touch with his brothers, but he was known to write letters often so it is possible. Two of his brothers, Henry and Thomas Edmund, were living in Australia by the 1860s. Henry was working as a medical doctor and married to Temperance Hoysted Toomey in Melbourne, Victoria, Australia on July 3, 1854, about a year after John left for America.[3] Henry lived in Australia the rest of his life, raising ten children with his wife. It appears that Thomas Edmund also immigrated to Australia after the loss of the Geary farm, as records show his young son, John Thomas Geary, died in Victoria, Australia in 1857. Thomas Edmund's wife, Jane, and daughter are also buried in Australia.[4]

In 1861, John's younger brother, Frederick, was still working as a Solicitor's Clerk in London, having moved to 75 Goulden Terrace in Islington. His older cousin, Charlotte Hall, continued to live with him; Fred was 30 and Charlotte was 49.[5] Fred and Charlotte lived next to Charlotte's sister, Rebecca Sarah Fuller and her husband, with whom the "deed trouble" occurred in 1852 (see

Chapter 3 herein).[6] By 1861, John's youngest brother, Elton, was married to Mary Ford, who was two years younger than himself. They lived in Leighton Buzzard, Bedfordshire, and Elton was still working as a Banker's Clerk.[7] Elton does not appear on any British Census after this time.

JOHN WRITES HIS LAST LETTER TO HIS CHILDREN

For at least some period during 1865-1866, John was separated from Sophia and his children, living back in Salt Lake City again. As shown in the preceding chapter, he submitted reports to the *Deseret News* from Toquerville during the summer of 1865 but we don't have an exact timeline of his whereabouts. John did record some bookkeeping transactions in Toquerville in January-February, 1866, as mentioned in the previous chapter, but nothing thereafter. During the summer of 1866, John was in Salt Lake and wrote this inspiring, yet heart-breaking, letter to his daughter, Sophia Ann, when she would have been 13 years old:

[JOHN TO SOPHIA ANN](#)

July 22, 1866
Great Salt Lake City

My Dear Sophia Ann,

I was very glad to receive your letter, but am sorry to say I am not able to make it all out. You delayed writing a long time after your mother promised you would write. Now I hope you will answer this letter at once, which is to say, by return of post. You have improved considerably since I saw you write last, though not so much in your writing as in your composition. I hope you and Echo still go to school. Be good girls, obeying your mother in all things and helping her all you can. Never think anything she asks you to do a trouble, but on the contrary, a pleasure. I will tell you how you can feel in this way all the time. Make up your mind to always be *willing* to oblige her and you will thus find that nothing will be a *trouble* to you which you do willingly. Be ever kind and affectionate to her and to your sisters.

When I was at home, you sometimes used to get angry with each other. Now, if you love your father, which I am satisfied you do, you will try to control your temper and not get angry. You will not always be able to avoid feeling angry, but try to be *silent* till you have got into a good temper. I will tell you how you may do this. When you feel angry, always count ten before you speak, and if you feel very angry, count a hundred. I used to tell you this sometimes when I was with you and I hope you will remember it. If you are tempted to do wrong at any time, which it is likely you may be, you must not encourage the *temptation* by nourishing and cherishing it, but rather walk swiftly away from it, so that it may not overtake you and that you may lose sight of it.

Do not cultivate the spirit of Revenge or Malice; if anyone does you an injury in word or deed, do that person all the good you can by seeking an opportunity to be extra kind to him. That way you will divest him all ill feelings toward you, at least if he has one spark of nobility or generosity in him. This is the best way, the surest and safest method, of conquering your enemies, which you are sure sooner or later to have, since you unflinchingly and perseveringly do right under all circumstances. But *never* return evil for evil, but on the contrary, good, and you will always have the satisfaction of a clear conscience on that head. Remember that Revenge is about the only debt which it is wrong to pay.

If you would wish to avoid misery, do in all things as your dear mother tells you. And neither say nor do anything which you fancy she may not like. If you are at any time desirous to do something, and yet, are in *doubt*, even a *little doubt* as to whether it is strictly right, be sure you don't do it without first asking her advice. By taking this course you will feel happy and lighthearted all the time; whereas by taking the opposite course you will gain only misery and a bitter experience, which you should avoid as much as possible. You can generally do this by noticing, and observing how some people get into trouble and then, avoiding your own account, of the course which led them into it.

You will find as you grow older that observation and the good instruction of those who are older than yourself will be far more pleasant teachers than bitter experience. Though you will, doubtless, have to learn to a greater or less extent by experience, too. If everything always went smoothly with us, we should not know how, we could not know how rightly, to fully appreciate the blessings which are constantly showered down upon us. We can appreciate and realize them in one way only, and that is by being deprived either temporarily or permanently of some one or more of these blessings.

The best way to retain all blessings is to feel thankful and grateful to our Father in Heaven for every one. The water we drink, the food we eat, the clothes we wear, and the houses which we live in, for all of these things come from Him. Pray, therefore, that these great blessings may be continued to your mother, to your sisters, yourself, and to fill those *who desire in their hearts* to do right. And withal, that the Spirit of Truth may dictate to us in using these blessings a right. You, perhaps, may not always have this spirit with you. When you have it, you will feel happy, lighthearted and desire to go good to all; if you will go good, not so much for reward which you may expect, or some punishment you may dread, as for the pure pleasure which doing good naturally produces within you.

Sometimes you will feel miserable and low spirited, and not so kind in your feelings as you have done in times past. Under such circumstances, you may conclude that some evil influence has been permitted to intervene, which for the time being, has deprived you of the Spirit of God. In fact, that this Spirit has been withdrawn from you for a season in order that you may realize and comprehend what a great blessing you formerly enjoyed, and which you have for a moment lost. At such times you will be much more liable to be led astray, I mean led to do wrong than when you were under the influence of the good, kind, gentle Spirit which you before enjoyed. But at these times never despair; do not give up, but in childish simplicity, ask your Father in Heaven, to give you that same spirit again. Though he may delay granting your prayer for days or weeks or even longer, still persevere, all the time doing right, or rather not do anything which you may have the *slightest doubt* is strictly right.

You will never do any *very great wrong*. After a trial of this kind, when the clouds which hung over you have been dispelled, you will actually feel *happier* than you did before. It is pleasant to have the sun shine upon us. But if there were no clouds we could not enjoy the sun. Would you like the hot sun to shine upon you always? I think I hear you answer. "No, I should like to have the sun hidden by a cloud sometimes." That is right, dear Sophia Ann. Whenever you get into the cloud, and have not the light of Truth to enlighten your path, be cautious where you step. And rather *stand still* than slip in doubt. You are no longer a little girl to be charmed and pleased with dolls and such like toys. Hence, I feel anxious, *very* anxious to warn you against saying or doing anything which may be cause for bitter repentance.

You may perhaps think that I am too particular and place undue *stress* on trifles, but I want you to understand that what you may call "trifles" will generally be found to be matters of great importance. If you never do anything which is in a small, *very* small degree wrong, you will see at once that you cannot possibly commit *any great evil*. But if you once open the door to a *little* vice, it will be almost a miracle if a *greater* one does not enter, also. Avoid, then the commission of the *first* wrong, shun and resist the first appearance of evil, and you will save yourself many a bitter pang. The first transgression makes us, to a certain extent, careless about the second and so go on from bad to worse, unless at length they are led completely captive by the spirit of evil which abounds in the world.

There is one thing here which I will speak about. I wish you to take my reproof in the spirit of kindness in which I can assure you it is given. I have noticed in you often, and hence I speak of it. A manifestation of strong dislike at being found at fault, the unfriendly knitting of the brow, the disdainful curl of the lip, and sometimes taken opposition in the shape of words. Now, my dear girl, I wish to see you a lady in the true sense of the word. No person who allows a bad spirit so far to influence them as to distort their countenance and speak harsh words can strictly lay claim to the title of being a lady. You like to be praised rather than be blamed and indeed, who is there who does not? But, dear Sophia, you should not *desire or expect praise* where *blame* is due, but in that case, feel to thank and love the person who kindly rebuked you for your good, for such a one is, I assure you, your true friend.

The best course to take is to never do or say anything to another which you would not be willing for that person to do to you under the same, or similar, circumstances. [This line is worn so badly that I cannot make it out. Next reads:] Do what is right and whether praise is bestowed or withheld, even where it is due or even though censure may be instead bypassed, endeavor to be satisfied, and to take comfort in the reflection that you have done your duty, the hope is sure which has its foundation in *virtue*. To tell you, my dear girl, what I really think. When I see a person who seems to *covet praise* for every trifling benefit which he may fancy he has conferred, and for the simple performances of the everyday duties of life.

I should sum the whole affair up in these words – I really have a doubt whether he or she actually *deserves* any praise at all. I have a kind of disagreeable suspicion about most of such characters. You must not suppose from this that I have any such feeling about you, for I have not. All you require is to have the matter properly explained, to see the folly of a (cause) as the one I have just been trying to picture to you. Esteem those who kindly point out to you your faults as your very best, your truest and most valued friends. And consider those as your most deadly enemies who come to you with flattering words and praise you for some quality you do not possess or, on another account, that is not sterling and genuine. Be sure when praise is bestowed upon you that you deserve it, and feel perfectly careless and indifferent whether it is given or withheld even where it would not be wrong to give it.

I will add but a few words more in this. I shall have neither time nor space to answer your truly welcome letter. But one thing I must insist upon you. That in all I have said, I have been guided by one motive only. That is your best good.

My heart feels to yearn after my children, I mean after their welfare. I earnestly desire to see them make virtuous and honorable women. I know that one way to bring about this result is to teach them good and righteous principles and the precepts while they are young and, therefore, the more susceptible of good, as well as of evil impressions. And now I will say one word, or maybe two or more, to all my dear daughters who are capable of understanding, their older sisters will tell them of their father's love for them and how earnestly he desired their well-being.

My dear daughters, I hope to see you all again in this life, but it is possible I may not do so. This letter may contain the last words of instruction and counsel from your father, thought I hope to write you many, very many times and as I said before, to see you face-to-face. But it will do you no harm, I am sure, to receive what I have said as though they were the last words which may come from me, and for this reason, that all I have said has been spoken from the purest of motives, and love for you though the main part of this letter seems to be intended for Sophia Ann, only it is not so. What I say to one, I say to all. If what I have said directly to her is calculated to her good, surely it can do no harm to any. I ask then that all of you will try to profit by the few broken hints which I have scattered here and there as if it were random. God bless you all – God bless you! Oft think of Father and pray for him that he might be sustained and strengthened under all the changes through which he might yet be called to pass. He prays for you, remember. I don't know how I feel, at least I can't describe my feelings. Surely I shall see you all again, it surely can't be otherwise.

I know not why should, "A child is the brightest ray in the sunshine of a parent's heart," so I once read somewhere, but the sunshine in my heart is well-nigh eclipsed. Trust, however, that a glimmering ray of hope will still be vouchsafed to me to guide me in my uncertain path. That I may under the painful circumstances and unfortunate and shameful influence which, for the present, surrounds me. Be enabled to take for my own guidance in the future, as I have endeavored to do in the past, the counsel which I have given you. And now I will refer to Sophia's letter and try to answer it, but before doing so I will ask that each of you kiss the other one for me and try to feel that you are all kissed by me, through each other's kisses – and bless each other and feel that you are all blessed by me, through each others blessing.

And now, my dear Sophia [Ann], I will try to answer your letter, and in the first place I may as well tell you that I cannot make out all the things you want. I will, however, tell you what I can make out and you must send me a fresh list of what you want. I find the ink I am writing with so pale that my writing is nearly illegible so I will use red ink for the remainder of my letter, as I cannot get any good black just now. As I remember it, you asked me to send a pair of shoes for yourself, your mother, and your sisters silk…[The rest of the letter is gone][8]

Many aspects of this letter are impressive, from John's picturesque and sophisticated language to his deeply heartfelt sadness. He displays a wonderfully wide vocabulary and a graceful turn of the phrase. For example, when he observes that "the sunshine in my heart is well-nigh eclipsed" he sounds both heartbroken and eloquent. Words such as "vouchsafed," "nobility," and "sterling" indicate John is a man who is well-read and gifted at written expression. He constructs paragraph after paragraph of detailed advice and inspiration in an organized manner. It is fascinating to think about how he might have explained himself verbally in person on the same subjects.

John's advice to his daughters tells us a great deal about his own philosophy of life and outlines his principles clearly. He is a man to whom honesty and ethics are of utmost importance. He warns about many of life's pitfalls, such as anger, pride, and stubbornness. He sets a very high standard of behavior for his young daughters, choosing to emphasize times when he has seen Sophia Ann give way to bad habits: "the unfriendly knitting of the brow, the disdainful curl of the lip."

John focuses on controlling one's temper, respecting one's mother, being grateful for one's blessings, and learning from others' experiences. His is a template for a highly ethical life. His advice about revenge and malice is particularly poetic: "Remember that Revenge is about the only debt which it is wrong to pay." One can't help but wonder if he, like most parents, is trying to help his children avoid mistakes that he made in his own life. He does write of wanting to take, for his "own guidance," the counsel he is giving them.

When it comes to vice and unwise choices, John advocates a strict standard: "rather *stand still* than slip in doubt" and "never do anything which is in a small, *very* small degree wrong." He is stern in his insistence that they avoid even the appearance of evil, because it is a slippery slope. In one sentence he even includes himself in the advice, noting that, "The first transgression makes us, to a certain extent, careless about the second…" implying he has some experience in the matter. John's insights are precise. He is hopeful about the faith he has in his girls: "You will never do any *very great wrong.*"

John also gives firm, frank advice about Sophia Ann's need for praise. This is intriguing, as one wonders in what situations he has seen her "covet praise" and refuse blame. His fatherly view is that his children should appreciate the rebukes they are likely to receive and he encourages them to "esteem those who kindly point out to you your faults." He clarifies with Sophia that, although the letter is addressed to her, it should be shared with all of his daughters.

The letter ranges from advice about practical items such as penmanship to advice about character traits such as humility, but by far the most powerful section of the letter deals with John's spiritual advice. He returns again and again to contrasting images of light and dark, sunshine and shadow, joy and despair. He bears testimony of a loving Father in Heaven who bestows blessings and spiritual strength, but then withdraws for a time. It is heart-wrenching to contemplate that John might have firsthand experience with this type of spiritual pain: "this Spirit has been withdrawn from you for a season in order that you may realize and comprehend what a great blessing you formerly enjoyed, and which you have for a moment lost." It is an unusually complex and honest description of religious dilemmas to share with a 13-year-old girl. John seems strong in his faith but in the midst of some personal suffering. He describes his circumstances as needing guidance on "my uncertain path" and he urges Sophia Ann to pray for him.

It is startling and alarming when John writes that this letter "may contain the last words of instruction and counsel from your father." He also writes that he may not see them again in this lifetime. Where does this dramatic prediction come from? Does John have a premonition of his own upcoming death? Or is he referring to the possibility that he and Sophia may get divorced and he will be unable to contact the children? What is behind his stark statement?

As soon as John mentions that ominous topic, he tries to reassure them (and himself) that it can't be true. He reiterates that he expects to write them many more letters. "Surely I shall see you all again, it surely can't be otherwise." But having introduced the idea of his disappearance, the letter takes on a somber tone. Each piece of advice is given additional weight as something he chose to address to them deliberately, feeling his time was short. He refers to mysterious changes through which he "might yet be called to pass."

John's letter ends with an emphasis on love. He feels deep love for his daughters and expresses it throughout the letter, from his admonition that they love each other to his own fatherly love. John believes in a loving Heavenly Father. He notes that the older daughters will tell the younger ones of his love for them, again implying he may not be around to do so himself. He is clearly a caring father trying to pour out his heart to his children in a time of trial.

Two months after writing this melancholy letter to his daughters, John wrote his own will. On September 10, 1866, he used his hard-won legal skills to draft and sign a will leaving all his earthly possessions to his wife, Sophia. The will was witnessed by Henry Oakley and Charles A. Herman, two young men living in the Salt Lake 14th Ward.[9]

SOPHIA REQUESTS A DIVORCE

Sophia's situation in 1866 was precarious. At this time, she had lived in the Utah Territory ten years, given birth to three additional children and resided in at least three different towns. Since marriage, Sophia and John seem to have spent more time living apart than together. Neither of them had consistent financial support. During the mid-1860s, Sophia was living in Toquerville in the home she and John originally shared at Lot 4, Block 15, at 76 Ash Creek..[10]

Sophia's brother, Richard, lived nearby while he was building a large stone home for his family, which included wife, Theresa, and two children.[11] Richard was apparently working as a builder and sometime schoolteacher in Toquerville. Sophia's sister, Jane, lived forty miles away in the small community of Pinto; it is unclear how often the sisters saw each other.

In October, 1866, Sophia took the drastic step of writing directly to her church leader, Brigham Young, the president and prophet of the Mormon Church. In her own handwriting, Sophia asks him to grant her a divorce from John Thomas Geary:[12]

SOPHIA TO BRIGHAM YOUNG

President Young

Dear Brother,

I have this week made application to Bishop Willis for a Bill of divorse [sic] the circumstances of wich [sic] he will make known to you by this week's mail. By granting me the favour wich [sic] I ask, you will greatly oblidge [sic] your sister in the gospel.

Sophia Geary

What prompted Sophia to request a divorce from John? Was it a question of financial need? There is no other circumstantial evidence of infidelity, disagreements about the children, religion, or morality. The couple had lived apart for long periods of time, but some of that seems necessitated by the frontier situation in which they found themselves.

Sophia's letter is marked "received" by Brigham Young on November 1, 1866 and there is also a notation at the bottom of the letter that states "October 16, 1866." The authors are unable to locate the letter Sophia describes to Young which was sent by Bishop Willis explaining the "circumstances" of Sophia's request. Various Geary descendants, including the authors, have made earnest efforts for many years to inquire at the Church History department for access to these Willis/Young files, but the authors were told in a series of May, 2021 emails from Church History Specialist/Archivist Jay Burrup that: "The Brigham Young office files do not contain a letter from Bishop Joshua Thomas Willis regarding the Gearys' marital situation in 1866." Burrup wrote, "we have noted large gaps of records in Brigham Young's office papers during the 1860s and 1870s." Burrup stated that the records may have been discarded from this period.[13]

"YOU CAN NOT DO ANY BETTER ANYWHERE ELSE"

During the fall of 1866, Mormon Church President Brigham Young conducted his own private investigation of the Gearys' marriage and wrote a letter back to Sophia.[14]

BRIGHAM YOUNG TO SOPHIA

President's Office
Gt. Salt Lake City
Nov 13th, 1866.
Sister Sophia Geary, Toquerville, Washington Co.

Dear Sister:

Bishop Willis' letter and your own on the subject of a divorce were duly received and a paper submitted to Bro Geary to sign. He afterwards came and saw me upon the subject and, at my request, wrote his wishes and feelings to me in a letter, which I wished that I might have something tangible to act upon. He acknowledges that he has done very wrong in his treatment of you, that he has indulged in unjust aspersions of your virtue, and that these have been long-continued and that his suspicions were entirely unjust and wholly without foundation. He expressed his willingness to make any reparation in his power for the wrongs he has committed. Your better course, I think, will be to accept his acknowledgements and be reconciled forthwith. You can not do any better anywhere else.

Your Brother
Brigham Young.

By this letter, Sophia was denied a divorce by the highest Church authority possible. Brigham Young was not only the president of the Mormon Church but he served as the "prophet, seer and revelator" for the entire church population. An answer from Brigham Young would have been profound. Jay Burrup, Church History Specialist/Archivist, told the authors that, "The last line in Brigham Young's letter to Sophia suggests that it would best for her and her husband to reconcile."[15]

President Young's letter contains some intriguing references to John's position on the divorce request. First, it is clear that President Young offered John a "paper submitted" for him to sign which may have represented John's potential consent to the divorce. If so, John apparently did not agree. Church History Library specialist Jay Burrup explained to the authors that the paper referred to here was likely a divorce/sealing cancellation certificate. It would need to be signed by both parties to the divorce and a $10 fee was required "before it was complete."[16]

Second, President Young met with John in person. It is not clear if John was invited to meet with the president or if John requested the meeting. President Young does not say in the letter what was discussed in the meeting but presumably John objected to the divorce and asked for another chance. President Young asked him to go home and write "his wishes and feelings to me in a letter." President Young had an open mind as to whether or not the divorce should be granted and was genuinely interested in hearing John's side of things. He tells Sophia in his letter that he asked John to write the paper, "that I might have something tangible to act on." Presumably, Young meant that, if John confessed to certain actions, Young might be justified in granting the divorce. That did not happen.

Again, it would be extremely valuable to have copies of the paper John submitted to Brigham Young, a record of the Brigham Young meeting with John, or copies of John's "wishes and feelings" in a letter to Brigham Young. As indicated with the Willis/Brigham Young letter above, the authors made repeated efforts to locate or access these documents in Church records. (See above and also footnote 13 herein.) It is our conclusion that the records no longer exist in Church records, which conclusion is supported by Church History Specialist/Archivist Jay Burrup.[17] Burrup was extremely responsive and thorough in dealing with our questions about the Geary marriage and the Brigham Young correspondence records. While he noted that the Brigham Young correspondence in Church history files is open for research, "the correspondence regarding marital problems, divorces, and ecclesiastical disciplinary situations is not available for public research, because of the confidentiality of those matters. However, as a courtesy to you I have closely examined all the pertinent records in those restricted groups and found no correspondence, reports, divorce proceedings, or entries related to the Gearys' situation."[18] Therefore, it is not a question of *access* to these documents; they simply do not exist in Church records.

John admitted some hard things to President Young, according to Brigham Young's letter to Sophia, even if they did not justify a divorce. John admitted to President Young that he had "done very wrong in his treatment" of Sophia. This alone is heart-breaking. Given John's high ethical standards for himself (as expressed in his 1866 letter to his daughters) it must have given him great pain to realize the extent of his errors. John specifically admitted to indulging in "unjust aspersions" of Sophia's virtue, that this behavior had "long-continued" and John also admits that "his suspicions were entirely unjust and wholly without foundation."

This is the first suggestion in any contemporaneous records that John treated Sophia unfairly and it comes from his own mouth. Sophia does not accuse him of this treatment in any of her surviving letters, nor do other observers make these comments. The aspersions may be consistent with an oft-told family story that John teased Sophia about being unfaithful. It should be noted that the story was told by women who did not know either John or Sophia while they were living.

According to one version from Bessie Snow, "Eva Page Higbee, Aunt Sophia's granddaughter, told me another thing that may have caused trouble between Aunt Sophia and Uncle John. When they were married, in London, the minister who married them told Uncle John that if their first child was a boy he would know it was his. But if their first child was a girl he would know it wasn't his child. Their first child was a girl and Eva says he was always 'twitting' her about it."[19] Another version was written directly by Eva Page Higbee: "He continually twitted her about being untrue to him. A doctor in England had told him that if their first child was a girl, he could depend on it that she had been with another man, which was not true, and it pained Sophia to be told that continually."[20]

Several things about these stories raise questions. The "minister" who married John and Sophia in the Anglican cathedral is unlikely to have opined with such a superstitious prediction. The Geary marriage certificate is signed by "R. Bickerdike, curate" and general research indicates Reverend Bickerdike performed marriages as an Anglican minister for at least a decade at St. Saviour's, later Southwark Cathedral.[21] A curate in the Anglican Church is similar to a priest and commits his life to a religious career. It would make no sense for a man in that position to perpetuate a type of folklore. Even if he had, why would John, as a devout Mormon, put stock in the opinion of an Anglican minister? And why would such a comment persist in upsetting their marriage for more than ten years on two different continents and through the birth of six children? As for the "doctor" in Eva's story, it would have been unusual for the couple married only five months to have seen a doctor in London; they were married in August, 1852 and left for America in January, 1853. Sophia became pregnant with Sophia Ann in late fall, 1852.

If a superstitious comment were made to the couple at the time of their marriage – not by a minister or a doctor – it could have been made by a fortune-teller at Rosherville Gardens. The Gearys and others, including fellow Mormon Curtis E. Bolton, traveled down the Thames River on the night of their wedding to attend festivities at the amusement park known as Rosherville Gardens. (See Chapter 2 herein.) Among the amusements at the gardens were "fireworks, tightrope walkers, balloon ascents, and a gypsy fortuneteller."[22] Curtis Bolton recorded in his diary that he had his own fortune told that same night involving how many children he would eventually have. The Gearys may also have had their fortunes told that night. We are currently unable to know the truth about the "aspersions" John said he cast upon Sophia's character, but there is no evidence from any source that she was unfaithful to him.

No records have been found as to how the parties reacted after Brigham Young denied Sophia a divorce. John was living in Salt Lake that winter and Sophia was in Toquerville. Did they see each other again? Did John plead for a reconciliation? Were they together for the holidays?

The authors investigated the possibility that a divorce - either civil or ecclesiastical - was granted for the Gearys between November, 1866 and January, 1867. There are no records of a Geary divorce being sought or granted in the Utah Territorial legal archives.[23] Less than two months' time passed between Brigham Young's letter and John's death so it is unlikely a civil divorce was pursued. Further, there are no records in the Church files of a sealing cancellation. Jay Burrup of the Church History Library told the authors, "I have closely examined the index to the divorces/sealing cancellations approved by Brigham Young during his lifetime and found no entry for the Gearys."[24]

Brigham Young was known as an ecclesiastical leader who *did* grant divorce decrees to Mormons who sought them, especially Mormon women. In Brigham Young's letterbook at the Church History Library, the letter immediately following his letter to Sophia is a letter to Bishop Willis granting a divorce for the wife of Wm. H. Hutchings, also a woman in Toquerville. According to the Encyclopedia of Mormonism:

> "For nineteenth-century Latter-day Saints, feelings about divorce were mixed. President Brigham Young did not approve of men divorcing their wives, but women were relatively free to dissolve an unhappy marriage, especially a polygamous union (see Plural Marriage). Such divorces were handled in ecclesiastical courts because polygamous marriages were not considered legal by the government. Records of the number of divorces granted between 1847 and 1877 show a relatively high rate of divorce for polygamous marriages."[25]

Therefore, it is somewhat unusual that President Young here declined to allow Sophia to divorce, although theirs wasn't a polygamous marriage. Perhaps John and Sophia's sealing in the Endowment House was a factor in his decision. Perhaps John's opposition to the divorce stopped things in their tracks.

The laws in the early Utah Territory allowed divorce liberally. If Sophia had filed with a local court, she might have been able to obtain a court-granted divorce under the above standards. The first set of laws passed in the territory in 1851 provided in part, "If the Court is satisfied that the person so applying is a resident of the Territory or wishes to become one; and that the application is made in all sincerity and of her own free will and choice…" a divorce may be granted.[26]

The use of the female pronoun in the law is interesting; in a later section of the law it states that "the husband may in all cases obtain a divorce from his wife for the like causes" but the Utah law contemplated that most requests for divorce would come from women. The law enumerated causes allowed to support a divorce including, "willful desertion of his wife by the defendant or absenting himself without a reasonable cause for more than one year" as well as "when it shall be made to appear to the satisfaction and conviction of the Court that the parties cannot live in peace and union together and that their welfare requires a separation."[27]

SOPHIA ALONE IN TOQUERVILLE

A week after Brigham Young denied Sophia's divorce request, Sophia wrote a letter to her sister, Jane, in the fall of 1866 describing herself as "a poor widow" unable to obtain necessary items for her family. Rather than indicating she was literally widowed, Sophia was apparently using the phrase to convey that she felt like a single mother trying to provide for her children by herself.[28]

SOPHIA TO JANE

Toquerville
November 20, 1866

Dear Jane,

I received your letter and was glad to learn you were all well. Make the best of the clothes. If you could have got me 3 lbs. of gray I would be very much pleased but if you cannot get them I will try and do the best I can. When I send the work and can get the pay try and turn it into cheese so that I can send it up to the city. I got the cheese 11 lbs. and the small one for Sophia. She says she will send and thank Sophia herself. Please send my cloth as soon as you can. I need it so badly. I would have like the gray roos made into jens for a pair of pants but if you cannot get them it will be all right. Do you think I can get some butter and cheese by Christmas. If I could I would like it very much. We are all very busy putting up poles that is to say the men folks are. When that is completed they say Brigham Young will be down south in Dixie for the winter.

I shall be after taking a journey on the wires some day. So if you lose me you will know I am going a visiting. I have been sick with a bad cold and the children are not very well and I have to go out so much to do needle work. What a Horrible thing it is to be a POOR WIDOW.

Our kind love to all
Your affectionate
Sister Sophia

Sophia's letter to her sister makes it clear that she is in dire straits. She is apparently not only in need of clothes for her family, but she needs food. She asks politely for "butter and cheese by Christmas." She is writing in late November and she knows the winter is coming. She does not mention where John is or whether he is sending her money. It is not clear whether the family was getting together for any of the holidays. Bessie Snow notes that in her book that "Sophia [Ann] who gets the small cheese is the daughter of Sophia [Geary] who wrote this letter, and the Sophia she is going to thank for the cheese is likely Grandfather Harrison's daughter by his wife, Mary Ann."[29]

In her letter, Sophia talks about the idea that she is earning some money through doing sewing or needlework for others. In later life, Sophia's daughter, Sophia Ann, remembered her mother as an expert seamstress often sitting at the sewing machine for many hours. She fondly described the skill her mother used in making custom gloves for people and selling them. Sophia writes that she expects she will be paid for some clothes she sewed and she hopes to turn it into food for her family.

Sophia refers to the men "putting up poles", which is a reference to the telegraph system that was built throughout Utah in the fall of 1866. In the November 9, 1865 edition of the *Deseret News*, Brigham Young issued a letter asking the residents to build the system:

> "Brethren: The proper time has arrived for us to take the necessary steps to build the Telegraph Line to run North and South through the Territory, according to the plan which has been proposed…scarcely a week passes that we do not feel the want of such a Line….we wish you to take the proper steps immediately in your several Wards and Settlements to have this part of the labor efficiently and entirely accomplished, so that we may be able to stretch the Wire as soon as it can be imported and put up next season…"[30]

Young gave detailed instructions about harvesting the 22-foot-long poles from local trees and placing them at 70-yard intervals across the sagebrush flats. Each settlement was given an allotment of miles to complete with poles and wire. The telegraph line was in its final stages of completion when Sophia wrote her letter to Jane. It opened between Logan and St. George on January 15, 1867.[31] The ambitious public works project was very important in linking the far-flung Mormon settlements with each other. As Sophia notes, it also allowed Brigham Young to spend winters in the warm climate of St. George while still staying in touch with Church administration.

TRAGEDY STRIKES

In early January, 1867, John's life came to an unhappy end. He was shot on a snowy winter day, December 31, 1866, in a Salt Lake City backyard. The circumstances of the shooting were inconsistently reported in the newspapers of the day. The *Deseret News* reported that John's shooting was an accident; the *Union Vedette* reported it as an attempted suicide.

DESERET NEWS

"SHOT – John T. Geary shot himself, on Monday morning, in the 11th Ward. He went out to fire at a mark and while a boy was putting up a board for him to shoot at, his pistol was discharged by some means, the ball passing through his body. He was living at last report, but not expected to survive." [32]

UNION VEDETTE

"Attempted Suicide – Yesterday morning John T. Geary attempted suicide by shooting himself with a pistol. Various reports were in circulation and we have taken much pains to ascertain the true statement of facts. Mr. Geary was formerly bookkeeper of the firm of Staines & Needham, is a married man and about thirty-eight years of age. He was met by an old acquaintance yesterday morning, about an hour before the occurrence, and conversed with him for a few moments on the weather, when they parted; the friend states that he noticed nothing unusual in either his appearance or his conversation to cause any suspicion that Mr. Geary was not in a perfectly sound state of mind. The only one present at the time of the perpetration of the act was a lad who lives at Mr. Cummings' on South Temple street, where the act was committed. The statement of the lad is that Mr. Geary called at the house and requested him to place a board up as a target. It was snowing at the time and Geary placed his pistol under his cloak, with the supposed object to protect it from the weather. While the young man was engaged in the erecting of the target he heard the report of a pistol and the exclamation of Geary, "Oh! I am shot!" It was first thought it was the result of accident but on inquiry, we find that a few evenings since a communication was received from Geary in which he expressed his intention to commit suicide, and he was for a few days constantly watched, but his friends were thrown off their guard by his apparent sanity. At the time of writing, it has not yet been fully ascertained that the wound will prove fatal, yet it is supposed that it will so result, the ball having entered his left side, and has not yet been extracted. We learned that some private family difficulty superinduced the act."

LATER: Up to the time of our going to press Mr. Geary was still living, with slight hopes of his recovery. His attending physician, Dr. Ormsby, informs us that upon examination, it was found that the ball had entered just below the left lung passing entirely through the body. We also learn from those who were acquainted with Mr. Geary, that he has been subject to frequent aberrations of the mind, and had quite recently made several attempts to destroy himself."[33]

A careful reading of both articles shows that some facts are similar in both reports but the conclusions reached are different. This may be attributable to the particular agenda of each newspaper. The *Union Vedette* was an anti-Mormon newspaper published at Fort Douglas by the military personnel from 1864-1867. The *Vedette* editors admitted the newspaper had a viewpoint: "This paper was established and has been conducted as to its typographical execution and otherwise, by soldiers—men thoroughly competent in their business, and that short of active service in the field they cannot better subserve the cause of their country than by thus devoting their time, talent, and energy to the objects above set forth, *viz.* the propagation of loyal sentiment and the development of a regenerated Utah!" [34]

The *Deseret News* was owned and published by the Mormon Church and was slightly less sensational in its coverage. Its agenda was more oriented to supporting the Mormons and the Mormon point of view. The *News* was only a weekly paper and the *Vedette* was a daily, so the latter provided more details. John was actually 43 years old, not 38, as the *Vedette* reported.

After the shooting, John was taken to the home of James Willard Cummings, with whom he may have been staying before the incident. Cummings lived on South Temple Street in the 11th Ward. Previously, John had mentioned Cummings as one of his friends in his September 13, 1860 letter; he noted Cummings helped him get the job at Staines, Needham & Co. as a bookkeeper. (See Chapter 5 herein.) Cummings knew John well enough to recommend him to another successful businessman. The *Vedette* mentions the "lad who lives at Mr. Cummings," but we don't know the identity of this young man.

Cummings (1819-1883) was a convert to the Mormon Church, having been born in Wilton, Maine. He lived in Nauvoo with the Saints and came across the plains with the initial group. He served a church mission in England during 1850-1851 and presided over a company of British Mormon emigrants who sailed from Liverpool on the ship *Ellen* on January 6, 1851. While he left England before John was baptized in the spring of 1851, John or Sophia may have known him while he served his mission in England. After he arrived in Salt Lake, Cummings established a successful tannery business. He served in several church and civic callings, including a seat on the Salt Lake City Council in 1859. Cummings was known for his charity. As his granddaughter, Clare Cummings Brown observed: "Though apparently of a rather stern nature, he was extremely kind-hearted and was especially good to the poor and the needy. On many occasions, he has taken the needy right into his own home and cared for them."[35] John was fortunate to be cared for in his final days by such a kind man as Cummings.

If Dr. John S. Ormsby was indeed John's attending physician, as the *Vedette* reported, John would have received excellent medical care. Dr. Ormsby (1806-1876) was a prominent non-Mormon physician who had recently returned to Utah from the California Gold Rush where he made a fortune. At the time of John's death. Dr. Ormsby was 60 years old, having had an illustrious career in California and Nevada during the 1850s. Dr. Orsmby received his medical degree from the University of Pennsylvania at a young age but later wandered west to seek his fortune. Shortly before John's shooting, Dr. Ormsby moved to Salt Lake City to join his son, Oliver, also a doctor, and to continue his medical practice there.[36]

Good medical care notwithstanding, John did not recover from his wounds. He died on January 5, 1867 at the Cummings' home. Both newspapers covered his passing, although the *Deseret News* incorrectly reported at first that John was recovering on January 9: "Mr. Geary, who shot himself on Monday, is recovering, we understand from Mr. J. Cummings, at whose residence he now is."[37]

UNION VEDETTE

"DIED: We learn with regret that Mr. Geary, who shot himself about a week ago, died from his wounds on Saturday last. The deceased leaves a wife and five children to mourn his loss."[38]

In the Sexton's Report for the *Deseret News Weekly* in January, 1867 it was reported that 15 persons were interred that week, one who was "shot accidentally," presumably John.[39] In the Salt Lake City Cemetery "Record of Deaths," John Thomas Geary is listed at entry 2928 without much other identifying information except the cause of death is listed as "shot by accidental discharge of pistol."[40] His attending physician at death is shown as Dr. Anderson, probably Dr. Washington Franklin Anderson, a prominent Salt Lake physician educated in Maryland and one of Brigham Young's doctors.[41] His burial spot is identified as D 7 4 in the "potter's field" at the Salt Lake City Cemetery.[42]

In the end, John Thomas Geary died while hundreds of miles away from his wife and daughters, with no family apparently visiting him or making funeral arrangements. The status of his marriage was left in limbo. No one came forward to claim John's body. It may have been that Sophia and his family were not informed of his death immediately, although his illness lasted a week and the shooting was publicly reported. Sophia may not have had the financial means to travel 300 miles or to provide for a memorial. John was buried in an unmarked grave in a potter's field at the Salt Lake Cemetery without any record of a memorial service.[43] A potter's field, paupers' grave or common grave is a place for the burial of unclaimed bodies and unknown or indigent people.

Many aspects of John's life remain mysterious and yet, his strong spirit and fierce intellect are undisputed. His considerable abilities, though they may not have resulted in a clear path to financial success in the Utah Territory, were used in honorable ways. His love of his wife and children is documented in tender, articulate letters. His friendship with a variety of people is a consistent theme throughout his life. His willingness to sacrifice is undeniable, having left his homeland, his extended family, and his profession to come to a wilderness in order to practice his strong religious beliefs. His devotion to the gospel of Jesus Christ guided his every move. In light of all his talents, efforts, and accomplishments, John's lonely death is a sad ending to the brief and brilliant life of a fascinating man.

ENDNOTES FOR CHAPTER SIX

1   Snow, Bessie, Fate of the Fryers, self-published, 1973, copy in possession of the authors, at page 32. Bessie explains, "The next part of my story is composed of stories that have been told by family members over the years. I don't know how nearly correct I may have it or how near it agrees with what others think. Aunt Sophia Geary was known for her beauty. Some people said she was the best looking woman they ever saw. The following story is told of the day she and Uncle John Geary arrived in Toquerville. It was quite the custom of that day for the church authorities to come out and greet new settlers when they arrived in town. Uncle John and Aunt Sophia's company arrived just as church was letting out on a Sunday afternoon. Joshua Thomas Willis was bishop of the Toquerville Ward. It is reported that when he looked up and saw Aunt Sophia sitting on the wagon seat beside Uncle John he said, 'My God that is the beautiful woman I ever saw in my life. I'm going to have her if I have to go to hell to get her.'" This is not corroborated by any contemporaneous records from the 19th century, but is repeated in 20th century family histories.

2   Gardner, Marie Higbee and Zeenati, Eva Louise Gardner, My Father Called Me Yebbie – Life Sketch of Eva Geary Page Higbee, Custom Family Publishers, St. George, Utah, 1997, pages 297-298.

3   www.familysearch.org, Henry Geary (1825-1880), K2FC-H3X. Henry and his wife raised a family of 10 children in Australia. He died in 1880 in Kew, Victoria, Australia. Patty Swenson Research Report 2019, copy in possession of authors.

4   www.familysearch.org, Thomas Edmund Geary, (1825-deceased), L7X2-R84. Patty Swenson Research Report, 2019, copy in possession of authors. The burial for Thomas Edmund's wife, Jane Ann Neal Geary, and son John Thomas Geary, are found in Geelong, Victoria, Australia. The obituary for Jane is published in the *Geelong Advertiser* (Vic: 1859-1929) on Monday April 20, 1875, page 2, National Library of Australia: Trove – digitized newspapers.

5   www.familysearch.org, Frederick Geary (1830-1901), K2FC-9NZ. By the 1880 British Census, Frederick was living at 266 Barnsbury Road, Finsbury Borough, Islington Township, London England. He was unmarried and living with his cousin, Charlotte Hall, who was 83. Fred was 50. They also had a housekeeper, Eliza Swainson. Fred was still listed as a Solicitor's Clerk.

6   Patty Swenson, *Genealogical Report on Frederick Geary 8 July 1830 to 4 July 1901, dated April 2020,* copy in possession of authors, "By 1861 Frederick Geary and Charlotte Hall are found in the Census at 22 Goulden Terrace, next door to Charlotte's sister Rebecca Sarah and her husband John Fuller at 21 Goulden Terrace. In 1863, these Goulden Terrace addresses were renumbered and renamed Barnsbury Road. The census of 1871 found Frederick Geary and Charlotte Hall living in the same residence but with a change of address, 58 Barnsbury Road. John and Sarah Fuller are still next door at 56 Barnsbury Road. This location was less than a mile from Duncan Terrace. Frederick Geary lived here for over 20 years until Charlotte Hall's death in May of 1881." Frederick did eventually marry when in his fifties to Sarah Wilmot, a woman about 15 years younger. They lived at 17 Ambler Rd. Finsbury Park in London until Frederick's death on July 4, 1901 at the Islington Infirmary, St. John's Road Workhouse, Middlesex. He was buried at Camden on July 9, 1901. See also Patty Swenson Research Report, 2019, copy in possession of authors.

7   www.familysearch.org, Elton Geary (1835-deceased), K2FC-W1M. Elton is not found on subsequent British Census records after 1861.

8   John Geary's 1866 letter to his daughters appears as a typed transcript on pages 296-299 of the Gardner/Zeenati book, My Father Called Me Yebbie – Life Sketch of Eva Geary Page Higbee. It is in the section of the book which is labeled "A Narrative of Daniel Richey Page and His wife Sophia Ann Geary Page, written by their daughter Eva Geary Page Higbee". The narrative is a story Eva wrote in the 1960s, beginning with the Fryers' history, then explaining a short version of the Geary history and her mother's birth in Keokuk, Iowa, then describing Sophia Ann's childhood and including the transcript of this letter. Because Eva was Sophia Ann Geary Page's daughter, it is possible that Sophia Ann, as the original recipient of the 1866 letter, handed the original down to her daughter, Eva. On the Family Search entry for John Thomas Geary, the typescript of this letter was posted by Marian Isom on 22 January 2017 with a notation that the original letter "was given to Francis M. Keele" in November, 1947 by Eva Geary Page Higbee. Frances was a descendant of John and Sophia's daughter, Eliza Jane Geary Keele. The original letter from John Geary to his daughters has not been located by the authors.

9   See Appendix herein for a copy of John Thomas Geary's will dated September 6, 1866. This copy was provided to Kaye Page Nichols by Charlie Martin of Hollister, California in February, 2010. Martin explained that he had read Nichols' research online about John Thomas Geary and thought the will would be of interest to him. At the top of the document it reads: "Last Will and testament of John Thomas Geary sent to Effie S. Keele in October 1939 by Marion Clawson. Richard Fryer, Grandfather of Marion Clawson, was a brother of Sophia Fryer (Geary) Grandmother of Marion Keele, (husband of Effie S. Keele.)"

10   At this book's writing in 2021, no evidence of the Geary's home remains at 76 Ash Creek in Toquerville. There is a modern home on the site with the property which is attractive and well-maintained.

11   As of this book's writing in 2021, Richard Fryer's original stone home still stands in Toquerville. After his 1875 death, it was briefly owned by the Presbyterian Church and used for a school, but is now a private home.

12   See a digital image of the letter at the end of this chapter. This copy of Sophia's handwritten letter to Brigham Young was provided by a family member to Kaye Page Nichols some years ago, likely by Vernetta Page Marshall or Melanie Jones. It was not located by the authors in the publicly available Church History online files. The copy contains a notation, possibly from President Young's clerk, at the top: "Oct 16, Rec'd. Nov 1/66, Sophia Geary about a divorce, President Young" and a notation at the bottom: "Tokerville October 16, 1866".

13   Email exchange dated May 7, 2021-May 13, 2021 from Jay Burrup, Church History Specialist/Archivist at the Church History Library to Kaye Page Nichols, in possession of authors. Burrup is an expert on Brigham Young's correspondence files. He explained in his emails that, "We do not know exactly why that gap of records exists. At some point in time many years ago, it appears that some records from his office during that time period were discarded. There is no trace of them in our current holdings." Burrup also explained that the information regarding the lack of records preserved from Brigham Young's office during the 1860s-1870s "is an observation from former employees, some of whom are retired…it is quite evident from an examination of his digitized office files in the Church History Library's online catalog (call number CR 1234 1) that what has survived from the 1860s-1870s is significantly less than the office files that have been preserved from the 1840s-1850s." Mr. Burrup went on to tell Nichols that there is a letter from Brigham Young to Bishop Willis on the page immediately following Young's response to Sophia's divorce request, but that it "involves a different couple's marital situation." He also said there are several letters from Brigham Young to Bishop Willis but they "involve business transactions". Jay Burrup summarized the authors' feelings well in his email when he states, "Lamentably, it appears that all the records related to Bishop Willis and the Gearys that may have existed in Brigham Young's office files at one time have apparently not survived the ages."

14   Brigham Young's letter to Sophia is found in the Church History Library archives, BY Letterbook, v.9, Nov. 13, 1866, page 235. Brigham Young office files, 1832-1878 (bulk 1844-1877); Letterbooks, 1844-1877; Letterbook, v. 9, 1866 June 21-1867 February 25; Church History Library, https://catalog.churchofjesuschrist.org/assets?id=954ebbd5-0620-40f5-86f3-97fa7dbab-8f6&crate=0&index=471 (accessed: May 14, 2021) A copy is also reproduced in the Gardner/Zeenati book My Father Called Me Yebbie at page 327.

15   Email dated May 7, 2021 from Jay Burrup, Church History Specialist/Archivist to Kaye Page Nichols, in possession of authors.

16   *Ibid.*

17   Emails dated May 7, 2021-May 13, 2021 from Jay Burrup, Church History Specialist/Archivist at the Church History Library to Kaye Page Nichols, in possession of authors. Burrup is an expert on Brigham Young's correspondence files. He told us in his May 7, 2021 email that, "If John Thomas Geary submitted a letter to Brigham Young regarding his feelings about his marital situation in the 1860s-1870s time period, it apparently has not survived the ages…" referring to the likely-discarded records from the Young correspondence described in footnote 13.

18   *Ibid..*

19   Snow, Fate of the Fryers at page 33.

20   Gardner and Zeenati at page 297.

21   R. Bickerdike is listed as performing marriages in the Anglican Church as early as 1851 and as late as 1866, according to the authors' cursory search of London marriage records, London Metropolitan Archives, Saint Saviour, Southwark, Register of Marriages, www.ancestry.com, London England Marriages and Banns, 1754-1921, GRO Ref. M1865-St. Saviour 1 d 14. R. Bickerdike is also reported in newspapers to have preached conservative sermons, for example, in the *Morning Post*, October 8, 1857, www.newspapers.com.

22   Curtis Bolton Reminiscences and Journal, 1849-1852, Journal MS_1424-Journal_1852_February-1853_ORIGINAL Curtis Bolton, Church History Library. https://catalog.churchofjesuschrist.org/assets?id=e251d241-3587-422b-8da8-e971a28a71f8&crate=1&index=23

23   Author Kaye Page Nichols researched the Utah State Archives for this information during 2010-2021 and found no such records.

24   Email dated May 7, 2021 from Jay Burrup, Church History Specialist/Archivist at the Church History Library to Kaye Page Nichols, in possession of authors. Burrup went on to say in that email, "Although Brigham Young's correspondence files have large gaps, the divorce files seem to be complete."

25   The Hutchings divorce letter from Bishop Willis appears at CR_1234_1_b0007_v0009_item_474-Letterbook_v_9_1866_June_21-1867_February_25 in the Church History Library online catalog. See also Encyclopedia of Mormonism, MacMillan Publishing, New York, 1992, "Divorce" entry, page 391, cited in Divorce article by Kristen L. Goodman on www.lds.org, accessed April 27, 2020. https://contentdm.lib.byu.edu/digital/collection/EoM/id/5684 https://eom.byu.edu/index.php/Divorce

26   An Act relating to Bills of Divorce, Section 2, First Legislative Assembly of the Territory of Utah 1851, page 83, https://collections.lib.utah.edu/details?id=71677, accessed April 27, 2020.

27   *Ibid.*

28   Snow, Fate of the Fryers at page 33.

29   *Ibid.*

30   *Deseret News*, November 9, 1865. http://digitalnewspapers.org

31   Arrington, Leonard J. "The Deseret Telegraph--A Church-Owned Public Utility." *The Journal of Economic History*, vol. 11, no. 2, 1951, pp. 117–139. *JSTOR*, www.jstor.org/stable/2113125. Accessed 14 Mar. 2020. The telegraph was embraced by the residents of the Utah Territory as a great boon to communication. The Church organized the effort and commissioned Captain Horton Haight to bring 500 miles of wire to Utah using 65 ox-drawn wagons in October, 1866. The telegraph system was built entirely by church members and using church funds. It was owned by the Church for many decades until it was sold to Western Union in 1900.

32   *Deseret News*, January 1, 1867. http://digitalnewspapers.org

33   *Union Vedette*, January 1, 1867, http://digitalnewspapers.org

34   *Union Vedette*, June 11, 1864, http://digitalnewspapers.org Meanwhile, on August 12, 1865, the *Territorial Enterprise* (Virginia, Nevada) wrote: "The *Union Vedette* of Salt Lake is a thorn in the side of Mormonism. It is a Daily journal, published under the guns of Camp Douglas, and the 'Destroying Angels' are not disposed to molest the audacious little sheet. It is the enemy of polygamy and the affects of its broadsides are beginning to be seen and felt. Were the Federal Troops to be withdrawn from Salt Lake City, the *Vedette* would not long be permitted to assault the sacred symbols of Mormonism."

35   https://www.geni.com/people/James-Cummings/352634616000006486. James Willard Cummings. *Deseret News*, May 23, 1883, "The Life of James W. Cummings." http://digitalnewspapers.org.

36   "Dr. Oliver C. Ormsby:The Dean of Early Cache Valley Doctors", by Larry D. Christiansen, According to this article written on www.rootsweb.com, Dr. John S. Ormsby was a graduate of the University of Pennsylvania where he received his medical degree. The medical school there was the first established in America and one of the most prestigious in the country. Dr. Ormsby and his brother left Pennsyvlania in 1849 for the California gold fields and were very successful there. Dr. Ormsby became prosperous and served in the California Legislature. His young family, including son, Oliver, lived in Sacramento and Oliver apprenticed with his father to learn medicine. Oliver later attended Rush Medical College in Chicago as part of a Mormon Church mission. Father and son eventually moved to Utah and established a thriving medical practice in Logan, Utah, where Dr. John S. Ormsby is buried. www.sites.rootsweb.com/-utcache/history/ormsby.htm. www.findagrave.com.

37   *Deseret News*, January 9, 1867, http://digitalnewspapers.org.

38   *Union Vedette*, January 7, 1867, http://digitalnewspapers.org.

39   *Deseret News Weekly*, 1867, BYU Library D45 Reel 4, page 48, Record posted on www.familysearch.org. John Thomas Geary (LLHM-Z2L) entry, by Roland L. Lee, 3 March 2019.

40   "Utah, Salt Lake City Cemetery Records, 1847-1976", database with images, *FamilySearch* https://www.familysearch.org/ark:/61903/1:1:Z6BK-F76Z : 9 December 2020), John Thomas Geary, 1867. Record posted on www.familysearch.org, John Thomas Geary (LLHM-Z2L) entry, by Earl Marshall on October 22, 2020.

41   www.familysearch.org, Washington Franklin Anderson, (1823-1903), K27T-WZ1. Dr. Anderson was converted to Mormonism as a young doctor in Yolo County, California. He emigrated to Utah in 1857 and befriended Brigham Young. Dr. Anderson served in many capacities in the Utah medical community, including being the first president of the Utah Medical Association and a member of the Utah House of Representatives. He and his wife, Isabella, had 13 children and three of his daughters received medical degrees. Dr. Anderson lived in the 13th Ward on 200 East, just a couple of blocks from where John was living after his shooting, at Cummings' house on South Temple. Dr. Anderson was one of the doctors attending Brigham Young during his last illness.

42   Salt Lake Record of Death listing was posted on www.familysearch.org John Thomas Geary (LLHM-Z2L) entry, by Roland L. Lee, 3 March 2019 and by Earl Marshall on April 6, 2014, "Utah, Salt Lake County Death Records, 1849-1949," database with images, *FamilySearch* (https://familysearch.org/ark:/61903/1:1:NQH2-GLK : 4 August 2017), John Thomas Geary, 05 Jan 1867; citing Ward 14, Salt Lake City, Salt Lake, Utah, Management and Archives, Salt Lake City; FHL microfilm 4,139,616.

43   The authors cannot determine what kind of a grave marker was originally placed on John's grave, or if one was placed at all. Nothing with any permanency survived from 1867. Geary descendants have since placed markers there.

In about 1945, two first cousins, Robert Geary Page and Francis Marion Keele, grandsons of John Thomas Geary through his daughter, Sophia Ann, went to the Sexton of the Salt Lake City Cemetery to locate John's burial place. The Sexton gave them the burial information on the cemetery records, which they recorded. Their record, now in possession of author Kaye Page Nichols (Robert's grandson), includes Robert G. Page's comment, "I am glad to know that he [John T. Geary] was ACCIDENTELY shot."

Another Geary descendant, Vernetta Page Marshall, a great-granddaughter through John's daughter, Sophia Ann, visited the Salt Lake City Cemetery in the 1990s looking for John's grave. She discovered the name of John Thomas George (not Geary) on the cemetery records and noted that all other details of the burial were consistent with those of John Thomas **Geary.** Vernetta tried to get the cemetery record corrected to the Geary name but was unsuccessful. Vernetta then talked with her sibling, Elwood Orton Page, and her cousin, Maree Higbee Gardner, and they decided to place a small tombstone marker in the pauper's section with John's name on it. Elwood's son, Michael Page assisted with this. In 1997, they raised the funds necessary for the marker, and having knowledge of the Geary Family Seal with its motto and symbol, had the marker made and put in place. It does not appear that the Salt Lake City Cemetery Sexton recorded this grave marker on cemetery records.

A third group of Geary descendants determined to place a marker on John's grave in a celebration of the 150th Anniversary of the exact date of 15 December 2006 when the Geary family entered into the Salt Lake valley. This family group included the Lee family, who are descended from John's daughter, Eliza Jane Geary Keele. The Lee family was similarly unable to find accurate grave information. When the Lees gathered to place their marker, they did discover the earlier 1997 marker placed by Marshall and her family, but placed their marker also as it contained additional information. They held a quiet ceremony on a cold December, 2006 and read a poem they composed to honor John and Sophia Geary. These details of the two gravestones were obtained by author Kaye Page Nichols in personal conversations and correspondence with Earl Marshall (Vernetta's son) and with Andrea Conley of the Keele family during the research for this book in 2020-2021.

> Oct. 16 Rec'd Nov 1/66
> Sophia Geary
> about a Divorce
> (President Young)
>
> Dear Brother
> I have this week made application to Bishop Willes for a Bill of divorse the Circumstances of wich he will Make Known to you by this weeks Mail by granting Me the favour wich I ask you will Greatly Oblidge
> your Sister in the Gospell
> Sophia Geary
>
> Takervill Oct. 16. 1866

Copy of the handwritten letter Sophia Fryer Geary wrote to Mormon Church President Brigham Young on October 16, 1866 asking for a divorce. The letter was apparently received by Young's office on November 1, 1866, as noted in the top right corner. This notation may have been made by a clerk. The original of this letter has not been located.

President's Office,
Gt. Salt Lake City,
Novr. 13th, 1866.

Sister Sophia Geary,
Toquerville, Washington Co.

Dear Sister:

Bishop Willis' letter and your own on the subject of a divorce were duly received, and a paper submitted to Bro. Geary to sign. He afterwards came and saw me upon the subject, and, at my request, wrote his wishes and feelings to me in a letter, which I wished that I might have something tangible to act upon. He acknowledges that he has done very wrong in his treatment of you, that he has indulged in unjust aspersions of your virtue, and that these have been long-continued and that his suspicions were entirely unjust and wholly without foundation. He expresses his willingness to make any reparation in his power for the wrongs he has committed. Your better course, I think, will be to accept his acknowledgments and be reconciled forthwith. You can not do any better any where else.

Your Brother Brigham Young

Copy of the handwritten letter Mormon Church President Brigham Young wrote to Sophia Fryer Geary on November 13, 1866 telling her he would not grant her divorce. The original of this letter is in the Church History Library files.

Local and Miscellaneous.

TO ADVERTISERS.—The VEDETTE is the pioneer daily newspaper of Utah. Its extensive circulation in every mining camp and city of Montana and Idaho, to which it gives the telegraphic despatches (a whole week ahead of the Pacific papers,) makes it the most advantageous medium for advertising in these four central Territories.

ATTEMPTED SUICIDE.—Yesterday morning John T. Geary attempted suicide by shooting himself with a pistol. Various reports were in circulation and we have taken much pains to ascertain the true statement of facts. Mr. Geary was formerly book-keeper of the firm of Staines & Needham, is a married man and about thirty-eight years of age. He was met by an old acquaintance yesterday morning, about an hour before the occurrence, and conversed with him for a few moments on the weather, when they parted; the friend states that he noticed nothing unusual in either his appearance or conversation to cause any suspicion that Mr. Geary was not in a perfectly sound state of mind. The only one present at the time of the perpetration of the act, was a lad who lives at Mr. Cummings', on South Temple street, where the act was committed. The statement of the lad is, that Mr. Geary called at the house and requested him to place a board up as a target. It was snowing at the time, and Geary placed his pistol under his cloak, with the supposed object to protect it from the weather. While the young man was engaged in erecting the target, he heard the report of a pistol and the exclamation of Geary, "Oh! I am shot!" It was first thought it was the result of accident, but on inquiry, we find that a few evenings since a communication was received from Geary, in which he expressed his intention to commit suicide, and he was for a few days constantly watched, but his friends were thrown off their guard by his apparent sanity. At the time of writing, it has not yet been fully ascertained that the wound will prove fatal, yet it is supposed that it will so result, the ball having entered his left side, and has not yet been extracted. We learn that some private family difficulty superinduced the act.

LATER—Up to the time of our going to press Mr. Geary was still living, with slight hopes of his recovery. His attending physician, Dr. Ormsby, informs us that upon examination, it was found that the ball had entered just below the left lung, passing entirely through the body. We also learn from those who were acquainted with Mr. Geary, that he has been subject to frequent aberrations of the mind, and had quite recently made several attempts to destroy himself.

Union Vedette article on January 1, 1867 regarding the shooting of John Thomas Geary.

> DIED.—We learn with regret that Mr. Geary, who shot himself about a week ago, died from his wounds on Saturday last. The deceased leaves a wife and five children to mourn his loss.

Union Vedette article on January 7, 1867 reporting John Thomas Geary's death from a gunshot wound.

> RECOVERING.—Mr. Geary, who shot himself on Monday, 31st ult., is recovering, we understand from Mr. J. Cummings, at whose residence he now is.

Deseret News article on January 9, 1867 incorrectly reporting that John Thomas Geary was recovering from his injury when, in fact, John had died on January 5, 1867.

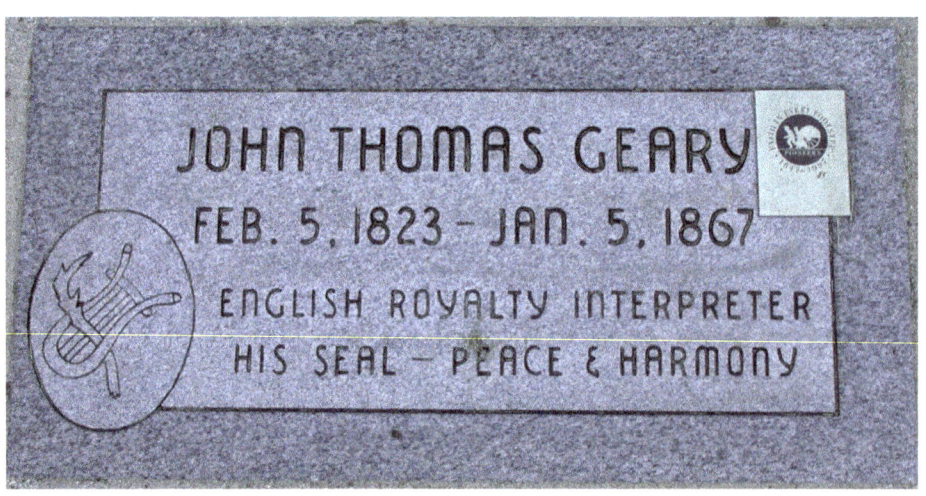

A grave marker placed at the Salt Lake City cemetery to commemorate John Thomas Geary in the 1990s. It was placed there by Vernetta Page Marshall and other family members as part of efforts to locate his unmarked grave.

Map of the Salt Lake City Cemetery in Salt Lake City, Utah with a star on the spot where John Thomas Geary is buried. It is in section D-7-4. This map was posted on the entry for John Thomas Geary on Family Search by Roland Lee, a Geary descendant.

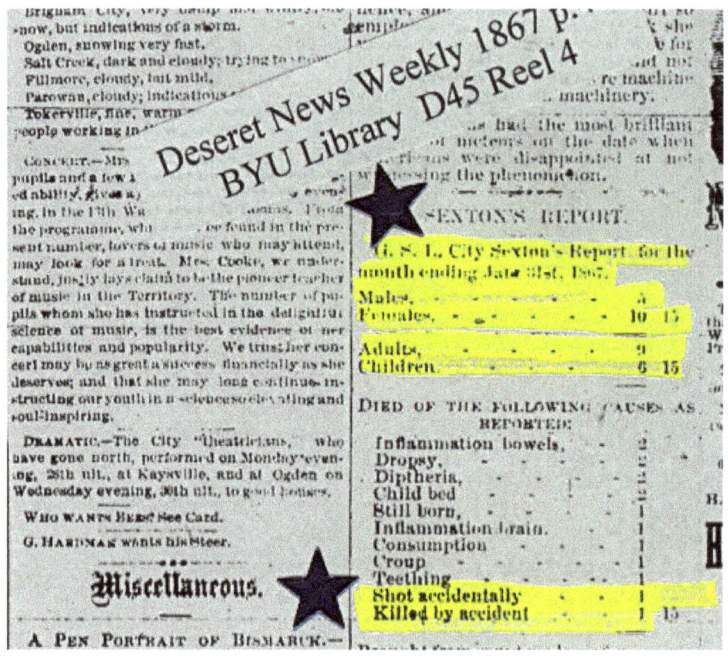

Deseret News Weekly for January, 1867 where the city's deaths were reported. John Thomas Geary is not listed by name but is presumably included in the listing of 1 person "shot accidentally." This was posted on the entry for John Thomas Geary on Family Search by Roland Lee, a Geary descendant.

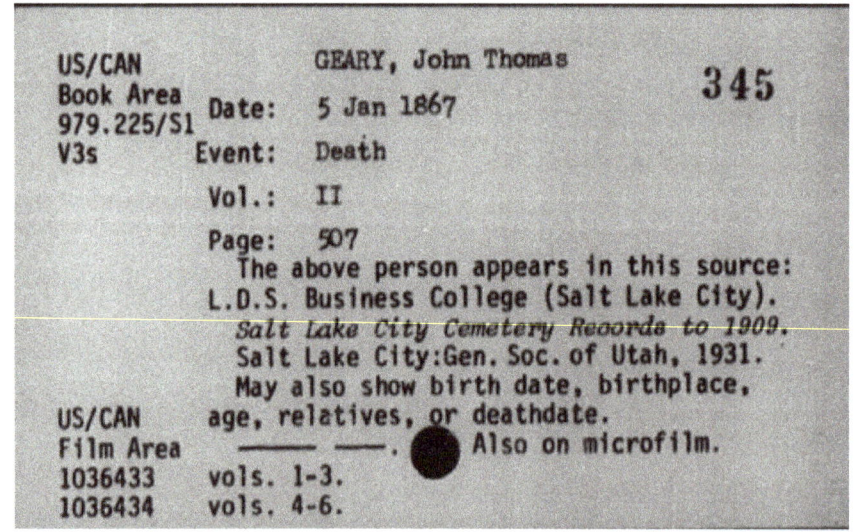

This is the information on John Thomas Geary's death located at the Church Family History Library.

This Record of Deaths document is shown in two parts.
<u>Above</u>, the left side of the page, showing John Thomas Geary as entry 2928.
<u>Below</u>, the right side of the same page, showing Geary was born in England, "shot by accident," attended by Dr Anderson, and buried in the Potter's Field at D 7 4.
This is posted on the John Thomas Geary entry on Family Search by Roland Lee, a Geary descendant.

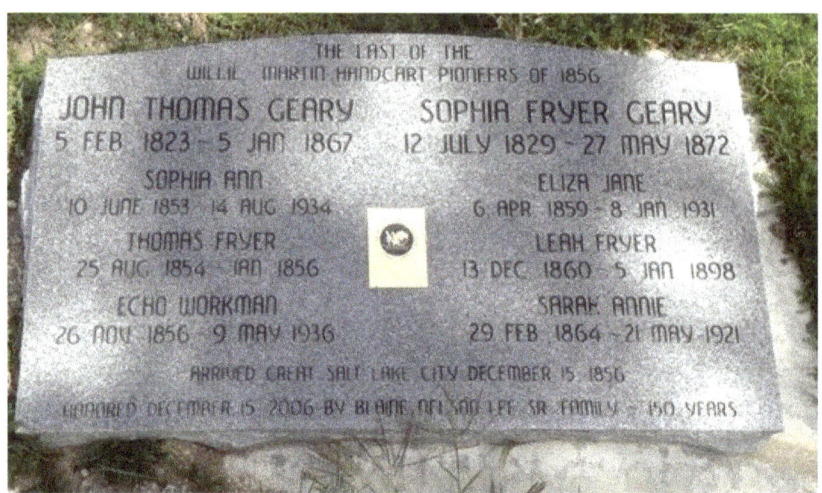

The grave marker placed at the burial site of John Thomas Geary in the Salt Lake City Cemetery, D 7 4. This stone lists both John and Sophia although Sophia is buried in the Toquerville, Utah cemetery. It also lists their children's names; they are buried in various other cemeteries. The lettering at the top reads, "The last of the Willie - Martin Handcart Pioneers of 1856" and the lettering at the bottom reads, "Arrived Great Salt Lake City December 15, 1856
Honored December 15, 2006 by Blaine Nelson Lee, Sr. Family - 150 years."
The Lee family descends from John and Sophia's daughter, Eliza Jane Geary Keele.
(Kelley Bollinger photo)

View looking west from the burial place of John Thomas
Geary at the Salt Lake City Cemetery. May, 2021.
(Lisa Michele Church photo)

AFTERMATH

"I request said wife to keep and transmit to our children and their children,
to the latest generation, my gold seal presented to me by my dear father..."
JTG

After John's death, thirty-seven-year-old Sophia was left with financial and family challenges as a single mother of five young daughters: Sophia Ann, 13, Echo, 10, Eliza, 7, Leah, 6, and Annie, 2. Although John had recently written a will leaving everything to Sophia, his will wouldn't be filed for probate for almost a decade. Sophia stayed in their Toquerville log home, located on a lot with fruit trees and grapevines. The other assets John listed in his will included a field lot containing two and a half acres in the "new fields" west side of Ash Creek, a silver watch in possession of St. George watch repairman, Charles Smith, two cattle, two or three steers on Smith's herd-ground, his trunk, wearing apparel, books and papers, his gold seal from his father and his other personal effects (presumably also the 1629 Geary Family Bible). None of these things would have provided financial stability for Sophia. Interestingly, in John's September, 1866 will, he specifically provided that the items he left Sophia "shall not be subject or liable to the control, debts, liabilities or any agreements of any husband or husbands with whom she may entrust it." In other words, John contemplated the idea that she might remarry.

SOPHIA REMARRIES

Indeed, Sophia began entertaining offers of marriage shortly after John's death. Family stories emphasize that Sophia's bishop, Joshua Thomas Willis, had previously made comments to the effect that he found Sophia attractive.[1] There is no first-hand documentation for these stories, but Sophia and Joshua did know each other. Toquerville was a small town of only about 41 families in the 1860s and Willis had been bishop since 1862. Willis helped Sophia with her application for a divorce from John Thomas Geary and reportedly submitted his own letter supportive of her request to Church President Brigham Young. He was the husband of two other wives (Sarah and Ellen) and the father to at least seven children by 1867. He was not wealthy, but he did have the means to support his families. He would have been familiar with Sophia's situation in that, after John's death, she had no means of support and several small children.

In the spring of 1867, Sophia wrote to her sister about some proposals of marriage. It was a light-hearted letter considering the circumstances, demonstrating Sophia's resilience.[2]

SOPHIA TO JANE

Toquerville
May 7, 1867
Dear Jane,

When Brother Willis returned from St. George he said Brother Harrison was coming here so I looked and waited but no, lo, Brother Harrison and now unless you come very soon I would like you to put off your visit until I come back from Salt Lake City, or I would rather see you when our peaches and grapes and all our fruit is ripe. Please send and tell me what you think of my choice (my young man). I rather think you will feel to say, Why you can suit yourself. Well I think I have done the best from the many hearts and hands offered. Brother Willis is the one I have chosen. Now is the time to speak or forever hold your tongue. I'll quit. Before going to the city I will send the work. My health of late has been very poor. I have done but very little. Sophia and the other children send their love to all your children. They say bring them with you when you come. Give my love to Mary Ann and tell her I will call and see her sisters. I passed by her brother in the city but he did not know me and I did not try to get in his way but I believe he would have treated me well if I had made myself known to him.

I suppose Heber has got married before this. Still I do not know where the young woman lives – I think in Pinto. Tell him to come here. There are quite a lot of fine-looking girls and good girls in Toquerville. Today I have sent a letter to Frank. Remember me to Brother Harrison. My kind love to all.

Your sister, Sophia

The letter displays Sophia's sense of humor, joking that Willis is her "young man" when in fact he was 49 years old at the time and she was in her 30s. She is also somewhat playful in imagining the conversation with her sister telling her "you can suit yourself." Sophia sounds excited at the remarriage prospect. The sisters would soon share the experience of being a plural wife.

Sophia also mentions several other people in the letter. "Mary Ann" is Jane's sister wife, the first wife of Richard Harrison, whom he had married when they were both young people in England. Mary Ann's story is an interesting one because she and four siblings joined the Mormon Church as young people in England; they emigrated to Nauvoo in the 1840s leaving their parents and other siblings behind. All came across the plains in 1847 and settled in Utah. Mary Ann was close to her brothers, Moses and George, who had families in Utah. Moses died in 1852 so presumably Sophia was referred to seeing George Whittaker "in the city." Mary Ann's sisters, Sophia and Harriett, were both plural wives of Apostle John Taylor and Sophia was planning to call on them during her Salt Lake trip. "Heber" is Heber Harrison, Jane's stepson. Heber was the 20-year-old son of Richard and Mary Ann; he did not marry until 1870 when he married Ellen Eldridge and established his home in Pinto. At the time of Sophia's letter, Jane, 59, and Mary Ann, 56, were sharing the Harrison home in Pinto and raising seven children between them. "Frank" is Jane's son Frank Jorden, Jr. with her first husband, who had left Utah as a young man.[3]

Sophia refers several times in the letter to her upcoming trip to Salt Lake City, which means she already planned her marriage trip with Willis before writing for her sister's blessing. A little more than a month after Sophia's letter to Jane, Sophia and Joshua traveled to Salt Lake City and were married at the Endowment House on June 15, 1867. Sophia became his third plural wife.

Joshua Thomas Willis was the fifth child of Merrill and Margaret Willis. He was born on December 21, 1818 in Gallatin County, Illinois. Joshua married as a young man and had two small children. Tragically, both his wife and two children died during the early 1840s. Shortly thereafter, Joshua, his parents, and some siblings joined the Mormon Church. They emigrated to the Utah Territory in the summer of 1847. Joshua was then 29 years old. He married Sarah Melissa Dodge on July 2, 1848 and they settled in Provo, where Joshua served as sheriff. Joshua and Sarah eventually had 16 children together, although some died in infancy.

In 1853, Joshua and Sarah were called by Church leaders to help settle Cedar City. After a few years there, Church leaders sent them to help establish the new settlement of Toquerville on Ash Creek near St. George. Joshua was called to be the first branch president in the community of nineteen families. He worked closely with Church President Brigham Young who gave him assignments to develop industries which would support the pioneer families, including raising cotton, silk worms, and grapes. Joshua built the first water-powered flour mill in southern Utah. He was called to be the bishop of the Toquerville Ward in 1862 when there were a few hundred people living there. In 1864 Joshua married a second wife, Ellen Aldridge, with whom he had three sons.

Sophia's remarriage decision could have been based on a number of practical reasons. Financial security certainly played a part, as well as religious commitment to marry within her faith. She may have wanted to stay in Toquerville, a familiar community for her children and still the home of her brother, Richard Fryer. She mentions being in poor health, so possibly she needed help with medical challenges. It is likely she felt respect or even affection for Willis. Whatever her reasons, she made her decision within a few months of being widowed. Willis was the bishop of Toquerville and a community leader with a direct relationship to Brigham Young. Willis' large brick home was located on the lot at modern-day 476 North Springs Drive in Toquerville. It appears that Sophia did not move into the Willis home but remained in the home on Ash Creek which she had shared with John. Sophia's life may have stabilized after her marriage to Bishop Willis, but she was still sewing buckskin and silk beaded gloves to make money. In an undated letter to her sister Jane, she describes the difficult economics of buying beading supplies for the gloves and trying to sell enough gloves to cover her costs and make a profit.[4]

SOPHIA TO JANE

Dear Jane,

I have at last sent you the gloves. Charge 50 cents. I would like the money if I can get it. I cannot buy my beading without money. I will send you the other gloves the next time. Get what money you can and the rest in store goods. I suppose it is not good to ask for cheese or butter. I could do with a few pounds of (illegible). Our fruit is about gone and I am glad of it. There is so much work with it.

I am kept busy making gloves for Duffins. It pays me very well but I do not get any money. I have to take my pay in such things as he brings in from Pioche. I think Heber ought to get himself a fine pair of gloves. Could I sell some ladies fine gloves among some of your friends. If you could sell some for me I should pay my agent for her trouble. But do not say anything to Duffins about it. Thanks for the cloth Dick brought me. All our love to you,

From your sister Sophia Willis

"Duffins" in Sophia's letter refers to Duffin's Store in Leeds, a town adjacent to Toquerville.

Isaac Duffin (1826-1883), the proprietor, was a long-time Mormon pioneer who was called to Dixie in 1862 to help build roads. There he started a mercantile business and freighted produce to Pioche, Nevada, a mining town. He had a silver mine (called the Duffin Mine) five miles southwest of Toquerville, near the Virgin River. He also had dealings in Silver Reef during its heyday in the 1860s and 1870s. Sophia would have been able to sell her gloves at the prosperous Duffin's Store or in the mining communities where Duffin hauled goods, but apparently she did not receive money, just goods in return. Sophia did not want Isaac Duffin to know she was also trying to sell gloves directly in Pinto through her sister.[5]

SOPHIA'S CHILDREN WITH JOSHUA WILLIS

In late 1867, a few months after remarrying, Sophia, 38, became pregnant with her first child with Joshua Willis. On May 22, 1868, she gave birth to a boy, William Richard Willis. It must have been an interesting change for Sophia to have a baby boy after raising so many girls. Even after Sophia's plural marriage to Willis, her older girls continued to go out to work in other people's homes to supplement the family income. Sophia's oldest daughter, fourteen-year-old Sophia Ann, was working for a "Mr. Birch" who apparently had a family in St. George. Other families for whom Sophia Ann worked included Ann Knell and Charity and Mary Thornton in Pinto. She earned $2.50 per week during this type of job, usually living with the families and helping with household chores.[6]

Sophia Willis wrote to her sister, Jane, in 1869 when she was pregnant with her second Willis baby. She was busy fighting grasshoppers in her garden:[7]

SOPHIA TO JANE

Toquerville
June 7, 1869

Dear Jane,

I thought I would send you a few lines to let you know that we are not dead yet. I have just come from the garden with a big mess of peas. I wish I could send you a sack full I would. We have plenty but some of the gardens are bare as if it were winter. The grasshoppers have eaten up everything. I got a letter from Dick. They will not be back for 2 months. He intends to stay and work if he can. I have his two children staying with me.

Sophie has come home again. Mr. Birch is played out. He is done up. Brown can't afford to keep a girl any longer. So you may expect Sophia over there the first chance she can get. I think in two weeks. I wish I could get my pan. I went in such a hurry to St. George or I could have taken some rags and the honey but I had no time to think. Tell me if there is any chance of selling any more work and what the chance of getting wool.

If the grasshoppers will keep away I think we will have some grapes and other fruit. But at present things look very strange. Bread seems all gone. All our people are planting cane seed and corn and cotton. But whether we will get a crop is yet to be seen. Our kind love to all the folks at home.

From your affectionate sister, Sophia Willis

Despite having a new husband and family, Sophia is still focused on where she is getting her food supplies and she is still sewing for money. "Dick" refers to Sophia's brother, Richard Fryer, who was apparently out of town working with his wife, Theresa. Sophia was keeping his two children, Eliza, 7, and Annie, 5. The girls would have fit in well with Sophia's younger girls, Leah, 10, and Annie, 4, and her one-year-old baby boy, William. Sophia was pregnant again by 1869; she gave birth to a baby girl, Laura Adina Willis, on February 17, 1870. She was busy with four small children to care for again, as well as watching her older girls find their way out into the world.

SOPHIA DIES IN CHILDBIRTH

Just as Sophia was beginning the second act of an already eventful life, she died in childbirth with her third Willis child. Sophia became pregnant again in 1871 when she was 42 years old. Having already borne two children in the past four years, Sophia's health might have been precarious during what would have been her ninth pregnancy. Sophia still had Leah, Annie, William, and baby, Laura Adina, to take care of at home, assuming her three older girls (Sophia Ann, 19, Echo, 16, Eliza, 13) were working outside the home.

A family story from her granddaughter, Eva, paints a poignant picture of Sophia's state of mind during the spring of 1872 as she watched her daughter, Sophia Ann, leave home one day:

> "Sophia Ann was making preparations to go to Long Valley[sic], to work for Mrs. Prime Coleman out at their ranch. She said goodbye to her dear mother and little sisters, took her bundle of clothes and strolled down the path to where her ride was waiting for her. It is said by one of her small sisters that Sophia, sitting at her sewing machine and watching her daughter go, laid her head on her folded arms at the machine. Weeping bitterly said, 'Oh, I shall never see that girl again.'"[8]

(This story misidentifies the residence of the Colemans as "Long Valley" when it was actually "Spring Valley" near the Nevada border.) Sophia was apparently still sewing for money during her last pregnancy. A few short months after Sophia Ann left home, her mother died. Both Eva Geary Page Higbee and Bessie Snow describe Sophia Fryer Geary Willis' death in heart-breaking terms:

EVA:

> "It was during Sophia Ann's stay at Long Valley that Sophia was confined and died in childbirth on May 27, 1872. The baby boy died, also. Mr. Willis buried Sophia and the baby in the same casket without letting Sophia Ann know one thing about her mother's death. He never did send word to her. Some three weeks later, a friend of Sophia Ann's was out in Long Valley and told her about this event. Sophia Ann, using her own words, said, "Grief and sorrow were terrible to bear, but there was nothing else for me to do but try and drown my sorrow in work."[9]

FATE OF THE FRYERS:

> "Not long before Aunt Sophia's last Willis child was born, her oldest child, Sofy, went out in Long Valley to work. She got a chance to ride out with one of the neighbors who was going there. She says when she got ready to tell her Mother goodbye, her Mother leaned her head over on the sewing machine, where she was working, and began to cry and said, 'Im sure I'll never see you again...Three weeks later Aunt Sofy met one of her Toquerville friends who told her of her Mother's death and burial."[10]

The idea that Sophia Fryer Geary Willis died without having her older girls with her is a difficult one to accept. She fought so hard to support her family and to make the best of her challenging pioneer life. For a woman who had traveled around the world from the Isle of Wight to Toquerville,

Utah in the name of love and religion, this was a tragic ending.

It is not clear what happened to Sophia's children or her possessions immediately at the time of her death. Joshua Willis, as her widower, would have had the right to make decisions about them. It does not appear that Sophia had written her own will. John's will from 1866 had not yet been filed for probate. Presumably Sophia Ann, as the oldest daughter, was able to reclaim her father's Geary Family Bible and his family seal, as those are still in possession of Geary family members to this day. Also a few other trinkets were preserved for posterity, such as a pair of embroidered leather gloves made by Sophia, the book she received at her marriage in the London cathedral, and the professional hand-tinted portraits of John and Sophia. These items and others remain in the family as precious treasures. With all the chaos of John's sudden death, followed by Sophia's untimely one a few years later, the children were left adrift. There was little chance that many of the Geary personal effects would be preserved into the next century.

One particularly touching family story about Sophia's deathbed scene deserves inclusion here. This version was told by Wilma Higbee (a great-granddaughter of Sophia) to one of the authors on June 14, 2000, but it has been told by various members of the family and even outsiders from the community for generations.[11]

WILMA HIBGEE KEMP STORY

"Told to Wilma Higbee Kemp by her Aunt Golda Page Smith, on 31 March 1973.

This came from Aunt Caddie Slack (Caroline Amelia Lamb Slack), who was Grandma Lorine Isabel Lamb Higbee's sister, concerning the death of Wilma's great-grandmother, Sophia Fryer Geary Willis.
This event took place 27 May 1872 in Toquerville, Utah.

Aunt Caddie told my grandmother, Sophia Ann Geary Page, that the night great-grandmother Geary [Willis], was confined, she had been terribly sick all day and they were afraid she was going to die. Grandma Lamb, Aunt Caddie's mother, asked her to go down the street to Sister Dodge's place, and get a start of yeast. So she took some sugar in a cup and sauntered down the street.

All of a sudden she looked up and there was a man standing in front of her, she knew he hadn't been there a minute before. She thought to herself, "Well if I didn't know that John Thomas Geary was dead I would say that was him." The more she looked at him the more she knew it was him, his walk, his build, everything about him. She didn't take her eyes off him and he walked in front of her until he got to Willis' house. The lower bar to the fence opening was down, and when the man got to this point he ducked down, going under and then straight to the door.

He didn't stop to knock, he opened the front door and went in. So she said she did the very same things he did, but when she got to the door she knocked and they opened the door to let her in. She looked around expecting to see a man, but there was none to be seen anywhere.

"Who was that man who came in here just before I did?" she asked the ladies who were present.

They said, "No man came in here that we saw."

She said, "Yes there was, I could swear that it was John Thomas Geary."

About that time she said Great-grandmother Geary [Willis] looked up with the most heavenly expression on her face and said, "Why, John Thomas Geary what are you doing here?"

Then she reached her arms up as if putting them around someone and fell back on her pillow dead.

With the deaths of both John and Sophia Geary, the epic that began with two Mormon converts being married in an elegant London cathedral in 1852 came to a sad end on the Utah desert. During their 14 years of marriage John and Sophia sailed across oceans, bid goodbye permanently to their families of origin, endured suffering and primitive conditions in the American wilderness, crossed the plains in one of the most desperate overland expeditions, persevered to help build a new community in the Salt Lake valley, pioneered another new community in the remote canyons of southern Utah, and raised beautiful and accomplished children.

Through it all, both John and Sophia Geary kept some of their most optimistic qualities, including Sophia's humor and John's poetic imagination. Their tremendous work ethic helped them survive against difficult odds and they displayed a fierce sense of making the best of things. John and Sophia embodied faith, courage and character that reverberates among their descendants, who still haven't forgotten them 150 years later.

ENDNOTES FOR CHAPTER SEVEN

1 The family story about Sophia and Bishop Willis is told in Snow, <u>Fate of the Fryers</u>, see footnote 1 in Chapter Six and also in Gardner, Marie Higbee and Zeenati, Eva Louise Gardner, <u>My Father Called Me Yebbie – Life Story of Eva Geary Page Higbee,</u> Custom Family Publishing, St. George, Utah, 1996, page 344, quoting from a December 22, 1974 Letter from Eleen Higbee Harris, Eva's daughter. The letter tells the family story about Sophia's arrival in Toquerville in the 1860s: "I have heard our mother [Eva Geary Page, daughter of Sophia Ann Geary Page] tell the story many times about the day John Thomas and Sophia pulled their wagon into the church yard at Toquerville. Joshua Thomas Willis, standing nearby, made this comment, 'That is the most beautiful woman I have ever seen and I intend to marry her someday.'" It is important to note that neither Eva nor Eleen would have met or spoken with Sophia Fryer Geary during her lifetime, so the most likely source of this story is Sophia Fryer Geary's daughter, Sophia Ann. Sophia Ann would have been a young girl when the alleged incident happened.

2 Snow, <u>Fate of the Fryers</u>, at page 34. The original letter has not been located.

3 Family history information found at <u>www.familysearch.org</u> Richard Harrison (1808-1882) KVP1-65G and Mary Ann Whittaker Harrison (1811-1898) KWV3-MWC.

4 Snow, <u>Fate of the Fryers</u> at page 34. The letter is not dated in the Snow book and the original letter has not been located. Because Sophia signs her name as "Sophia Willis" and because she speaks of her fruit harvest being "about gone" it is reasonable to estimate the date of the letter as the fall of 1867.

5 <u>http://wchsutah.org/people/isaac-duffin.php</u>

6 Gardner and Zeenati at pages 302-304.

7 Snow, <u>Fate of the Fryers</u> at page 35. The original letter has not been located.

8 Gardner and Zeenati at page 303, quoting from Eva Geary Page Higbee's story "A Narrative of Daniel Richey Page and His Wife Sophia Ann Geary Page," contained in the book.

9 *Ibid.*

10 Snow, <u>Fate of the Fryers</u> at page 36. It is notable that both Bessie Snow and Eva Geary Page Higbee personally associated with Sophia Ann Geary Page throughout their lives and so likely heard this story from Sophia Ann directly.

11 Original document written by Wilma Higbee Kemp in the possession of Lisa Michele Church, copy in the Appendix herein.. Wilma told Lisa Michele this story in person during a June, 2000 visit to Wilma's home in Santa Clara, Utah.

Handmade leather glove sewn by Sophia Fryer Geary and passed down to Geary descendants through her daughter, Sophia Ann. Sophia sewed clothes and gloves to raise money to support herself and her children while living in Toquerville during the 1860s. She sold some of the gloves at Duffin's Store in Silver Reef.

Handmade knit baby booties, made by Sophia Fryer Geary and passed down to her descendants through her daughter, Sophia Ann. Sophia was known for her excellent skills in knitting, sewing, and embroidering. She sold her items for income to support herself.

Antique wooden wall pocket which was among John Thomas Geary's personal effects which he left to his family. It was passed down to his descendants through his daughter, Eliza Jane. The pocket was brought from England and used for filing paperwork or other documents.

The women in this photo are identified on the back of the original photo, reportedly scratched into the metal surface of the tintype. Theresa Revel Fryer, sitting on the left, was the wife of Richard Fryer. She is holding her baby, John, on her lap. Sophia, sitting on the right, is identified as "dau. of Sophia Fryer" meaning it is Sophia Ann Geary.

The photo could have been taken no earlier than 1871, as John Fryer was born in 1870 and he is not a newborn here; William Willis was born in 1868. It was likely taken in later 1872 after the death of Sophia Fryer Geary Willis in May, 1872.

The children shown are, <u>left to right</u>, Echo Workman Geary, born 1856, (sitting at the far left), Theresa's daughter, Annie Fryer, born 1864, (standing behind and between the women), and William Willis, next to Sophia. The blurred image of the girl standing behind and to the right of the group with her arm on Sophia's shoulder is identified as Theresa's daughter, Eliza Fryer, born 1862.

Joshua Thomas Willis (1818-1886) in a photo posted on the Family Search entry for him. Willis became Sophia Geary's second husband in 1867.

The Joshua Thomas Willis home in Toquerville, Utah when he was serving as bishop. This photo was posted on the Willis Family Search entry by C.G. Naegle on August 4, 2016.

View of the Toquerville Cemetery taken from the location of the Sophia Fryer Geary Willis grave. She was buried with her baby boy, named James.

This photo of Sophia's grave marker in Toquerville was posted on her Family Search entry by WillisKeevin1 on March 14, 2014.

HONORABLE REMEMBRANCE

Though John and Sophia both died within 15 years of their arrival in the Utah Territory at relatively young ages, they are honored by thousands of descendants throughout the country even today, 150 years later. Family members tell and re-tell stories about the Gearys' younger lives to keep them alive in hearts and minds. Many of these stories became embellished in the endless re-telling, but the essence of the man - John Thomas Geary - remains. He was unusual. His intellect and manner of expressing himself were far above average and his sacrifice for the gospel of Jesus Christ in which he believed was astounding.

Many things draw us to the story of John Thomas Geary: his ancestry in Leicestershire, his rise to become a London lawyer in Victorian England, his poetic and earnest writings, his pride in his family, his willingness to remake his life dramatically by coming to America, his trip across the plains in desperate conditions, his tireless work ethic trying to survive in a frontier community, and finally, his unwavering faith that God would provide for him. His short life and mysterious death leave us with a sense of unfinished business. More complete answers elude us for the time being. And yet, we are also left with a sense of a brilliance surrounding the man, a life well-lived, his promises kept.

Certainly, John's devotion to his five daughters was heartfelt. Each of them went on to become unusual and outstanding women in their own right, despite being orphaned in tragic circumstances. Sophia's children with Joshua Willis also lived honorable lives. It is reassuring to see the Fryer and Geary family traits echo through the decades.

THE GEARY GIRLS

After their mother's May 27, 1872 death in childbirth, the older Geary girls – Sophia Ann, 19, Echo, 16, and Eliza, 13 – were already working outside the home for other families, so they remained in those situations. There was no Toquerville home for them to return to and they needed to support themselves. The younger children, Leah, 10, and Annie, 8, were taken in at first by Sophia's brother, Richard Fryer, and his wife, Theresa Revel Fryer. A letter survives from one of the distant Fryer siblings who wrote to inquire about "my sister's death" and asked "why does my brother have her children?"[1]

The two surviving Willis children lived with their father, Bishop Joshua T. Willis, and were reared by his first wife, "Aunt" Sarah. William was 4 when his mother Sophia died and Laura Adina was turning 2.

SOPHIA ANN GEARY

Sophia Ann (or Sophia) was working in Spring Valley, Nevada at a ranch owned by the Prime T. Coleman, Sr. family when her mother died.[2] The Colemans previously lived in Pinto and may have known Richard and Jane Fryer Harrison. Coleman was a British immigrant and Mormon convert as Sophia's parents had been; he was called to help settle southern Utah by church leaders. In the mid-1870s he moved his family into Kanab and probably no longer needed Sophia's services, so she looked for a new situation.[3]

Sophia then moved to St. George and went to work in The Big House, a large hotel operating in the former home of Erastus Snow in the center of town. This was a demanding job. The hotel was a four-story building that housed many visitors each day. Dinners could be held there to host up to 80 people. At the time that Sophia worked there, The Big House had a group of boarders that were helping to build the St. George Temple. According to her daughter, Eva Geary Page, Sophia was required to be up at 4 a.m. every morning and work until midnight. One day she ran a needle through her foot at work and had to keep working. "After working several days to try and extract the needle and failing to do so, some fellow suggested that they put a cow manure plaster on her foot, which they did, and this drew the needle to the surface and they were able to get it out," wrote Eva.[4]

Sophia lived and/or worked with the family of Alexander Findlay MacDonald in St. George during the early 1870s. MacDonald (1825-1903) was a Scottish convert to the Mormon Church who served many missions and church leadership positions. From 1870-1877 he served as the head of the Church Tithing Office in St. George and worked on the temple building project. Prior to this MacDonald had served a similar role in Provo during construction of the Provo Tabernacle. The MacDonald family was a large family with multiple wives and children. It is understandable that they could have used Sophia's help in exchange for her room and board.[5]

Sophia contracted typhoid fever while working at The Big House due to caring for her younger sister, Eliza, who also caught the fever while working in St. George. All of Sophia's hair fell out and she was "bald as an eagle", according to stories she told her daughter, Eva.[6] This was hard on her because Sophia's hair had normally been thick and wavy. Sophia continued to work while ill. A kind woman, Sister Haskell, saw how dangerously sick Sophia was and she arranged for her to leave her job at The Big House and move to Pinto, Utah where Sophia's aunt, Jane Fryer Harrison, could care for her.

Sophia was living there in Pinto recovering when she met Daniel Richey Page, who worked at nearby Irontown. Daniel was born May 27, 1855 in Salt Lake City to Daniel Page and Mary Ann Richey.[7] At the time Daniel and Sophia met, Daniel was living at the ranch homestead of his Grandfather Robert Richey. The beautiful cattle ranch was called Richey Ranch, just north of Pinto. Daniel and Sophia courted for a few months and fell in love. They were married at the ranch on April 12, 1876 and Daniel inherited what later became known as Page Ranch. Sophia was to live there the rest of her life.[8]

Sophia and Daniel raised seven children on the ranch and built a large Victorian mansion there in 1899 to serve as a boarding house and way station on the original route of the Old Santa Fe Trail. The spot was known far and wide as a welcoming place to get a clean room and a delicious meal. It was an operating cattle ranch and farm. Daniel made money on mining claims in the nearby hills and was able to support his family in grand style. The Victorian mansion was furnished with fine furniture ordered from Chicago stores and shipped by rail. Sophia inherited her father's love of words and religion. She was fiercely loyal to the Mormon faith, a fact which eventually came between her and Daniel. They divorced in 1906 and Sophia ran the ranch alone for the next 20 years. Her children helped her stabilize the operation. She was known as a wonderful grandmother who enjoyed the visits from her numerous family members.

Her daughter, Eva, remembers Sophia this way:

"Our mother was about 5 feet, 6 inches, weight 156 lbs., eyes of blue, light brown or yellow hair, very wavy and long, it fell below her waist, she could sit on it, very fair skin, rather corpulent. A square chin like her father…She was always very jolly, always playing pranks and tricks, was a dancer, danced jigs, and was the smoothest dancer on the floor when she promenaded, she did it so smoothly that she looked as if she were being carried around on a piece of glass…"

Mother was a lover of the beautiful and as I have stated before, she understood music and as she was churning or working in the garden she could puzzle out the tunes of different songs…As a child she was quite gifted in singing and often sang solos in Sunday School meetings, at dances, and at holiday entertainments… Mother would take me out into the garden where she was working and teach me one note at a time, until I got so I could keep along with her quite well. I am indebted to dear Mother for a great many things. We spent many enjoyable evenings in the winter, singing, roasting apples on the hobs of the old fireplace, roasting beef steaks over burning embers, popping corn and grinding it in the coffee grinder, then mixing it with sugar or molasses…

She was honest and taught her children honesty, obedience, courtesy, kindness and to be charitable to all people, to respect the aged and people in authority whether secular or ecclesiastical. In short, she taught her children all the grand principles that Mormonism implies…She had a strong testimony of the divinity of Mormonism and was constantly led and guided by the Holy Ghost…I will say Mother was deserving of all and any praise I have given her. It was she who taught me to pray, to my Heavenly Father. She who built up my faith in my Heavenly Father and taught me to believe in Him and love Him that I might always have his spirit with me, to direct my feet to heaven."[9]

One of Sophia's grandchildren, Maree Higbee Gardner, wrote these memories of her trips to Page Ranch as a child:

"We soon climbed the beautiful stairway leading to Mother's (Eva's) bedroom, #6, as all rooms were numbered. Mothers' would be on the front, southeast corner. We were not tall enough to open or see out of the beautiful stained-glass window at the first landing, but stopped long enough to admire its beauty. Our Grandma Page would open it wide and call out, 'Geary-eee, come to dinner.' Those in the fields would do so.

Our second dash was back down the stairs, sliding down the banister if Grandma Page wasn't in sight, on through the dining room, through the kitchen and into the pantry, where we could smell the goodies, cookies, cake and pies. Large pans of milk and cream, pounds of butter, cheese and other good things to eat were always in abundance."[10]

Sophia treasured some of her parents' mementos which she inherited from them, including the 1629 Geary Family Bible, the small hand-sewn child's booties and a set of beautifully embroidered leather gloves made by her mother. Sophia, as the eldest, also inherited the Geary Family Seal depicting a musician's lyre with an olive branch. In some surviving photos, Sophia can be seen wearing the family seal around her neck on a ribbon. Sophia had a reverence for the items she and her parents brought across the plains from England so many years before. She kept her ancestors' memories alive by telling her children and grandchildren the stories she remembered. Sophia died in her bedroom at Page Ranch on August 14, 1934 at the age of 81. She is buried in the Pinto Cemetery next to her sister, Leah.

THE WILL OF JOHN THOMAS GEARY

During her lifetime, Sophia pursued the probate of her father's Last Will and Testament.

The real estate owned by John Thomas Geary in Toquerville was sold at Public Auction on October 4, 1880, more than thirteen years after John's death.[11] The Probate Court appointed Charles Stapley, Jr. as administrator of John's estate and sold the house at Lot 4, Block 15, in the official Map of Toquerville Town to Ashton Nebeker, the highest bidder, for the sum of $160. It is not clear why the sale took so long or where the money went.

The Kane County Probate Court also tied up one other loose end in 1880 relating to the estates of John Thomas Geary and Sophia Fryer Geary Willis. At the same time as the Court ordered the sale of Geary's land, Sophia Ann Geary Page was appointed as the legal guardian for "Anna Geary" or Sarah Ann Geary.[12] In 1880, Annie Geary would have been almost 16 years old. Her mother had been dead for eight years. It is not known who was consulted about this guardianship, but it probably did not have much effect on either woman's life as Annie Geary was living in Panaca, Nevada working as a servant for the Christian and Amelia Ronnow family in 1880. She married James Davis in September, 1882.[13]

On July 24, 1882, Sophia wrote a letter to an attorney and family friend, John W. Brown in Parowan, to inquire about the will. Apparently, Sophia and Mr. Brown had been corresponding about the will for some time and Sophia mentions that Mr. Brown recently sent her a letter with a copy of what he claimed was the will of John Thomas Geary. Sophia disagreed. She wrote that she originally had her father's will in her possession after his 1867 death, but she gave it to a "Mrs. McDonald" in the 1870s and it was never returned to her.

The way Sophia tells the story in her 1882 letter, this incident occurred when she was living with the MacDonald family in 1876 while working at The Big House in St. George:[14]

"In the year 1876 when I was living with Mrs. McDonald, she came into the kitchen, where I was, & said to me, Sophy look what a nice present Mr. Mack has given me. At the same time showing me a silver watch. 'Oh', said I, 'that is just like my Father's watch.' Oh no, said she, it cannot be, for Charley Smith brought it to Mr. Mack saying, 'some person, years ago, brought me this watch to clean & never called for it & I forget who brought it, so I donate it to the Temple.' She said Mr. Mack put means into the Temple, kept the watch & gave it to her. I felt positive then as I do now that the watch she had was my Father's. I told her I thought [he] mentioned his watch in his Will.

'Where is your father's Will,' said she. And that was how I came to show the Will. I gave it into the hands of Mr. Macdonald & Lawyer Jackson & I have never seen it from that day to this. I gave with the Will some blue papers, I think they was from My father's father, relating to what was due to Father in England."

The story makes sense given that Alexander Findlay MacDonald was in charge of the St. George tithing office. It is plausible that a person who came into possession of John Thomas Geary's watch could have donated it to MacDonald as a form of tithing to support the St. George Temple construction.

John does mention his silver watch in the only copy we have of a John Thomas Geary will, dated September 10, 1866 three months before he died: "my silver watch now or lately in the possession of Charles Smith of St. George, Watchmaker."[15] John clarifies that he gave it to Smith for cleaning in St. George but does not say when. If it was in 1866 or before, it would have been at least nine years before MacDonald received it for tithing in the 1870s. John died in 1867 and Charley donated it in 1876, at least according to Sophia's story. In any event, the watch has never reappeared among the Geary family descendants.

Sophia also told Brown in her 1882 letter that she was convinced the Will which Brown had was not a correct copy. Sophia remembers her father's Will included the words, "I make my Will so that it will cope with the iron laws of England" or similar wording, and such words are not in Brown's copy.

In her letter, Sophia reviews the items mentioned in Brown's copy of the Geary Will and details where she thinks they are:

- "The bin that is mentioned in his Will I thin[k] Mrs. Batty the old Lady that lives in Toker has it. The bin, cupboard, and a large chest, is all that I care about, of the household goods. I have been told they was auctioned off…but his children nor any of us never received one dime for them."
- "Father had one or two cows…the old cow's name was Rose, the young cow's name was Frosty. Mother gave Frosty to me & Willis sold her for fifty dollars in Cash & kept it."
- "Father had a good wagon, that is not mentioned, in the Will. Willis used or sold it…"

Sophia's additional criticism of the Will is that Sophia believes John Thomas Geary was entitled to an inheritance from his father, Thomas Geary, back in England. Sophia writes Brown that, "Relating to what was due to Father in England. I know there was property coming to Father in England." This may have been Sophia's impression, but we now have information about Thomas Geary's will (see Chapter 5 herein) and John was specifically not included in his father's estate, nor were his other brothers who left England.[16]

Sophia concludes by telling Brown that she understands that her father's Will was filed April

15, 1875, presumably with the Probate Court, but that she has written three times for it and was told it cannot be found. No letter response from Attorney Brown can be found.

Twelve years later, on April 13, 1894, Sophia writes John W. Brown, attorney, again about her father's Will, reminding him that, "It is about now going on twelve years since I heard from you in regard to Father's Will & property." Sophia notes that Brown told her the Will was "destroyed in some way" and she suggests that John Thomas Geary's brother, Fred Geary, destroyed it. (Fred Geary was the brother living in London whom John feared was after him as John was departing for America in Liverpool.) Sophia reminds Brown that she sent him copies of some letters from John Thomas Geary in 1882 and she would like them returned. It is not known whether the letters were ever returned, nor do we know if Brown ever responded to Sophia.

The authors have diligently researched the John Thomas Geary Will in the records of the State of Utah Archives and have not found a probated copy of his Will. Kaye Page Nichols confirmed with the State of Utah that a Will for John Thomas Geary was recorded on April 15, 1875 but record-keepers cannot find a copy of the Will nor a record of its probate.

It was honorable of Sophia Geary Page to so diligently pursue a proper settlement of her father's estate, but she could have been hampered by the fact that she was a child when her father died and her recollection of the circumstances may be flawed. It is possible that John Thomas Geary had drafted an earlier Will which Sophia saw as a child. Maybe that Will referred to the laws of England where he previously resided as well as referring to a possible inheritance from his father in England. That Will could have been in Sophia's possession at one time but not necessarily be the valid Will.

It is also possible that the 1866 Geary Will came into Richard Fryer's possession after John and Sophia both died. We know that Richard and Theresa Fryer took Sophia's younger children for a period of time after her 1872 death; maybe they took some of her personal possessions and paperwork as well. Richard Fryer and his wife both died tragically and suddenly in March, 1875. According to Bessie Snow in *Fate of the Fryers*, after Richard Fryer's death, his sister, Jane Fryer Harrison was called to Toquerville to claim Fryer belongings and returned with Richard Fryer's journal.[17] This indicates Jane had access to Richard Fryer's papers and possibly access to papers from John or Sophia Geary. The Will may have stayed with Fryer family members until it resurfaced in 2010 and a copy was sent to Kaye Page Nichols.

Charlie Martin of Hollister, California, a Fryer descendant, became aware in 2010 that Kaye Page Nichols was researching the John Thomas Geary will and he sent it to Nichols. It is a Will dated a few months before John's death, as described in Chapter 6 herein. It is possible that Sophia, being a 13-year-old girl when her father died, was never given a copy of that particular Will. Her parents were living 300 miles apart at that time in September, 1866.

The Geary descendants are eternally grateful that, despite the Will mix-up, some treasures of John's life were preserved for posterity (see images and Appendix herein) and are proudly displayed to and passed down among family members today.

ECHO WORKMAN GEARY HANLEY

Echo, was born December 9, 1856 as the family came across the rugged plains in a terrible snowstorm. She was named after Echo Canyon, the site of her birth near the Salt Lake Valley. She lived an adventurous and colorful life which took her far from her Utah roots. About the time of her mother's death in 1872, Echo was living and working at the mining boom town of Silver Reef, Utah, a few miles from Toquerville. She was only 16 years old but she had been working as a domestic helper in order to support herself.

As a teenager during the 1870s, Echo met and married Kennedy James Hanley in Silver Reef, Utah. Hanley was at least 12 years older than Echo and was born in Ireland. He came to America as a 16-year-old boy, settling first in Ohio but then moving to Virginia City, Nevada to seek his fortune in 1865.[18] In the 1880 Census, Hanley was living in Silver Reef, Utah and is shown as married to Echo. Their two children were born in Silver Reef – Robert Emmet Hanley on February 13, 1882 and James Geary Hanley on March 15, 1885.

Silver Reef was a rollicking boom town when Echo and Kennedy lived there. "During the height of activity at the mining district from 1877 to 1888, the Barbee and Walker Mine, the Leeds, Leeds Number 2, McNally, Nichols, Newton, South and other mines produced thousands of dollars' worth of silver. It is estimated that from 1875 to 1910, when the last efforts were made to extract silver from the sandstone, some $7.9 million worth of silver had been mined from the district."[19] By the time Echo and Kennedy left Silver Reef, they were prosperous and looking for new adventures.

From 1888 to 1907, they lived in Idaho where Kennedy operated the Wardner and Mullen Mines in the Coeur D'Alene district of Idaho. He was originally an investor in those mines when his partners tried to cheat him by representing that the mine had no worth. Actually, it was producing millions of dollars of ore.[20] Kennedy sued and lost at the lower court but the judgment was reversed in 1901 by the US Court of Appeals and eventually Kennedy won a large victory totaling $175,867.02 from his partners. He became a wealthy man.

In 1906, Kennedy bought 25,000 acres in eastern Oregon for $300,000, a very large timber deal for the time. Kennedy and Echo's older son, Robert, lived with them, and their younger son, James, was attending Gonzaga College in Spokane, Washington. The family moved to Spokane in 1908 where Kennedy then bought the Hotel Spokane. The family lived there from 1907-1909, apparently with a luxurious lifestyle. The local newspaper covered an automobile wreck in 1907 involving Hanley's $3,500 vehicle being driven by a chauffeur.

The 1910 Census shows them living in the Altadena Apartments in Spokane, having been married 31 years; Kennedy is 65 and Echo is 50. The family continued to live in Spokane until moving to Los Gatos, California in 1920. Their oldest son, Robert, joined them in Los Gatos and worked as a real estate agent. Kennedy died on October 31, 1921 at the age of 76. He is buried in the Los Gatos Cemetery. His obituary describes him, in part, as "a pioneer of the northwestern mining states" and that he "enjoyed a large circle of acquaintances."[21]

After becoming a widow, Echo built a lovely Spanish-style home at 15 Loma Alta in Los Gatos which she shared with her adult son, Robert. Robert was a well-known businessman in Los Gatos and a frequent golfer. He never married. The younger Hanley son, James, joined the military and served in World War I. He married a woman named Nellie in about 1923 when he was 28 years old and she was 65 years old. They lived in various places around the country, including Virginia and Washington, D.C. Echo had no known grandchildren.

Echo lived with Robert at the Loma Alta address for the rest of her life. Robert became ill in 1936 and died April 10, 1936. He was living in California's Agnews State Hospital, otherwise known as the "Great Asylum for the Insane," at the time of his death.

Echo died one month to the day after her son, Robert. She had been diagnosed with arteriosclerosis in 1932 and other heart problems. She died of a heart attack on May 19, 1936 and is buried in the Los Gatos Cemetery. Until recently, Echo's grave was unmarked, as she had buried her son, Robert, in the spot next to his father, Kennedy. When the authors and other relatives researched Echo's burial, it was determined that Echo was buried a few feet away from her husband and son and a marker was placed there in 2018 by the family.

It is not known if Echo kept in touch with any of her siblings during the years she lived outside of Utah. Her older sister, Sophia, records one interaction she had with Echo while Sophia lived at Page Ranch. It occurred after Echo had her two children but before she moved to Idaho, so it probably occurred about 1886 or 1887, when both women were in their thirties. The two sisters reminisced and then Echo asked to see the Geary Family Bible. Sophia obliged and as the two sisters looked at the family heirloom, Echo threw it into the fire that was burning in the fireplace. Sophia was shocked and alarmed by this – she immediately seized the Bible out of the flames largely intact. It is difficult to understand this incident but we have only one person's side of the story so judgment should be withheld.

Echo's only remaining son, James, died a few years after his mother, on May 19, 1940 and he is buried in beautiful seaside surroundings at The Presidio military cemetery in San Francisco, California.

ELIZA JANE GEARY KEELE

Eliza Jane was a girl of 13 when her mother died and she was left an orphan. She was not a happy child during Sophia's nearly five-year marriage to Joshua Thomas Willis. According to a family story, "Willis was not very fond of his wife's first family. Eliza Jane had reddish gold hair and freckles and he always called her 'Freckles.' She resented this very much, and she would go up to the garden and sit on the ditch bank and cry by the hour. She really missed her father [John Thomas Geary.] She had very little schooling after that, yet it would be hard to find a better educated person."[22]

Eliza left Toquerville when she was fourteen years old and began to work as a household helper. At first, she worked for Ashton Nebeker in Toquerville and later she worked for the Walter Erastus and Eleanor Malone Dodge family in St. George. While Eliza was working for the Dodges, in about 1876, she contracted typhoid fever. This was when her older sister, Sophia Ann, was also working in St. George at The Big House so Sophia Ann nursed Eliza back to health. The two orphan girls cared for each other.

Eliza then moved to Panaca, Nevada where she and her younger sister, Annie, both worked for the Christian Ronnow family. The Ronnows had several children in their large Danish family. According to Eliza's family, "She liked the Ronnows very much, they were kind to her, but the boys teased her and would not chop wood, so she quit and went to work for Jim Wadsworth."[23]

After working for several other families, Eliza was introduced to David Keele by Liza Langford (grandmother of Ruby Keele). They began dating and were married in the St. George Temple by David H. Cannon on March 29, 1877. This would have been shortly after the St. George Temple was dedicated as the first Mormon Temple in Utah. David Keele was 24 years old and Eliza Jane was 18.

Some other interesting details were recorded by her family members about Eliza:

Eliza Jane Geary Keele, called Eliza by her husband David, was a striking woman with wavy auburn-red tresses, ample bosomed and a trim waist line. Only age added to a more statuesque build. Her figure was typical of the stalwart pioneer woman, whose stamina and vigor raised large families, and provided well for their off-spring during the trying times of the pioneer days of Eastern Nevada.

Entertainment was a community affair, and Eliza was gifted with a voice reflection which she used to help make the music and rhythm for the youngsters as they danced the quadrilles at the church functions.

A religious background provided her foundation for her diligent work in the L. D. S. Ward at Panaca, where she was President of the Mutual, very active in the Relief Society and other affairs. Her parents were converts to the Mormon faith, coming from England in a sailing ship, the trip taking three months.

David and Eliza were parents of twelve children, six boys and six girls. Following is a list of the children: Elzada, Annie Eliza, Eathel, John David, Mary Pearl, Jessie William, Leah, George Quincy, Francis Marion, Howard Geary, Iretta, and Arville. David built a log cabin on a lot in Panaca for he and his wife and they lived there for many years, adding rooms to it at different times. It is believed that all of the children were born there. It was just across the street from the Samuel Keele home.

In 1912, Eliza and David bought the old Turnbaugh home in the center of Panaca, (across from Dotson's store). It was a large two story "T" constructed type home, which Eliza Keele opened to the public for room and board. Known as a compassionate woman, and overly generous with her tasty dishes, the Keele home prospered as a boarding house for transients. With the income from her business, she bought new wicker type furniture, rugs and other household items to make her family more comfortable.

The cellar of Eliza Keele would be an oddity in this modern day of deep-freezes, for crocks of sauerkraut, mincemeat, jams, pickles, dried fruits and jars of other foods were abundant, as her husband and boys kept a fine garden. David had fine gardens at both places, and the earliest ones in town. Many a person walked by his garden because they knew he would always have a bunch of vegetables to give them. Eliza started canning and preserving all vegetables when they were young, sweet and in their prime. One of her best preserves was the potowatamy plum, and no one could prepare rhubarb like she could.

They raised their beef, pork, and chickens and these were cured in a number of ways. Her pickles were outstandingly good: chow-chow, bread and butter, sweet and sour, dill and others put in salt brine to be soaked out later and put into sweet and spiced vinegar. There were not many salads, only when they had fresh vegetables and lettuce in the garden, and her dressing for cabbage slaw was super. Her baked beans were a must at church socials and she always had good homemade bread. Her big black wood cook stove always shone like a mirror.

When asked by one of her boys why she worried so much about her family, [Eliza] answered: 'That's a question that I cannot answer, I will only say that when you become a parent and your children get the age you are now, then you will know'. Growing old in age, but not in spirit, she often was sentimental over incidents and objects of her children's pupilage period. Although she was not outwardly affectionate, she showed her love to her family by the many endowments of life she instilled in her children.

She was as ready to help a neighbor in need as to care for her own. Her beds were always perfectly made with the big feather mattresses which to us would be so hard to make look nice, and no one ever sat on her beds. She was a good nurse, a good seamstress, made many quilts, and dyed and sewed rags for rugs, and carpets; crocheted lace and knitted, mostly socks and mittens. Everything she did was done right. After the sheep would go through town and leave a bunch of wool on the barbed wire fences, she would have the children gather it, then she would wash and cord it, and put it in quilts and comforters.

Eliza and David celebrated their Golden Wedding Anniversary on March 29, 1927 at the family home in Panaca, with all the family in attendance. The three-tiered cake was made by Iretta (Rita) and Vern Fitzgerald, a daughter and son-in-law of the Keeles. Although some of her children had passed on during the years, by accidents and illnesses, Mother Keele was still the proud figure she had been at the time of her marriage to David. She had added with the years, some slight poundage and her beautiful natural wavy, auburn hair was flecked with silver, changing her hair color to flaxen blond.

In January 1931, Eliza went to Cedar City and was operated on, came home and was apparently doing very well. Her granddaughter, Fawn Lee, was with her as well as Father Keele. The morning of January 8th, she asked for water. As Fawn gave it to her, a blood clot struck her heart and she was gone. She died at 4:30 AM in the morning, January 8, 1931."[24]

There are similarities between Eliza Jane and her older sister, Sophia Ann. Both women raised large families and ran challenging households. Both women established their homes as boarding houses and were known far and wide for their excellent homemaking skills, always making travelers and strangers feel welcome. Both were devoted, faithful Mormons and Eliza was fortunate in finding a companion that shared her conviction.

It appears from some correspondence that Eliza Jane and Sophia Ann wrote letters and visited each other when circumstances permitted. Eliza must have inherited a few precious possessions from John and Sophia, her parents. In her family history it is noted that one of her descendants inherited "an antique wall pocket brought from England and across the plains in a handcart by Eliza Keele's mother. It must have been a very treasured piece to come such a long way" and her son, Quincy Keele, inherited some of John Thomas Geary's records and a copy of his shorthand.[25] (The John Thomas Geary records are described in Chapter 5 herein and copies of the shorthand are included in the Appendix herein.)

In one poignant comment, Eliza Jane Geary Keele reportedly told her daughter-in-law, Roxy Keele, "Quincy is so much like my father in all of his ways, and also his build." It is both a happy and a sad memory.

LEAH FRYER GEARY

Leah was 10 years old when her mother died. She and her younger sister, Annie, were temporarily placed with their uncle, Richard Fryer, and his wife, Theresa. The Fryers lived in Toquerville and the families had been close, so this was likely a good result. However, Richard and Teresa died three years later in a family tragedy, after which Leah and Annie were forced to work for others in their homes.

According to her niece, Eva Geary Page Higbee, Leah was treated badly by a few families but finally found a good situation working for the Chauncey MacFarlane family in St. George. Leah was known for being a hard worker, washing, ironing, cooking, cleaning, sewing, sweeping, scrubbing and tending children with the best of them. [26]

One of the unusual things about Leah is that she had a birthmark (what family members called "a port wine stain") on the left half of her face. According to Eva, this was considered disfiguring for Leah and was the reason she never married, although a surviving photograph shows her to be very beautiful.

During her adult life, Leah was often living with her sisters, Sophia Ann at Page Ranch or Eliza Jane at Panaca. If she was needed to work for another family for money she would go, but otherwise she enjoyed helping her sisters with their large families. "When my mother married Daniel Richey Page, she had Leah come live with her when she wasn't working," remembers Eva. "When a woman had a new baby and needed someone to help her do her housework they would send for Aunt Leah because they knew she could be depended on. She charged $2.50 per week, which was a very small wage."

Eva recalled an incident when she was a child at Page Ranch and Leah was there:

"She was a very dear aunt, a good worker and a good cook. She always demanded $2.00 to $3.00 per week when she worked out. Leah was very dependable and kept things clean. She was a favorite aunt of mine and I will tell you how she treated me. One morning, she called me to get up and help with the milking. It was our custom to arise between five and six to milk, and it was very cold.

When she called me, I did not get up right away, so she came back, pulled me out of bed, and took all the covers off and left me. You must know that I was soon dressed and on my way. However, as I was going out of the hollow toward the corral, I heard Aunt Leah and the rest scolding about me being so slow getting there. I just listened for a minute and turned back and hid myself in the brush, and remained there until I heard all the milk hands coming. They were still scolding about me, so I remained there until breakfast was over, and then went to the house. Believe me, I was up and at the corral on time thereafter."[27]

Leah was living with her first cousin, Eliza Fryer Baxter, in St. George when she became ill. Eliza was the daughter of Richard and Theresa Fryer and Leah had grown up with her in Toquerville. The doctor diagnosed Leah with a tumor in her abdomen. He recommended surgery be performed in Salt Lake City, because they did not have the medical facilities in St. George.

In December, 1897, Sophia Ann and her husband, Daniel Page, drove Leah up to Salt Lake in a lumber wagon. She went to St. Mark's Hospital where abdominal surgery was performed, but she died on January 5, 1898 while still at the hospital. She was only 36 years old. Sophia and Daniel brought her back to Pinto, Utah where she was buried in the Pinto Cemetery. Sophia was later buried next to her.

Leah's sister, Eliza Jane Geary Keele, wrote Sophia a letter about the death:[28]

ELIZA TO SOPHIA ANN

Panaca, Nevada

January 8, 1898

Dear Brother, Sister, and all,

I am sorrowful enough this night you may be assured. It seems so sad and dreary to think that our dear blessed sister has left us and to make it worse, that we can't come out. I can hardly stand it. I just imagine I can see the team traveling along with her at such a slow, dreary pace. Then again, I see her in health, bustling around and so jolly and good.

I then see the Dear thing suffering as she did before she left here, and the long months she suffered after that. It makes my head ache and sink within me to think that one so good and self-sacrificing should suffer so much. But even this I guess we should not complain at, for we know not why it is.

May peace and rest be with the blessed thing. When you write tell me how she was dressed and if she was conscious all the time. We will still continue to help settle the bills as fast as we can. I wish I could get this to you in time to tell you to kiss her for me but it will be too late.

It seems to me if we could have been there to see her and had a good cry together I could feel better satisfied, but I will try to stop complaining and do the best I can about it.

I will stop for tonight, hoping this will find you well as it leaves, us, with the exception of the terrible shock we have had.

Write soon to your loving sister,
Eliza Keele

SARAH ANN (ANNIE) GEARY DAVIS

Annie was 8 years old when her mother died and Annie went to live with her Uncle Richard Fryer's family at first. After Richard and his wife died in 1875, Annie worked for various families in exchange for room and board. In 1880, when she was 16, Annie was living in Panaca, Nevada working for the Christian Ronnow family.[29] Ronnow was a Danish immigrant who converted to the Mormon Church in 1855 when he was 22 years old. He served in the Danish Army as a sharpshooter and then served a Danish mission. He and his wife immigrated to Utah in 1862, but his wife died shortly thereafter, leaving him with small children. He remarried and went on to have seven more children. The Ronnows were called by Brigham Young to settle Panaca, Nevada and lived there the rest of their lives. Ronnow was a successful farmer and owned the Co-Op Store in Panaca. They hired Annie and her sister, Eliza, to help with their large family.

On September 11, 1882, when Annie was 18 years old, she married James Davis in Panaca. They moved around the west after that, living in mining towns such as Orangeville, Utah where their first son, Robert, was born in 1883. Their next two sons were born back in Panaca, Nevada – Heber in 1885 and Walter in 1887. They moved to Star Valley, Wyoming in the 1890s and had a set of twins, Ernest and Effie, born there in 1891. Finally, they moved to the Big Horn Basin in Wyoming in 1894 and had their last child, Grace, in 1896 at Burlington, Wyoming. The family homesteaded a ranch along the Greybull River near the early Mormon settlement of Burlington/Otto.

Sadly, Annie's husband died on the ranch in early 1900, reportedly from a wagon accident as he was freighting.[30] This left her a 36-year-old widow with six children all under 17.[31] Her son, Heber, died two years later in 1902 at the age of 17. She continued to live on the ranch, filing a Homestead Claim in 1906 and obtaining a deed to 80 acres in her own name on June 30, 1906, with a deed signed by U.S. President Theodore Roosevelt.[32]

Annie farmed and raised her children there on the Wyoming ranch. She is listed on the 1910 census as a farm owner and a carpet weaver.[33] Her son, Robert, is married and gone from Burlington by then, but her son, Walter, is living there and working as a well driller. Annie's son, Ernest, served in the U.S. Army in World War One. Annie was a valiant Red Cross worker in Burlington during the war, along with her youngest daughter, Grace. An article in *The Basin Republican* on January 10, 1919 notes that the mother-daughter pair "made the following articles: 55 suits of pajamas, 57 bed shirts, 20 pairs of socks, 17 chemises, 12 underskirts, 11 outing flannel shirts for men." They were dedicated war workers.

Another tragedy struck in 1919 when Annie's daughter, Grace, died suddenly of peritonitis at the age of 23. Annie lived another two years, dying herself of chronic heart disease at age 57 in 1921. Her obituary in *The Big Horn County Rustler*, dated May 27, 1921, notes that Annie died on Saturday, May 21, 1921 at her home. "She had been confined to her home but a short time, and the news of her death came as a shock to her many friends." The article goes on to say that a funeral was held at her house conducted by Rev. Edwin Bowling. She was apparently not connected to the Mormon Church at that time. "Mrs. Davis, during her residence in this section had won the enduring friendship of all with whom she came in contact. She was a woman of splendid character, a good mother and went to her grave with a knowledge of having reared a good family. She will be greatly missed by all friends and relatives and the sorrowing ones have the sincerest sympathy of all." Annie's four surviving children married and had children of their own. Some lived in Powell, Casper, or Lovell, Wyoming and others went as far as Santa Ana, California, Oahu, Hawaii, or Washington, D.C.

It is fascinating that two of John and Sophia's daughters – Sophia Ann Geary Page and Annie Geary Davis – ended up as single women running ranches in the west for many years. Their character and strength were in evidence during their entire lives.

WILLIAM RICHARD WILLIS

William was only 3 years old when his mother, Sophia, died and he was taken in by his father, Joshua T. Willis, and raised by his stepmother, Sarah. He was likely named "William" for his father's brother and "Richard" for his mother's brother. Joshua T. Willis had several plural wives and many children so William was raised in a large family. After serving for 14 years, Willis asked to be released as the Toquerville bishop in a letter to Brigham Young written January 1, 1874.[34] He then moved his family to Taylor, Arizona in May of 1879.[35]

At that time, eleven-year-old William would have joined several other young children in the Willis family – Mary Mocellia, Mary Agnes, Richard Merrill, Franklin Joshua, Hyrum Alonzo, and Laura Adina – in their new Taylor residence. William's father's home in Taylor was known as one of the finest and most attractive in the relatively new settlement. His father was sixty years old at the time of the move. Joshua was feeling pressure from the federal authorities about living in polygamy, which was against the law. He had to make several trips to Mexico to avoid arrest on cohabitation charges.

William wrote his life sketch which includes the following stories:[36]

I was reared by Aunt Sarah Willis, father's first wife. She was a good mother to my sister Laura and I. She reared a family of her own; eight of her children were living at the time, six of them were married when she took my sister and I to care for.

When I was eight years old I was baptized by Charles Stapley, Feb 11th 1875 and confirmed by James Jackson. We moved to Arizona when I was about 11 years old arriving in Taylor Arizona in November of 1879. As near as I remember we were about 5 weeks on the road from Toquerville Utah to Taylor. On our arrival in Arizona we turned all the horses and cattle on the range. Some of them were never seen again. We nearly always had plenty to eat, although the first year or two in Arizona we didn't have wheat flour for bread. But we were thankful for cornmeal and barley flour for bread. We had brought plenty of dried fruit with us from Utah.

I went to school in a little log house where my sister, Mocellia Maria ("Dolly" as she was called by the family) was teacher. She was the daughter of Aunt Sarah, father's first wife. In the spring of 1880 I helped father and others make a ditch from Shumway to our farm, which is now the Alma Hunt place. It was nearly two years before the ditch was finished, because of the work was done with shovels... After being in Arizona a few years, I went back to Utah with father and Aunt Sarah who went to do Temple work in the St. George Temple.

As a 20-year-old, William married Harriet Rachel Thompson, who was 19. They were married by William's half-brother, Merrill Willis, bishop of the Taylor Ward, and later sealed in the St. George Temple in October, 1888. William and Harriett had ten children during the years 1889-1911. They raised the family mostly in Taylor, although they lived briefly in other places such as the Gila Valley and Espanola, New Mexico.

William was active in the Mormon Church for his entire life, serving in many callings including in the bishopric. He played in local bands and enjoyed serving as Ward Choir Leader; he was musical as Sophia had been. William was proud to be very active in civic affairs.

In later life, he lived in Taylor and worked as a stonecutter making monuments at the cemetery. He wrote in 1945, "In our present home north across the street from the Taylor ward chapel we are very happy. And I find great pleasure in making head stones for relatives and friends. Some of them bring me remuneration; a good many I've been happy to furnish without pay."[37]

William wrote occasionally to his oldest half-sister, Sophia Ann Geary Page, and appears to have had a lifelong relationship with her, as well as with other siblings. He named his first daughter "Rachel Sophia." The surviving letters to Sophia show a man with a folksy sense of humor and a wry understanding of the ups and downs of life:[38]

[WILLIAM TO SOPHIA ANN]

Taylor, Navajo County, Arizona
Dec 15th, 1914

Dear Sister Sophia,

I thought I would write you a few lines to let you know that we are still alive and well…When I have not had a letter from any of you girls for over a year now I think it carelessness than anything else. I know it is with myself. If you have Annie's address I wish you would send it to me. I think I will write to Eliza in a few days. Have you ever been to see Lolly? Gee whiz I wish I was closer to all of you…Our baby is three years old. We call her Echo. She is a sweet little girl. I guess Echo would have objected to having her <u>named</u> Echo, but she cannot help that. I hope that Echo will live long enough to Repent of what I think is foolishness. Do you ever heat from her? I would like to meet with her if she did not know who I was…I wish you all a Merry Xmas and a happy New Year.

Love to all
WR & HR Willis

Taylor, Navajo County, Arizona
January 15, 1934

My Dear Sister and Family,

I guess I will try to write you a few lines to let you know we are still alive. I think it has been two years since I wrote a letter to anyone…I hope you are all well and doing well…I have been working on the highway for nearly two months, nearly every man I the county is working somewhere. It sure seems good to earn a little money…I go to bed cussing and get up cussing. I am so body out of patience I could pull on a rope to hang the worthless cuss. It seems possible to get the rascal in the pen where he belongs but I am still trying to land him in the pen…Ma just keeps going, it seems like the back is built for the burden. Well I guess I have said enough. I will close. Hoping to hear from You soon,

Love to all
WR Willis

William lived to be 86 years old and died at home in 1954 in Taylor, Arizona.

LAURA ADINA WILLIS

Laura Adina (sometimes listed as Adina Laura or Lolly) was a toddler when her mother, Sophia, died in 1872. She was taken in by her father's family, Joshua T. Willis and his plural wives. Like her brother, William, she moved with the family to Taylor, Arizona when still young and was raised there.

Laura met Samuel Larkin Lewis as a young woman; he was from Harrisburg, Utah near

Toquerville. They were married in St. George on October 21, 1885 when Laura was 15. They lived most of their family life in Kanab, Utah, about 70 miles south of Toquerville. Laura gave birth to ten children but several of them died young. Her first son died at 12 and her second daughter died of appendicitis at 21 years old. She had a baby girl, Alice, who died at 8 months. Her son, Leslie, was killed in a car accident near Kanab when he was 21.

    Six other children lived into adulthood. She had a daughter, Laura Lewis Bruce, who spent her adult life in Amherst, Massachusetts and another daughter, Emily, who resided in Chicago, Illinois where she raised her family.[39]

    While Laura was visiting her daughter Emily in Chicago in 1938, she became ill. She was diagnosed with liver cancer and had surgery. She recovered enough to return to Kanab but died shortly thereafter, on the 20th of November, 1938, at the age of 68.

    Laura Adina was active in the Mormon Church throughout her life. She was lauded as a "pioneer" in her 1938 obituary, one who had "done her work well."

ENDNOTES FOR CHAPTER EIGHT

1   Snow, The Fate of the Fryers at page 36. Bessie Snow published this letter dated October 8, 1872 from St. Albans, Vermont, written by Eliza Fryer Forward to Jane Fryer Harrison. Eliza was another Fryer sibling from the Moses and Eliza Miller Fryer family in the Isle of Wight. Eliza temporarily moved to America from England in the 1870s but then returned to England due to her husband's employment. Eliza Fryer Forward did not join the Mormon Church. According to Bessie Snow's book, Eliza regularly corresponded with her sister, Jane Fryer Harrison – and possibly other siblings – but the original letters have not been located. In this 1872 letter she writes, "I feel anxious to hear from you also the particulars of my sister's death. Tell me why my brother has the care of her children. Where is her husband and is her older girl married. It was sad to hear of her death so soon after Mother's and so many deaths. "

2   Church, Lisa-Michele, Sunshine and Shadow – The Page Ranch Story, Stevenson Publishers, Provo, Utah, 2017, page 23. This book contains the story of Sophia Ann Geary Page and her life at Page Ranch in southwestern Utah.

3   https://ourheywoodfamily.blogspot.com/search/label/David%20Evans%20Coleman%20-%20his%20Family%20History. www.familysearch.org. Prime T. Coleman, Sr. (1831-1905) L5DS-BWZ.

4   Gardner, Marie Higbee and Zeenati, Eva Louise Gardner, My Father Called Me Yebbie – Life Story of Eva Geary Page Higbee, Custom Family Publishers, St George, Utah, 1996 at page 304-305.

5   https://www.familysearch.org/photos/artifacts/5986576. Citing an article written by Taylor MacDonald entitled "Alexander F. MacDonald – Man of Three Nations" at the Alexander F. MacDonald Family Search entry (1825-1903) KWN2-385. The MacDonalds only lived in St. George for a few years, as MacDonald was called on a mission to Scotland in 1877.

6   *Ibid.*

7   www.familysearch.org Daniel Richey Page (1855-1933) KWZC-3PF

8   Church at page 23.

9   Church at page 37.

10   Church at page 128.

11   Geary descendents Roland Lee, Richard Lee, and Andrea Lee Conley located the records in the Utah State Archives regarding the disposal of the John Thomas Geary real property. The record indicates that on August 26, 1880, the Probate Court for Kane County in the Utah Territory appointed Charles Stapley, Jr. as the Administrator of the Estate of John Thomas Geary and ordered Stapley to sell the property at Public Auction. The Administrator's Deed appears in the Utah State Archives, Kane County Probate Court Record of Deeds, Book C, page 579-582. Copies in the possession of the authors.

12   See Appendix for a copy of the Annie Geary Guardianship papers dated October 1, 1880. Original in possession of Kaye Page Nichols.

13   www.familysearch.org, Annie Geary Davis, (1864-1922) KWVP-DLT, "United States Census, 1880," database with images, *FamilySearch* (https://familysearch.org/ark:/61903/1:1:MDCZ-TZJ : 19 February 2021), Anna [sic] Geary in household of Christian Ronnow, Panaca, Lincoln, Nevada, United States citing enumeration district ED 30, sheet 356B.

14   See Appendix for a transcription of the 1882 letter Sophia Geary Page wrote to John W. Brown, attorney; original is in the possession of Kaye Page Nichols. Nichols, Kaye Page, "Research Report on the Will of John Thomas Geary," February, 2010, unpublished, copy in the possession of authors.

15 See Appendix for the September 6, 1866 transcribed copy of John Thomas Geary's Will. A copy is in the possession of authors.

16 See Appendix for a copy of the July 20, 1860 Will of Thomas Geary (1792-1872). A copy is in the possession of authors.

17 Snow, Fate of the Fryers at page 40.

18 *Los Gatos Mail News*, Thursday, November 3, 1921, page 1, "Death of Kennedy J. Hanley Here." www.newspapers.com.

19 Alder, Douglas D. and Brooks, Karl, The History of Washington County – Isolation to Destination, Utah State Historical Society, Salt Lake City, Utah, 1996, pages 114-115.

20 www.familysearch.org, Kennedy James Hanley (1845-1921) KFRL-TTN, Kennedy James Hanley Life Sketch posted by Elaine Young of the Silver Reef Foundation, which references a US Circuit Court of Appeals case No. 934 and various newspaper articles.

21 *Ibid.*

22 www.familysearch.org. Eliza Jane Geary Keele, (1859-1931), LLHM-Z2B. quoting "A Sketch of the Life of Eliza Jane Geary Keele" by Roxa and Effie Keele.

23 *Ibid.*

24 *Ibid.*

25 See images at the end of Chapter 7 for a photograph of the "wall pocket," provided to Kaye Page Nichols by Jill Keele in 2020. See Appendix herein for copies of John Thomas Geary's shorthand and writings, provided to Kaye Page Nichols by Jill Keele, 2020. It is unknown if any other Geary records are in Eliza's family.

26 Handwritten document entitled "A Sketch of Dearly Beloved Aunt Leah Geary's Life" by Eva Geary Page Higbee, August 11, 1970. Copy in possession of the authors. Eva was Leah's niece, a daughter of Sophia Ann Geary Page. This Life Sketch was written by Eva because she was giving her granddaughter, Rosalee Harris Hunt, a large framed portrait of Leah Fryer Geary to hang in her home in California. As Rosalee had never known Aunt Leah, she asked her grandmother to write a life story for her. The large Leah Fryer Geary portrait still hangs in the home of Rosalee's daughter, Lisa Michele Church, as of 2021.

27 Gardner and Zeenati at page 28.

28 Original Letter from Eliza Jane Geary Keele to Sophia Ann Geary Page dated January 8, 1898 is in the possession of the authors. See image and transcription in the Appendix herein, which includes a section from David Keele also.

29 www.familysearch.org., Sarah Anne (Annie) Geary Davis, (1864-1922), KWVP-DLT.

30 Email from Sandy Cutter, great-granddaughter of James Davis, to Kaye Page Nichols dated February 26, 2021, in possession of authors.

31 "United States Census, 1900," database with images, *FamilySearch* (https://familysearch.org/ark:/61903/1:1:M3V5-5WZ : accessed 26 February 2021), Anna Davis, Fenton, Burlington, Otto, Basin, Alamo, Embar, Anderson Precincts, Big Horn, Wyoming, United States; citing enumeration district (ED) 70, sheet 7A, family 124, NARA microfilm publication T623 (Washington, D.C.: National Archives and Records Administration, 1972.); FHL microfilm 1,241,826.

32 See Appendix herein for a digital image of Annie Davis' land deed to her Burlington, Wyoming ranch, found on the website for the U.S. Department of Interior, Bureau of Land Management, General Land Office Records, Document Number 1363, BLM Serial Number WYWYAA 020140, issued June 30, 1906. https://glorecords.blm.gov/details/patent.

33   "United States Census, 1910," database with images, *FamilySearch* (https://www.familysearch.org/ark:/61903/1:1:MP-JV-32Q : accessed 26 February 2021), Sarah A Davis, Burlington, Big Horn, Wyoming, United States; citing enumeration district (ED) ED 17, sheet 3A, family 37, NARA microfilm publication T624 (Washington D.C.: National Archives and Records Administration, 1982), roll 1745; FHL microfilm 1,375,758.

34   Letter from Joshua T. Willis to Brigham Young, dated January 1, 1874, Church History Library, CR 1234, 1 box 35 fd. 11 item 1. Willis was submitting his resignation as Toquerville bishop.

35   Rice, Shareene K. Strem, "When You Know Your Past You Understand Yourself, The Joshua Thomas Willis Story," A Closure Project Submitted to the Degrees by Independent Study Program, Brigham Young University, December 2002, copy in possession of authors.

36   www.familysearch.org, William Richard Willis, (1868-1954), DWZN-WK5.

37   *Ibid.*

38   See Appendix herein for copies and transcriptions of the William Richard Willis letters dated December 15, 1914 and January 15, 1934, original letters are in possession of Kaye Page Nichols.

39   www.familysearch.org, Laura Adina Willis Lewis, (1870-1938) KZMH-97X. See images at end of the chapter for a copy of the Lewis obituary in the *Kane County Standard,* November 11, 1938.

Above, the Daniel and Sophia Ann Geary Page family about 1903. They were a prosperous family at the time due to Daniel's mining ventures. This was shortly after the family built their red brick mansion near Pinto, Utah, operating it as a boarding house along the Old Spanish Trail.

Standing, l. to right: Amy, Daniel, Sophia Ann, Eva
Sitting, l. to right: John, Golda, Dettie, Robert
Sitting in front: Geary

Right, Sophia Ann Geary Page as a young woman. Note she is wearing the Geary family seal around her neck on a chain or ribbon.

203

Two photos of Echo Workman Geary Hanley as a young woman. In the bottom photo she was living with her husband and two sons in Idaho in the early 1900s. She lived in several places in the northwest and eventually settled in Los Gatos, California.

Above, David and Eliza Jane Geary Keele, probably in the late 1800s. They lived in Panaca, Nevada where they raised a large family.

Right, Frances Marion Keele and his mother, Eliza Jane Geary Keele, probably in the 1920s.

Leah Fryer Geary died at age 36 from stomach cancer. She never married; she worked for others and often lived with her sisters to help raise their children. Leah had a birthmark on the left side of her face that was considered disfiguring but she was obviously a beautiful woman.

Annie Geary Davis as a young woman.

Annie Geary Davis

Christian Ronnow, the man who hired both Eliza Jane Geary and Sarah Ann (Annie) Geary when they were teenagers to work as household servants in Panaca, Nevada. He was a Danish convert to the Mormon Church who raised a large family.

DEATH OF MRS. ANNIE DAVIS

Mrs. Annie Davis passed away on Saturday, May 21, at her home in Basin, death being due to chronic heart disease. She had been confined to her home but a short time, and the news of her death came as a shock to her many friends.

Funeral services were held at the house on Tuesday morning, conducted by Rev. Edwin Bowling, after which the remains were taken to Burlington, where after another service, they were laid to rest beside those of her husband.

Annie Geary was born on February 20, 1864, at Panaca, Utah. Her parents died when she was a small child. She was married to James Davis September 11, 1882, and to them were born six children. Robert of Powell, Wyo.; Walter of Lovell, Wyo.; Ernest of Basin, Wyo.; Mrs. Elmer Gould of Powell, Wyo.; Heber and Grace, deceased.

The family moved from Utah to the southwestern part of Wyoming in 1889, where they spent five years. They came from there to the Big Horn Basin in 1894. Mr. Davis passed away at their ranch on the Greybull river in the year 1900. The widow and surviving children have continued to live in the Big Horn Basin since that time. Mrs. Davis had lived in Basin for the past seven years.

Mrs. Davis, during her residence in this section had won the enduring friendship of all with whom she came in contact. She was a woman of splendid character, a good mother and went to her grave with a knowledge of having reared a good family. She will be greatly missed by all friends and relatives and the sorrowing ones have the sincerest sympathy of all.

Above, the James and Annie Geary Davis family in about 1898-1899, prior to the 1900 wagon accident that killed James. Annie homesteaded a ranch on the Greybull River in Big Horn County, Wyoming and raised her family there.

L. to right, James, Heber (born 1885), Robert (born 1883), Walter (born 1887), Annie. The twins, Ernest and Effie are in the center (born 1891) and baby Grace, in front, (born 1896).

Left, the newspaper clipping dated May 21, 1921 from The Big Horn County Rustler, reporting on the death of Annie Geary Davis at age 50 from chronic heart disease.

William Richard Willis and his family.

Above, about 1912:
 Standing, l. to right, Jennie, Carl, Archie, William Albert, Leo.
 Sitting, l. to right, Clarence, Harriet with Echo Bea on her lap, Hyrum, William Richard, Ella Mae.

(Note: William Albert died in October, 1912 of typhoid; Echo Bea was born in 1912.)

Below, about 1950:
 Standing, l. to right, Carl, Hyrum, Clarence, Leo, Archie.
 Sitting, l. to right, Harriet, William Richard, Ella Mae.

Laura Adina (Lolly) Willis and her husband, Samuel Larkin Lewis.

Report of Adina Laura Willis Lewis' death in The Kane County Standard, November 11, 1938

Adina Willis Lewis Passes At Kanab

After an illness of several weeks, Adina Willis Lewis of Kanab, died at the hospital Monday morning, November 21. Funeral services were held Tuesday afternoon at 2 p. m. at the North Ward chapel. Melvin S. Haycock, of the North Ward bishopric, took charge of the services.

The choir beautifully rendered "Rock of Ages", the opening song, "Thou Doest Not Weep Alone" and the closing hymn, "I Know That My Redeemer Lives". An appropriate violin solo was given by Ray B. Young.

Speakers were Bishop Joseph S. Johnson and Osborne Brown. The opening prayer was by Fred A. Lundquist and the benediction by Ami Judd.

Many tributes were paid to the deceased by the speakers. Bishop Johnson mentioned the fact that both Brother and Sister Lewis were pioneers who had done their work well.

Mr. Brown, in remarks made, spoke comforting words to the family.

Many beautiful flowers from relatives and friends covered the casket and were banked on a table in front of the stand. Interment was in the Kanab cemetery.

Adina Willis was born at Toquerville February 17, 1870, but later lived in Arizona. She married Larken Lewis when a young woman and to them were born many children. The greater part of her life she has lived at Kanab. She was a true pioneer mother and with her husband helped in the pioneering of this county. She was a woman of good judgement, kind, sympathetic and appreciative. Her husband, Larkin Lewis, died only a few months ago.

She was visiting her daughters in the east when she became ill and at Chicago underwent an operation. She came home in a very weakened condition and remained in the hospital under the care of Dr. Aiken until the end came last Monday.

Mrs. Lewis is survived by three sons and two daughters, Mrs. Millie C. Crummery of Chicago, Ill.; Mrs. Laura L. Bruce and Roy Lewis of Salt Lake City, and Charley and Sheldon Lewis of Kanab. She is also survived by nine grand children.

Out-of-town relatives who came to Kanab to attend the funeral services were, Mr. and Mrs. Roy Lewis of Salt Lake City and Charley Lewis of House Rock, Arizona.

ACKNOWLEDGEMENTS

We would like to acknowledge all the assistance and support we received over the years from so many Geary descendants and family members in creating this book. We honor the valuable work and prior contributions of Bessie Snow, Eva Geary Page Higbee, Maree Higbee Gardner, Eleen Higbee Harris, Shirlee Harris Graff, Suzanne Swindle Johnston, Andrea Lee Conley, Roland Lee, Richard Lee, Francis Marion Keele, Robert Geary Page, Melanie Jones, Jill Keele, Wilma Higbee Kemp, Karma Kemp Wasden, Brian Kemp Bowler, Eva Louise Gardner Zeenati, Paul Tooke, Kirk Bailey, Jill Keele, Vernetta Page Marshall, Earl Marshall, LaJean Carruth, Keevin Willis, Yvonne Stone, Kelley Bollinger, Valerie Kortenber, Dale Clawson, Jay Burrup, and Charlie Martin, without whom this book would not have been possible. We are also indebted to so many family members who shared their Geary family treasures with us so they could be documented in the book.

We appreciate the support of our spouses and immediate family members who patiently endured and enhanced our project, especially our adult children who helped immensely with computer and internet questions. We relied on many outside sources such as the Utah State Historical Society, the Family Search website, the Ancestry website, the Church of Jesus Christ of Latter-day Saints Church History Library and Family History Library, professional genealogists, independent scholars, historical journals and publications, and several academic institutions. We did not include everything relevant from those sites and we encourage readers to explore those sources on their own.

The book was a labor of love intended to bring together as much verified historical information as we could to illuminate the life of John Thomas Geary. We know there are unanswered questions, but we feel strongly that this is the story that needed to be told at this time. In the future, other items may come to light and new discoveries will be made which we will gladly add to the record.

Finally, we would like to acknowledge the role of the gospel of Jesus Christ in our lives that gives us such a powerful connection to our ancestors. Through our religious beliefs we were able to feel support from both sides of the veil separating the living from the dead. For this we are grateful.

Lisa-Michele Church and Kaye Page Nichols
July, 2021

APPENDIX

Selected Excerpts from Patty Swenson Research Report
Original 1712 Will of John Geary
Transcription of 1712 Will of John Geary
1712 Inventory of John Geary Property
2008 Letter from the Royal Archives
Transcriptions of Articles of Clerkship - John Thomas Geary 1838/1843
1845 Admittance of John Thomas Geary to Queen's Bench
Transcription of 1845 Admittance of John Thomas Geary
Transcription of 1849 Thomas Geary Mortgage
The Geary Family Bible
John Thomas Geary Calling Card
Excerpts from the Diary of Richard Fryer
July 15, 1860 John Thomas Geary Letter to Sophia
Complaint in Geary v. Stambaugh Lawsuit 1860
September 13, 1860 Cross-Hatched Letter
Transcription of September 13, 1860 Cross-Hatched Letter
The 'Writings' of John Thomas Geary
Will of Thomas Geary July 20, 1860
Transcription of Will of Thomas Geary July 20, 1860
Trnascription of Will of John Thomas Geary September 10, 1866
Family Story regarding Sophia Geary Willis' Death
1880 Guardianship Paper for Annie Geary
Transcription of 1882 Letter from Sophia Geary Page to John Brown
Transcription of 1894 Letter from Sophia Geary Page to John Brown
January 8, 1898 Letter from Eliza Geary Keele to Sophia Geary Page
1906 Deed to Annie Geary Davis on Wyoming Ranch
December 15, 1914 Letter from William Willis to Sophia Geary Page
January 15, 1934 Letter from William Willis to Sophia Geary Page

Selected Excerpts from the Patty Swenson Research Report on the Geary Family - April, 2019

Research Report Geary Family

By: Patty Swenson

For: Kaye Page Nichols and Lisa Michele Church

Introduction

My research for the Geary Family of Leicestershire, beginning with John Thomas Geary (1823 – 1867), began years ago as I helped Kaye Page Nichols with research on his family when we found each other by realizing that our ancestors, John Thomas Geary and John C. Hall, were contemporaries and mentioned each other in letters, journals, and other documents. They were also likely related, as family members were listed in the 1851 Census as cousins. After some pretty extensive research, the first report I wrote about John Thomas Geary for Kaye Page Nichols was delivered in 2010, so it has been some time since I have revisited this family. There have been huge advancements in the availability of indexed records since that time and it has been easier to find original documents that allow for the detailed research necessary to locate, identify, and analyze the data needed to document the ancestors of John Thomas Geary.

Over time I have seen a large amount of evidence that many descendants, primarily members of the Church of Jesus Christ of Latter-day Saints, have tried to compile the genealogy for their ancestor, John Thomas Geary. Even from the early time of the ancestral file where records were kept on long paper forms and held by the Family History Library in Salt Lake City, there were errors and information that just wasn't accurate. I know those looking for their beloved ancestors were doing their best, but with the frequency of the Geary surname in the county of Leicestershire and lack of available records, even with the best intentions, it was nearly impossible to compile an accurate record. Kaye Page Nichols and Lisa Michele Church want to go beyond the names and dates and misinformation to tell the real story of John Thomas Geary and his family and have gone to great lengths to acquire all available documents and reliable information to set the record straight.

This report prepared for Lisa Michelle Church and Kaye Page Nichols is my attempt to identify the Geary males and their families for a few generations, with supporting documentation, and to share my impression of the situations and the socioeconomic status of the family of John Thomas Geary that had resided in Leicestershire, England for generations.

A big order, and believe me I have felt the overwhelming complexity of this project since resuming the Geary research in January of 2019. Great success has ensued with relentless research and detailed analysis, resulting in more research, more documents, and a clearer picture of this family. The research is not complete but the report is still full of hundreds of dates, facts, and documents, and is significantly lengthy to tire even the most enthusiastic reader. Considering that there are no less than seven different John Geary's, I have written the report in sections to avoid confusion as much as possible and so it can be read a little at a time and referred back to as necessary. It is my wish that my research and subsequent report will provide the basis for the interesting story that Lisa Michelle Church and Kaye Page Nichols plan to tell about the Geary family.

Patty Swenson

The Socioeconomic Status of the Geary Family who lived in Atterton, Witherley and Ratcliffe Culey, and Dadlington in Leicestershire England from about 1680 to 1880.
Patty Swenson
April 2019

The story of the socioeconomic status of the Geary Family from one generation to the next is the same as the story of the land they held. Owning land meant wealth, social status and influence, and control over the livelihood that supported the family. The story of the Geary land holdings, especially the land in Atterton in Witherley Parish and Ratcliffe Culey, began at least in the later part of the 1600's.

John Geary of Atterton who died in 1712, left a will in which he mentioned his land in Atterton. His parentage is uncertain. He called himself 'yeoman' which means that he was commoner who owned the land that he farmed or cultivated. He would definitely have been part of the middle class. The top of society in England were the nobility, those with a title or knighthood. Below them were the gentry. Gentlemen were not quite rich but they were most often well off. To be called a Gentleman it was a requirement that one did not work. Below them were yeomen, farmers who owned their land. Yeomen were usually comfortably well off but they often worked alongside their men. Below them came the mass of the population; craftsmen, tenant farmers and laborers.

Hoskins states in 1939 that:

Leicestershire was, until the early eighteenth century, an almost purely farming county with no towns of any size (Leicester itself had about 4,500 to 5,000 people at the end of the seventeenth century) and no industries beyond those of the local crafts and trades; and it was until the later decades of the seventeenth century a great corn county. As one early seventeenth-century writer put it, Leicestershire's 'great manufacture was tillage'. Leicestershire was small even as the English counties go, just about 800 square miles, but there was very little waste in this area. Fully 95 per cent of Leicestershire was being cultivated in some form or other in this period. Leicestershire had been one of the most highly cultivated and densely peopled regions of England from the thirteenth century onwards.

So, farming the land was the primary occupation in Leicestershire and was significant, and owning the land one farmed was even more significant.

John (Gearie) Geary - 1698 to 1754, his son, also called yeoman, inherited the land from his father. During his lifetime and possibly with his influence the land in the hamlet of Atterton was re-appropriated by the act of enclosure. This began about 12 June 1726, and ended about 25 April 1729 by the consent and agreement of all the landholders in Atterton, including John Geary. The enclosure allowed for each landowner to make exchanges of small parcels of land that weren't contiguous and were "*in and amongst the other in the Common & open fields of Atterton, insomuch that no man cod make the best profits of his own lands*", (as noted in Estate Doc #2, abstract by John Thomas Geary).

Found in Local Histories.org online:

During the 18th century agriculture was gradually transformed by an agricultural revolution. Until 1701 seed was sown by hand. In that year a seed drill was invented, which sowed seed in straight lines. Furthermore, until the 18th century most livestock was slaughtered at the beginning of winter because farmers could not grow enough food to feed their animals through the winter months. Until the 18th century most land in England was divided into 3 fields. Each year 2 fields were sown with crops while the third was left fallow (unused). The Dutch began to grow swedes or turnips on land instead of leaving it fallow. (The turnips restored the soil's fertility). When they were harvested the turnips could be stored to provide food for livestock over the winter. The new methods were popularized in England by a man named Robert 'Turnip' Townshend (1674-1741). Under the 3 field system, which still covered much of England, all the land around a village or small town, was divided into 3 huge fields. Each farmer owned some strips of land in each field. During the 18th century land was enclosed. That means it was divided up so each farmer had all his land in one place instead of scattered across 3 fields. Enclosure allowed farmers to use their land more efficiently.

Enclosure allowed that parcels of land previously held by a few owners, as well as much of the land that was common pasture or the waste of the manor which had traditionally been used by everyone, be transferred to the land owners and made available to them for fencing, hedging, or ditching to enclose the land for their own benefit. Under this act the land owned by the Parish, called glebe land, was also surveyed and set aside for the benefit the Rector of the Parish by establishing the collection of a quarterly payment of Tithe money in lieu of the customary tythes & tenths of hay and grain. Enclosure required that one or more surveyors be chosen to map the land, and three to five independent commissioners or referees appointed to set out and allot specific plots to each land holder...

In Estate Documents #4 – John Thomas Geary mentions that John (Gearie) Geary (1698 to 1754) "departed this life intestate, leaving his son John Geary (1730 – 1817) "eldest son and heir at law" to inherit the property of Atterton by fee simple in possession. This is very interesting because John (Gearie) Geary (1698 to 1754) yeoman did not die intestate, but did leave a will dated 11 March 1754 that was proved 30 March 1754. This will named his grandson, John Neal, and daughter, Mary Neal, wife of Thomas Neal. It also named his wife, Sarah Geary, and finally his son, John Geary, was to receive, 'all the residue and remainder of my personal estate whatsoever'.

John Geary (1730 to 1817) was 24 years old when he inherited the land at Atterton, in the parish of Witherley, from his father. Four years later at age 28, he married Ann Sharman. He had two sons, John Geary born 1763, and Thomas Geary born 1767. He did not leave his land to either of these sons. As a young child, his oldest son, John Geary (1763-1826) inherited the estate of Ann Sharman's father, John Sharman, but did not inherit anything from his own father's will. His second son, Thomas Geary (1767-1853), did not inherit property but received money from this maternal grandfather as well an annuity provided for him from his father's will. He did not own land and it seems he did not have any children. He lived to the old age of 86.

John Geary (1730 to 1817) added extensively to the estate inherited from his father as described in John Thomas Geary's Estate Documents #1-5... He was likely the wealthiest of the Geary men included in this report. At the time of his marriage he was identified as a farmer, but by the end of his life, his will gave him the title of a Gentleman. As mentioned, John Geary did not leave any of the land or property of Atterton, Witherley, and Ratcliffe Culey to his sons, John (Sharman) Geary (1763-1826) & Thomas Geary (1767- 1853). However, by his Will, created a lifetime annuity to provide for the support of his son Thomas from the profits of his estate, but willed the actual land & property to his grandson, Thomas Geary, second son of his eldest son, John Geary. The will proves the relationships between each of them, supported by dates found in the parish registers and other documents. (See individual reports for each male member of the Geary family.)

John (Sharman) Geary (1763-1826) was a landowner at Dadlington, Leicestershire, and later at Higham on the Hill. He inherited the estate of his paternal grandfather John Sharman at age 8, which was managed for him by his grandfather's executors until he became of age. Known as a farmer and grazier to the town of Higham on the Hill and his eldest son probably was left to manage the estate. His will gave him the title of Gentleman. He left this estate to his eldest surviving son, also the eldest of twins, **John Geary (1792-1868)** who farmed and grazed the land until his own son, John Abell Geary (1826-1907), took over. The land at Dadlington was sold in 1881 when John Abell Geary decided to retire from farming.

Thomas Geary (1792 -1865) the youngest of twin sons born to John (Sharman) Geary (1763 – 1826) inherited the land at Atterton, Witherley and Ratcliffe Culey from his grandfather, John Geary. The land was mortgaged in 1849, the mortgage was transferred in 1852, and probably the land was eventually foreclosed on or sold as a result of non-payment. Thomas was the father of five sons including his oldest son, John Thomas Geary, (1823 to 1867) the ancestor of Kaye Page Nichols and Lisa Michelle Church. All but one of these five sons left their birth country of England by 1861. It seems unusual that four young men from a well-connected family of some prosperity that had owned land in the county of Leicestershire for around two hundred years would all be leaving England around the same time. The question has been: What happened to the Geary family to change the course of their lives?...

My thoughts about possible contributing factors:
- at the end of the life of John Geary (1730-1817) changes in Britain created financial hardships for many land owners. Taxes were high and were being assessed more frequently.

- The depopulation of the rural areas of Leicestershire reduced the availability of workers. This was caused at first by the act of enclosure that took away the use of shared common lands and the ability for laborers to support their families. And later by the industrial revolution which required that the poor move to places where they could get work. Some of the land had been farmed without rotation and didn't produce as well. Partly because of this, and partly for the lack of laborers, much of the farmland of Leicestershire had been converted to pasture for the grazing of animals.
- There is always the possibility of financial risk taking or gambling. Even investing was done at high risk. Speculation holds a prominent place in English history, both in society and among the working classes.
- The circumstances that Thomas Geary (1792-1865) found himself in: supporting his uncle Thomas Geary from the profits of the land, high taxes, low profits, and five sons to provide for, may have been too much for him to be able to stay out of debt.
- Certainly, there is evidence that there was some displeasure about how his uncle Thomas Geary (1767-1853) was supporting his own wife.
- It is also possible that Thomas Geary (1792 -1865) believed that using the money that could be raised by mortgaging the land for the education of his sons would have a greater benefit than the land itself could provide for them.
- The death certificates for Sarah Ann Geary and Thomas Geary indicate they may have been under a lot of stress. Sarah at age 49, died from Apoplexy caused by a cerebral hemorrhage or stroke. And Thomas at age 72, died from Asthma, Debility, and Exhaustion…

I found a reference to an investment Thomas may have made around 1846 in a proposed railway spur between Coventry and Nuneaton. The company was called the **Oxford, Coventry, Burton on Trent Junction Railway,** which in November 1845 published a **Book of Reference Containing the Names of Owners, Lesses, and Occupiers of the Lands, Houses, and Hereditaments to be taken for the purposes described on the Plans of a Line of Railway**. Thomas is listed on three pages concerning land in Witherley, Atterton, and Ratcliffe Culey. It seems there was a lot of competition in the railway business and companies were competing for the right to build connecting lines. There was some controversy about the amalgamation of railway lines and about a disagreement and deadline that was missed with the Great Western Railway Company and The Oxford, Coventry, Burton on Trent Railway was shut out.

Eventually, The Oxford, Coventry, Burton on Trent line made an agreement with the London and North Western Company, and their obsolete script was traded or marked and their required signature written on a 'Suplemtary Subscribers Deed'. A notice in Bradshaw's Railway Manual Shareholders Guide for 1854 records '*that the company [Oxford, Coventry, Burton on Trent Railway] was incorporated in July 1847 for a line between those towns, 10 miles – gauge 4 feet 8 1/2 inches; and by the same act the London and North Western obtained powers to lease it, at 5 per cent, per annum in perpetuity, and half surplus profits of working. This company's shares were issued to holders of scrip in the late Oxford, Coventry, Burton on Trent Railway Company, who withdrew their bill in 1846, on those conditions: shares in the London and North Western Company being issued in exchange entitled to the above mentioned*'.

I don't know for sure that Thomas Geary bought shares in this railway line, but he certainly had an interest in it. I believe the line proposed by the Oxford Coventry and Burton on Trent Railway Company was never built. In 1847 The House of Commons addressed a Bill proposed by the North-Western Company to build a branch railway diverging from their main line, between Coventry and Nuneaton. The House struck out part of the proposal reciting terms of an arrangement with the Oxford, Coventry and Burton on Trent Railway Company relative to providing the necessary funds for construction, as recorded in the March 1847 edition of The Monthly Railway Record, ed. By J. Robertson and J. W. Brooke. I am not sure if this was the cause of Thomas losing his land, but I feel it has to be a contributing factor. Based on the time period this was happening, the indication of stress in the family, and the fact that most of his sons left England soon after, the Railway situation has to have had some impact…

Original 1712 John Geary Will on file in the British records

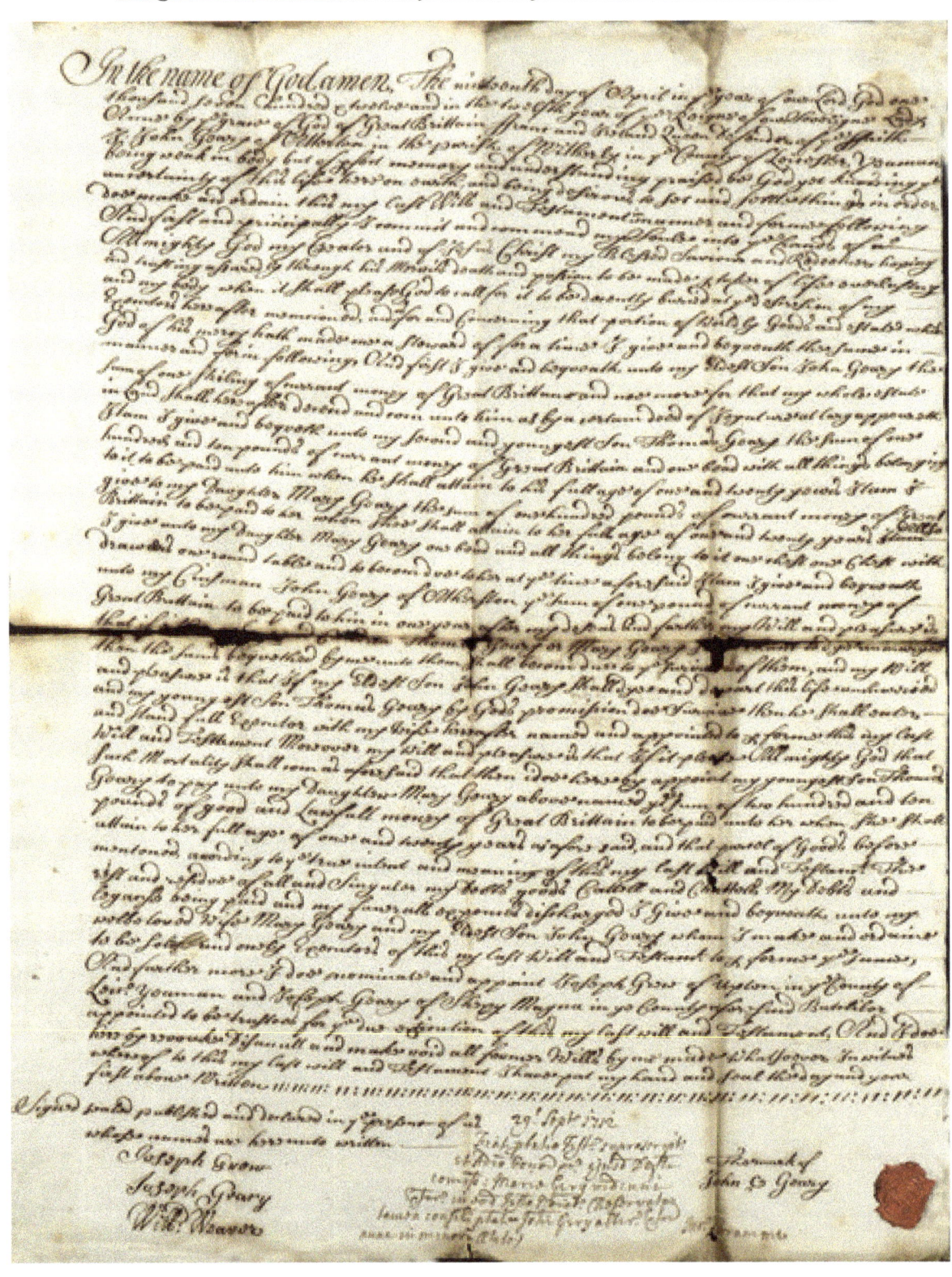

Source: Record Office for Leicestershire, Leicester & Rutland. Leicestershire Wills and Probate Records, 1712 (VG A-W). John Geary of Atterton parish of Witherly. Find my Past Collection: Leicestershire Wills and Probate Records, 1500 – 1939. Digital image. Transcribed by Patty Swenson – February 2019 original spelling left uncorrected, punctuation added.

Transcription

Will of John Geary of Atterton Leicester, yeoman:
dated 19 April 1712; proved 29 September 1712.

In the name of God amen. The nineteenth day of April in ye year of our Lord God one thousand seven hundred & twelve and in the twelfth year of ye Reigne of our Soverigne Lady Anne by ye grace of God of Great Brittain France and Ireland Queen Defender of ye faith,

I, John Geary of Atterton, in the parish of Witherly in ye County of Leicester yeoman being weak in body but of sound memory and understanding praised be God yet knowing the uncertainty of this life here on earth and being desirous to set and settle things in order, do make and ordain this my last Will and Testament in manner and forme following. And first and principally I commit and commend my soule into ye hand of All mighty God my Creator and of Jesus Christ my Blessed Savior and Redeemer hoping and trusting assuredly through his merit death and passion to be made a taker of life everlasting and my body when it shall please God to call for it, to be decently buried at ye discretion of my Executors here after mentioned and for and concerning that portion of Worldly Goods and estate which God of his mercy hath made me a steward of for a time, I give and bequeath the same in manner and form following:

And first, I give and bequeath unto my Eldest son John Geary the sum of one shilling of current money of Great Brittan and noe more for that my whole estate in Land shall hereafter descend and com unto him as by a certain deed of joynture at large approacheth.

Item - I give and bequeath unto my second and youngest son, Thomas Geary, the sum of one hundred and ten pounds of current money of Great Brittain and one bead [bed] with all things belonging to it to be paid unto him when he shall attain to his full age of one and twenty years.

Item - I give to my Daughter, Mary Geary, the sum of one hundred pounds of current money of Great Brittan to be paid to her when she shall attain to her full age of one and twenty years.
Item - I give unto my Daughter, Mary Geary, one bead [bed] and all things belong to it, one shelf, one chest withdrawers, one round table, and to become due to her at ye time aforesaid.

Item - I give and bequeath unto my kinsman, John Geary of Atherston, ye sum of one pound of currant money of Great Brittain to be paid to him in one year after my decease and farther my Will and pleasure is that if ---[unreadable]---said children Thomas Geary or Mary Geary ---[unreadable---] do dye unmaryed then the sum bequeathed by me unto them shall become due to ye survivor of them, and my Will and pleasure is that If my eldest son, John Geary, shall dye and depart this life unmarried and my youngest son, Thomas Geary, by god's permission does survive then he shall enter and stand full Executor with my wife hereafter named and appointed to forme this last Will and Testament.

Moresoever, my Will and pleasure is that, If it please All mighty God, that such Mortality shall com as aforesaid that then I doe hereby appoint my youngest son, Thomas Geary, to pay unto my Daughter, Mary Geary, above named ye sum of two hundred and ten pounds of good and lawful money of Great Brittain to be paid unto her when she shall attain to her full age of one and twenty years as aforesaid, and that parsol of Goods before mentioned according to ye true intent and meaning of this my last Will and Testament.

The rest and residue of all and singular my debts, goods, Chattel and Chattels, My debts and legacys being paid and my funeral expenses discharged, I give and bequeath unto my well beloved Wife, Mary Geary, and my eldest son, John Geary, whom I make and ordaine to be sole and only Executors of this my last Will and Testament to and forme ye   .

And farther more I doe nominate and appoint Joseph Grow of Upton, in ye County of Leic [Leicester], yeoman, and Joseph Geary of Shepy Magna, in ye County aforesaid, Batchilor, appointed to be trusted for ye due execution of this my last will and Testament. And I do hereby revoke, disanull, and make void all former Wills by me made Whatsoever. In witness whereof to this my last will and testament, I have put my hand and seal the day and year first above written.

Signed sealed published and declared in ye presens of us whose names are hereunto written
Joseph Grow
Joseph Geary   The mark of John Geary
Will. Weaver
29 Sept 1712
First pbatio Test – appeared Marie Gery one of the executors Johi Gery another extor

1712 Inventory of the Goods, Cattle and Chattels of John Geary of Atterton, Parish of Witherley, County of Leicester.

Aprill ye 20th 1712

An Inventory of the Goods Cattle and Chattels of John Geary of Atterton in the parish of Witherley in the County of Leicester yeom.

	£	s	d
Imprs His purse and Apparell	05	10	00
In the Dwelling House five Irons one Cupboard one Table Six Chaires and other old things	01	10	00
In the parlor two beds one Chest one Table three Chaires and other old things	06	00	00
In the Kitchen pewter Brass one Dresser Tubs pailes one Churne and other old things	01	10	00
In the Chamber over the Kitchen one bed one Table one Chest of Draws one Box one Coffer 3 boxes a pairs woole & other things	09	00	00
In the Chamb: ov: the House three beds and some oth: things	03	00	00
In the Chamb: ov: the parlor wheats & oats and Mault	10	00	00
Linings	05	10	00
Bacon on the Bacon Cratch	02	05	00
Corne In the Barne	10	00	00
Six Mares	36	00	00
Three year old Colts	09	00	00
Eight Cowes	32	00	00
Two thirk Heffers two Rearing Calves	09	00	00
Fifty Sheep	16	00	00
Two pigs	01	10	00
Implem:ts for Husbandry	15	00	00
Corne on the Ground	45	00	00
with other Lumber	00	15	00
	222	10	00

Wm Weaver
Jos: Grew
Jno Geary

2008 Letter from The Royal Archives clarifying the family stories about Queen Victoria

APPENDIX B

THE ROYAL ARCHIVES   4 December 2008

Dear Dr. Nichols,

Thank you for your letter of 18 October and I must apologise for the delay in replying to you; we have been very busy lately and therefore unable to answer your enquiry as quickly as we would have liked. I hope this delay has not caused you too much inconvenience.

I have searched our various indexes for the names **John Thomas Geary**, **Moses** and **Sophia Fryer**, but regret to say that I found no reference to any of them. In particular, I searched the index for Queen Victoria's Journal, but there is no mention of the surname Fryer or of a visit to the Fryer home. In fact, the Queen did not have a residence on the Isle of Wight in 1840, as she did not purchase Osborne House (near East Cowes) until 1845 (having first stayed in the original house in 1844), so some years after the birth of the twins.

As can be found in printed sources such as *Burke's Guide to the Royal Family*, biographies of Queen Victoria and newspaper reports, Queen Victoria did indeed marry Prince Albert on 10 February 1840, in the Chapel Royal at St. James's Palace, London; and according to a press cutting, the time of the service is said to have been around 1 in the afternoon. The wedding was reported in some detail in the national press, and it is perhaps possible that this gave the Fryers the idea of naming the twins Victoria and Albert as they were born on the same day as the Royal wedding.

While I fear we have not been able to be of much assistance to your enquiry, I hope that the above information may perhaps prove of some interest and help to your family history.

Yours sincerely,

A Dewett
pp Douglas Sulley
Archives Assistant

Dr. Kaye P. Nichols
114 W. Innsbruck Lane
Midway
Utah 84049
U.S.A.

The Royal Collection Trust, Windsor Castle, Berkshire SL4 1NJ.   Tel. 01753 868286.   Fax: 01753 854910.

The Royal Collection Trust is a company limited by guarantee registered in England and Wales
Registered No. 2713536. Registered Charity No. 1016972
Registered Office: Stable Yard House, St James's Palace, London SW1A 1JR

Kaye Page Nichols wrote to the Royal Archives in Britain during 2008 seeking to clarify whether Queen Victoria named the twin children of Moses Fryer, father of Sophia Fryer Geary, and whether John Thomas Geary served as a royal interpreter.

Transcriptions of the Articles of Clerkship for John Thomas Geary by which he embarked on his Law Career - 1839 and 1843

ARTICLES OF CLERKSHIP FOR JOHN THOMAS GEARY TO STAFFORD STRATTON BAXTER 1839

In the Queen's Bench

Leonard Gisborne of Atherstone, in the County of Warwick, Clerk to Stafford Stratton Baxter of the same place, Gentleman, maketh oath and saith that by Articles of Agreement bearing date the twenty fourth day of November now instant and made between Stafford Stratton Baxter of Atherstone, aforesaid Gentleman, One of the Attornies of Her Majesty's Courts of Queen's Bench Common Pleas and Exchequer of Pleas at Westminster of the one part, and Thomas Geary of Atterton in the County of Leicester, and John Geary of Atterton, aforesaid Son of the
said Thomas Geary of the other part, the said John Geary for the considerations therein mentioned did put, place, and bind himself Clerk to the Stafford Stratton Baxter to serve him in the Profession of an Attorney at Law from the day of the date of the said Articles for the term
of five years thence next ensuing and fully to be complete and ended and which said Articles were in due form of Law executed by the said Stafford Stratton Baxter, Thomas Geary, and John
Geary in the presence of this deponent and of one John Baker of Atherstone aforesaid and that the names Thomas Geary and John Geary "Leonard Gisborne" and "John Baker" set and subscribed to the said Articles as Witnesses to the due execution thereof are the proper hands writing of this deponent and of the said John Baker

    Sworn at Atherstone in the County
    Of Warwick the twenty fourth day of
    November One thousand eight hundred
    and thirty eight
           Before me   Leonard Gisborne
       A Commissioner etc.

Sworn at Atherstone in the County of Warwick
The seventh day of December One thousand eight
Hundred and thirty eight
        Before me   Leonard Gisborne
        Henry Pooh (signed)
        A Commissioner etc.

Sworn at Atherstone in the County
of Warwick the Fifteenth day of
February One thousand eight
Hundred and thirty nine.
Before me Leonard Gisborne
Henry Pooh (signed)
A Commissioner etc.

           Geary
         Re   Geary
Herewith I send you affect of the execution of said Geary's Articles for you to file which
be pleased to do on Monday I am gentn for SS Baxter
Your able Servt Leo Gisborne (signed)
Atherstone 17 Feby 1839

ARTICLES OF CLERKSHIP FOR JOHN THOMAS GEARY
ASSIGNED FROM STAFFORD STRATTON BAXTER TO ROBERT MICHAEL BAXTER
1843

page 224 of 1763 & page 278 of 1763

In the Queen's Bench

Stephen Pilgrim of Atherstone, in the county of Warwick, gentleman, maketh Oath and saith that by a certain Indenture of assignment bearing date the thirty first day of March last [1843] and made between Stafford Stratton Baxter of Atherstone, aforesaid gentleman, one of the Attorney's of Her Majesty's Court of Queen's Bench Common Pleas and Exchequer of Pleas at Westminster and a Solicitor of the High Court of Chancery of the first part, Thomas Geary of Atterton in the county of Leicester, farmer, and John Thomas Geary, son of the said Thomas Geary of the second part, and Robert Michael Baxter of Lincoln's Inn Fields in the county of Middlesex, one of the Attorney's of Her Majesty's Courts of Queen's Bench at Westminster and Solicitor in the High Court of Chancery of the third part, the said Stafford Stratton Baxter, for the consideration therein mentioned and with the consent and approbation of the said Thomas Geary and John Thomas Geary, did assign over the said John Thomas Geary and also certain Articles of Clerkship bearing date the twenty fourth day of November one thousand eight hundred and thirty eight of the said John Thomas Geary with the said Stafford Stratton Baxter for the Term of five years unto the said Robert Michael Baxter for the remainder of the said Term of Clerkship then to come and unexpired and which said Indenture of assignment was in due form of Law executed by the said Stafford Stratton Baxter and Thomas Geary in the presence of this deponent and that the Name "Stephen Pilgrim" set and subscribed

page 225 of 1763

to the said Indenture do witness to the due execution thereof by the said Stafford Stratton Baxter and Thomas Geary in the proper handwriting of this Deponent.

      Sworn at Atherstone in the
      county of Warwick the first   Stephen Pilgrim
      day of April One thousand   (signed)
      eight hundred and forty three
          Before me
              John Thos Pilgrim (signed)
      A Commissioner for taking Affidavits
      in Her Majesty's Court of Queens
      Bench at Westminster

ARTICLES OF CLERKSHIP FOR JOHN THOMAS GEARY
ASSIGNED FROM STAFFORD STRATTON BAXTER TO ROBERT MICHAEL BAXTER
CLERKS OATH
1843

In the Queen's Bench

Charles Cooke the younger, Clerk to Mefs^{rs} Baxter of Lincolns Inn Fields in the county of Middlesex, gentleman, maketh oath and saith that by a certain Indenture of Assignment bearing date the thirty first day of March last and made between Stafford Stratton Baxter of Atherstone in the County of Warwick, gentleman, one of the Attornie's of Her Majesty's Courts of Queens Bench Common Pleas and Exchequers of Pleas at Westminster and a Solicitor in the High Court of Chancery of the first part, Thomas Geary of Atterton in the County of Leicester Farmer and John Thomas Geary, Son of the said Thomas Geary and Clerk to the said Stafford Stratton Baxter of the second part, and Robert Michael Baxter of Lincolns Inn Fields in the County of Middlesex one of the Attornie's of Her Majesty's Courts of Queen Bench at Westminster and Solicitor in the High Court of Chancery of the third part, the said Stafford Stratton Baxter for the consideration therein mentioned and with the consent and approbation of the said Thomas Geary and John Thomas Geary did assign over the said John Thomas Geary and also certain Articles of Clerkship bearing date the twenty fourth day of November One thousand eight hundred and thirty eight of the said John Thomas Geary with the said Stafford Stratton Baxter for the term of five years unto the said Robert Michael Baxter to serve him the said Robert Michael Baxter for the remainder of the said Term of Clerkship then to come and unexpired and which said Indenture of Assignment was in due form of Law executed by the said John Thomas Geary and Robert Michael Baxter in the presence of this Deponent and that the name "C Cooke Junr" set and subscribed to the said Indenture as witness to the due execution thereof by the said John Thomas Geary and Robert Michael Baxter is the proper handwriting of the Deponent.

Sworn at my Chambers Rolls Garden Chancery   C Cooke Junr
Lane this 5th day of April 1843 Before me   (signed)
                  J Paltym

SOURCE: John Thomas Geary Articles of Clerkship with Stafford Stratton Baxter https://www.ancestry.com/family-tree/person/tree/10612501/person/6404827772/facts John Thomas Geary Articles of Clerkship with Robert Michael Baxter https://www.ancestry.com/family-tree/person/tree/10612501/person/6404827772/facts

1845 Admittance of John Thomas Geary as an Attorney at the Queen's Bench

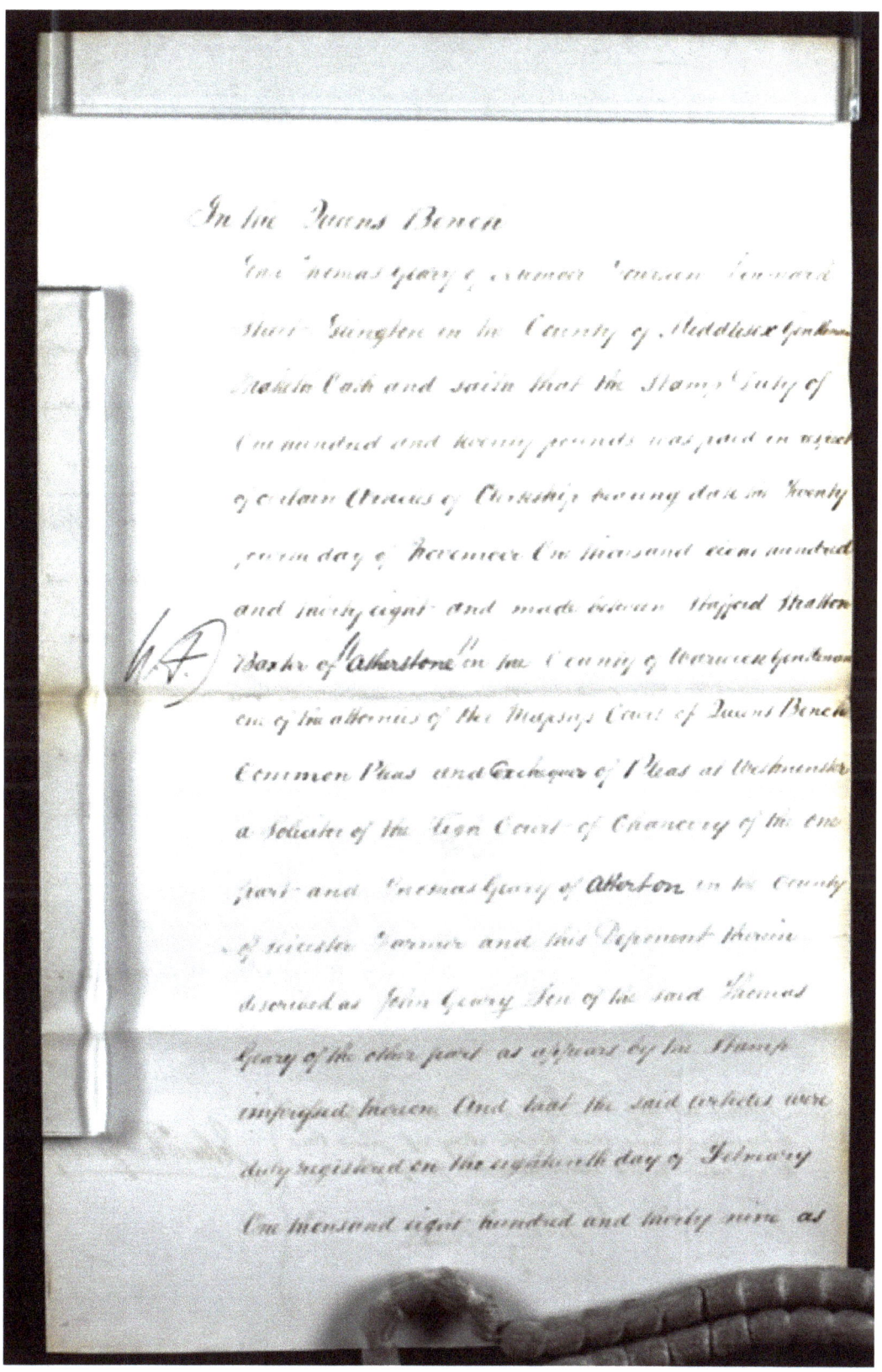

appears by the Certificate of the Proper Officer endorsed thereon And this Deponent further saith that the Stamp Duty of One pound fifteen shillings was paid in respect of a certain Assignment of the said articles bearing date the Thirty first day of March One thousand eight hundred and forty three and made between the said Rassoul Shatten Poster of the first part the said Thomas Geary and this Deponent of the second part and Robert Michael Basker of Lincolns Inn Fields in the County of Middlesex, one of the attornies of Her Majesty's Court of Queens Bench at Westminster and Solicitor in the High Court of Chancery of the third part as appears by the Stamp impressed thereon and that the said Assignment was duly registered on the fifth day of April One thousand eight hundred and forty three as appears by the Certificate of the Proper Officer endorsed thereon

Sworn at my Chambers in Rolls Garden
Chancery Lane this tenth day of June One
thousand eight hundred and forty five
Before me
Wm Wightman

John Thos Geary

Transcription

2958
John Geary
To Stafford Stratton Baxter

Rec. 11 June 1845
Filed this day of 18 February 1839
Messrs. Baxters
Lincoln's Inn Fields, London

In the Queen's Bench

John Thomas Geary of Number Fourteen Denmark Street Islington in the County of Middlesex, Gentleman, maketh Oath and saith that the Stamp Duty of One hundred and twenty pounds was paid in respect of certain Articles of Clerkship bearing date the Twenty fourth day of November One thousand and eight hundred and thirty eight and made between Stafford Stratton Baxter of Atherstone in the County of Warwick, Gentleman, one of the attornies of Her Majesty's Court of Queens Bench Common Please and Exchequer of Pleas at Westminster a Solicitor of the High Court of Chancery of the one part and Thomas Geary of Atterton in the County of Leicester Farmer and this Deponent therein described as John Geary son of the said Thomas Geary of the other part as appears by the Stamp impressed thereon.

And that the said Articles were duly registered on the eighteenth day of February, one thousand eight hundred and thirty nine as appears by the Certificate of the Proper Officer endorsed thereon and this Deponent further saith that the Stamp Duty of One pound fifteen shillings was paid in respect of a certain assignment of the said articles bearing dated the thirty first day of March One thousand eight hundred and forty three and made between the said Stafford Stratton Baxter of the first part the said Thomas Geary and this Deponent of the second part and Robert Michael Baxter of Lincoln's Inn Fields in the County of Middlesex, one of the attornies of Her Majesty's Court of Queens Bench at Westminster and Solicitor in the High Court of Chancery of the third part as appears by the Stamp impressed thereon, and that the said assignment was duly registered on the Fifth day of April One thousand eight hundred and forty three as appears by the Certificate of the Proper Officer endorsed thereon.

              Signed by John Thomas Geary

Sworn at my chambers in the Rolls Garden Chancery Lane this tenth day of June one thousand eight hundred and forty-five before me, Wm. Wyhteman.

Transcription of Thomas Geary 1849 Mortgage

Abstract of Mortgage
Of the whole of Mr. Geary's
Property

11 Jany 1849   By Indre of mortgage made betw^n Thomas Geary of Atterton in the parish of Witherley in the coy of Leicester Esq of one part & Thomas Thorpe Fowke of Midgham in the Coy of Berks Esq. of the other pt.

After recit^g the Indre of 5 Octr 1733 set out at commencement of Abstract No. 2.
And recitg that John Geary (in such abstract parly mentioned) aftwd departed this life intest^e[in testate] leaving John Geary (in the now abstracting Indre after called "John Geary the Son") his Eldest Son & heir at law who thrupon because entitled to the heredits & premes described in & limited & assured by the said therein lastly recited Indre for an absolute estate in fee Simple in posson.
And also recit^g 2 sev^l Indres of Lease & Release resp^{ly} dated 15 & 16 Feby 1779 15 & 16 Feby 1779 & 4 & 5 April 1800 resp^{ly} set out at pages 1,5 & 7 in Abstract No. 2.

And also reciting that sd John Geary the Son ~~aftwards deptd this life~~ being so seised or entitled as aforesaid did in such manner as was then by the law ^{regd} for the validity of Devises of Real Ested duly sign seal & publish his last will & testam^t in ^{writg} bearing date <u>1 Nov.1809</u> being the will of that date set out at page 12 of Abstract No. 2

And also reciting that sd John Geary the Son aftwds departed this life with having altered or revoked his said will other than & except as the same was altered or revoked by 2 Codicils but which Codicils did not affect the thereinbefore recited Devise of said Testator's real Este & that said Will & Codicils were on 8 May 1818 duly proved by sd Thos. Geary the surviv^g Exor thereof in the Prerogative Court of the Archbishop of Canterbury

And also reciting that upon the applicon & request of the said Thomas Geary party to now abstracting Indre said T. T. Fowke had agreed to advance & lend him L5000 upon the terms that the repaymt thereof with Int for the same at the rate of L5 for evy L100 for a year (but reducible as thrinafter mentioned) shod be secured to him his exors ads & ass by a mtg^e in fee of the messuages farms lands tenem^{ts} & hereds comprised in the sd Indres & will resp^{ly} in the now abstracting Indre after conveyed or otwise assured or intended so to be & by the power of Sale & ot powers & by the Trusts covenants provisions

[end of page 1]

& agreemts thrinar[thereinafter] covt^d [covenanted].
It is witnessed that in pursuance & performce of the sd Agreem^t & for & in conson of L5000 to the sd Thos Geary party to now abstract Indre paid by said T. T.Fowke (the receipt &c) The said T. Geary party thereto Did by those presents grant release & convey unto sd T.T.Fowke his heirs & assigns.

All & singular the messes or tenements pieces or pcels of land farms & heredits thrinbefe described or ment^d & comprised in sd thrin recited Indres with & which were then in the posson of sd Thos. Geary party to now abstract Indre the site of which sd messes or tenm^{ts} & sd lands & heredits were then divided into the sev^l fields closes & pcels of land & were called & known by the sev^l names & cont^d the sev^l quantities mentioned & set forth in the Schedule to those presents

And also all other (if any) the lands tenm^{ts} & heredts described or comprised in the said Schedule
And all houses &c And the revon &c And all the Estate &c

To hold same with the appurts unto & to the use of sd T.T.Fowke his hrs & ass subject nevertheless to the proviso or agreem^t for redemptn of sd heredits in now abstract Indre afr cont^d

Proviso for redemption & reconveynce of sd heices & premises on paym^t by sd Thos. Geary party to now abstract Indre his hrs exors admors or ass some or one of them unto sd T.T.Fowke his exors admnors or ass of L5000 on 15 Jany 1850 & in the meantime half yearly on 15 July & 15 Jany in each & every year during the continuance of sd sum of, L5000 on that Security Int for sd Sum of L5000 at L5 for every L100 for a year with^t[without] any deduction or abatem^t whats^r out of the same or any part throf for or in respect of any present or future taxes charges rates assessm^{ts} paymts or imposons whatsr by authority of parly otwise hows^r (the property or Income tax only Excepted).

Proviso for entry by sd T.T.Fowke his exs ads or ass into posson or rect of rents & profits of & to demise for 21 yrs sd heres & premes on default in paym^t of sd Princip or Int: & on other events in the now abstracting Indre ment^d

Usual Power of Sale (which has not been exercised) on Notice sub^j to annuity payable to sd Thos. Geary the Son as thrin aforesd and

[end of page 2]

Declaron as to the mode of applicon of the proceeds of such Sale & that purchaser shod not be bound to see to the applicon of purchase may &c & that his receipts shod be a good dischg^e
Power of dishes & entry in case int:in arrear for 1 Cal^r month.

Cov^{ts} by sd T. Geary (pty to now abstract Indre) with sd T.T.Fowke his exs ads & ass for paym^t of princ^l & int: as aforesd

That he had good right to convey
For quiet enjoym^t by sd T.T.Fowke after default
Free from incumb^s (the sd Anny excepted)

And recit^g that sd T. Geary (pty to now abst^g Indre) many years ago caused sd messes or tenemts erections or build^{gs} upon sd premes to be insured ags^t loss or damage by Fire in the Phoenix Fire Office in the City of London by a certn Policy of Ins^{ce} No 299501 & dated the 5 day of March 1808 for L500 & that same policy was then in full forced & virtue.

The sd Thos. Geary (pty thrto) Did by those prest^s bargain sell assign transfer & set over unto sd T.T.Fowke his exs ads & ass.

All that the same policy & all benefit & advantg^e
    To be derived thrfrom.

And all & evy sums & sum of moy due or to become due or payable in respect throf.

To hold same unto sd T.T.Fowke his exors admors & ass to & for his & their own use & benefit but subj nevertheless to the befe cont^d conc^g sd premes.

Cov^t by sd T. Geary (party thrto) for himself his hrs exors & admors with sd T.T.Fowke his exs ads & ass to keep sd premes insured during cont^{ce} of now abstract Sec^y in L500 at the least & to pay premiums produce receipts &c with the usual power for Mr. Fowke to insure in case of Mr. Geary's neglect & any moy pd by him for pms &c to be a chg^e on the prop^y.

Declon that insce moy shod be applied in rebuildg &c or in part paym^t of sd princ^l & int: in Mgee's discron.

Cov^t by sd T. Geary for further Assurance
Power for mtgee to appoint receiver (which has not been done) afr default in paym^t of Int for 3 cal^r mos.

Declon that such Receiver's rects should be suffic^t dischg^{es} with a provon as to applicon
of moys rec^d by him & sev^l or Clauses & especially an agreem^t on the pt of the

[end of page 3]

Mtge^e reducing the int: from L5 to L4..10..0 percent on punctual payment & for quiet enjoymt by the Mtgo^r until default.

Cov by sd T.T.Fowke that the said principal sum of L5000 should remain on secy of those present for 5 yrs from the date throf except in the event therein ment^d & that he would not proceed to a sale or enter into posson or receipt of the rent or in- - - - - any proceeding at law or - - - equity until the expiron of sd term or until default in paym^t of the int: or until default in princp^l of some or cov^t or agr^t therein cont^d or unless or until said thos Geary should become Bankrupt or take the benefit of the Insolvent adm

Cov^t from said T. Geary not to redeers sd premes or pay ass adm or any part of said L5000 during sd time of 6 yrs without consent of sd T.T.Fowke his exors &c & hrs or therin agr^t to accept same.

The Schedule to which the above abstracted Mortgage refers

Name or description	State of cultivation	Quantity		
In Atterton		Acres	Roods	Perches
1. Site of Buildings Yards & Gardens	--- ---- ----	2	1	29
2. Ringstone Hill	Pasture	24	2	33
3. Darbys Meadow	Meadow	4	1	14
4. Hill Meadow	Meadow	2	2	11
5. Dinner Meadow	Meadow	1	0	28
6. Far Linpit	Arable	6	2	17
7. Near Linspit	Arable	8	3	13
8. Top Meadow	Meadow	2	1	1
9. Far Acres	Arable	8	1	25
10. Near Acres	Pasture	10	3	3
11. Townsends Leys	Meadow	3	1	29
12. Home Close Site of Cottages	Pasture	8	0	1
13. Garden at Village	-----------	"	"	36
14. Slade Meadow	Meadow	5	2	20
15. Middle Close	Pasture	11	1	1
16. Bush Close	Arable	7	3	5
17. Roberts Hill	Arable	8	1	34
18. Ozier Beds	---------	"	2	11
19. Two Doles in Town Meadow	Meadow	1	3	14
20. Lane	---------	1	2	34

	Sub-total	<u>120</u>	<u>3</u>	<u>39</u>
In Witherley				
21. Little Atterton Close	Pasture	6	1	32
22. Great Atterton Close	Arable	9	2	26
23. Atterton Meadow	Meadow	4	1	20
24. Lane		1	0	18
	Sub-total	<u>21</u>	<u>2</u>	<u>16</u>
In Radcliffe Culey				
25. Far Close	Arable	2	3	16
Middle Close	Arable	5	0	1
Far Hill	Arable	5	1	3
Near Hill	~~Arable~~ pasture	2	1	36
House Close with site of Bldgs	Pasture	4	1	10
Ratcliffe Close	Patsure	4	2	30
Lexall Close	Arable	3	0	38
Long Meadow	Meadow	4	1	35
Hunters Meadow	Meadow	7	0	0
Hinckley Leys	Pasture	2	3	27
		<u>42</u>	<u>0</u>	<u>20</u>

Executed by Thomas Geary & Thomas Thorpe Fowke duly attested & receipt for conson Indorsed.

The Geary Family Bible

BY KAYE PAGE NICHOLS

This material is presented with the intent to have the descendants of John Thomas Geary aware of the treasured family Bible and Seal, and other items, which were brought from England to America in 1853. Many are not aware of the Bible and its history and significance. Since the Bible is kept in a bank vault, it is not available for easy viewing or handling. Therefore, it is hoped that this presentation will serve as a vicarious experience with the treasured Bible. Enjoy your reading and enlightenment. (Full report is posted on www.familysearch.org)

The Geary Family Bible

We descend from early Mormon Pioneers who braved the trials and hardships of the plains during that fateful winter of 1856. John Thomas Geary, his four month pregnant wife Sophia Fryer Geary and their three year old daughter Sophia Ann Geary began their journey to 'Zion' on July 15, 1856 from Iowa with the Willie Handcart Company. We have read of their conversion to The Church of Jesus Christ of Latter Day Saints in 1851 and the difficulties they endured travelling from England to the developing, but primitive, Utah Territory. They brought with them a few treasures from their families in England as a remembrance and tie to their own roots, knowing that they were probably leaving England and their families for good. It is the 'few treasures' that they brought with them that is the subject and purpose of this dialogue.

The 'few treasures' of which we are aware, consist of the following items which have been passed down for the past 160 years or longer among Geary family descendants:

1. The Geary Family Seal
2. The Geary Family Bible
3. Knit booties by Sophia Ann Geary
4. The pocket watch of John Thomas Geary (missing)
5. The will of John Thomas Geary
6. The professional business card of John Thomas Geary
7. The Wall Pocket from the Gearys
8. The Wedding Gift Book of Poems
9. The 'writings' of John Thomas Geary
10. The framed portraits of John and Sophia Geary
11. Personal histories of either John Thomas or Sophia Geary
12. Handmade gloves by Sophia Geary
13. Correspondence to or from the Gearys:
14. Personal letters between John Thomas & Sophia.
15. Letters from relatives, both in the United States as well as from England
16. Letters to and from Church authorities.

The Geary Family Seal: It is not known who was the first owner of the Seal, but we can trace it to at least Thomas Geary. Thomas' son, John Thomas Geary being an Attorney in London in the 1840's and 50's, probably had reason to use the seal in his professional correspondence. The seal is of carved Onyx stone set in a gold casing with a bell- shaped top for ease of handling. On the top is a gold loop with a purple ribbon coursing through it. It was used by placing hot wax on an envelope and pressing the seal into the wax. When the wax hardened, the letter could not be opened without breaking the wax, thus it was used to assure that the correspondence was private. "Paiz Et Harmonie" is engraved into the stone suggesting "Peace and Harmony". A musical lyre with an olive branch coursing through the lyre strings occupies the center of the stone.

The **Geary Family Bible**, is central to the story of the Geary family. At first glance, one could say, "It's just a family bible!"   As we then start asking questions and researching aspects of the bible, we begin to discover the place in history that this particular bible occupies. We come to a realization that this is not just 'another' bible. The purpose of this section of the book is to give us a sense of just how special this bible is to our family, and as a volume of scripture in the English language. As you read, keep in mind the history as to how we came to be in possession of this volume. It is a treasure far beyond the first sight of 'just a Holy Bible'.

The known history of the Geary Family Bible in England.

The Geary Family Bible is a First Edition Cambridge printing of the 1629 King James Bible with Thomas and John Buck as printers for the University of Cambridge. It is the FIRST King James Bible that was specifically printed to be used by the average person in their personal religious studies. On the spine of the book, and the inside page of the bible, one can see the year that it was printed, MDCXXIX, A. D. 1629.

For over 160 years after Johannes Gutenberg invented the moveable print type, the same method of setting the individual type letters was used. After the first King James Bible was printed in 1611, other compositors varied spelling, capitalization and punctuation. Some 1,500 unintentional misprints were introduced into these early printed bibles.

The two Cambridge editions of the King James Bible, those of 1629 and in 1638, attempted to restore the proper texts. They introduced over 200 revisions of the original work.

King James I of England ruled from 1603 until his death in 1625. Following his death and the ascension of King Charles I to the throne, the Cambridge University printers cultivated a relationship with the new King and they were able to obtain the authority to be the first printers of the King James Bible besides the king's printers. This led to the first printing of the King James Bible in 1629 by Thomas and John Buck, both of whom served as official printers at the University of Cambridge, as well as Esquire Bedell for the University.

What do we know about this particular copy of the Bible?

In researching what we know about The Geary Family Bible, there are some elusive facts that we just do not have at our disposal. We can follow its known provenance. Just when the bible first came into possession of the Geary family is not definitively known. The Geary family line can be traced to about 1565. It is conceivable that the Bible came into the Geary Family soon after the Bible was printed in 1629, however, we just don't know when it made its first appearance in the family. There is a gap of approximately 200 years between the printing of the bible in 1629 and when we are certain that the Bible was in possession of Thomas Geary in the early 1800's.

The following custodianship of the Bible is current as of January 2020:

1. Thomas Geary (1792-1865) gave it to his son John Thomas Geary.
2. John Thomas Geary (1823-1867) gave it to his wife, Sophia Fryer Geary.
3. Sophia Fryer Geary (1829-1872) at her death, gave it to her daughter Sophia Ann Geary. Sophia Ann had the Bible repaired in the early 1900s after some fire damage occurred, and it was re-bound with her name on the spine.
4. Sophia Ann Geary Page (1853-1934) gave it to her son Robert Geary Page.
5. Robert Geary Page (1877-1945) gave it to his daughter Reta Page Bailey Bartell.
6. Reta Page Bailey Bartell (1905-1988) gave it to her son Kenneth Rone Bailey
7. Kenneth Rone "Sonny" Bailey (1929-2010) gave it to his son Kirk Matthew Bailey.
8. Kirk Matthew Bailey (1955-living) presently has the Bible, which he keeps secured in a bank vault, as of 2021

NOTE 1: One source reports that when wealthy owners of the 1629 Bible obtained their copy, they would employ artisans to use red ink and with a straight-edge draw the decorative red lines as a customization of their copy. Many of the 1629 Bibles in existence are without the "red ruled" markings. The Geary Family Bible has the "red ruled" markings throughout the Bible. It is not known who had these markings made or when they were performed.

NOTE 2: Some persons have asked what the monetary value of this edition of the King James Bible of 1629 might be. A person could go online and review some of the sales figures for themselves, but in 2019, a value of $50,000 would be in the ballpark. This would be for a marketable volume without a particular provenance. **In this case, there is a sentimental value that cannot be denominated with a monetary value. It is irreplaceable. It rightfully holds an esteemed position amongst the descendants of John Thomas Geary.**

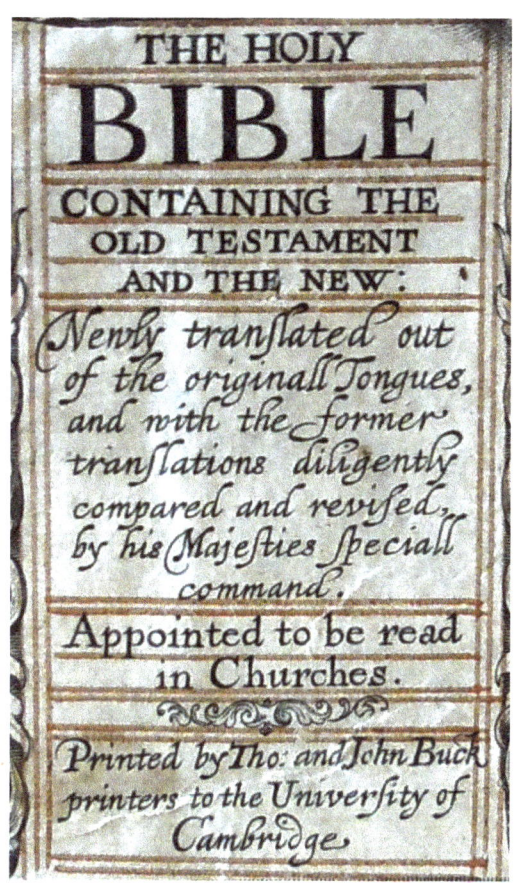

The Title Page of the Geary Family Bible reads: "The Holy Bible Containing the Old Testament and the New: Newly translated out of the original Tongues, and with the former translations diligently compared and revised by his Majesties Special command. Appointed to be read in Churches. Printed by Tho. and John Buck, printers to the University of Cambridge."

From The King James Bible and the Restoration, Edited by Kent P. Jackson. Published by the Religious Studies Center, Brigham Young University, Provo, Utah, in cooperation with Deseret Book Company, Salt Lake City. Chapter VIII, page 118-119: The phrase "Appointed to read in Churches" announced a fundamental function of the King James Bible. It was intended to be read, meaning read aloud, in church. It was meant for the ear and not simply for the eye. The King James Bible was originally a lectern Bible. It was made for the pulpit, as a Bible to be read as part of public, communal worship. . . . What strikes one first is the size of an original King James Bible. It is huge. It is heavy, weighing in at over twenty pounds. . . . From the start, the translators understood that their assignment was to produce a translation suitable to be read aloud. Indeed, the whole notion of a new translation began with John Rainolds's petition to King James for "authentical" new translation "to be read in the church.". . . . Thus the translators were aware from the outset that the new translation needed to read well aloud."

When one reads the "Names and Order" page below, we can see that this Bible includes the books of the Apocrypha.

The wood carver for the Title Page of the 1629 Edition was engraver John Payne (1607-1647). Each image represents an important story or character appearing in the books of the Bible.

John Thomas Geary Calling Card

This item of John T. Geary's is in the possession of one of his descendants, Paul Tooke.

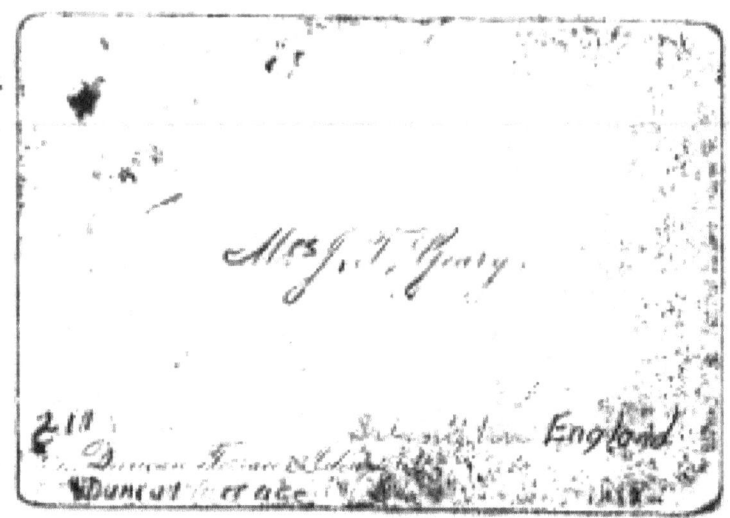

This below rendition of the Calling Card has been enhanced by removing much of the static and noise, thereby making it a little more readable. Someone at some time tried to write over the lettering and so it is damaged. It was originally used by John when he lived in Islington, England at Duncan Terrace. He must have brought it to America and it could have been altered by his wife, Sophia, as the 's' was added to "Mr." in handwriting. Possibly Sophia Geary used it as her calling card as well.

Excerpts from the Diary of Richard Fryer

It is not known if this is Richard Fryer's complete journal; it does match some entries quoted by Bessie Snow in *Fate of the Fryers*. It has also been posted on Richard Fryer's Family Search entry. This copy was provided to Kaye Page Nichols by Don Clawson, a descendant of Richard Fryer.
1853-1857.

A Journal from England to Great Salt Lake City

January 3, 1853. We left London at 7 p.m. and after a journey of ---- miles arrived in Liverpool, at 1/2 past 8 p.m. went to Wilton St. and Brother Samuel was not at home. We inquired for lodgings, and they directed us to Grant Crosshall St. where we found lodgings.

January 4th. I went to the General Post Office to enquire for a letter but there was none.

January 5th. Brother Walker and me went to the Railway Station to meet a friend and a Gentleman came and asked Brother Walker what was his object in coming there. He said that he had come to meet a friend. The Gentleman said people were not allowed to come into the station to meet their friends, and he ordered us out. We went back to Great Crosshall St.

January 6th. I went to the Railway Station to see if the luggage was there, but it was not come. I then went to the General Post Office and from there to the ship.

January 7th. Went to the Railway Station, the luggage was come. Brother Orson Spencer arrived.

January 8th. Brother and Sister Geary and myself went to look at the ship.

January 9th. Went to the meeting and heard Brother Orson Spencer preach on Plurality of Wives.

January 10th. Took the luggage on board the ship. Brother Young had forgotten to secure a berth for me and I was obliged to do without one.

January 11th. The Saints were very busy today getting their boxes ready to be put in the hold. A man took his wife away.

January 12th. A Sheriff's Officer and Policeman came on board and examined the ship. Mr. Geary and me went on shore in the evening to get some necessary's for the voyage. He also got his head shaved.

January 13th. The surgeon came on board and examined us. The ship was cleared and we were ready for sea. In the afternoon a woman came on board to look for her son, but she could not find him.

January 14th. This morning as I was in the steerage waiting for our provisions a man came on board with a letter directed to me, but I knew better than to take it, and I informed Mr. Geary of it. There was a policeman on board the rest of the day.

January 15th. Mr. Geary, thinking that his brother and policeman would come on board, resolved upon going to Holyhead and meet the ship there. He left the ship about 1 o'clock and went over the River to New Brighton Ferry. After it was dark we went to Berkenhead Railway Station. On our way we met a man, who remarked that Brother Geary was very much like a gentleman he had took over to Liverpool during the day. Brother Geary, thinking it was his brother, asked the man several questions about this gentleman and he gave a correct description of Mr. Fred Geary, however, we walked on to the Railway Station, took our tickets separate and got into a carriage for Chester; while we were there a man came and looked into the carriage and went away again; we waited about a quarter of an hour before the train started. We arrived at Chester about 9 o'clock. We enquired for lodgings and a porter took us to a house where we found lodgings; we had some tea, and Brother Geary paid the woman for our lodgings, saying, he should like to go into the City, but instead of going into the city, we went to the Railway Station, but on our way we met the porter who took us to our lodgings. We asked him what time the train started for Holyhead; he said there was one going in a quarter of an hour, so we walked on to the Railway Station and took our tickets. We were very glad to see the train come, for this reason. A man and a policeman followed us about, and asked Brother Geary if he was going to Ireland and several more questions, but we got into the train and were soon on our way to Holyhead.

January 16th. We arrived at Holyhead about 1 o'clock in the morning, but Mr. Geary thinking he was . . . telegraphed to Holyhead, resolved to go on to Ireland and on inquiring about the fare from Holyhead to Ireland found we could have got from Chester

241

to Dublin for the same money that he paid from Chester to Holyhead, however, we went on till we came to the steamer and went aboard. We had a rough passage and were sick. We arrived at Ringstown about half past 6 o'clock, and we were much surprised to find that we had to pay £1 O fares. We went to the railway station, took our tickets and got into the train to Dublin. We arrived at Dublin about half past 7 o'clock and after walking about 2 hours we found some comfortable lodgings, we being tired went to bed and slept till 3 o'clock in the afternoon; we then had some tea and went out into the town.

January 17th. Mr. Geary thinking that he was not safe, went to a Law Station to read the English Common Law Act, but he found he was quite safe. Then we went strolling about and seeing some very high mounds in the distance, I thought we might see a great distance but it was getting dark and I thought it was time to go home to our lodging and we turned back to the town.

January 18th. We went to Gt. Ship St. and found some Latter-Day Saints and stopped there.

January 20th. Mr. Geary and a Brother went to some reading rooms to look for advertisements of shipping but they could not find one for New Orleans. We left Dublin for Glasgow at 2 o'clock in a steamer.

January 21st. This morning it was very rough and the wind was ahead, which delayed us very much. We had been without food for twenty-four hours and were very hungry, so we went into the Cabin and had breakfast for which we paid 2 shillings. We arrived at Glasgow at six this evening and had considerable difficulty in finding a Saint. We went to Charlotte St. and from there we were directed to another Charlotte St. When we got there we could not find the house but meeting with a Policeman we obtained some information. He directed us to a factory where a Saint worked. We went to the factory but he was gone home. They directed us to the Saint's house and we tried to find it, but we could not. We had to go back to the factory and the woman very kindly took us to the house, but after all this trouble we found this man was not a Saint which was very provoking. However, Brother Geary was two hours talking to the old man about Mormonism. While we were there this man's daughter said there was a woman at the factory where she worked they called a Latter-Day Saint and they sent the boy with us to show us the house and we were very glad to find that this was the L.D.S. Saint. Well, he took us to Brother Lyons. We had some supper and then went to bed.

January 22nd. Brother Geary was looking for a ship for New Orleans but could not find one.

January 23rd. This evening I went to the meeting which was held at the British School Room.

January 24th. Brother Geary had a walk with Brother and Sister Lyons.

January 25th. Writing letters, etc.

January 26th. We were out nearly all day looking for a ship but could not find one.

January 27th. Brother Geary decided upon going to Liverpool but we tried once more to get a ship and found there was one going to start in the afternoon. We went to the dock and found the ship but we could not secure passage. The Owner said the ship was cleared and he could not take us. We went back to the office to see if they could procure a passage for us. They said that we could not get a passage. However, Brother Geary was determined, if it was possible, to procure a passage. He went to the Mate and got a little information. The Mate said he thought we could procure a passage by offering the Captain a trifle of money, which Brother Geary succeeded in doing, but the owner kept so close to the Captain that Brother Geary could not make an appointment with him. However, we understood that the ships in general stopt at Greenock a few days so Brother Geary decided upon going to Greenock the next day.

January 28th. We packed up our clothes and started for Greenock about midday and just as I was getting out of the train at Greenock, who should I see but the owner of the ship. I don't know if he saw me for I got among the crowd and was soon out of the station. I did not stop to look for Brother Geary. I was afraid of the Owner seeing me. I walked some distance down the street before I looked around thinking that Brother Geary was following me, but I was greatly mistaken. I kept walking to and from the station and on the warf, out of one street and into the other for 2 or 3 hours, but I could not find him until late in the evening as I was passing by the station. Now I found out how we had lost each other. Brother Geary immediately he saw the Owner went back into the station until the owner went and then as he was passing out of the station he met the Captain who said it was impossible for him to take us because the Owner had put his Nephew on board, but Brother Geary would not give it up. He asked the Captain the third time and the Captain said he wanted three sailors and he would take us for two of them. Well, Brother Geary thought this was a first rate chance, so we engaged with him to be there without fail at 12 o'clock the next day so we went back to Glasgow thinking that we would be sailors the next day.

January 29. We rose early next morning and were soon on our way to the railway station, but as we passed the Post Office I remarked to Brother Geary that there might be a letter for us. He put down his bundle and went into the Post Office to see and there was a letter from Brother Samuel Richards informing Brother Geary of Brother John Hall's arrival and also counseling him to go to

Liverpool. So we left Glasgow for Liverpool about 4 o'clock in the afternoon. We had a very rough night. The wind was blowing right ahead. We were up all night.

January 30. It was tremendous rough today and we were both very sick until we arrived at Brother John Hall came and met us and took us to a lodging house. We were very tired and went to bed.

January 31. Brother Hall went to the Office and brought back some stars.

February 1st, 1853. Brother John Hall went to London and Brother Geary went to the office.

February 2nd. Brother Geary went and got the tickets.

February 3rd. Brother Geary went to the ship; and secured his berth.

February 4th. Brother Piercy and Brother Geary took the bundles to the ship and in the afternoon Brother Geary came in a cab and we went to the ship. After we had passed the Doctor, Brother Geary, Piercy and Hyde went on shore to buy provisions for the journey. They came on board late in the evening with bedding etc. and they intended going on shore in the morning to buy the rest, so we all went to bed. However, we had not been in bed long when Brother Piercy said he would have a joke with Brother Hyde making him believe it was morning. Well he got out of bed and dressed himself then Brother Piercy and Brother Geary jumped into bed again and we had a good laugh at him.

February 5th. All hands were called on the quarter deck to count them and tug towed us out of the dock. I failed to keep a journal on the sea, but anyway we had a pleasant voyage of six weeks endurance and enjoyed it very well having a few days of sea sickness. We were 3 days and nights clearing the Irish Channel. Then we rolled over the swells of the Atlantic. I thanked God I had escaped from that land of oppression, although I could not but feel that I had left my native country, my home, and all that was near and dear to me. Yet, I felt a calmness of mind and looked forward to the end of my journey as something that would create my happiness. The company of Saints that came in the same ship (Jersey) enjoyed good health, and to all human appearances were happy and jovial under the circumstances.

The President George Halliday behaved well to them, endeavoring at all times to make them as comfortable as possible. We had a fine voyage. Every Sunday the sea was calm and we had studding-sails set and we had one death and 2 births. We arrived in Belees (America) at daylight on the morning of the -------- instant. There was a number of ships lying here and amongst them we discovered the Golconda with topmasts gone. The Pilot anchored us very close to her so that we learned by the aid of the Spy Glass and Blackboard that they had been here 10 days unable to cross the bar. At dusk a Steamer took us in tow in company with 2 others and in an hour we were gliding up the Mississippi River, the color of which is dark stone color. After two days and nights pulling and grunting we arrived at New Orleans "March 21, 1853" and set our feet once more on Terra Firma here.

While strolling about, I came in contact with a n----- establishment. It quite amused me to see the n----- strutting about looking as big as life. They were in separate houses, the males in one, and the females in the other. Today the Saints were busily employed getting their luggage on board the John Simonds Steamboat, and left New Orleans at dusk on our way up the Mississippi. The next day presented to our view such a scene as I have never witnessed, to see the Steamers going up and down the River, the N---- at work in the Plantations, the thick long woods as we passed, with now and then a large piece of Farming land with a bustling little town. It was truly beautiful.

We were 6 days coming up the River, during which time John was our President, and we had a good time. We arrived at St. Louis on the morning of the ----, met my sister Sophia, who I was very glad to see, she having come in the same ship that we intended coming in. I stayed in the city of St. Louis about six weeks during which time I worked at painting, receiving one dollar per day wages. The time for us to leave being close at hand Geary started up the River to get cattle and wagon. In a few days I received a letter from him wishing me to come to Keokuk. Consequently I started by the next boat and arrived at Keokuk late in the evening of the next day, found Geary who delivered into my hands 2 yoke of cattle which I found to be troublesome. There was about 1200 of the Saints camped here in their wagons and tents and on arrival of Geary and my sister, we joined with them.

We stayed here a fortnight during which time they organized 3 companies but Geary not being ready we organized in the last company. John Brown Captain, after considerable trouble yoking up the cattle, owing principally to our want of experience in that line. We succeeded however in making the start. We traveled over a considerable extent of country chiefly prairie land, distance about 500 miles which took us about a fortnight to travel and during which time I had some little experience in driving team, watching cattle and camping out in tents. We arrived at Council Bluffs on the Missouri River on the 17th of July 1853, camped just below the city and drove the cattle 2 miles off to feed.

July 18th. Herding cattle till noon, afternoon helping my sister Jane to remove to another wagon. Geary was making preparations to stay because his wife was sick. Jorden was trying to induce Jane to stay but could not.

July 19th. Mr. Stewart came to camp inquiring for men. I engaged myself to him to drive team across the plains for my board, preferring this to staying another year, which Geary intended doing. Today he sold his cattle and wagon, and moved into the city. I also went to Stewards company, about 1 1/2 miles further down the River.

July 20th. Hunted up the Cattle, drove through the City where Geary run after me and bid me farewell, travelled through a sood and arrived at came at dusk. Drove 6 miles.

July 21st. Owing to our cattle being so wild we were under considerable trouble in getting the train started. Had 2 accidents on the road and reached the Ferry (Missouri River) in the evening. Brown's Company was here. Drove 6 miles.

July 22nd. Brown's company crossed over excepting the cattle.

July 23rd. The remainder of Brown's company ferried over and in the afternoon we crossed over our wagons.

July 24th. We got the cattle over and was organized into 2 nesses.

July 25th. The cattle were very unmanageable. 3 hours yoking up. Made a start about noon. Passed by Winter Quarters. A company of Gold diggers passed us. Camped 8 miles from the Missouri.

July 26th. Crossed Pappae Creek, Ferryed over the Elk Horn and camped. Drove 13 miles.

July 27th. Traveled through a bottom, very sandy road, drove 21 miles.

July 28th. Good traveling, took in wood and camped a little farther on . Drove 25 miles.

July 29th. We arrived at the Main Platte at noon, very sandy road for 6 miles. Ferryed over the Loup Fork and camped on the opposite bank. Drove 25 miles.

July 30th. Sandy Road, very hard on the teams.

July 31st. Passed a camp with a large herd of sheep on their way to Oregon.

August 1st. Traveled through San Bluff to Prairie Creek, no wood.

August 2nd. Rough road. Saw Brown's Company 6 miles ahead. Crossed over Prairie Creek, which had very steep banks, met a company of gold diggers.

August 3rd. Fine day, bad road, camped close by Brown's Company.

August 4th. Made a bridge over a creek, crossed over and camped at Wood Creek.

August 5th. Made a bridge over Wood Creek.

August 6th. Crossed over Wood Creek, and overtook Brown's company. Here we met some Indians who were very saucy, stealing, and threatening us. Camped with Brown's Company to secure us from the Indians. Kept the cattle in the Corral, and kept double guard.

August 7th. This morning while herding the Cattle, I discovered a few Indians coming up the road; they were all armed with spears, bows and arrows and guns and they came thicker and faster until the Captain being alarmed set men out to help us drive in the cattle to the corral. By the time we came to camp the Indians had gathered to the amount of 5 or 600 and demanded we pay for traveling through their land. Our Captain consulting on the matter gave them flour, coffee, sugar and all that we could spare. But they were very dissatisfied with it and upon finding they could not get any more began jumping from their horses, loading their guns, yelling and said they would fight us. Consequently they moved out and we passed on but they tormented us along the road running among the teams pricking us with their arrows and doing all the mischief they could until the Chief called them away leaving us traveling peaceable on until dark, when we camped.

August 8th. Very good traveling, separated from Brownes Company.

August 9th. Crossed Buffalo Creek, saw several herds of Buffalo, killed 1 and passed on. Camped on the Sandy bluffs, no wood, stinking water. Cooked some buffalo meat, which was very good.

August 10th. Passed Brown's Company, crossed over Sandy Bluffs, struck off the road and camped on the banks of the Platte.

August 11th. Crossed Sandy Bluffs. Cold Spring.

August 12th. Very bad road. We crossed the Platte 15 miles below Fort Laramie, the Sioux were very peaceable and friendly. Just before we crossed 5 of our teamsters left the trail on account of the Captain acting so mean to us and threating 2 men who were sick with fever and ague, if they did not get out of their beds and work he would make them pay when they got to the valley, for boarding and hauling them. We camped at the first Trading Post. Traded for Oxen staid 1 1/2 days fixing our wagon tires. 2 trains of Merchandise crossed on their way to the Salt Lake. The next morning we proceeded on. Passed Fort Laramie where we bought some flour and bacon, our supply being almost exhausted - traveled over the Black Hills where we passed a large Camp of Sioux - very peaceable. Crossed the Platte at the upper crossing and camped at the last trading post on the Platte and exchanged and bought cattle. Met Mr. Bridger, an old mountaineer, and his gang on the way to the States. Passed Independence Rock and camped at Devil's Gate.

Colonel Babbit camped with us on Greasewood Creek - Traveled on up the Sweetwater, crossed the south pass - Cattle very weak - camped at Pacific Springs and shod some of the cattle. Several cattle died on Big and Little Sandy. Camped at Green River 2 or 3 days trading merchandise for cattle, sheep and flour, bought a little flour at Fort Bridger. Crossed Bear River out of provisions. Killed a small steer and sheep. Cattle very weak. Scarcely averaging 7 miles per day. Wagons breaking down all the time. Met a wagon with provisions from the valley. Met a man at the top of Big Mountain with flour. Traveled to the foot of the little mountain and camped. Proceeded over the little mountain through Emigration Kanyon into the Valley of the Great Salt Lake being over a fortnight from Fort Bridger. Being unable to reach our destination that day, we camped a little beyond Kanyon Creek.

The Captain went back to Brigham's Mill and bought flour for our supper. Next day proceeded on to Big Cottonwood, unloaded the wagons, stayed there a few days and then went to G. S. L. City, slept at Samuel Burgess's. Walked about the City and went to the 16 Ward. Stayed over night. Next day tried to obtain work but could not. Mr. Staples offered me every 7th bushel if I would dig his potatoes which I accepted and in a few days earned 15 bushels. I then tended Mr. Staples plastering a few days, during --- which time he proposed (as I could not get work at my own trade, viz. painting) to take me as an apprentice, which I finally accepted. The first house we built was Mr. John Tharpe which we finished a little before Christmas. The winter set in very severe. I boarded with Jorden.

Cut my foot choping wood which laid me up 6 weeks. I had nothing more to do through the winter but to draw my provisions from the Tithing Office and try to keep warm which however, was no trifling thing to do. The winter was so severe that the water would freeze at times upon the hearth, and anything left at night upon the cupboard would freeze solid by morning. In February I began boarding with Mr. Staples and was ordained a Priest on the 16th in the school house. I was ordained an Elder on the 26th of March.

In April (1854) I worked at the City Hall and at Mr. Merchant's in the big field In May of that year my brother in law (Jorden) denied Mormonism and went to California leaving my sister and children entirely to the mercy of those around her. I left my lodgings forthwith and took up my abode with them, and supplied their wants to the best of my ability. I worked very hard during this month, digging and planting potatoes and other vegetables.
On the **28th** there was quite deep snow fell and very cold indeed.

In **June** we put a small room for Mr. Jas. Rupeell.

On the 12th began laying the foundation of large building called the Big House for President Brigham Young. In July we removed from the 4th ward to Bro. Bakers in the 17th Ward.

On the 4th the Militia paraded the principal streets. In the afternoon repaired to the Tabernacle and heard many speeches made by principal men of the territory.

On the 24th, the Mormons celebrated the anniversary of their exit into these vallies. The procession formed at the Tabernacle consisting of all the young gents and ladies between the ages of 7 and 18 years with some of the twelve and chosen men for the occasion.

In August, Jane presented us with a fine baby which took sick about a fortnight after its birth and in the early part of October it died. Annie was taken very sick. The latter part of the month Jane and the children were rebaptized.

In November, Jane received a letter from Jorden wishing her to come to Sacramento, California.

During **September** I learned the Deseret Alphabet.

In the early part of **October** Jane's baby died and Annie was taken very sick. In the latter part of the month Jane and the children were rebaptized.

In November we had a deep snow which suspended work for a time. We also received a letter from Jorden wishing Jane to go to him in Sacramento, California. We continued to work, although it was pretty cold until Christmas. Upon this day there was quite a disturbance caused by some drunken soldiers disturbing the Nauvoo Bros. Band and insulting persons in the Street until it became a general fight between Mormons and the soldiers, using fists, stones, selalieghs, or whatever came first, but the soldiers finding they would come off second best resorted to their guns and succeeded in firing a few shots which however did no hurt. It was however stopped at this point by the Civil and Military Officers and strict guards kept on both sides the remainder of the day. It was afterward reported that 1 soldier was killed.

New Year's Day (1855) was very cold and windy but the inhabitants of the City enjoyed themselves at parties and dancing. Jane became acquainted with Mr. Harrison, a delegate from Iron County.

In March we left Mr. Bakers and went to Mrs. Stevenson 14th Ward.

At the April Conference many of the young men were called to take missions among the Lamanites. Jane was also married to Mr. Harrison and left on the 10th for Iron County. There was a grand celebration on the 4th of July in which the Nauvoo Legion and the Government Authorities paraded the principal streets and at 2 o'clock met at the Bowery north end of the Tabernacle. Speeches were delivered by Judge Kinney, Docture Hart, I.S. Governor Young and others.

On the 23rd we finished the Big House, the dimensions of which is 110 feet long by 6 inches wide, 3 stories high. At this time we were put on rations at the tithing office, 1 lb. of flour and take your chances for other things. I left Sister Stevensons and boarded with Br. Staples 15th Ward. Build a house for Mr. Marten - Shoemaker.

In August we built a house for Mr. Wm. Martin.

In September we went 10 miles north to Sessions Settlement and build a house for President J. M. Grant.

In October built a house for Mr. Davidson, shoemaker. On the --- of November we went to Kays creek and laid out for the foundations of a large meeting house, put a room for them to meet in during the winter, and worked laying up the foundation until the winter set in. We left on the 19th of December for the City, in which place there was quite a scarcity of provisions, owing to the drouth and grasshoppers eating the crops off. At Christmas I joined a dancing school at the Pioneer Hall.

April 12, 1856. Drove cattle to Willow Creek. Wagons did not come to camp. Made a fire and roasted some beef we had and eat it. Drove on to the Hot Springs. Slept at the house at the point of the mountain.

April 13, 1856. Hunted up the cattle and put them in the corral. Went to the house and eat breakfast - counted the cattle - 2 missing - hunt them up - at 2 o'clock it began to storm - let the cattle loose and they went back on the road.

April 14. Went 2 miles back, met the wagons, hunted up the cattle and traveled on round the point of the mountain into the Utah Valley. Passed Lehi City and camped this side of American Fork Settlement.

April 15. Drove through the settlement. Passed through Battle Creek Settlement. Crossed over the Provo Bench and camped on Provo River.

April 16. Passed through Provo City, Springville and Spanish Fork and got to the farm about sunset. There was about 100 men at work intending to fence in and cultivate 1000 acres, which the Indian Agent had named the "Indian Reserve."

April 17. Received my pay and started home on foot with 2 others. The Bishop of Springville wanted $10.00 per cwt for flour.

April 18. Went on to Lehi City, where I stayed the remainder of the day trying to buy provisions but could not at any price.

April 19. Passed around the mountain into G. S. L. Valley and arrived in Great Salt Lake City at 9 o'clock at night.

1856. Brother Jedeiah Grant with 4 missionaries came to Kays Ward where they preached 4 days and baptized the inhabitants. They called a meeting in the evening. Brother Grant called a vote of the meeting to know if they wished to repent of their sins and be baptized, and it was carried unanimously. Preaching by Brother Grant, Hunt, Young and others and they chastized us. We were all baptized.

April 30, 1856. I wrote to Mother, Geary and Jane.

August 3, 1856. I received a letter from Geary.

August 5, 1856. (Sunday) I received a letter from Jane.

November 6, 1856. Received another note from Geary saying they were short on provisions.

November 9, 1856. I met a church company who arrived in Salt Lake. They said Geary was in the next company.

November 10, 1856. I wrote to Jane.

Jan 18, 1857. Attended a Welch concert in the store house. There was a 15th Ward dancing in the evening.

Jan 19. Attended the Bishop's meeting in the Tabernacle. A great deal of instructions were given to the people and bishops in regards to our future movements as people. Presented a charter for establishing a bank. The spirit of it was accepted. Brother Pratt, Benson, and Kay and others arrived from England through California. Benson spoke at length upon the feelings of the world to this people, and U.S. was sending troops round California to come in the spring. The names of officers of the standing army was read and accepted. Many songs were sung and we had a first rate meeting.

Feb. 25. Colonel Thomas L. Kane arrived from Washington City (likely means Washington D.C.) under the name of Dockur Osborne. Came by California in 51 days, his object to lay our case before the Government in a different way.

March 12, 13. Working tithing.

March 11, 1857. I received a letter written from Geary December 15, 1855.

March 17, 1857. I spent the afternoon writing to Geary and Jorden.

March 23, 24, 25. Working tithing on the temple. They were packing up the organ.

March 27, 1857. I posted a letter to Mother.

July 24, 1857. Was a beautiful day and according to arrangements made the previous year, President Brigham Young, his counselors and a large group of Saints had gathered at Silver Lake, at the headwaters of Big Cottonwood Creek to celebrate the 10th anniversary of the arrival of the pioneers in Salt Lake Valley.

All day long on the 23rd, a continuous line of wagons, carriages, people on horseback and mule back had wended their way up the canyon, until by nightfall, there were, by actual count, two thousand five hundred and eighty seven persons four hundred sixty-four wagons, and carriages, one thousand twenty-eight horses and three hundred thirty-two oxen and cows on the camp ground. Captain Ballo's band the Nauvoo Brass Band, the Springville Brass Band, the Ogden City Brass Band, and the Great Salt Lake City and Ogden City Martial bands were on hand to gladden the festivities. There were also many infantry displays. What a celebration it was. Three spacious boweries with floor planks, had been provided by the Big Cottonwood Lumber Company, and a large number passed the evening in joyous dance. **The 25th** was spent in joyous festivities beginning with three rounds fired from a brass howitzer, for the First Presidency of the Church of Jesus Christ of Latter-Day Saints, and our rights and independence. At fifteen minutes past 10:00 a.m. three rounds were fired for the Hope of Israel. The stars and stripes were unfurled on two of the highest peaks in sight of the camp, and on top of two of the tallest trees.

July 15, 1860 Letter from John Thomas Geary to Sophia Geary

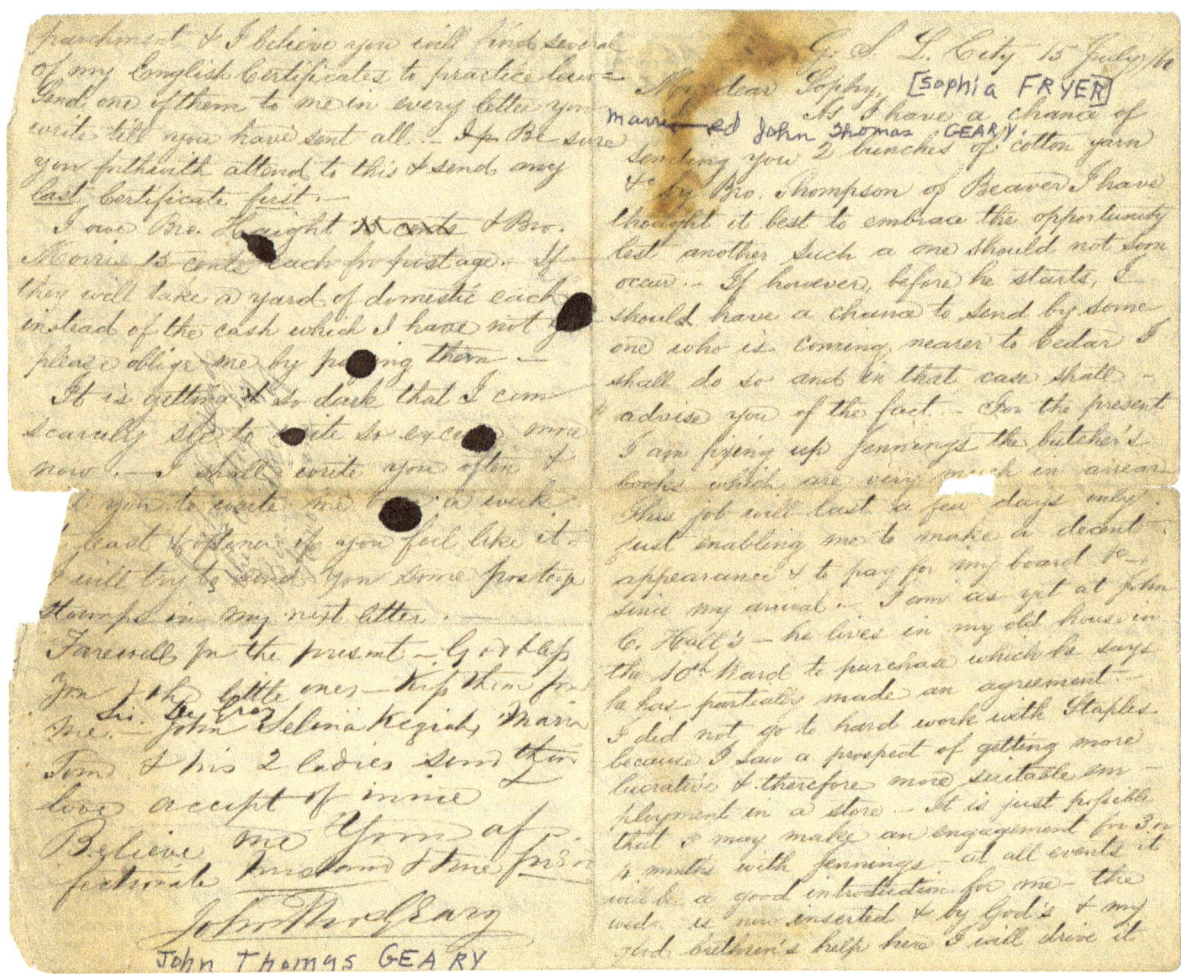

July 15, 1860 handwritten letter from John Thomas Geary in Great Salt Lake City to his wife, Sophia, in Cedar City. The letter is an excellent example of John's handwriting and his thinking at this critical time in the Geary family. This image shows the first page of the letter on the right and the last page of the letter on the left. The other two pages are shown on the following page. A full transcript of this letter is included in the text of Chapter 4 herein. This is only one of two original letters of John's which are still in the possession of a Geary descendant.

The original July 15, 1860 letter is in the possession of Geary descendant, Brian K. Bowler.

Complaint filed by John Thomas Geary in Utah Territorial Court against Samuel Stambaugh, 1860

In the Probate Court
Great Salt Lake County
Territory of Utah, U. S. A.

Complaint made and filed 1st October 1860

Between John Thomas Geary ———— Plaintiff
and
S. C. Stambaugh ———— Defendant

Great Salt Lake County to wit — John Thomas Geary (the plaintiff in this suit) complains of S. C. Stambaugh (the defendant in this suit) in an action of Debt and the plaintiff demands of the defendant the sum of forty-nine dollars and seventy-five cents which he owes to and unjustly detains from him. For that the defendant heretofore to wit on the twenty-ninth day of September in the year of our Lord One thousand eight hundred and sixty was indebted to the plaintiff in the said sum of forty-nine dollars and seventy-five cents (as shewn or evidenced by the particulars of demand hereunto annexed) for the work and labor care and diligence of the plaintiff before that time done performed and bestowed by the plaintiff for the defendant at his request which said sum of money was to be paid by the defendant to the plaintiff when he the defendant should be thereunto afterward requested whereby and by reason of the same sum of money being and remaining wholly due and unpaid an action hath accrued to the plaintiff to demand and have the same of and from the defendant yet the defendant hath not as yet paid the said sum of forty-nine dollars and seventy-five cents or any part thereof to the plaintiff but hath hitherto wholly refused and still doth refuse to pay the same To the damage of the plaintiff of forty-nine dollars and seventy-five cents and therefore he brings his suit &c.

Subscribed & sworn to before me this 1st day of Oct. 1860.   John Lynch   John the Gray

The Stambuagh court documents were located by Kaye Page Nichols at the Family History Library, Series 373, Reel Number 9, Box Number 07, Folder Number 089. Also on FHL US/CAN Film No. 2258957, Box 7, Folder 66, No 387.

September 13, 1860 Cross-Hatched Letter of John Thomas Geary to his wife, Sophia

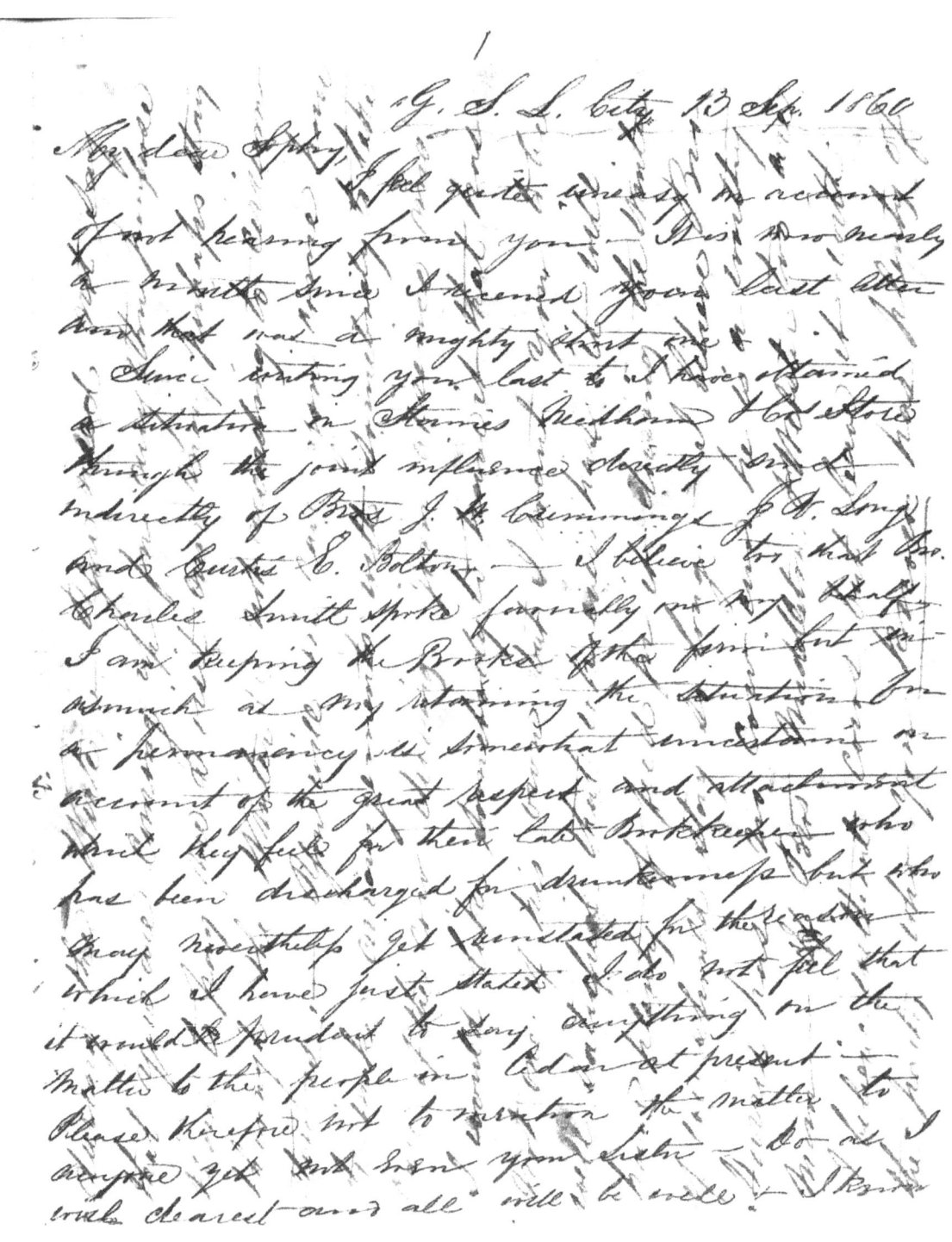

2

you wish to keep posted as to my affairs which is the reason why I tell you about this matter now. It is just possible that in the next letter which I write I may not have to inform you that I am out of employment altogether. But pray for me dearest that I may be prepared and that all things may work together for our mutual good. I should much like you to come on at Conference. I were perfectly certain of keeping my present situation I would say come upon no condition — that you make satisfactory arrangements about everything at home so that if we should have [return] at home or that if we should have [return] nothing would be destroyed during our absence.

I think before posting this I will feel disposed S. W. & Co. pulse to find out if what there is of permanent employment & may perhaps ask the plain question whether I shall be justified in sending up for my family. If I can manage to stay where I am now I shall of course leave Ogden altogether — but keep this secret at present. In case you do not come up at Conference in Oct. you will most likely have to wait till next April Conference and for my own part I do not wish to act hastily but to do what will really turn out for the best. Ask the Father to direct us both in the matter & feel in your

5

G. S. L. City 13 Sep. 1860

My dear Sophy,

I feel quite uneasy on account of not hearing from you. It is now nearly a month since I received your last letter and that was a mighty short one.

Since writing you last to it I have obtained a situation in Hennies Meikham & Co Store through the joint influence directly and indirectly of Bros J. H. Cummings J. V. Long and Curtis E. Bolton — I believe too that Bro. Charles Smith spoke favourably on my behalf. I am keeping the Books of the firm but inasmuch as my retaining the situation on a permanency is somewhat uncertain on account of the great respect and attachment which they feel for their late Bookkeeper who has been discharged for drunkenness but who may nevertheless yet be reinstated for the reasons which I have just stated, I do not feel that it would be prudent to say anything on the matter to the people in Cedar at present. Please therefore not to mention the matter to anyone yet but when you listen — do as I write dearest and all will be well. I know

6

you will to keep priest as to my affairs which is the reason why I tell you about this matter now. It is just possible that in the next letter which I write I may not have to inform you that I am out of employment altogether. But pray for me dearest that I may be prepared and that all things may work together for our mutual good. I should much like you to come at Conference & I were perfectly certain of keeping my present situation I would say yes — come upon no condition — that you make satisfactory arrangements about everything at home so that if we should have to return nothing would be destroyed during our absence. I think before posting this I will feel S.N. & Co's pulse to find out if there there is of permanent employment & may perhaps ask the plain question whether I shall be justified in sending up for my family. If I can manage to stay where I am now I shall of course leave Cedar altogether — but keep this secret at present. In case you do not come up at Conference in Oct. you will most likely have to wait till next April Conference and for my part I do not wish to act hastily but to do what will really turn out for the best. Ask the Father to direct us both in the matter & feel in your

The original cross-hatched handwritten letter is in the possession of Geary descendant, Vernetta Page Marshall.

Transcription

1

Dear Sophy, G. S. L. City 13 Sep. 1860

I feel quite uneasy on account of not hearing from you. It is now nearly a month since I received your last letter and that was a mighty short one. Since writing you last I have obtained a situation in Storme's Needham & Co Store through the joint influence directly and indirectly of Bros. J. W. Cummings, J. A. Long and Curtis E. Bolton. I believe too that Bro. Charles Smith spoke formally on my behalf. I am keeping the Books of the firm but in as much as my retaining the situation for a permanency is somewhat uncertain on account of the great respect and attachment which they feel for their late Bookkeeper who has been discharged for drunkenness but who may nevertheless get reinstated for the reason which I have first stated. I do not feel that it would be prudent to say anything on the matter to the people in Cedar at present. Please therefore not to mention the matter to anyone yet and even your Sister. Do as I wish dearest and all will be well. I know

2

you wish to keep posted as to my affairs which is the reason why I tell you about this matter now. It is just possible that in the next letter which I write I may have to inform you that I am out of employment altogether. But pray for me dearest that I may be prospered and that all things may work together for our mutual good. I should much like you to come up at Conference & if I were perfectly certain of keeping my present situation I would say come up on one condition – that you make satisfactory arrangements about everything at home so that if we should have to return nothing would be destroyed during our absence. I think before posting this I will feel Messrs. S. N. & Co's pulse to find out of what chance there is of permanent employment. I may perhaps ask the plain question whether I shall be justified in sending up for my family. If I can manage to stay where I now am I shall of course leave Cedar altogether – but keep this secret at present – In case you do not come up at Conference in Oct. You will most likely have to wait till next Conference and for my own part I do not wish to act hastily but to do what will really turn out for the best. Ask the Father to direct us both in the matter. I feel in your

3

heart at the time submissive to his will – My prayers since I have been here have been fully answered because I have not asked for anything except what I felt I really needed. Act on the same principle and you shall be blessed with your heart's desire. In case it should be decided that you remain for the present I want you by return of post to send me a full list of **all** you require and I will try to supply your wants – Send the list anyhow so that if necessary I may send the things by Bro. Lunt [Henry W. Lunt] or somebody else who may be here at next Conference as I have lost the list I brought with me. I wish you would send me some sealing wax & a seal the next chance you have as it is useless to buy when I have plenty at home & I wish to spend nothing foolishly. I wish also you would send "Crittenden on Bookkeeping" which you will find amongst my books. Wrap it up very carefully as it is a borrowed book – I wish to get it as soon as possible. You had better send it by post if Bro. Lunt should not start in a day or so after you receive this. The possession of this book is a matter of importance to me in my present situation. If you send it by Bro. Lunt wrap it up carefully so that it's nature cannot be discovered. Know this be sure. 15 September – my chance of keeping my situation seems to me more certain every day though I do not hold that or anything else otherwise than with a loose hand as I

4

know how in times past my expectation have not always been realized. I like Messr's Storme's & Co. much so far and do not feel to desire any more comfortable or lucrative Employment in this Territory. I have not yet made any particular arrangements about Salary only that in case I should not remain. I am to receive $ 3 per day for the time Employed and I have no idea they would think of offering me less than this by the year if I should continue with them. All things seem working together for our good and if they continue prosperous as at present I think and hope we shall both know how partially at all events to appreciate the blessing by contrast with just occasional hardships. I will tell you what has just occurred to me – It is this – If you can make arrangements with Bro. Lunt or Bro. Harrison or anybody else who is coming for Conference to come with him –do so on the condition that you are allowed to return with him if I cannot make arrangements to make you comfortable here

5

during the Winter. You need not say that you are coming up for any other purpose than to pay me a visit and may perhaps stay through the Winter or not according to circumstances. You will in case you come, know to make arrangements with somebody to take care of the cow during your absence and I would like somebody to have it that has not one of his own, but I want you to be well satisfied that whoever has it will have plenty of feed for it during the Winter if you should stay so long. I believe Bro Harris has no cow and he is a worthy man. Also Bros. Middleton & Webster too are I believe without cows but leave it with the party who you know has plenty of

6

feed on hand even though you should have to leave it with somebody who has cows. I shall of course expect the party to pay the herd bill for the time he has the cow but he is quite welcome to the use of her free in every other respect if he will take good care of her. I suppose John Adams has herded the cow since I left. I would like to know how much I owe him and will try to send him something at Conference but make no particular promise for fear I should not be able to perform it. You will have to make arrangements for the calf to be herded so that it canbe fed during the Winter. I am willing to pay for it if it can be well attended to.

7

If you cannot get this done in Cedar which to incur? I should think you can do perhaps some of the people at Session would oblige me by taking the oversight of it in connection with their own. As I said before I will pay them for their trouble. I want it put into the hands of a careful man who takes good care of his own stock for it is of great importance to me that I should not lose it . I presume my cattle will be safe on the range. Both of the sheep will remain with Bro. Seth Johnson as per agreement with him and now about the house and the things therein. You will have to nail up or get nailed up the windows and doors. You had better empty the cellar and put everything into the house Be sure the house is made secure. Bring with you my double barreled rifle and moulds

8

also bring with you the silk velvet belonging to your basinet and all the other good clothing you have. Of course I will be last. By the bye I have said nothing about the pig and chickens I think you had better let them out on shares – on halves. I don't think of anything else just now but set to work and do your best to come along and may God help and prosper us both. I am well and feel well though I have not yet got my money from Stambaugh. I shall sue him as soon as I can find a little spare time. As ever Your most affectionate John The moment anything sad come up I will write you again in case you should not be able to come. Good bye

The 'Writings' of John Thomas Geary

When John Thomas Geary died in 1867 and his wife Sophia Fryer Geary Willis died in 1872, their personal effects appear to have been scattered amongst family members and perhaps some of them just abandoned, lost or just thrown away. Their daughters were young women and the importance of family memorabilia to preserve for following generations would not have been a high priority in their chaotic lives.

In pursuing research, there were several references made to the *'writings of John Thomas Geary'*. What were these 'writings' about? Who had them? Were there personal histories written by John or Sophia? During the writing of this book, the authors made a concerted effort to contact as wide a variety of family descendants as possible, in order to locate these things. One email contact was made to a cousin in the fall of 2019 and was followed up by a personal phone call. Kaye was assured that she had no personal items from John Thomas Geary, but that she would inquire further with family members she knew who were doing or had done genealogical research on the family. Eight months went by, when Kaye received an email that contained the *'writings of John Thomas Geary'*. She said that she was going through a box of her deceased mother's things, when she came across some papers that had been put into plastic folders. She didn't know what they were or their significance, and as she examined them closely, she wondered if indeed these may be the papers of which we had inquired many months before. When Kaye received the images of these papers, he immediately knew what they were, and this elicited further research and transcription of John Thomas' record books and shorthand. "*The jewel*" discovered treasures that we have been seeking for years. The presentation of the *'writings of John Thomas Geary'* gives us insight into the lives of our ancestors in the 1850's and 60's.

There are ten pages of writing total. Four pages of these images are full-sized pages without printed lines for accounting purposes. Other pages are specific accounting registers, as the lines and columns for debit and credit are printed on the pages. Some have torn corners, contain watermarks from moisture at some point and they appear to be accounts of items received from various persons and their value. Some pages seem to have been written in two colors of ink, with considerable fading in some cases, making it difficult to read. One page contains about 2/3 of the page written in shorthand. Another image contains about 1/3 of a page of shorthand. Some pages contain numbers either in the middle top of the page, and others in the corners of the pages, and it would appear that the pages are taken from more complete registers, suggesting that we only have portions of the full registers. Are there more pages among some of us? Because of the aging process of the papers, and the discoloration and faintness of some of the ink writings not everything was able to be fully transcribed, but we transcribed most of them.

The shorthand, or as it was known in the mid 1800's 'phonography', is written on several of the pages. Finding someone who could read this shorthand was quite a task. After several months of inquiries, we found a woman employed at The Church History Library[1] who was busily engaged in transcribing phonographic records from various early Church scribes. She was more than happy to assist in transcribing these writings. After seeing what we had, it was somewhat disappointing to know that the writings we had contained no information of historical benefit to us, other than to know that John T. Geary was proficient in the use of phonography. Some of the shorthand John used, turns out to be doodling or just practicing his strokes in forming the sound icons. It turns out that the one shorthand item of John T. Geary's writings that is complete is a record of Psalm 67. Perhaps the message of this psalm reflected the mood of his feelings at the time. The shorthand version of Psalm 67 appears upside down on Image #4 hereafter.

---

[1] The Church History Library, Salt Lake City, Utah. LaJean Carruth personal correspondence with Kaye P. Nichols, August 2020.

PSALM 67
A messianic psalm – The Lord will cause His face to shine upon men – He will judge and govern in righteousness

To the chief Musician on Neginoth, A Psalm or Song

1 God be merciful unto us, and bless us, and cause his face to shine upon us; Selah.
2 That thy way may be known upon earth, thy saving health among all nations.
3 Let the people praise thee, O God; let all the people praise thee.
4 O let the nations be glad and sing for joy: for thou shalt judge the people righteously, and govern the nations upon earth. Selah
5 Let the people praise thee, O God; let all the people praise thee.
6 Then shall the earth yield her increase; and God, even our own God, shall bless us.
7 God shall bless us; and all the Ends of the earth shall fear him.

Summary of the 'writings of John Thomas Geary'

1. The 'writings' confirm that John Thomas was a school teacher both in Salt Lake City and in Toquerville. His pay was in large part derived from goods or services from the parents of his students. These are delineated in the papers that are preserved.

2. The 'writings' confirm our timeline of where John Thomas was living:
1856 -57   Salt Lake City
1857- 61   Cedar City
1861 – 66   Toquerville
The above dates would mostly be correct for where the Geary family lived, however, we do know that John Thomas himself is back and forth between all of these locations, mostly looking for more permanent employment.

3. In Toquerville, he is keeping books for the Tithing Office, at least part of the time.

4. John Thomas records a transaction with "Staines N. & Co. for mate[rial]". This would be Staines - Needham & Company, for whom he would later be employed keeping books.

5. A Bro. Horne is mentioned, most likely Joseph Horne, with whom his family lived in the 14th Ward in Salt Lake City.

6. One entry made in early 1857 records putting new soles on boots and shoes, which would indicate the condition of their footwear that they had during this difficult trek.

7. We also learn that Sophia Geary is having tooth difficulty. Dr. Richardson then "draws 2 teeth for Sis. Geary". This refers to the extraction of diseased teeth. In the 1850's dentists were known as 'Barber Surgeons", which indicates to us the evolution in the practice of dentistry.

8. John Thomas is writing in shorthand. This is another impressive skill which he possessed that would qualify him for additional employment.

9. In the Oct. 19, 1857 entry is mentioned "Bro. J. C. Hall". This would be John Thomas Geary's cousin, John Charles Hall, whose mother, Charlotte, lived with John Thomas Geary in his home in Islington, a suburb of London. John Hall is also identified as a mail carrier.

10. Another entry identifies "Willis J. T". This would be Joshua Thomas Willis. He was called by Brigham Young to be the first Bishop in Toquerville. He also is the man who married Sophia Fryer Geary after John Thomas Geary died in 1867.

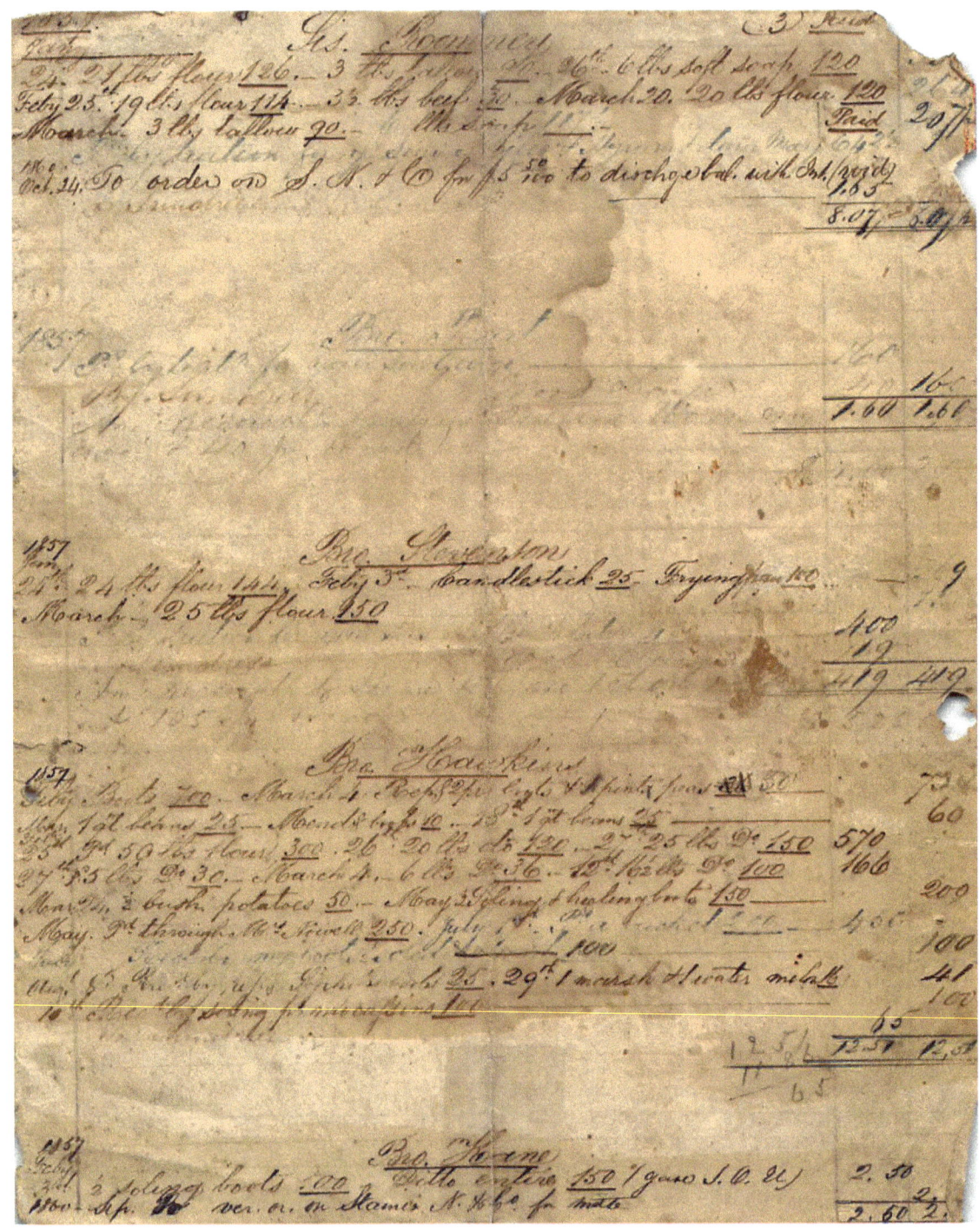

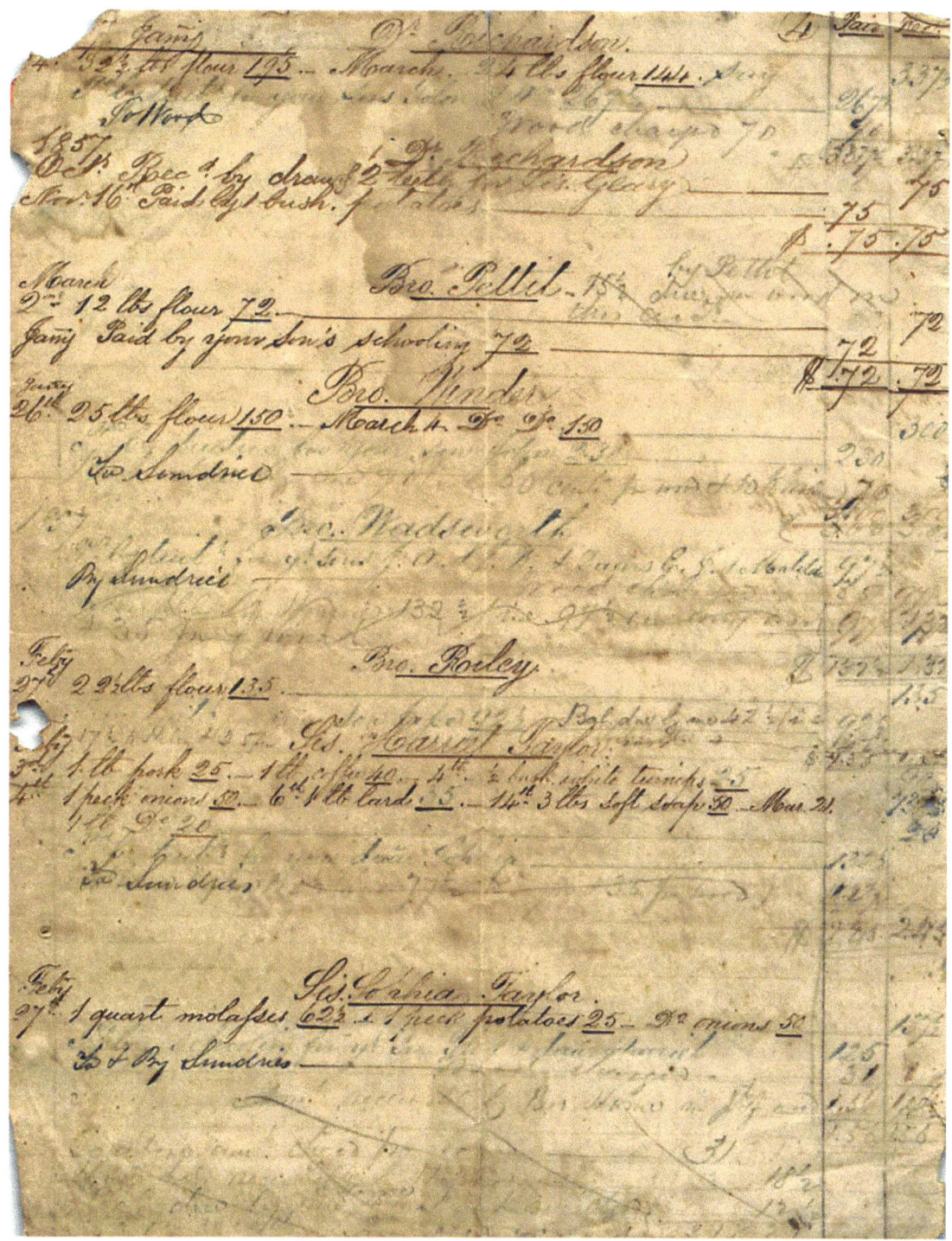

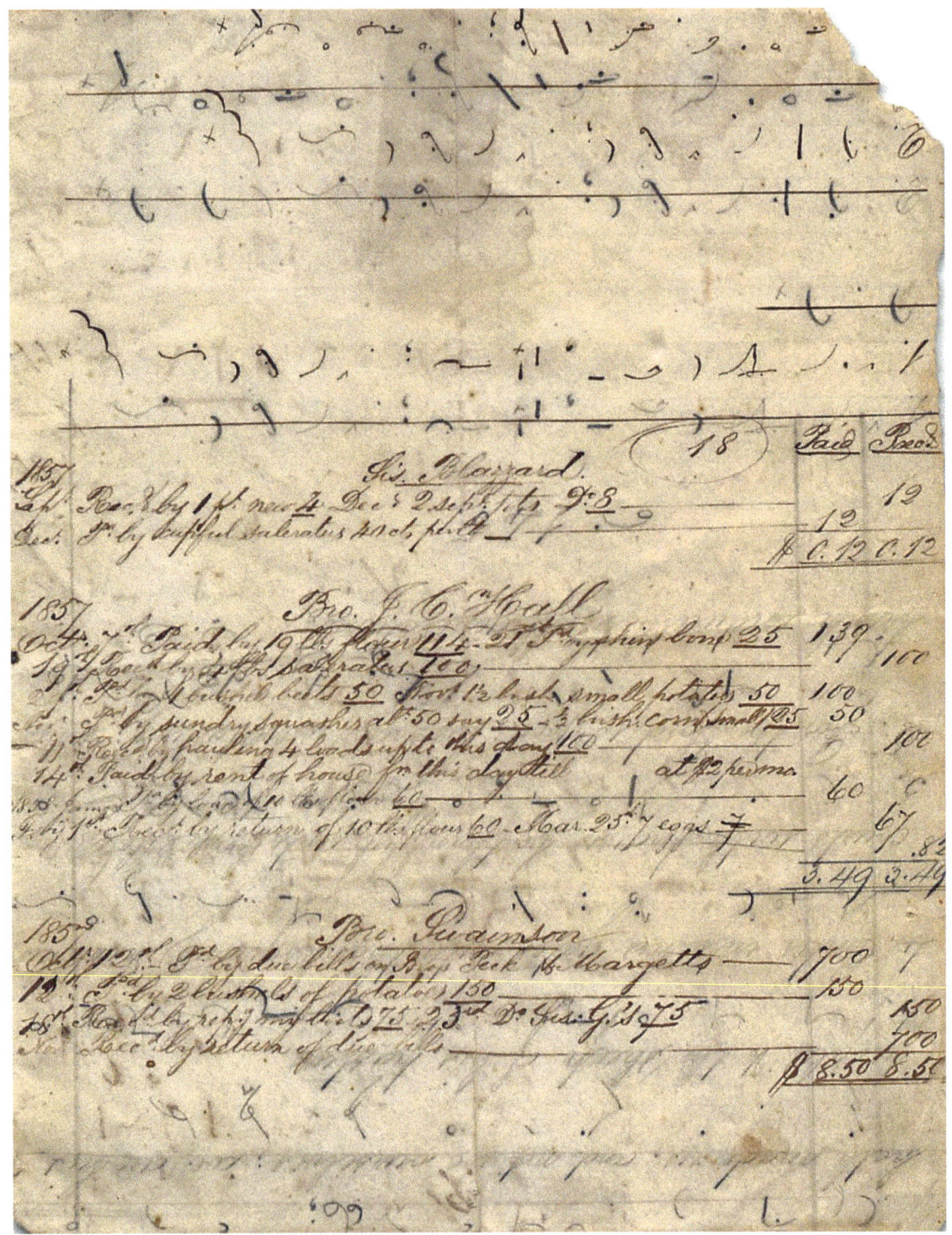

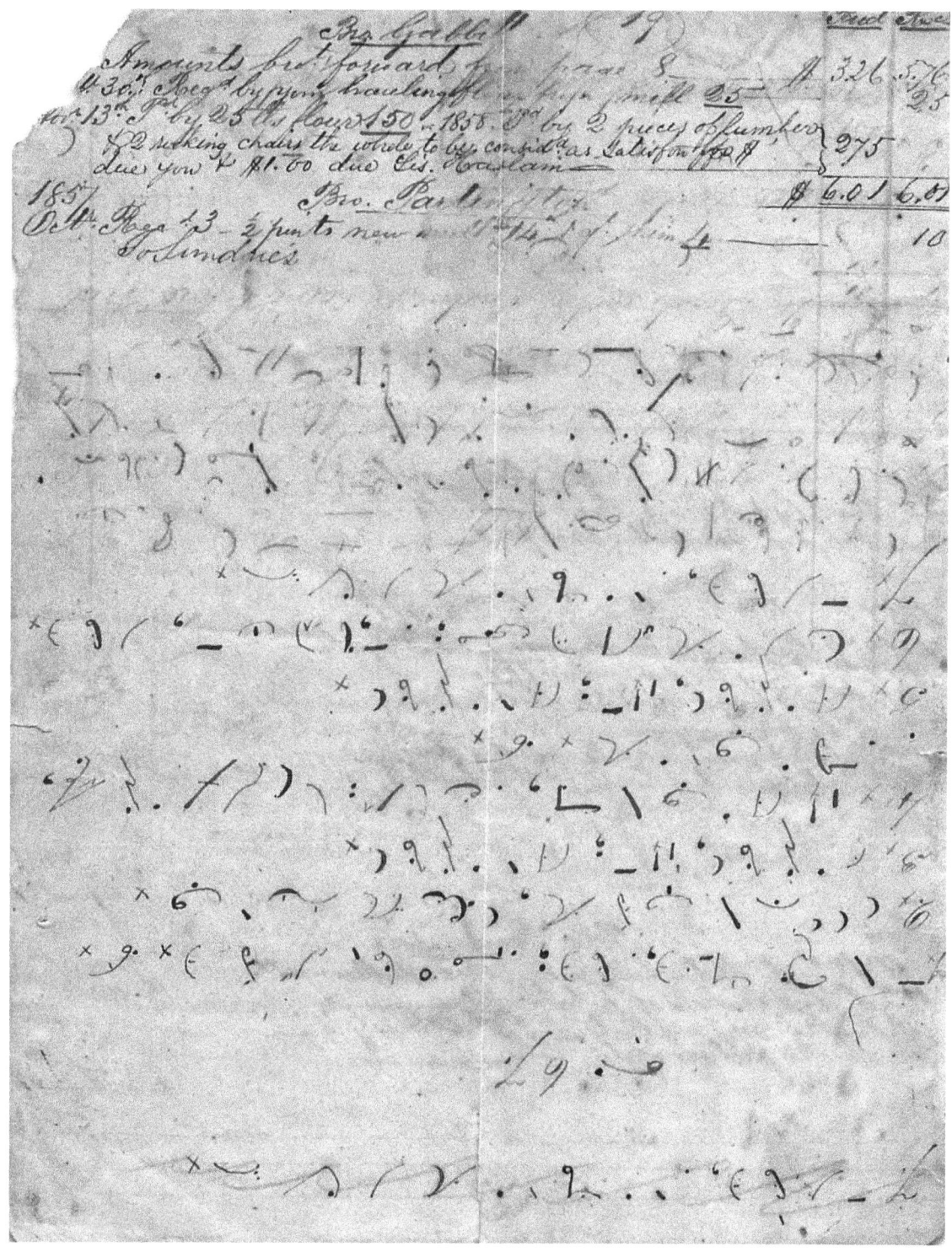

Bro. Gall——

Amounts bro't forward   page 8 $326.??
30th Reg'd by your hauling flour to your mill 25 —   25
Oct 13th Feb by 25 lbs flour 150 — 1858. Feb by 2 pieces of lumber
& 2 rocking chairs the whole to be consid'd as satisfact. $2.8   2.75
due you & $1.00 due Bro. Haslam

1857   Bro. Parkington $6.01 6.01
Oct. Reg'd ½ pints new ?? 14 ?? of skim 4 —   10
To Sundries

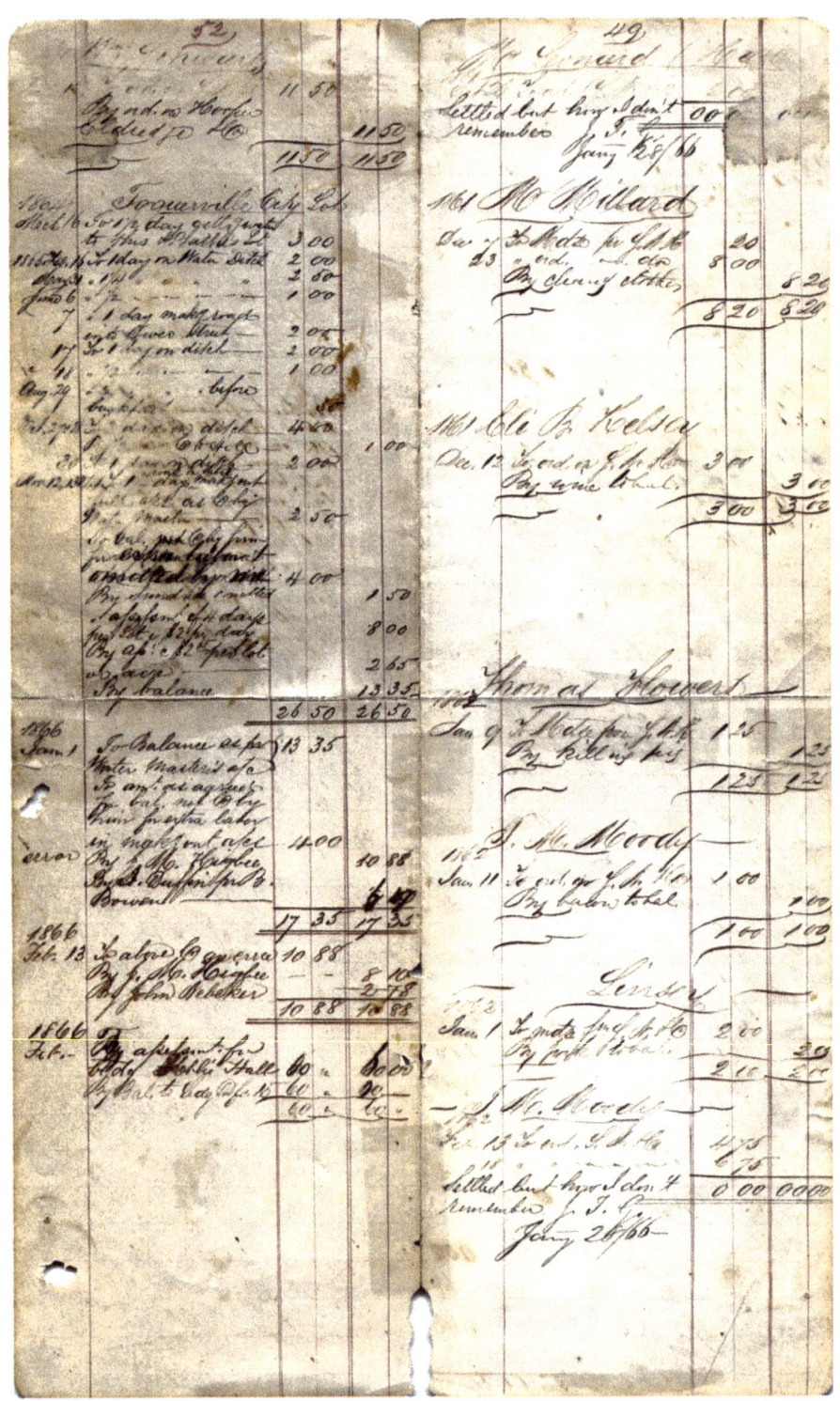

Image #6

	Soquewille Wednesday Sept. 16 1863			(34)
91				
84				68
7od	Minnerly A.	12½ beef Rd	10	0 00
102	"	5¾" "	12	1 52
102	"	beef shank	" 25	25
		2½ " "	25	63
103	Clark H.	15 bac 12" Aug 6		1 80
103	"	5 " c 11" heart	50	1 05
105	Hepeker John	1 canteen Aug 12		50
00				
91	Sundries	Dr To Stock		

Image #7

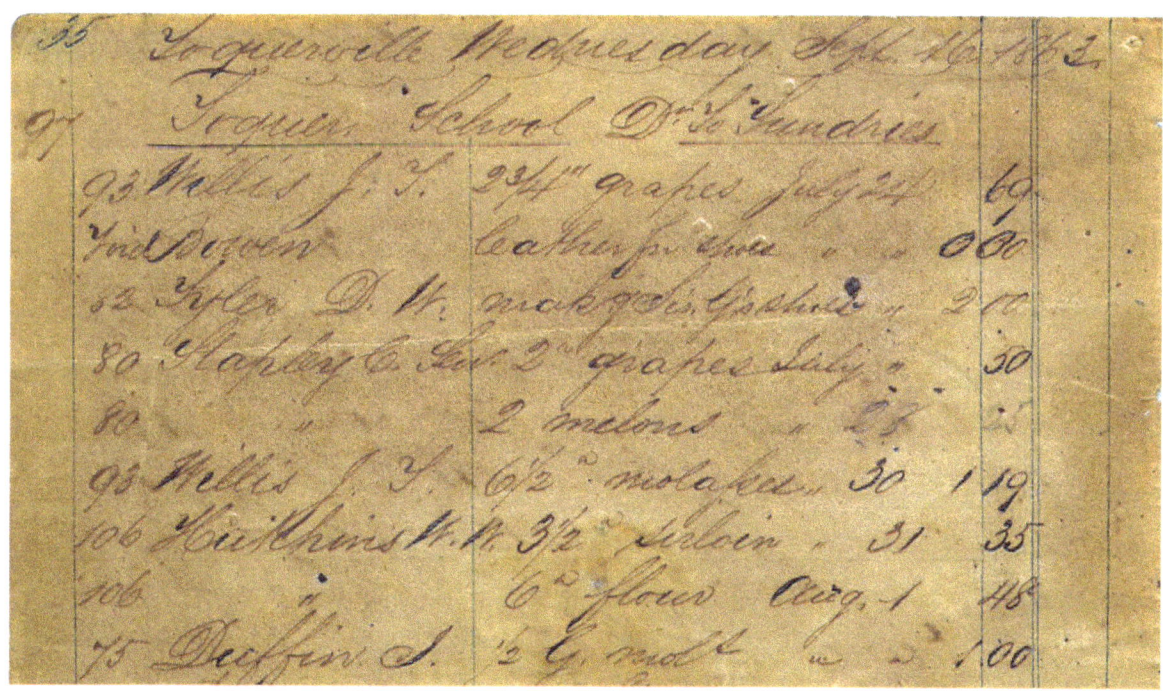

55	Soquewille Wednesday Sept. 16 1863			
97	Soquin School	Dr to Sundries		
93	Willis J. S.	23¾" grapes July 24		69
7od	Brown	leather shoe		0 00
82	Tyler D. W.	making girls shoes		2 00
80	Stapley C. Sen	2 grapes July		30
80	"	2 melons "		25
93	Willis J. S.	6½" molases 30		1 19
106	Hutchins W. R.	3½" sirloin 31		35
106	"	6" flour Aug 1		48
75	Duffin S.	½ G. malt "		1 00

Quiroille Tuesday December 1, 1863

Stock Dr To Sundries

87	Hannon A. M.	5½ bar⁵⁵ 1 lb Suet²⁵	80
99	Joquer Jg Office	2¾ lbs butter at 20	55
99	"	½ Pa onions	75
95	Bunker Edw'd	12½" cotton to bal a/c	

Monday February 1, 1864

Sundries Dr To Stock

99	Joquer Jg Of	3 hours on Books Jan 11	
99	"	3½ " " " " 15	
99	"	3½ " " " " 16	
99	"	2½ " " " " 17	
	Fryer Rich'd	¼ gal. molasses	0.00
96	Smith P. H.	4 lbs inferior cotton	15
104	Allen C. M.	126¼ lb flour	
99	Joquer Jg Of	2 hrs on Books Jan 21	
99	"	3 " " " " 22	
99	"	9 " " " " 23	
99	"	6 " " " " 24	
99	"	3 " " " " 28	
99	"	10 " " " " 30	
99	"	3 " " " " 31	
99	"	2 " " " Feb 1	

Image #9

Loquerville(?) Florida February 1, 18__

Stock Dr. To Sundries

76	Hill Wm	½ G molt	Jan 17	1 00
96	Smith J.H.	2½ B ashes @ 150	" "	3 75
92	Player Joseph	draw'g out axle	" "	75
92	"	weld'g (sint?) chain	" "	20
92	"	cotter for tongue bolt	" "	20
92	Steel John	new hound to tongue &		
92	"	fix'g splice to tongue of cart		
92	"	ox wagon some time ago		2 00
92	"	Half sol'g & heeling shoes		
92	"	at same time		1 00
92	"	Half sol'g shoes Jan 17		60
87	Harmount M.	Weld'g bolt to tongue &		
87	"	put'g on irons some time ago		1 00
87	"	1 G molasses Jan 22		2 00
75	Duffin S	butter some time ago		25
75	"	2 B. potatoes last Nov		3 50
75	"	1 " turnips " Dec		1 50
76	Hill Wm	Milk as agreed		1 50
77	Harrison R.	10 lbs cheese per Frank		2 50
80	Stapley Thos	Repairing public drum		1 00
81	Dodge A.E.	Saleratus on (some time ago)		1 00
82	Infer D.W.	Soft Soap do		40

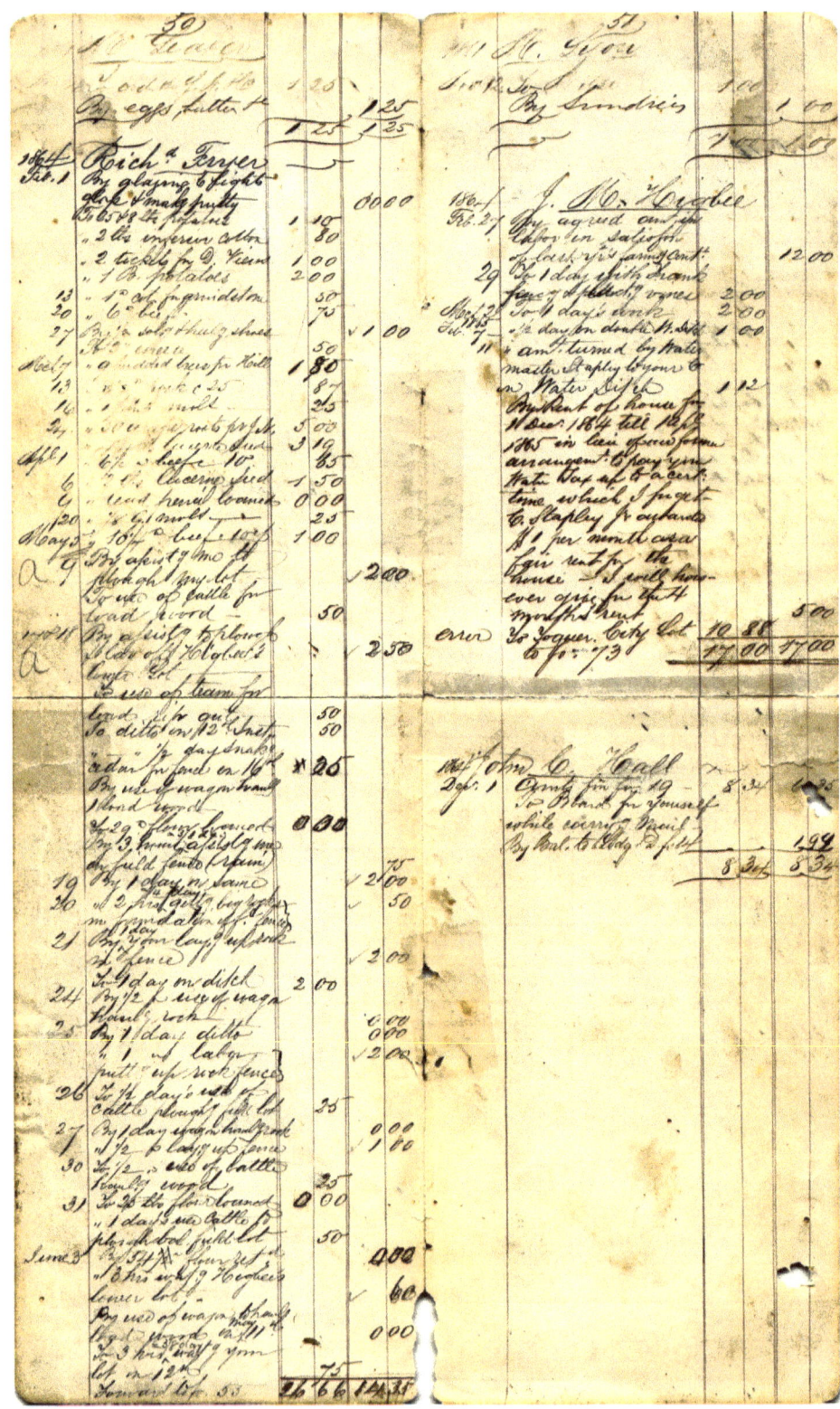

Transcriptions of Writings of John Thomas Geary by Kaye P. Nichols, July 2020

Image #1

<u>1857</u>
Jany   Sis Romney   [3]   Paid
 24   21 lbs flour <u>126</u>._   3 lbs tallow <u>90</u>._   26th 6 lbs soft soap   <u>120</u>
Feby 25th 19 lbs flour <u>114</u>. -   31/2 lbs beef <u>30</u>.   March 20. 20 lbs flour   120   264
March   3 lbs tallow <u>90</u>._   6 lbs soap <u>117 ½</u>   Paid   <u>207/2</u>
        P^d by tuition for y^e son   c ??? iles Hymas   ???   May   642 1/2
1860
Oct. 24. To order on S. N. & Co for $5 50/100 to dischge bal. with Int. (void)
            & Sundries.   <u>1.65</u>___
                                                                            8.07 ½   8.07 ½

1857   Bro. Pearl
        Pd. By tuitⁿ for   your Son George _____   160
            By Sundries   Wood charge   40   160
            In Receivable by the ? ? ? 160 on my   <u>1.60</u> <u>1.60</u>
            A co of ? 40 Jr   8   8.00   2.00

1857   Bro. Stevenston
Jan,
24th. 24 lbs flour <u>144</u>.   Feby 3rd Candlestick <u>25</u>   Frying pan <u>100</u>   9
        March 25 lbs flour <u>150</u>   400
            Feb tuition for year Son   ??? to Febry 430   <u>19</u>____
            In receipt by Ltr recd   ???? and ?? 1 ct on   419   419
            Sent 105 In wood   5.25   5.

1857   Bro. Hawkins
Feby Boots <u>700</u>.   March 4 Reps 2 pr boots & 9 pints peas <s>30</s> <u>50</u>   750
Mar   1 gl beans <u>25</u> - Mends books <u>10 -</u>   18th 1 qt beans <u>25</u> _____   60
Feb 25 Pd 50 lbs flour <u>300</u>. 26th 20 lbs do <u>120</u>.- 27th . 25 lbs Do <u>150</u>   570
27th P^d 5 lbs Do <u>30</u>. - March 4.- 6 lbs Do <u>36</u>. - 12th . 16 ½ lbs Do. <u>100</u>   166
Mar. 24. ½ bush. potatoes <u>50</u>. - May 2. Soling & healing boots <u>150</u> _____   200
May.   P^d through M^{rs}. Nowell <u>250</u>. July 17. P^d a bushel <u>200</u> _____   400
July   Rec. my boot. ½ soled <s>& ?????</s> 100 _____ 100
Augt. 8th   Rec ^d by rep & Sophi's boots <u>25</u>.   29th. 1 marsh & 1 water mils <u>16</u>   41
10th   Rec^d by soling pr. Moccasins <u>100</u> _____   100
                                                                            __65___
                                                                           12.51 12.51

1857   Bro. Horne
Feby 3rd 2 soling boots <u>100</u>   Ditto entire <u>150</u> (gave I. O. U)   2.50
1860 - Sep. 20 ver. or. on Staines N. & Co. for mate[rial]   <u>2.50</u>
                                                                            2.50   2.50

273

Image # 2

Jany	Dr Richardson	(4)	Paid	Rec^d
4. 32 ½ lbs flour 195. - March. 24 lbs flour 144		say		337₂
P^d by tuit^n for your Sons John & W^m 267 ½			267₂	
To Ward	Wood charged 70		70	
1857	1 Dr. Richardson		237 ½	337/2
Octr. Rec^d. by draws 2 teeth for Sis. Geary				75
Novr. 16 . Paid by 1 bush. Potatoes			.75	
		$	.75	.75

March	Bro. Pettit	by Pettit		
2nd 12 lbs flour 72		15 ½ drw on Ward in		72
Jany Paid by your Son's schooling 72		their acct	72	
		$	.72	.72

Jany	Bro. Winder			
26th 25 lbs flour 150. - March 4. Do Do 150				300
P^d by tuition for your son John 230			230	
To Sundries	60 cents for wood & 70 to (to Mid??)		70	
			100	300
			300	300

1857	Bro. Wadsworth			
P^d by tuitit^n for ye Sons J. A. & W. I. Davis E. J. A. Matilda			97 ½	
By Sundries	Ward children		35	97
		$	132 ½	132 ½

Feby	Bro. Riley.			
27th 22 ½ lbs flour 135				13.5
P^d by tuition for ye Son Jake 42 ½ - Bal. due by me 42 ½ /i.e.			92 ½	
17 ½ B. Riley 42.5 p^d	??		42 ½	

Feby	Sis Harriet Taylor		$ 135	135
3^d 1 lb pork 25. - 1 lb coffee 40. – 4th . ½ bush. white turnips 25				90
4th . 1 peck onions 50. - 6th 1 lb lard 35. – 14th 3 lbs soft soap 50. – Mar 2.1				135
1 lb Do 20				20
P^d by tuition for your dau. Sophia			132 ½	
Yd Sundries 112 ½ 77 ½ 35 for wood			112 ½	
			245	245

Feby	Sis. Sophia Taylor			
27th 1 quart molasses 62 ½ . - 1 peck potatoes 25 - Do onions 50				137 ½
P^d by schooling for ye Son Thad & dau Harriet			125	
To & By Sundries	Ward charged		31	
Am^t. receivable by Bro. Horne in p^t of and			1.56	18½
To also am^t chged fr ??			1.56	1.56

Image # 3

[Top third of page is in shorthand; Doodling]

| 1857 | Sis. Blazzard. | [18] | Paid | Recd |

1857   Sis. Blazzard.   [18]   Paid   Recd
Sep*t*   Recd by 1 pt. new 4   Dec & 2 sept. pts D°. 8   12
Dec.   P*d* by cupful saleratus 40 ct, per lb   12
                                                                                     $ 0.12   0.12

1857   Bro. J. C. Hall
Oct*r*   7*th* Paid by 19 lbs flour 114 - 21*st* Pd by shin bone 25   139
      19*th*   Rec*d* by 4 lbs saleratus 100   100
      20*th*   P*d* by 1 bushel beets 50 Nov*b*. 1½ bush. small potatoes 50   100
      Nov*r*   P*d* by sundry squashes ab*t* 50 say 25. ½ bush. corn mall 25   50
      11*th*   Rec*d* by hauling 4 loads up to this day 100   100
      14*th*   Paid by rent of house fm this day till   at $2 per mo.
1858   Jany   P*d* by load of 10 lbs flour 60   60
Feby   1*st*   Rec*d* by return of 10 lbs flour 60 March 25*th* 7 eggs 7   67
                                                                                                      .82
                                                                                    3.49   3.49

1857   Bro. Swainson
Oct*r*   12*th* P*d* by due bills on Bros Peck & Margetts   700
      12*th*   P*d* by 2 bushels of potatoes 150   150
      18*th*   Rec*d* by rep.g my boots 75   23*rd* D°. Sis.G.'s 75   150
      Nov*r*   Rec*d* by return of due bills   700
                                                                             $ 8.50   8.50

[bottom portion of page in shorthand]

Image #4

                           Bro. Gabbell   [19]   Paid   Rec*d*
             Amounts br*t* forward from page 8 $ 3.26   5.76
--*th*   30*th*, Rec*d* by yem hauling flour from mill 25   25
Nov*r* 13*th* P*d* by 25 lbs flour 150 - 1858. P*d* by 2 pieces of lumber
          & 2 rocking chairs the whole to by consid*d*. as satisfaction for $ }275
          Due you & $1.00 due Sis. Haslam
                                                                             $ 6.01   6.01
1857   Bro. Parkingston
Oct*r*   Rec*d*. 3 - ½ pints new milk - 14   19*th* skim 4   10
        To Sundrie's

[bottom part of page in shorthand]   Psalm 67

Image #5

49
Mr. Leonurd Hall

1861			
Oct 26	To ord. (Lent H)	2.00	
	Settled but how I didn't remember T.G.	0.00	0.00
	Jany 28/66		

1861 Mr. Millard

Dec 7	To Mdse pr L. A. H.	.20	
23	" ord. " do	8.00	
	By cleaning clothes	8.20	
		8.20	8.20

1861 Eli B. Kelsey

Dec. 12	To ord. on L.A.H.	3.00	
	By wine to bal.		3.00
		3.00	3.00

1862 Thomas Flowers

Jan 9	To Mdse from L.A.H.	1.25	
	By killing pig		1.25
		1.25	1.25

1862 T. M. Moody

Jan. 11	to ord. on L.A.H.	1.00	
	By bacon to bal.		1.00
		1.00	1.00

1862 Mr. Linsey

Jan. 1	To mdse. Fm L.A.H.	2.00	
	By ork to bal.		2.00
		2.00	2.00

T. M. Moody

1862			
Feb. 13	To ord. L.A.H.	4.75	
18	" " " "	6.75	
	Settled but how I don't Remember J. T. G Jany28/66	0.00	0.00

52
Wm Schwartz

	To ord.	11.50	
	By ord. wHooper Eldredge D		
	11.50		
			11.50
	11.50		

1864 Toquerville City Lot

Mch 16	To 1 ½ day get.g water To this & Battie's Lot		3.00
1865 Feb. 16	To 1 day on Water Ditch	2.00	
May 31	To 1 ¼ " " " "	2.50	
June 6	" ½ " " " "	1.00	
7	" 1 day mak.g road Into tower street		2.00
17	To 1 day on ditch		2.00
18	" ½ " " "		1.00
Aug. 29	" ½ " " " before Bankfail		.50
Oct.27 & 28	To 2 days in ditch		4.00
	By ½ & to Hill		1.00
30	To 1 day on ditch	2.00	
Nov. 12,13th & 14	Work in ditch days makg out Full a/cs as & by Water Master		2.50
	To bal. // ? by him For barter labor & Omitted by me		4.00
	By Sundries omitted 1.50		
	" assesst of 4 days Pres Lot c $2 pr day 8.00		
	By asst c $ 2.65 per lot Or acre 2.65		
	By balance 13.35		
1866			26.50
	26.50		
Jan 1	To Balance as pr Water Master's a/c		13.35
	To amt as agreed Fn bal. not & by Him fr extra labor In mak.g out a/cs		4.00
error	By J. M. Higbee 10.88		
	By J. Duffin pr B. Bowen 6.47		
1866			17.35
	17.35		
Feb. 13	To above & an erred		10.88
	By J. M. Higbee 8.10		
	By John Nebeker 2.78		
			10.88
	10.88		
1866			
Feb.	To assessmt. fr blde Hollie Hall 60.00		60.00
	By Bal. to Ledg &fo. 15		60.00
	60.00		
			60.00
	60.00		

Image # 6

	Toquerville Wednesday Sept. 16, 1863		(34)	
91				
	84			66
	Void Minnerley A.	12 ½ beef (July 21) c 10		000
	102 "	11^a (" ") 12		132
	"	beef Shank (" ")	25	
	102 "	2/2 Suet (" ") 25		63
	103 Clack H. Y.	15^a beef c 12" Aug. 6	180	
	103 "	5^a " c 11^{55} heart^{50} "	105	
	105 Nebeker John	1 canteen Aug 12	150	
	00			
	91 Sundries	Dr. To Stock		

Image # 7

35		Toquerville Wednesday	Sept. 16, 1863.	
97		Toquer School D^n To Sundries		
	93 Willis J. T.	2 ¾" grapes	July 24	.69
	Void Bowen	leather fr shoes	" "	0.00
	82 Tyler D. W.	makg Sis. G's shoes	"	2.00
	80 Stapley C. Sen.	2^w grapes	July "	.50
	80 "	2 melons	" 28	.25
	93 Willis J. T.	6 ½^w molasses	" 30	1.19
	106 Hutchins W. W.	3 ½ Sirloin	" 31	.35
	106 "	6^w flour	Aug. 1	.48
	75 Duffin J.	½ G. mol^s	" "	1.00

Image # 8

		Toquerville Tuesday December 1, 1863		44	
00		Stock	D^r To Sundries		
	87	Harmon A. M.	5 ½ Beef^{55} 1 lb suet^{25}	80	
	99	Toquer. T.g Office	2 ¾ lbs butter at 20	55	
	99	"	½ B. onions		75
	95	Bunker Edwd	12 ½ cotton to bal. a/c	624	
	00				
	00	Monday	February 1, 1864		
	00	Sundries	D^r To Stock		
99		Toquer. T.g Of.	3 hours on Books Jan. 11		
99		"	3 ½ " " "	15	
99		"	3 ½ " " "	16	
99		"	2 ½ " " "	17	
Void		Fryer Rich^d	¼ gal. molasses " "	000	
96		Smith P. K.	4 lbs inferior cotton " "	150	
104		Allen O. M.	126 ¼ lbs flour " "		
99		Toquer. T.g Off.	2 hrs on Books Jan 21		
99		"	3 " " " "	22	
99		"	9 " " " "	23	
99		"	6 " " " "	24	
99		"	3 " " " "	28	
99		"	10 " " " "	30	
99		:	3 " " " "	31	
99		"	2 " " " Feb. 1		
00					

Image #9

45		Toquerville	Monday February 1, 1864.	
00		Stock	D^r To Sundries	
	76	Hill, W^m	½ G. mols Jan 17 100	
	96	Smith P. K.	2 ½ B. ashes c 150 " " 375	
	92	Player Joseph	chan.g out axe " "	75
	92	"	weld,g Lunt's chain " "	20
	92	"	cotter for tongue bolt " "	20
	92	Steele John	new howrd to tongue &	
	92	"	fix,g splice to tongue of un-	
	92	"	o^r. wagon some time ago	200
	92	"	Half sol.g & heeling shoes	
	92	"	at same time	100
	92	"	Half sol,g shoes Jan 17 60	
	87	Harmon J. M.	Weld,g bolt to tongue &	
	87	"	putt,g on irons some time ago 100	
	87	"	S G. molasses Jan 22 200	
	75	Duffin, I.	butter some time ago 25	
	75	"	2 B. potatoes last Wood 350	
	75	"	1 " turnips " Dec 150	
	76	Hill W^m	Milk as agreed	150
	77	Harrison R^d	10 lbs cheese per Frank 250	
	80	Stapley Thos	Repairing public drain	100
	81	Dodge A. E.	Saleratus oru.^{d} Some timepiece 100	
	82	Tyler D. W.	Soft soap delt	40

	50			
	Mr. Leaker			
	To ord. fm L. A. H.	1.25		
	By eggs, butter, etc	1.25		
		1.25	1.25	
1864	Richd Fryer			
Feb. 1	By glazing 6 lights			
	Glap & makg putty7		00.00	
	To 25 & 8 lbs potatoes	1.10		
	" 2 lbs inferior cottⁿ	.80		
	" 2 tickels fn D Views	1.00		
	" 1 B. potatoes	2.00		
13	" 1[@] Cot. Fn grindstone	.50		
20	" 6[@] beef	.75		
27	By ½ sol.g & heel.g. shoes		1.00	
	To 3[#] cheese	.50		
Mch 7	" 9 budded trees fn Hill	1.80		
13	" 8 lb pork c 25	.87		
16	" 1 pint mol^s	.25		
24	" 50 gray he roots pr J. A.	4.00		
	" 4'lbs Lucerne seed	3.19		
Apl 1	" 6 ½ d beef c 10	.65		
6	" lead pencil loaned	0.00		
9	" 1/8 G. mol^s	.25		
May 5	" 10 ¼ ^d beef c 10 ct	1.00		
9	" By assist.g mo to			
	Plough my lot		2.00	
	To use of cattle fm			
	Ward wood		.50	
17 & 18	By assist.g to plough			
	& lay off 7 big beet's			
	Lower Lot		.50	
	To ditto un 12th Inst.	.50		
	" " ½ day snak'g			
	Cedar fn fence on 16th	.25		
	By use of wagon haul			
	1 load wood			
	To 29th flour Graned	0.00		
	By 3 hours asstg me			
	On field fence (rain)		.75	
19	By 1 day in same & 4 day		2.00	
20	" 2 hrs gettg big rocks			
	in foundation off fences		.50	
21	By your lay.g up rock			
	In fence		2.00	
	To 1 day on ditch	2.00		
24	By ½ da use of wagn			
	Hauling rock		0.00	
25	By 1 day ditto		0.00	
	" 1 day in labor		2.00	
	Putting up rock fence			
26	To ½ day's use of			
	Cattle plough.g field lot	.25		
27	By 1 day wagon haul.g rock		0.00	
	" ½ da lay.g up fence		1.00	
30	To ½ w use of cattle			
	Haul.g wood	.25		
31	To 25 lbs flour loaned	0.00		
	"1 day's use cattle fd			
	Plus and bal field lot.	.50		
June 3	By 54 # flour ret^d		0.00	
	" 3 hrs wat.g Higbee's			
	lower lot		.60	
	By use of wagon w/haulg			
	That wards on May 11th			
	Fr 3 hrs =38 day u at g ynn		0.00	
	lot on 12 shs		.75	
	Forward to lv .55	26.66.	14.35	
	51			
1861	M. Lyon			
Nov. 12	To Mdse		1.00	
	By Sundries			
	1.00			
			1.00	
	1.00			
1864	J. M. Higbee			
Feb. 27	By agreed amt in			
	Labor in satisfn			
	12.00			
	Of last yr's farm.g cont^r			
29	To 1 day with Frank			
	Fenc.g & plant.g vines		2.00	
Mch 2	To 1 day's work		2.00	
1865				
Feb 7	" ½ day on double W. Ditch		1.00	
11	" amt. turned by Water			
	Master Stapley to your ?			
	In Water Ditch		1.12	
	By Rent of house fm			
	1 Dec. 1864 till 1 Apl			
	1865 in lieu of our former			
	Arrangement to pay you			
	Water Tax up to a certⁿ			
	time which I for get.			
	C. Stapley Jr. awarded			
	$ 1 per month as a			
	fair rent for the			
	house – I will how-			
	ever give for the 4			
	months rent			
5.00				
error	To Toquer. City Lot		10.88	
	to fo: 73	17.00	17.00	
1864	John C. Hall			
Dec. 1	Amts. fm fo. 19-	8.34	6.35	
	To Board for yourself			
	while carry.g mail			
	By Bal. to Lodg. D. fo 14		1.99	
		8.34	8.34	

Last Will and Testament of Thomas Geary
Written July 20, 1860

This copy of John's father's will was located by professional researcher Patty Swenson in the Family History Library, as found in the Principle Probate Registry Will Index, FHL film #0251177 for his absolute use and benefit and as to the other moiety or equal half part of the monies of such proceeds Upon trust to pay the same unto my son Elton for his absolute use and benefit And I hereby declare that until the said freehold estate farm lands tenements hereditaments and premises and other real estate shall be sold the net income thereof or of the unsold part thereof, after payment of all outgoings, shall be paid to the persons for the purposes and in the manner to whom and for and in which the net moneys received by the sale thereof would have been payable if such estate farm lands tenements hereditaments and premises and other real estate had been sold & bequeath unto the said Mary Brown all my household goods furniture linen and china absolutely And as to all the use residue and remainder of my Real and Personal Estate and Effects what soever and wheresoever and of what nature or kind soever I devise and bequeath the same unto and for the use of my said sons Frederick and Elton in equal shares as tenants in common for their absolute use and benefit And I declare that the receipts or receipt in writing of the trustees or trustee for the time being acting in the execution of any of the trusts hereof for the purchase money of premises sold or for any money payable under the trusts of this my Will shall effectually discharge the purchasers or purchasers or other the person or persons paying the same therefrom and from being concerned to see to the application or from being answerable for the misapplication or non application thereof And I further declare that if the trustees hereby appointed or either of them or any trustee or trustees to be appointed as hereinafter is provided shall die or be desirous of being discharged or refuse or become incapable to act then and so often the said trustees or trustee and for this purpose any retiring trustee shall be considered a trustee, may appoint any other person or persons to be a trustee or trustees in the place of the trustee or trustees so dying or desirous to be discharged or refusing or becoming incapable to act and upon every such appointment the said trust premises shall be so conveyed and transferred that the same may become vested in the new trustee or trustees jointly with the surviving or continuing trustee or trustees or solely as the case may require and every such new trustee shall have the same powers authorities and discretions as if he had been hereby originally appointed a trustee And I also declare that the trustees or trustee for the time being of this my Will shall be chargeable only with such moneys as they or he shall actually receive and shall not be answerable the one for the other of them nor for any Banker Broker or other person in whose hands any of the trust moneys shall be placed nor for the insufficiency or deficiency of any stocks funds or securities nor otherwise for involuntary losses And that the said trustees or trustee for the time being may reimburse themselves or himself out of the moneys which shall come to their or his hands under the trusts aforesaid all expenses to be incurred in or about the execution of the aforesaid trusts And I further and lastly declare that every such trustee who is or may be a barrister solicitor and solicitor shall be at liberty to retain and be allowed the same compensation for loss of time and exercise of skill in the performance of the trusts aforesaid or in relation thereto as if he had not been such trustee but had been professionally employed by my trustees and had acted in such trusts in that capacity And hereby revoking all Wills by me theretofore made I declare these to be my last Will and Testament In witness whereof I the said Thomas Geary have hereunto set my hand this twentieth day of July in the year of our Lord one thousand eight hundred and sixty. Signed and declared by the said Thomas Geary as and for his last Will and Testament in the presence of us present at the same time who at his request in his presence and in the presence of each other have hereunto subscribed our names as Witnesses Thomas Crane, Brewer Brunswick Street Joseph Walmuff, Willow Street.

Transcription

Transcription of the Will of Thomas Geary (1792 -1865)
Will of Thomas Geary – written 20 July 1860, codicil 23 June 1863, proved 18 Aug 1865
He died 28 July 1865
Transcribed by Patty Swenson 2010 (spacing added)

This is the last Will and Testament of me Thomas Geary of Number 86 Stanley Street Leicester. I nominate and appoint my friend Mr. John Orton farmer of Witherley in the County of Leicester farmer and grazier and my son Frederick of Number 22 Gouldon Terrace Barnsbury Road Islington in the County of Middlesex Trustees and Executors of this my Will. I devise unto my said Trustees and Executors their heirs executors and administrators all my freehold estate farm lands tenements hereditaments and premises situate in the parish of Ratcliff Culey in the said County of Leicester and now in the tenure or occupation of James Wood Esquire and all other my real estate whatsoever and wheresoever upon trust, as soon as conveniently my be after my decease to sell the same either together or in parcels and either by public auction or private contract and subject to such conditions of sale as to them shall seem proper and with power for them to vary or rescind any contract for sale and if necessary to buy in and resell without being responsible for any loss or damage that may be occasioned thereby and to do and execute all such acts and assurances for effectuating any such sale as they shall think fit and put out of the proceeds of such sale upon trust in the first place to pay my debts and funeral and testamentary expenses and after payment thereof upon trust account to pay unto Charles Geary Browne the son of Mary Browne of Stanley Street aforesaid the sum of two hundred pounds for his own use and benefit absolutely and after such payments as aforesaid upon future trust to pay one equal moiety or half part of the residue of the proceeds of such sale unto my said son Frederick for his absolute use and benefit and as to the other moiety or equal half part of theresidue of such proceeds upon upon trust to pay the same unto my son Elton for his absolute use and benefit.

And I hereby declare that until the said freehold estate farm lands tenements hereditaments and premises and other real estate shall be sold the net amount thereof or of the unsold part thereof (after payment of all outgoings) shall be paid to the persons for the purposes and in the manner to whom and for and in which the net moneys produced by the sale thereof would have been payable if such estate farm lands tenements hereditaments and premises and other real estate had been sold. I bequeath unto the said Mary Browne all my household goods furniture linen and china absolutely.

And as to all the residue and remainder of my real and personal Estate and Effects whatsoever and wheresoever and of what nature or kind soever, I devise and bequeath the same unto and for the use of my said sons Frederick and Elton in equal shares as tenants in common for their absolute use and benefit. And I declare that the receipts or receipt in writing of the trustees or trustee for the time being acting … [legal jargon about administering the trust]…

And hereby revoking all wills by me heretofore made I declare this to be my last Will and Testament in Witness whereof I the said Thomas Geary have hereunto set my hand this twentieth day of July in the year of our Lord one thousand eight hundred and sixty.   T. Geary.

Signed and declared by the said Thomas Geary as and for his last Will and Testament in the presence of us present at the same time who at his request in his presence and in the presence of each other have hereunto subscribed our names as Witnesses. Thomas Crane, Brewer Brunswick Street. Joseph Watmuff Willow Street.

CODICIL –

Whereas I Thomas Geary of Number 86 Stanley Street Leicester have made my last Will and Testament in writing bearing date the twentieth day of July one thousand eight hundred and sixty and have thereby directed that my trustees and executors therein named shall out of the proceeds of the sale of my real estate pay unto Charles Geary Browne the son of Mary Browne of Number 86 Stanley Street aforesaid the sum of two hundred pounds for his own use and benefit absolutely, now I do hereby declare this present writing to be a codicil to my said last will and testament and I direct the same to be amended thereto and taken as part thereof accordingly. I direct that the said legacy or sum of two hundred pounds shall _?_ and be payable at the expiration of twelve calendar months from the day of my decease and that by reason of the minority of the said Charles Geary Browne the same shall be paid unto the hands of the said Mary Browne to be by her applied and expensed for his education benefit and preferment as occasion may require. And I further direct and declare that the receipt in writing of the said Mary Browne for the said legacy or sum of two hundred pounds shall be a good valid and sufficient discharge to the trustees or trustee for the time being acting in the execution of the trusts of my said Will who shall not be bound to see to the application of the said legacy or be answerable or accountable for the nonapplicaton or misapplication thereof by the said Mary Browne or by any other person or persons whoinsoever. And that the said receipt shall be binding and conclusive upon the said Charles Geary Browne and upon all persons claming or as claim thru with or under him and shall be as good value and conclusive in all respects as his receipt for the said legacy would be on his attaining the age of twenty one years if the payment of such legacy were postponed until he should attain that age. I hereby confirm my said will and except as it is altered by this codicil In Witness whereof I have hereunto set my hand this twenty third day of June one thousand eight hundred and sixty three. Thomas Geary - signed by the said Thomas Geary as and [to] be a codicil to his last Will and Testament in the presence of us present at the same time who in his presence and in the presence of each other have hereunto subscribed our names as Witnesses – Joseph Denton, Humberstone , Leicester – Robert Parr, N.135 Upper Brunswick , Liecester.

Proved at London with a codicil 18 August 1865 by the oath of Frederick Geary the son, one of the executors to whom admon was granted, John Orton farmer the other executor having renounced the probate and execution of the said will and codicil.

10

Transcription of the September 10, 1866
Last Will and Testament of John Thomas Geary

"Last will and testament" of John Thomas Geary.(sent to Effie S. Keele in October 1939 by Marion Clawson: Richard Fryer, Grandfather of Marion Clawson, was a brother of Sophia Fryer (Geary), Grandmother of Marion Keele, Husband of Effie S. Keele).

"This is the last will and testament of me the undersigned Jn Ts Gy (John Thomas Geary) formerly of Toqr (Toquerville) in the Co of Wash (Washington) in the territory of Utah but now of G S L City (Great Salt Lake City) in the same Territ (Territory). I give devise and bequeath unto my dear wife Sophia G. (Geary) her heirs, executors, admins (administrators) and assigns all that my Town lot in Toq (Toquerville) affords with the log house Fruit Trees grape vines and all the things now or lately or which at the time of my decease may be standg and growg on the s Lot. And also my Field Lot containg by admission two and a half acres be the same mor or less situate in the Toqr (Toquerville) New Fiels on the West side of Ash Creek and also all those the debts or sums of money except the sum of two dollars from Bro Porsamon due me as per list of or schedule then delivered by me to my wife and dated on or about the twenty seven day of Feby 1865 last and also my sill ver watch now or lately in the possession of Charles Smith of Saint George Watchmaker And also my yoke of Cattle named respectively Soph and Bright And also my two or three old Steer on Smith herd-ground And also the store and flour bin and all other things in the house. And also my trunk wearg apparel books and papers And also my gold seal (devised "The Olive Branch and Syn" surrounded with the words "Paix et Harmonia") presented to me by my dear father and which seal, as a momento on his account as well as on my own I request said wife to keep and transmit to our Children and their children to the latest generation And I give devise and bequeath to her heirs exetutives administrators and assigns my real and personal estate and effects whatsoever and wheresoever not hereinafter specifically devised and bequeathed and whether in possession reversion remained or expecting To and for the absolute use and benefit of my said wife her heirs executors administrators and assignees and so that the entire property estate and effects hereby devise and bequeathed or intended to be shall not be subject or liable to the control debts liabilities or any agreements of any husband or husbands with whom she may entrust it being my intention and desire that such property estate and effects will be and to and for the sole and separate use of my wife her heirs executives administrators absolutely. In witness whereof I have hereunto set my seal and subscribed my name this tenth day of Sept 1866
    (Signed) Jn Ts Gy (John Thomas Geary)
Said seal publicly declared by the said Jn Ts Gy the Testator as and for his last will and Testament in the presence of us who in his presence at his request and in the presence of each other present together at the same time have hereunto subscribed our names as witness

Henry Oakly 7 mo G.S.L.C.   Charles A Herman 14 do
       ****

This a copy of the Will given to Kaye P. Nichols by Charlie Martin of Hollister, California in 2010.

Family Story Regarding Sophia Fryer Geary Willis' Death as told by Wilma Higbee Kemp, a great-granddaughter

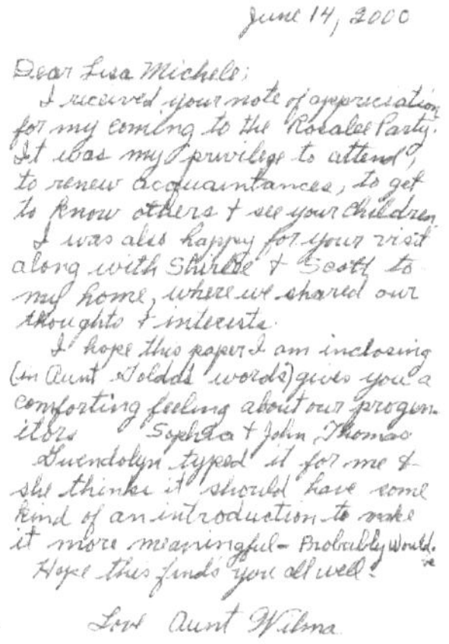

[Handwritten letter:]

> Santa Clara Ut
> June 14, 2000
>
> Dear Lisa Michele;
> I received your note of appreciation for my coming to the Rosales Party. It was my privilege to attend, to renew acquaintances, to get to know others & see your children. I was also happy for your visit along with Shirlee & Scott to my home, where we shared our thoughts & interests.
> I hope this paper I am inclosing (in Aunt Golda's words) gives you a comforting feeling about our progenitors — Sophia & John Thomas. Gwendolyn typed it for me & she thinks it should have some kind of an introduction to make it more meaningful — probably would. Hope this finds you all well!
>
> Love Aunt Wilma

Jun 14, 200

Told to Wilma Higbee Kemp by her Aunt Golda Page Smith, on 31 March 1973.

This came from Aunt Caddie Slack (Caroline Amelia Lamb Slack), who was Grandma Lorine Isabelle Lamb Higbee's sister, concerning the death of Wilma's Great-grandmother, Sophia Fryer Geary Willis.

This event took place 27 May 1872 in Toquerville, Utah.

Aunt Caddie told my grandmother, Sophia Ann Geary Page, that the night Great-grandmother Geary [Willis], was confined, she had been terribly sick all day and they were afraid she was going to die. Grandma Lamb, Aunt Caddie's mother, asked her to go down the street to Sister Dodges' place, and get a start of yeast. So she took some sugar in a cup and sauntered down the street. All of a sudden she looked up and there was a man standing in front of her, she knew he hadn't been there a minute before. She thought to herself, "Well if I didn't know that John Thomas Geary was dead I would say that was him." The more she looked at him the more she knew it was him, his walk, his build, everything about him. She didn't take her eyes off him and he walked in front of her until he got to Willis' house. The lower bar to the fence opening was down, and when the man got to this point he ducked down, going under and then straight to the door. He didn't stop to knock, he opened the front door and went in. So she said she did the very same things he did, but when she got to the door she knocked and they opened the door and let her in. She looked around expecting to see a man, but there was none to be seen anywhere. "Who was that man who came in here just before I did?", she asked the ladies who were present. They said, "No man came in here that we saw." She said, "Yes there was, I could swear that it was John Thomas Geary."
About that time she said Gr-grandmother Geary [Willis] looked up with the most heavenly expression on her face and said, "Why, John Thomas Geary what are you doing here?" Then she reached her arms up as if putting them around someone and fell back on her pillow dead.

Guardianship Papers issued for Sarah Ann (Annie) Geary in 1880

In the Probate Court of the County of Kane.
Territory of Utah —

In the Matter of the Estate } Letters
and Guardianship of   } of
Anna Geary, a Minor   } Guardianship

Territory of Utah } ss.
County of Kane   }

Sophia A. Page is hereby appointed Guardian of the person and estate of Anna Geary, a minor —

Witness, Martin Slack, Clerk of the Probate Court of the County of Kane with the Seal of the Court affixed this first day of October A.D. 1880

By Order of the Court.

Martin Slack, Clerk

Territory of Utah } ss.
County of Kane   }

I do solemnly swear that I will support the Constitution of the United States and serve the Laws of the Territory of Utah, and that I will faithfully perform the duties of my office as guardian of the person and estate of Anna Geary, a minor, according to law.

[Sophia GEARY PAGE]

Sophia A. Page

Subscribed and sworn to before me this first day of October A.D. 1880

Wm. A. Bringhurst
Probate Judge

Transcription of 1882 Letter from
Sophia Geary Page to Attorney John Brown

Little Pinto, July 24th 1882
Mr. Brown,

Kind Friend,

Your welcome letter was duly received, glad you have succeed so far, But sorry to say, I do not think it a correct coppy of my dear Father's Will Nor <u>would</u> I believe it, <u>unless</u> I went to St. George, & took some of my Father's letters & compaired the writing. Fore some cause ~~they have not sent~~ you have not received a correct coppy, As well as I can remember the Will is correct, with the exception of the property that is due to my Father in England, as I am almost <u>sure</u> it was mentioned in Father's Will, I remember my dear Mother reading these Words to me, as well as if it was <u>yesterday,</u> (I make my Will so that it will cope with the iron laws of England) & these ~~was~~ was my
                                                                              there
Father's words in his Will. & ~~these~~ is no such words in this Will they send. What was the need of using those words if there was nothing coming to him and I am <u>positive,</u> I have heard my dear Mother read these <u>very</u> <u>words</u>. & where would these words be except in the Will, "Well, they are not in <u>this</u> Will" that is <u>sure.</u> & I would like to know where they are, In the year 1876, when I was living with Mrs. Mcdonald, she came into the kitchen, where I was, & said to me, Sophy look what a nice present Mr. Mack has given me. At the same time showing me a silver watch, "Oh", said I,"that is just like my Father's watch". "Oh no", said she, "it cannot be, for Charley Smith, brought it to Mr. Mack, saying, Mr Mack, "some person, years ago, brought me this watch to clean, & never called for it & I forget who brought it, so I donate it to the Temple", she said. Mr. Mack ~~putt~~ put means into the Temple, kept the watch & gave it to her, I felt <u>positive then</u> as I do know, that the watch she had was my <u>Fathers</u>, I told her her I thought mentioned his watch in his Will. Wher is your Father's Will said she, & that was how I came to show the Will, I gave it into the hands of Mr. Mackdonald, & Lawer <u>Jackson</u> & I have never seen it from that day to this. I gave with the Will some blue papers, I think they was from my Father's Father. Relating to the what was due to Father in England. I know there was property coming to <u>Father,</u> in England.

The bin that is mentioned in his Will, I thin[k] Mrs. Batty, the old Laddy, that lives in Toker, has it. The bin, cupboard, & a large chest, is all that I care about, of the household goods. I have been told, they was ~~d~~ auctioned off, with Uncl Dicks, but his children nor any of us, never received one dime for them, the City Lot, & farming land. & what Willis ~~used~~, I <u>simply want</u>. I think we have been <u>cheeted,</u> out of them long <u>enough.</u> Father had one or two cows, that is not mention in this Will. The old cows name was Rose, the young cows name was Frosty Mother gave Frosty to me, & Willis sold her for fifty dollars in Cash, & <u>kept</u> it. We never got one cent. The watch I want also, I take a correct Copy of this Will at the same time, I feel positive it is not ^(thank you for it) a correct Copy of my dear Father's writing My being young I may be mistaken in regard to the them words being in the Will, if not in the Will, I am positive they are on some other papers. After reflecting, & studying on these words, perhaps they refer to the England Property (and I give, devise, and bequeath, to her & her hairs, Executors administrators and assigns all my real and personal Estate and effects whatsoever and wheresoever not thereinbefore specifically devised bequeathed and wether in possession reversion, remainder, or expectancy)

Does not these above words refer to the England property. I know there is some there, for Grandfather had what they call there, a free hold of Land. He did not have his land on <u>Lease</u>, it was his own. I think it was in or about Lestershier. I gave with the Will the blue papers, & some of Father & Mother's correspondence, Lawer Jackson, & Mr Mack said they would take them as they refered to the Will & Property before mentioned, Father's Will was filed April 15th, 1875, & I have written three times for it, since that time. My answer was, it cannot be found, if, or when It is found, I should have it. I asure you I do not like the way they have acted about it.

Pleas tell me, did you receive any paper, or papers with the Will.

Please answer as soon as^ ~~posable,~~ convenient it may be some time before I get an answer as the Iron Town mail is discontinued, we don't get our mail regular. All well, Rember us to your wife & family, as ever your friend.

Sophia G. Page.

P.S. Mr. Brown, which do you think should be the best, for to get the money, or the lot back, as far as I am concerned, if Mr. Hanley would have our money, I would be satisfied, I have written to him for the money. So that if he will let us have what justly belongs to us, all right, if not, we want the lot, I do not want any ill feelings if posable, & so give him a chance, he has had the use of the money for almost two years what do you think would be the best. For I don't much expect the money. Father had a good wagon, that is not mentioned, in the Will. Willis used or sold it, hopeing to hear from you soon, as ever your friend.

Sophia G. Page

(The original handwritten letter is in possession of Kaye Page Nichols as of February 2021. The original spelling and grammar have been preserved in transcription to enhance the feel and the personality of the original format.)

Transcription of 1894 Letter from Sophia Geary Page to Attorney John Brown

Little Pinto Utah
April 13, 1894
John Brown Esq.

Dear Friend,

It is about now going on twelve years since I heard ~~fr~~ from you in regard to Father's Will & property. The last time I seen, & talked, with you about it; You said about the same as Uncle. Saying, the most you could find out about it was; That Grandfather Geary's Will was destroyed in some way.

Have you done any more in regard to it. Or ~~have~~ can't you find out any more about it. If it is, as is supposed, that Uncle Fred has destroyed the Will, I think he will have it to answer for, If he can live in ~~pa~~ peace having What rightfully belongs to us, we can live without it. & if permitted hereafter to see him I for <u>one</u>, can honestly meet his gaze <u>knowing</u>, that I have <u>never</u>, wronged him in any way. At the same time I am sorry if we can't have our just dues.

I Hope you self & wife family are well as this leaves us. If you remember in your letter of Aug. 22nd, 1882. You requested me to send you any letters, I might have that would be of any use to you in regard to Father's property, & that you would look them over, & then return them to me. I gave you several letters. & as I want to keep Father's correspondence. Will you please return to me the Letters that I gave to you. Grandmother is about as usual. She has had two strokes

With best wishes & respects to yourself wife & family.
I remain as ever,
Yours respectfuly, Sophia G. Page
P.S. please register the letter back, & I will return the cost of registering. S. P.

(The original handwritten letter is in possession of Kaye Page Nichols as of February 2021. The original spelling and grammar have been preserved in transcription to enhance the feel and the personality of the original format.)

January 8, 1898 Letter from Eliza Jane Geary Keele to her sister, Sophia Ann Geary Page including a section from David Keele

Panaca Jan 8 98

Dear Brother and sister and all wee received the sad news of Dear Leahs death wee never could exersize mutch faith as the complaint looked too grave wee are disapointed in knott being able too come and see her. The weather is so cold and Eliza not well I dare knott undertake it please write us all the perticulars and let us help all wee can too pay the bills that have acrued I sent Leah 20 Dolars she received it on the 31 Dec I guess it will bee ahard matter too meet the expence on my

part any way as I aint been able yet too pay father bills wewille strugle an doo the best we can
god bless you all good by
Dave

Panaca Jan the 1898
Dear Brother sister & all
I am sorrowfull enough this night you may be ashured it seems so sad & dreary to think that our dear blessed sister has to left us & to make it worse is that is we cant come out I feel as though I can hardly stand it I just imagian I can see the team traveling along with her at such a slow dreary pace; then again I see her in health hustling about and so jolly & good I one then see the Dear thing suffering as

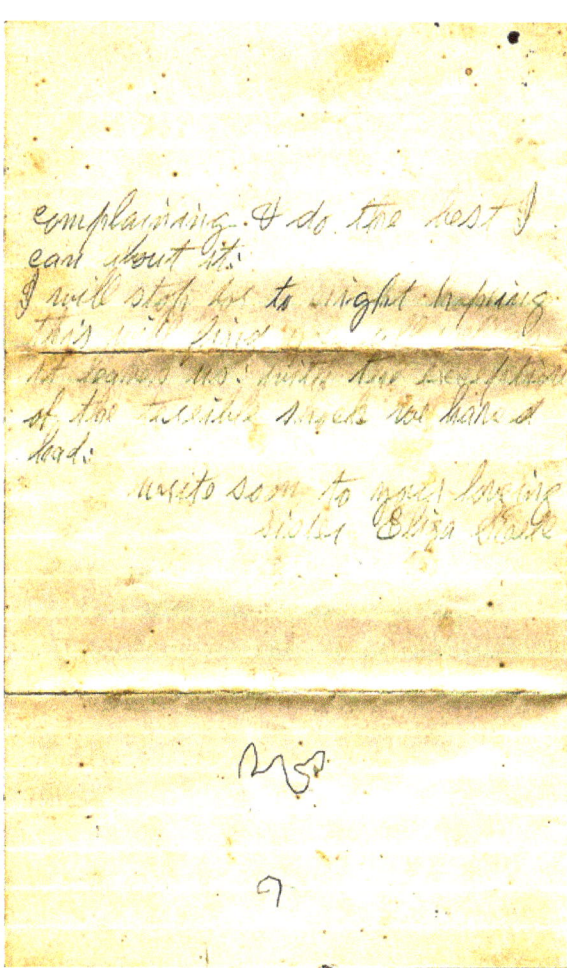

Transcription

A full transcription of Eliza's portion of the letter appears in Chapter 8 herein.
The original handwritten letter is in possession of Lisa Michele Church.

Transcription of David's portion of the letter:

Dear Brother and Sister and all, wee received the sad news of Dear Leahs death. wee never could exersize mutch faith as the complaint looked too grave. wee are disappointed in knott being able to come and see her. The weather is so cold and Eliza not well. I dare knot undertake it. please write us all the particulars and let us help all we can too pay the bills that have accrued. I sent Leah 20 Dolars she received on the 31 Dec. I guess it will be a hard mater too meet the expence on my part any way as I aint been able yet too pay fathers bills. Wee will struggle an doo the best we can god bless you all. Good by Dave

291

June 30, 1906 Deed to Annie Geary Davis establishing her Homestead on the Greybull River in Wyoming

34

Homestead Certificate No. 1363

4-773 A.

Application 3463

THE UNITED STATES OF AMERICA.

To all to whom these Presents shall come, GREETING:

Whereas, There has been deposited in the General Land Office of the United States a Certificate of the Register of the Land Office at Buffalo, Wyoming, whereby it appears that, pursuant to the Act of Congress approved 20th May, 1862, "To secure Homesteads to actual Settlers on the Public Domain," and the acts supplemental thereto, the claim of Annie Davis has been established and duly consummated, in conformity to law, for the West half of the South East quarter of Section twelve in Township fifty-one North of Range ninety-six West of the Sixth Principal Meridian in Wyoming containing eighty acres

according to the official plat of the survey of said land, returned to the General Land Office by the Surveyor General.

Now know ye that there is, therefore, granted by the United States unto the said Annie Davis the tract of land above described: **To have and to hold** the said tract of land, with the appurtenances thereof, unto the said Annie Davis and to her heirs and assigns forever; subject to any vested and accrued water rights for mining, agricultural, manufacturing, or other purposes, and rights to ditches and reservoirs used in connection with such water rights as may be recognized and acknowledged by the local customs, laws, and decisions of courts, and also subject to the right of the proprietor of a vein or lode to extract and remove his ore therefrom, should the same be found to penetrate or intersect the premises hereby granted, as provided by law, and there is reserved from the lands hereby granted a right of way thereon for ditches or canals constructed by the authority of the United States.

In testimony whereof, I, Theodore Roosevelt, PRESIDENT OF THE UNITED STATES OF AMERICA, have caused these letters to be made patent, and the seal of the General Land Office to be hereunto affixed.

Given under my hand at the city of Washington, the thirtieth day of June, in the year of our Lord one thousand nine hundred and six, and of the Independence of the United States the one hundred and thirtieth.

By the President: T. Roosevelt

By F. M. McKean, *Secretary.*

C. H. Bush, *Recorder of the General Land Office.*

This record was obtained by Lisa Michele Church from the records of the U.S. Department of Interior, Bureau of Land Management, General Land office https://glorecords.blm.gov/details/patent/default.aspx?accession=WY0340. Accession Number WY0340_.034, State Volume Patent, 6/30/1906.

December 15, 1914 Letter from William Willis to Sophia Geary Page

1

Taylor Kansas
Dec 15th

Dear Sister, I thought I would write you a few lines to let you know we are all alive and well. We have not good health for some time. My Myrs health is improving. It has been so long since we heard from you I cannot tell when I have not had letters from any of you girls for over a year now. I think it careless more than anything else I own it so with myself. If you have Dan's address I wish you would send it to me. I think I will write to Eliza in a few days. Have you ever been to see Letty yet. Sadly I wish I lived near to all of you. How are you getting along any way. Have the children write if we could get them to writing perhaps

2

we would hear from each other oftener. I will enclose a picture of our youngest boy. It was taken Last 4th of July. Just as he was dressed to take part with our two neither little girls his name is Byron Richard. Well we are but as poor as ever though I don't like to complain as long as we have good health, that is the greatest wealth we can enjoy. Jennie is quite a help now to her mother now I wish you's would all come and spend Xmas with us. Lee is going to the Eastman this winter he is doing well speaks in mass, he is Learning to Play the violin and can Play common music right off he taken 1st Prize last year at the State contest and trying for it again he is a good steady boy. I sold what little I had left

Both Willis letters are fully transcribed in Chapter 8 herein.
The original handwritten letters are in the possession of Kaye Page Nichols.

January 15, 1934 Letter from William Willis to Sophia Geary Page

Taylor Nargo Co
Aug Jan 15

My Dear Sister and Family I guess I will try to Write you a few lines to let you know We are still alive I think it has been two years since I wrote a letter to any one I have not heard from any of you folks for a long time I hope you are all Well and doing Well. We are all Well except colds I have ben Working on the highway for nearly too months nearly every man in the county is Working somewhere it sure seems good to earn a little money I have not taken in $25.00 in the last too years. Though We have got along

nicely Jenney our oldest girl has Worked nearly 4 years at Whiteover and We keep her children here with us 5 of them so you see We have plenty to do her man left he Without any thing to go on and ran away with one of our neighbors girl. We have only had $60.00 from him in too years. Geary What are you doing I put in a lot of time thinking of you folks Sophia uncle Peter Jensen died last Summer I hope some of you Will Write and let Me know how you are getting along I would sure love to see all of you but cannot see any chance

3

I go to bed cussing and get up cussing. I am so body out of patience I could pull on a rope to hang the worthless cuss. It seems imposible to get the racell in the pen where he belongs but I am still trying to land him in the pen. My health is not verry good I have a cold so much of the time Ma just keeps going it seems like the back is built for the burden. Well I guess I have sed enough I will close hopeing to hear from you soon love to all

W R Willis

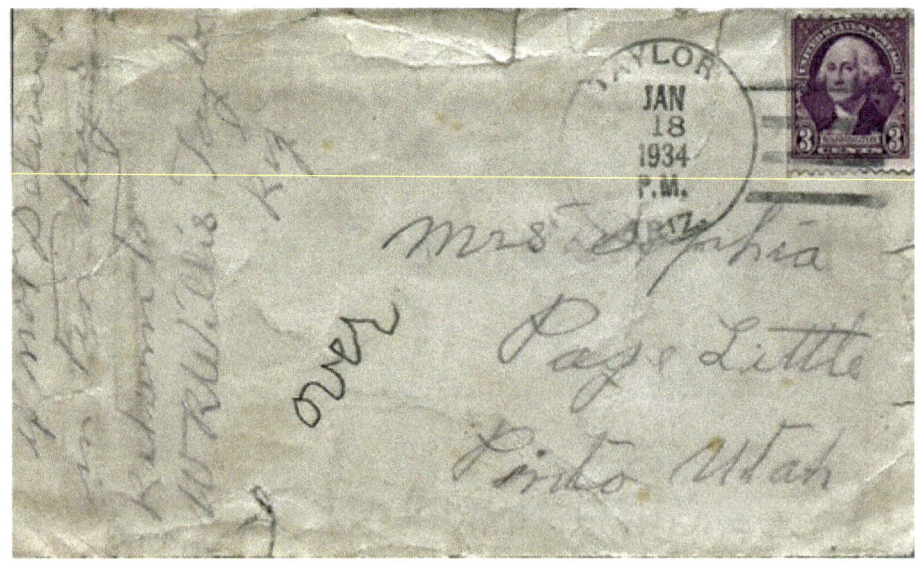

www.ingramcontent.com/pod-product-compliance
Lightning Source LLC
Chambersburg PA
CBHW061804290426
44109CB00031B/2932